Mexico

Also from Westphalia Press
westphaliapress.org

The Idea of the Digital University

Gems of Song for the Eastern Star

Bulwarks Against Poverty in America

Crime 3.0

Treasures of London

Anti-Masonry and the Murder of Morgan

Avate Garde Politician

Understanding Art

L'Enfant and the Freemasons

Spies I Knew

Baronial Bedrooms

Lodge "Himalayan Brotherhood" No. 459 C.E.

Making Trouble for Muslims

Philippine Masonic Directory ~ 1918

Ancient Masonic Mysteries

Collecting Old Books

Paddle Your Own Canoe

Masonic Secret Signs and Passwords

Opportunity and Horatio Alger

Careers in the Face of Challenge

Death Valley in '49

Bookplates of the Kings

Lariats and Lassos

The Boy Chums Cruising in Florida Waters

Mr. Garfield of Ohio

The Wisdom of Thomas Starr King

Freemasonry in Old Buffalo

Original Cables from the Pearl Harbor Attack

The French Foreign Legion

War in Syria

Social Satire and the Modern Novel

Naturism Comes to the United States

The Essence of Harvard

The Genius of Freemasonry

New Sources on Women and Freemasonry

A Definitive Commentary on Bookplates

Designing, Adapting, Strategizing in Online Education

James Martineau and Rebuilding Theology

Gunboat and Gun-runner

No Bird Lacks Feathers

Meeting Minutes of Naval Lodge No. 4 F.A.A.M ~ 1812 & 1813

Mexico

The Wonderland of the South

by W. E. Carson

WESTPHALIA PRESS
An imprint of Policy Studies Organization

Mexico: The Wonderland of the South
All Rights Reserved © 2014 by Policy Studies Organization

Westphalia Press
An imprint of Policy Studies Organization
1527 New Hampshire Ave., NW
Washington, D.C. 20036
info@ipsonet.org

ISBN-13: 978-1633910300
ISBN-10: 163391030X

Cover design by Taillefer Long at Illuminated Stories:
www.illuminatedstories.com

Daniel Gutierrez-Sandoval, Executive Director
PSO and Westphalia Press

Devin Proctor, Director of Media and Publications
PSO and Westphalia Press

Updated material and comments on this edition
can be found at the Westphalia Press website:
www.westphaliapress.org

MEXICO

THE WONDERLAND OF THE SOUTH

A TEHUANTEPEC BEAUTY,
Wearing her elaborate costume, starched head-dress, and necklace of gold coins.

MEXICO
THE WONDERLAND OF THE SOUTH

BY

W. E. CARSON

ILLUSTRATED

New York
THE MACMILLAN COMPANY
1909

All rights reserved

PREFACE

MEXICO is preëminently a land of picturesqueness, of romance, and of wonderfully strange contrasts. A period of twenty-five years has witnessed a general progress there which might easily have occupied centuries. But this very rapidity of evolution has worked against a completeness of development and has left fragments of the ancient order that give to the country, in patches, the fascinating interest of olden days. The automobile, electric traction, electric light, and the promoter have come; the Indian with his *burro*, the *cargador* with his burden, and the old-fashioned village priest have remained. Thus it is that in Mexico the old and the new are everywhere to be seen side by side.

It is this strange mixture of the ancient and mode n that produces such queer phases of life as exist in Mexi o to-day. And it can be truly said, moreover, that no country of Latin America is so full of interest as the land of the Aztecs. With a wonderful past and an equally wonderful present, peopled by an ancient race with strange customs and traditions, it is also a land of magnificent scenery, of superb climates, and amazing natural resources.

In the following pages will be found a concise account of my wanderings in Mexico, a description of the Mexican capital and other old cities, of the great haciendas, of the gold and silver mines, of some quaint health resorts, and of my experiences in mountain climbing, tarpon fishing, and ranching.

While dealing with all these subjects I have exerted every effort to make my book a book of human interest. I have tried, in short, to give an accurate pen-picture of Mexico as I saw this wonderful country in journeying from place to place, — the everyday life of the people, the sights and scenes that I witnessed, and the various incidents which marked my travel.

During my stay in the Republic I had ample opportunities to observe, in active process, the Americanizing of Mexico, which is destined to have such a far-reaching effect on the country's future. It was also my good fortune to be brought into sympathetic touch with Mexican affairs, and to learn much concerning the progress of the people, the policies of President Porfirio Diaz, the conditions of labor and the church, and the great agricultural and mining resources of the land.

Such, in brief, is a summary of this book, the aim of which is to give a pen-picture fresh, accurate, and inclusive of Mexico to-day.

CONTENTS

CHAPTER		PAGE
I.	The Tropics in a "Norther".	1
II.	From Orizaba to the Capital	19
III.	Mexico City by Night	44
IV.	Mexico Past and Present	67
V.	The Sights of the Capital	86
VI.	Churches and Miracles	111
VII.	The Life of the People	123
VIII.	The Mexican Woman	157
IX.	The Foreign Invasion	170
X.	The White Man's Burden-bearer	184
XI.	Mexico's Great Dictator	198
XII.	The Machinery of Government	210
XIII.	A Mexican Paradise	219
XIV.	The City of the Angels	235
XV.	A Mexican Carlsbad	249
XVI.	The Valley of Oaxaca	258
XVII.	Luxurious Life at a Gold Mine	272
XVIII.	Christmas at Los Reyes	287
XIX.	Prehistoric Mexico	300
XX.	Life in an Old Mexican Town	314
XXI.	In the Crater of Popocatepetl	328
XXII.	Guadalajara the Wonderful	339
XXIII.	"The Silver City"	355

CHAPTER		PAGE
XXIV.	THE TITIAN AT TZINTZUNTZAN	370
XXV.	THE ISTHMUS OF TEHUANTEPEC	378
XXVI.	TARPON FISHING AT TAMPICO	394
XXVII.	IN NORTHERN MEXICO	404
INDEX		429

LIST OF ILLUSTRATIONS

A Tehuantepec Beauty	*Frontispiece*
	FACING PAGE
Map showing Author's Route	1
Mexico's Chief Seaport	5
A Street in Vera Cruz	12
The Blind Beggar	19
A Typical Peon	23
Mexican Riding Costume	23
A View in Orizaba	30
Wonderful Engineering	33
Watching the Train	39
Mexico's National Drink	42
An Aguadore	42
Calle del Reloj, Mexico City	48
Reminiscent of the Past	53
Calle Cinco de Mayo, Mexico City	60
Ancient Picture Record	71
Hernando Cortés	74
The Emperor Maximilian	82
Cathedral and Plaza, Mexico City	87
The Mexican National Palace	90
Pyramid of the Moon	90

LIST OF ILLUSTRATIONS

	FACING PAGE
THE AZTEC CALENDAR STONE	94
ANCIENT AZTEC POTTERY AND STATUE OF THE GOD OF WAR	99
THE PASEO DE LA REFORMA	110
STONE FIGURES OF THE GOD OF FIRE AND THE SAD INDIAN	117
CHURCH AT TEPOZOTLAN	120
CHURCH OF GUADALUPE	124
TYPICAL MEXICAN WOMEN OF THE UPPER CLASS	130
PUBLIC SCHOOL CHILDREN	130
"PLAYING THE BEAR"	162
THE ANCIENT RACE — TYPES OF MEXICAN INDIANS	186
PRESIDENT DIAZ	197
MADAME DIAZ	204
MEXICAN STATESMEN	211
THE RURALES	214
THE AWKWARD SQUAD	214
A "BIT" OF CUERNAVACA	222
A VIEW FROM CUERNAVACA	227
AZTEC ARCHITECTURE	230
IN OLD PUEBLA	238
THE PYRAMID OF CHOLULA	238
A VIEW OF PUEBLA	246
THE PLAZA, OAXACA	257
TORTILLA MAKING	272
MEXICAN REBECCAS	272
A VALLEY IN THE SIERRAS	282
WITHIN THE RUINS OF MITLA	282
RUINS OF MITLA	312

LIST OF ILLUSTRATIONS

	FACING PAGE
ASCENT OF POPOCATEPETL — VIEW FROM HALFWAY HOUSE	330
THE JOURNEY'S END — ON SUMMIT OF POPOCATEPETL	330
CATHEDRAL AND MAIN PLAZA, GUADALAJARA	343
AN OLD STREET, GUADALAJARA	346
QUAINT OLD GUANAJUATO	355
A CHAMBER OF HORRORS	362
SILVER MINING	366
MEXICO'S ART TREASURE — THE TITIAN AT TZINTZUNTZAN	373
THE MEXICAN TROPICS	380
THE ROCKY ROAD	396

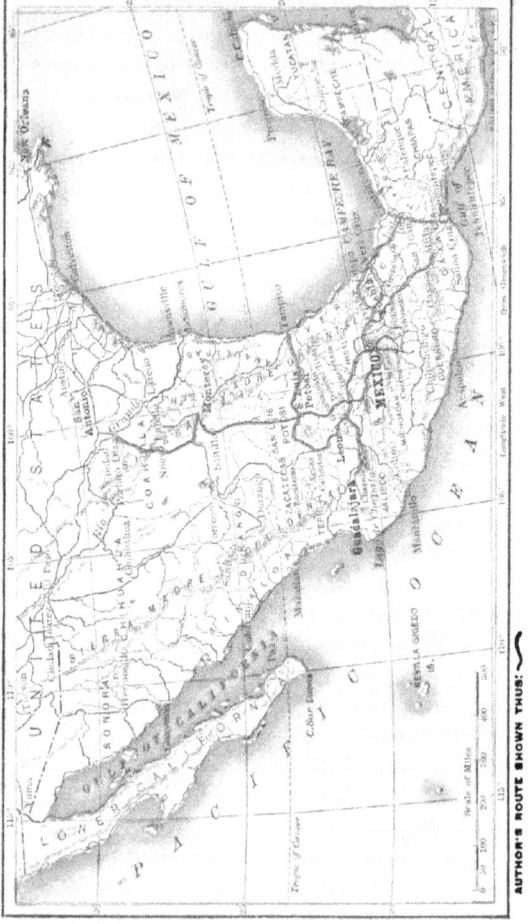

AUTHOR'S ROUTE SHOWN THUS:

MEXICO: THE WONDERLAND OF THE SOUTH

CHAPTER I

THE TROPICS IN A "NORTHER"

A LONG line of flat, sandy coast with numerous sand-bars stretching seawards over which the surf was breaking. The land, covered with scrubby bushes and here and there a melancholy group of cocoanut palms, lay forlorn and desolate under the dark sky. Farther off along the coast I could distinguish a long, gray, straggling city, an islet crowned by the time-worn turrets of a white fort, and two great stone jetties branching out from the shore. We were running through a stormy sea in the teeth of a strong head-wind; and this was my first glimpse of Mexico from the deck of a Ward liner in the early hours of a November morning.

From New York to Havana and thence into the Gulf of Mexico our voyage had been through seas that were beautifully blue, under a cloudless sky; and although it was winter, the air was as balmy as in June. But on the seventh day there came a sudden change. The tropical sky and warmth disappeared; dark clouds veiled the sun, a strong wind began to blow, the leaden-tinged sea was covered with white-caps. Then came a wireless message from Vera Cruz, warning us that a "norther" was playing havoc all along the coast. These "northers" are the winds which at frequent intervals during the winter swoop down from the ice-bound regions of the north and harry the Gulf coast shipping.

The breakers were dashing and the spray was flying about the narrow harbor entrance, but inside was smooth water. In the old days there was no harbor at Vera Cruz and the only protection from the sea was a low coral reef. Then vessels in the roadstead were obliged to lie with steam up, ready to put out to sea the moment a "norther" began to blow; collisions were frequent. Within the last few years a fine harbor has been built, at great cost, by S. Pearson & Sons, the English engineers, consisting of a system of great stone jetties which extend round the reef and completely break the force of the sea. Now vessels can lie safely alongside in any weather and discharge directly on to the wharves.

Bleak and mournful under the dark November sky, Vera Cruz had yet at closer quarters an extremely picturesque, old-world aspect. For about two miles along the shore stretched the city of low, flat-roofed houses; from among them rose the domes and towers of several churches. Conspicuous in the foreground was the new custom-house, a handsome structure of white stone, and not far off were the gray towers of the old cathedral. On a clear day, the distant snow-tipped peak of Orizaba forms a magnificent background for the port, but the famous volcano, when we arrived, was shrouded from view.

Lying at the wharves were three American and two English steamers, a big German liner, and three small revenue cruisers, painted light gray, and flying the Mexican ensign of red, white and green. A large and cosmopolitan gang of stevedores — Spaniards, Mexicans, Italians, negroes, Chinese, Japanese — were busily loading one of the American ships with bags of coffee and great bunches of green bananas; the German liner was taking in from two lighters at once a cargo of bright red dyewood logs. For Vera Cruz is a busy port, despite the "northers"; the bulk of Mexican trade passes in and out over its wharves. In years to come the northern port of Tampico is likely to rob the old town of much of its trade; but at the present time Vera Cruz handles over a million tons of imports annually, brought mostly from the United States and Germany, and including machinery, textiles, and such things as Chicago beef and bacon and tinned meats; for Mexico, notwithstanding its wonderful soil and climates, is not yet a self-sustaining country. The exports are chiefly sugar, coffee, tobacco, rubber, dyewoods and various tropical fruits.

Our liner went easily to her berth hard by the little island of San Juan de Ulloa, with its quaint battlements of gleaming white; beneath the walls a group of tall palms covered with their masses of fan-shaped leaves of vivid green gave a touch of the tropics to the scene. Upon this island Cortés landed on April 21, 1519, and here he continued his wonderful career of conquest by burning his ships and marching away to the Aztec capital. The first fort, of which not a vestige remains, was built by the Spaniards. In the reign of Queen Elizabeth, it was seized by that bluff English hero, Sir John Hawkins, when he entered the harbor to obtain provisions and repair his storm-beaten vessels. Treacherously attacked by a large Spanish squadron which afterwards arrived, he was driven from the port with the loss of most of his ships, many men, and much treasure. The ancient stronghold, enlarged and rebuilt at various times, remained in Spanish hands for over two centuries. In later times it was successively captured and occupied by the Americans in 1847 and by the French in 1864. It is now used as a prison. Vera Cruz was originally named La Villa Rica de la Santa Vera Cruz (the Rich City of the Holy True Cross) from the reputed richness of the land in gold and the fact that Cortés landed on Good Friday. Since the Conquest it has always been Mexico's most important seaport.

We were not allowed to land before the Mexican health officers had come aboard and examined us. Havana is regarded by the Mexican authorities as a hotbed of yellow fever, and the Havana authorities regard Vera Cruz in the same light. During the winter months there is no yellow fever in either city, but that makes no difference in their fear of each other. Our steamer had touched at Havana, and the doctors accordingly subjected us to a rigorous examination, putting thermometers in our mouths to take our temperatures and otherwise overhauling us. As each thermometer ran the gantlet of several mouths, and was only slightly washed with antiseptic between each, this ordeal was not a pleasant one. Some of us began to fear that we might have yellow fever without knowing it, and should be hurried off to some dismal quarantine hospital to end our days. It was a real relief to find that we had not.

In the meantime a mob of gesticulating porters or cargadores had gathered on the wharf, clamoring loudly for patronage. They were yellow-skinned fellows with the coal-black, beady, furtive eyes of the Indian half-breed. Most of them simply wore a shirt and trousers of dirty white cotton, scanty and ragged; a few had a loose jacket of the same material; all looked half frozen in the "norther." Some had wrapped a tattered piece of blanket about their shoulders to keep out the cold. Some were barefooted, others wore sandals of a rough-and-ready kind.

These cargadores, or burden-bearers, are familiar objects throughout Mexico. They are trained from childhood to

MEXICO'S CHIEF SEAPORT.
A view of Vera Cruz, showing one of the great stone jetties.

carry heavy weights, and might also be said to inherit their wonderful capacity. The Aztecs had no beasts of burden, and the baggage of their armies was always carried by cargadores. The Spaniards, having few horses, continued this custom. Though most cargadores are not particularly sturdy in appearance, they can lift and carry enormous loads. It is not uncommon to see a couple of them carrying a piano through the streets. A trained cargador will carry a load of one hundred and fifty pounds over rough mountain trails and cover more miles in a day than a mule. The load is held in place by either a forehead strap or a breast strap or a shoulder strap, or by two or more of these combined. As the cargador moves along with his heavy load, there is a good deal of straining of the straps, reminding one of the line in Omar Khayyam: "Now for the porter's shoulder-knot a-creaking." In the towns the cargadores are licensed, and carry brass plates on their breasts showing their numbers.

I stepped ashore, and instantly two cargadores seized my luggage. One took my bags; the other, quite a slight man, lifted my heavy trunk on his shoulders and trotted off to the custom-house. After the examination he trotted off with it to the railway station about a mile away.

Leaving the water front, I walked out into the city of Vera Cruz, where I found that outside the principal thoroughfares the streets were almost deserted. This seemed strange for a city of thirty thousand inhabitants until I remembered the "norther," likewise the midday siesta which is still preserved as a sacred custom even in this busy seaport. A queer, dingy old place it looked, for the most part, the business places being ancient and grimy; the sign-boards with their Spanish wording were faded and battered. The buildings and houses are nearly all low, two-storied structures of solid stone or stucco, seldom white, but generally tinted pink, yellow or blue; on the second stories are bright green wooden or iron balconies where the dark-eyed señoritas love to sit at their needlework and watch the passers-by. Oil paint is seldom used here or anywhere else in Mexico for the exteriors of buildings, and the water-color or kalsomine quickly fades. After one rainy season it becomes soft and streaked, so that even a new building soon looks quite antiquated.

The narrow streets were at that time (this has been altered since) paved with rough, unevenly laid cobblestones, and had open gutters in the centre. Small streetcars, painted bright yellow and drawn by two sturdy mules, ran through most streets, but there were no ordinary carriages of any kind to be seen. I was told that the bad paving made it almost impossible to use them. On Sundays I heard it was quite the custom for the townsfolk, even of the better class, to ride up and down the streets in the cars, enjoying the air and gossiping with friends who passed in other cars — the Vera Cruzan substitute for the Champs Elysées or Rotten Row.

In the centre of the town is a small plaza, planted with palms and various tropical shrubs, where the local military band plays several nights a week, as is the custom in all Mexican towns. On one side of the plaza is the cathedral, built in 1734, though it looks much older. Not far away is the church of San Francisco, founded in 1568; its tower is now used as a lighthouse. Adjoining it is a convent which has been converted into a public library. The other sides of the plaza are occupied by the portales or arcades found in every Mexican town. Here are various shops and cafés and one or two hotels. On the sidewalk outside the cafés groups of men sit all day and almost all night at small iron tables, forever drinking refrescos, which are cool Mexican drinks, or, alas, the fiery American cocktail.

In this quarter of the town are the theatres, the exchange, and two or three public buildings.

Having to change some money, I went into a hotel where I was accommodated with Mexican coin in return for a small discount. To my joy I found that for every American dollar I received two Mexican. These Mexican dollars, called pesos, are not only larger than the American dollar, but contain a greater percentage of silver, yet their value — such are the freaks of monetary systems — is only fifty cents. However, that doesn't matter much in Mexico, because the purchasing power of the money is on a Mexican basis too. Thus, railway travel, hotels and most of the necessaries of life are somewhat less than in the United States. On the other hand, as Mexico, like this country, goes in severely for protection, most imported articles are extremely dear.

Notwithstanding the delight of having one's supply of money automatically doubled, there is a dark side to this bright picture. On this occasion, part of my Mexican small change consisted of twenty-five silver dollars, each weighing nearly an ounce. I carefully distributed these throughout my various pockets, and thus burdened, felt like an ancient Spanish galleon loaded with pieces of eight. Notes and gold are in circulation, but they are not always easy to get; the notes, too, when you get them, are often in a filthy condition. Silver, however, seems to be preferred by the Mexicans, and they frequently carry their available funds in a handbag strapped over the shoulder.

The design of the Mexican dollar is on the obverse the cap of liberty, bearing the word "Libertad," surrounded by the rays of the sun; on the reverse is the traditional eagle perched on the cactus, with a serpent in his talons. Although the engraving is very crude, it is impossible to improve it, because the Chinese, who use the Mexican dollars very largely in their own country, as being the purest silver coin in existence, would not accept them if the design were changed. At the same time, the roughness of the design makes counterfeiting very easy and its detection difficult, with the consequence that there is much bad money about the country. Other silver coins are the half and quarter dollars, and the ten and five centavo pieces, the centavo being worth half a cent.

A negro who was lounging conveniently outside the hotel heard me asking my way, and promptly stepped up with a polite bow and a cheery smile. "Let me show you round the city, boss," he suggested. He was a dapper colored gentleman of middle age, and had that half-familiar, half-deferential manner which distinguishes the average negro who has been employed in any serving capacity. Like most negroes, he was full of good humor, and he spoke Spanish like a native. I accepted his offer, and we walked on. As we strolled through the streets, my companion exchanged smiles and greetings with sundry Mexican acquaintances, one or two of them good-looking girls of the humbler class. He bowed with exaggerated politeness and lifted his hat with the words, "Que tal? señor" (How goes it, sir), or "Buenas dias, señorita" (Good day, miss).

"You seem to be very well known here," I remarked.

"Yes, sir," replied the negro, with an air of pride, "I guess I do know quite a few people in Vera Cruz."

"How do you like the Mexicans?" I asked.

"Well, boss," was the reply, "it's dis yer way: dere's some mighty fine folks in dis town, but Lordy! most of de poor people are trifling and no account. But," he added, in a patronizing tone, "what else can you expect of dese yer half-breeds? No, indeed, sir, you won't find no such low-down, no-account people in any part of the States, 'deed you won't, tank de Lord.

"Dey's mean, too, dese yer Mexicans," he went on; "dey count deir centavos like dey was gold. Give me a genleman from New York or Boston. You never see 'em counting of deir dollars."

This gentle and diplomatic hint was thrown in, I presume, as our walk was about to end. As we were parting company, the colored gentleman, with a grin which would have made the fortune of any negro comedian, remarked: "I's proud o' meeting a genleman from New York or Boston, boss; dey jest naturally know how to travel. Dey ain't like dese yer Mexicans. Dey's all right."

It is a curious fact that, although Mexico adjoins the United States, few negroes ever cross the border; and most of these are found in Vera Cruz and other towns along the coast. With the exception of a few employed by railway companies as porters for Pullman cars, there are almost none in the interior. The "nigger" in Mexico, too, is far from being the subservient creature that he generally is in this country. The Mexicans, perhaps naturally, do not feel the color horror so general among Americans. A negro is granted equality in a way which astonishes an American; and he is something of a curiosity, too, exciting more or less wonder in Mexico wherever he goes. In small towns the natives stare at him and children follow him. Mexicans call negroes "negritos," and think them very amusing. A woman of Indian blood would not lose caste by marrying one.

The reason why negroes are so scarce in Mexico is that they cannot compete with the Indian population as laborers, and the wages are so small that no American negro could live on them. Some years ago an American company brought down two thousand negroes to work on a Mexican plantation, paid them good wages and fed them well. At first they were very industrious, and did more work than the peons. Then they became lazy, many of them took Indian wives, loafed about and refused to work; so they were discharged, and soon became destitute. The Mexican government compelled the company to take them back to the United States.

After my stroll round the city, I sat down outside a café near the plaza to take, at my leisure, a first survey of real Mexican life. The scene was full of vivid contrasts. Across the street was quite a smart-looking costumier's shop, in the windows of which were displayed some dainty gowns and hats. This was the centre of attraction for many well-dressed women and girls, who stopped to feast their eyes on the fashions. Only a few doors away was a battered, tumble-down drinking den, cavernous in its gloominess, reeking of stale liquor, where scantily dressed, barefooted natives perpetually passed in and out; at the door stood a lumbering old wagon, drawn by two oxen, loaded with bananas — such a cart as might have come over from Spain with Cortés. Then there was civilization again in the shape of a bank, quite a substantial stone building, where much business was apparently being done. Now and again, a Mexican from the country would ride by on a spirited horse, his feet deep in the national pocket stirrup, on his head the steeple-crowned sombrero, or a native milk vendor, sitting almost on the tail of his mule, its back loaded with clattering milk tins; jolting baggage trucks passed, driven by Indians, cracking their whips and calling down perpetual encouragement to their mules of "Mula, mula!" Then at noon, from the neighboring police barracks, trotted out a patrol of rurales or mounted police in their neat gray, silver-braided, tight-fitting uniform and huge sombrero, Winchesters slung on their backs, revolvers and swords at their sides.

But perhaps the most curious sight in Vera Cruz is

the city's unpaid scavengers. Hopping about the streets, outside the smart costumier's, by the cathedral, alongside the cafés — everywhere, in fact — were groups of zopilotes or turkey buzzards, equalling in size the largest American species. These ungainly birds act as public scavengers, and are protected by law; the fine for killing one of them is five dollars. Hundreds of them can be seen perched on the roof tops or the church towers, waddling about the streets, fighting over all sorts of offal, or hurrying after the street-cleaners to claim the choicest bits of garbage. What with the zopilotes and their human assistants, the streets of the town are kept quite decently clean.

Until recent times, Vera Cruz was a town of bad drainage and evil smells, and yellow fever raged there perpetually. During the summer months each year the mortality was often frightful. Whole ships' crews were sometimes swept away by this scourge, and an unacclimatized traveller visiting the city literally took his life in his hands. A few years ago the city authorities set vigorously to work to stamp out the pestilence. Much of the old city was demolished, and a new sewerage system was constructed, the sewage being taken out to sea, and contamination of the harbor thus avoided. A new water supply was installed, and a relentless war was waged against mosquitoes. This thoroughgoing hygienic campaign ended in a victory for the city's health authorities; and now there is practically no yellow fever in the winter months, and even in the summer the cases are few and far between. There were only 21 deaths from the disease in 1908, according to government reports. Unacclimatized travellers who observe the usual precautions are generally safe nowadays at all seasons.

Strangely enough, now that Vera Cruz has lost its evil reputation as a plague-stricken city, it has actually achieved a new character as a health resort. During the winter months large numbers of people flock thither from Mexico City in search of sunshine and warmth. Situated as it is in the tropical region of Mexico, Vera Cruz, even when a "norther" is blowing, rarely has a temperature below sixty degrees Fahrenheit, the normal winter heat being between seventy and eighty. The "norther" which was blowing through the town when we arrived was not actually a cold wind; it was simply bracing. But the thin-blooded natives are so accustomed to tropical heat that a sudden drop in the temperature to sixty degrees causes general suffering, and keeps every Mexican indoors as much as possible while the wind is blowing.

The greater part of the thirty thousand inhabitants of Vera Cruz are true Mexicans, that is to say, people of mixed Indian and Spanish blood. There is a fairly large foreign element in the city, consisting mainly of business men, American, English, German, Spanish and French. In the surrounding country there are a good many foreign planters cultivating sugar-cane, coffee, bananas, etc. In Vera Cruz, as in all parts of Mexico, Spanish is the only European language known to the mass of the people, although owing to the increasing number of Americans in the country a knowledge of English is gradually becoming more general among Mexican business men.

Vera Cruz with the "norther" blowing was a place to hurry away from, so in the afternoon I took the train to Orizaba. This mountain town, situated 4026 feet above sea-level, amidst beautiful scenery, is a favorite health resort for the Mexicans. The gradient is so steep for the greater part of the way that the train takes about five hours to cover the eighty miles from Vera Cruz.

On Mexican railways the trains are arranged in the usual American style, and American rolling stock is generally

A STREET IN VERA CRUZ.
On the roofs are perched the street-cleaning turkey-buzzards.

used. The Mexican Railway, however — the line between Vera Cruz, Orizaba and Mexico City — uses some big Fairlie engines made in Glasgow. The trains are invariably divided into first, second, and third-class cars, the first-class car corresponding to what is usually called in this country "a day coach." Only the night trains have Pullman cars attached to them.

Compared with an American train, the Mexican Railway's day train seemed rather shabby; the first-class car was old and worn, and furnished with black leather seats.[1] It was, however, no worse than the ordinary first-class cars in which I afterwards travelled on other Mexican railways. The companies, I was told, could not afford to run Pullman cars on their day trains at present, as there are not enough foreign passengers to make it pay, and Mexican travellers are usually too parsimonious to pay any additional fare for the sake of more comfort.

About twenty passengers from the steamer had taken tickets for Orizaba, so that the single first-class car was fairly well filled when the train started.

The Mexican Railway, which is owned by an English company, has the distinction of being the first railway ever built in Mexico; it was begun in 1858 and finished in 1873. The track runs from the lowlands of Vera Cruz up through the mountains, and is a marvel of engineering. Some of the gradients are stupendous; at one point the line reaches an altitude of over ten thousand feet; in some places it runs along the mountain side on terraces cut out of the solid rock. Owing to the magnitude of the work and the enormous difficulties of laying the track, the con-

---

[1] A change for the better has since been made. The Mexican Railway Co. now runs some comfortable, reclining chair cars for the accommodation of first-class passengers, and for which no extra fare is charged.

struction cost over $35,000,000, or about $125,000 a mile. The Mexican Railway is not only regarded as one of the best railroads in the world, but as a scenic line it is surpassed by none, the views for most part of the way being magnificent.

The country for miles round Vera Cruz is a vast sandy waste interspersed with swamps, the haunt of herons, wild ducks, alligators and snakes. This, at intervals, is broken by dense woods filled with aromatic shrubs and gorgeous wild flowers peculiar to the tropics. Leaving this unwholesome region, the line runs through a succession of banana and cocoanut plantations, miles of coffee trees, with their dark, glossy leaves and bright red berries, forests of palms and palmettos, groves of oranges and lemons, fields of pineapples and green sugar-cane. Novel as all this was, I must confess that, without the glare of sunshine and the heat which we have a right to expect from the tropics, the tropical vegetation lost most of its charm.

We passed a number of small stations, mostly crude structures of wood, usually set in the midst of a grove of palms or cocoanut trees. Outside these a few yellow-skinned, barefooted natives would be seen, with their sarapes or blankets drawn tightly about them, looking half frozen in their thin cotton clothing and straw sombreros. Some Americans who appeared to live in the district boarded the train, and their talk was all about banana- and coffee-growing. But with the cool weather and the dark sky it seemed impossible to realize that one was actually in the tropics.

The first important station at which we stopped was Cordoba, about sixty miles from Vera Cruz. This town has an altitude of 2713 feet and a population of ten thousand, and is just on the border of the sub-tropical zone. It is noted for its fruit and flowers as well as for its fine coffee, of which there are numerous plantations in the neighborhood. It is quite an old town, having been founded in 1618 as a place of refuge from the malarial fevers of the coast.

Numerous beggars, picturesque in their tattered garb, clamored round the train for centavos. Two or three of them carried queer-looking old harps and mandolins, and entertained us with a verse of the Spanish song, La Paloma, which they sang in rather high-pitched nasal tones. One blind man, with a most saintly expression, stood by our car, sombrero in hand, beseeching us to be generous for God's sake — "por el amor de Dios." Another blind beggar, led by his much-wrinkled, sad-visaged Indian wife, gave an excellent imitation of various sounds peculiar to animal life, such as the quacking of a duck, the clucking of a hen, the grunting of a pig, and the whistling of a mocking-bird.

Standing a little removed from this motley swarm of mendicants, I noticed a melancholy looking Mexican wearing a rather battered brown felt sombrero, his limbs encased in skin-tight trousers of thin gray cloth, adorned with numerous patches. Over his shoulders was a bright red blanket. He was strumming away at an old-fashioned mandolin and singing some mournful Spanish song. Catching sight of me, he stopped playing, and lifted his sombrero. I went out on the car platform and handed him five cents. To my astonishment, he politely declined my humble offering. "Señor," said he, in choice Spanish, with some emotion, "you must pardon me for being unable to accept your gift, but I am a ten-cent beggar, señor (un mendigo de diez centavos), and never, never accept a smaller gratuity." Drawing himself up with an air of pride, he continued, "I shall be honored to sing for your entertainment a song of old Spain or one of our noble Mexican airs, but always for a fee of ten cents, never for less, for I am a ten-cent beggar, señor, poor as I am."

It was impossible to resist this touching protest, so with an apology I handed the courtly vagrant his proper fee, which he acknowledged with "a thousand thanks" (Mil gracias, señor) and a graceful bow. At the other end of the car the mob of beggars were scrambling for copper coins thrown to them by my fellow-passengers. The melancholy minstrel glanced at them, shrugged his shoulders and waved his hand deprecatingly. "Ah, señor," he observed, "those poor people, they have to work hard for their bread; good folk, worthy folk, well deserving of your charity; but they give you a very bad impression of Mexico. Pray, señor, do not class them with poor musicians like myself." With these words he commenced twanging his discordant instrument again, and once more burst into a song so dismal that it seemed to make the gloomy weather even more depressing. Fortunately, our train commenced to move on a few moments later, and Cordoba and the courtly ten-cent beggar were soon lost to view.

During our short stop at the station, Indian women and children had offered us fruit and flowers at tempting prices; large bunches of camellias for a few centavos, luscious pineapples of six to eight pounds for ten cents apiece, all the bananas and oranges you could carry, for a few cents. Cordoba well maintained its reputation as a place of fruit and flowers.

As we travelled farther from Vera Cruz there was a noticeable drop in the temperature, and while it was not cold, still one would have welcomed the prospect of arriving at a comfortable country house with a cheerful wood fire blazing in the hall. No doubt the black sky and the rain which began to fall had something to do with this feeling, but the altitude probably had much more.

THE TROPICS IN A "NORTHER" 17

In Mexico almost everything depends on the altitude, and it is to altitude that Mexico owes its three climates. Being well within the tropics and near the equator, it is naturally always thought of as a warm country, but only parts deserve this character. Geographically speaking, Mexico is situated in North America. It has a maximum length of 1990 miles, is 540 miles across at the widest point, and has a coast line of over 6000 miles.

On one side of this great country is the Atlantic or Gulf Coast, and on the other the Pacific. Along both coasts there is a broad, flat tract called the tierra caliente or "hot land," which is wholly tropical. In this region grow tropical fruits and flowers of all kinds. Here, too, are vast forests with a jungle of creeping plants, where are found mahogany and numerous valuable dyewoods, which are exported to all parts of the world. Much of this tropical region is unhealthful, though the winds from the sea generally mitigate the heat during the middle of the day, and the nights and mornings, as a rule, are pleasantly cool.

As you travel inland from the Atlantic or Pacific coasts, the country constantly rises, until in the interior it reaches an altitude of six or seven thousand feet. A good idea of this peculiar topography is given by the following cut, which shows the profile of the country between the ports of Tampico and Manzanillo on the eastern and western coasts.

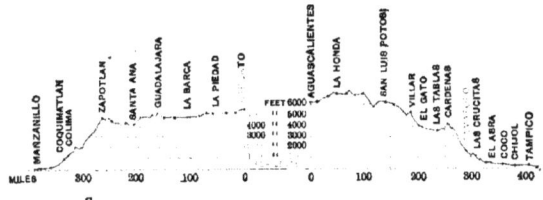

At an altitude of four thousand feet or more, a subtropical region known as the tierra templada, or temperate land, is reached, where the climate is perpetually delightful.

A third region, six thousand feet or more above sea-level, is called the tierra fria or cold land, although it is not actually cold, for the mean temperature is not lower than that of central Italy. In brief, perpetual summer, eternal spring, and a temperature rarely cold enough for snow or ice are the climatic joys which Mexico offers to the shivering American who travels southward in midwinter to escape from the blizzards of the north.

THE BLIND BEGGAR.
"One penny, señor, for God's sake."

CHAPTER II

FROM ORIZABA TO THE CAPITAL

NEARLY four centuries ago the soldiers of Cortés, marching over the mountains from the coast to the Aztec capital, came to an Indian town situated in a beautiful valley, intersected by rushing streams which kept it forever green. The natives called the place Ahauializapan or "joy in the waters." The Spaniards, with their usual avidity, took possession of this attractive spot, but after heroic efforts to pronounce its name, they wisely changed it to Orizaba. Under Spanish rule, a new town arose on the site of the old, and this became, in time, one of the most important places in Mexico. For generations Orizaba was a haven of refuge for people who fled from the pestilent coast during the yellow-fever season to seek health in the pure mountain air. In later times it was a favorite resort of the Emperor Maximilian, who, during his brief reign, often sought rest and quiet in the quaint old town. To-day it is a popular health resort, and has a host of visitors the year round, its climate being perfect and its scenery charming.

I did not see Orizaba under its best aspect, for like many other places, it has its dreary days. Pursued by the "norther," I reached the ancient city at seven in the evening, to find a heavy rain falling, while the chilly air was reminiscent of an American November rather than what one expects in the Mexican sub-tropics. Some Indian urchins, looking pinched and cold in their ragged clothing and bare feet, surrounded me as I left the train, offering to carry my bags. They were pushed aside by a picturesque-looking ruffian wearing a huge steeple-crowned sombrero and swathed in a heavy red blanket drawn up to chin height. He was an Orizaban cab driver, and he undertook to drive me to my hotel in his cab or *coche*, a heavy, lumbering vehicle of the station-fly order, with a capacious leather hood. It was drawn by two vigorous mules, and it needed them, for the paving of Orizaba's streets was even worse than that of Vera Cruz.

I took a seat in the *coche* and was soon jolting through some narrow streets lined with low, flat-roofed houses and buildings, seldom over a story high, and quite Moorish-looking. All were of the same washed-out tints of pink, yellow and blue. The upper windows, I noticed, were rarely glazed, but simply provided with wooden shutters; while the lower windows were crossed with thick, prison-like bars of iron, not only as a protection against thieves, but to guard the Juliets of the household from their swarthy Romeos. This, of course, applies to the habitations of the well-to-do. The poor in Mexican towns invariably live in mere hovels of unbaked brick of only one story, looking like rows of stables. They have no windows, and light is admitted through the doorway only. When a norther is blowing, the door is kept tightly closed, and the shivering inmates endeavor, by excluding the fresh air, to keep life in their thin-blooded bodies. I noticed that very few of the shops of Orizaba had glazed windows, but were mostly open to the street somewhat after the fashion of English butchers' shops; some were lighted with flaming oil lamps, and others with gas. All the streets were well lit with electric light. It was Saturday night, and despite the rain, the streets were crowded with dark-skinned natives in their picturesque attire.

The dress of the poorer classes, the Indians, called peons,

is much the same throughout Mexico. Men wear a loose suit of white linen, coat and trousers, sometimes no coat, the shade of whiteness varying in accordance with the cleanliness of the owner. Sometimes the clothing is white (soon after washday), sometimes it is a cream hue, but usually it is a dark gray! The trousers are often rolled up to the knee, and the native goes about with bare legs and feet. Sometimes the trousers reach to the ankles, and he is provided with sandals strapped over his bare feet. Stockings are never worn. On his head the peon wears a huge steeple-crowned straw sombrero, with the brim anything up to two feet wide. This is sometimes used as a basket. I often saw Indians in the market buying fish or vegetables and carrying them off in the brims of their hats.

In addition to his linen suit and straw sombrero, the peon has a woollen blanket or *sarape* (pronounced *sah-rah-pay*). This is usually of bright red, with black stripes at each end. Sometimes it has a slit in the middle through which he thrusts his head, the blanket falling over the body like a shawl. During the heat of the day the sarape is folded and carried over the left shoulder. It serves the double purpose of a garment by day and a blanket by night, for the peon sleeps under it.

Mexicans of a higher class, when they can afford it, will often buy a felt sombrero — the felt about a quarter of an inch thick — decorated with gold and silver tinsel embroidery. In country places the wealth of a man is usually shown by the style of his hat. Some of the finer embroidered sombreros cost over a hundred dollars. For riding, extremely tight skin-fitting trousers, edged with small metal buttons, are commonly worn, accompanied, in some cases, with a heavily braided, short bolero coat ornamented with bright buttons. This, with the gorgeous sombrero, makes a very picturesque costume. In the towns and cities, however, the middle and upper classes dress like Europeans.

The Indian women are usually dressed in some cheap kind of calico, the favorite material being a plain blue dotted with white, or white dotted with blue, and all of them wear a shawl or mantilla called the *rebosa*. This is generally of some thin woollen or cotton stuff, and is always of a faded blue tint. It is usually draped tightly over the head, leaving only the face exposed. Thus attired, they have a strong resemblance to the women of the East, and this is especially noticeable when you meet one of them coming from a village well, bearing a pitcher gracefully poised on her head. As a rule, the women have an unkempt, bedraggled appearance, and their coarse black hair is worn in two untidy plaits.

The children of the poor have a very queer appearance, looking exactly like little men and women. Boys dress just like their fathers, having the same linen suits, big straw sombreros and red sarapes; girls wear the same long dresses and blue rebosas as their mothers.

At first sight, the Mexican Indians seemed to me to be a very melancholy race, and this first impression was confirmed by what I afterwards saw of them. As we drove through the streets of Orizaba, filled with the passing throngs of natives, moving silently, barefooted or shod with noiseless sandals, there was rarely the sound of laughter; nor was there any roughness or horseplay such as one would have noticed in an American street filled with Saturday-night shoppers. Strings of children glided along silently after their parents, wonderfully subdued and grave, rarely exchanging a word.

The shops were, of course, decorated with Spanish signboards, the fondas (grocers) and dulcerias (confectioners) being the most noticeable. Here and there, however, there

A TYPICAL PEON
Wearing the sarape and sombrero.

MEXICAN RIDING COSTUME.
Still popular in country districts.

were indications of an American invasion, for over some of the buildings were big sign-boards advertising "Dr. Dash, American Physician," or " Dr. Blank, American Dentist." In most Mexican cities nowadays there are several American doctors and dentists. Some of the shops, apparently American, had English as well as Spanish signs, and proclaimed themselves "The United States Grocery Co.," with "Goods at cut prices," or the "American-Mexican Canning Co."

In less than ten minutes my *coche* took me to the Hotel de France, which I found to be an excellent establishment; in fact, it has the reputation of being one of the best hotels in Mexico. It is conducted by an enterprising Frenchman.

Arranged on much the same plan as many Spanish hotels, this Mexican hotel was a large, square, stone building having a central courtyard or patio, paved with tiles, open to the sky, and centred by a fountain surrounded with palms and flowers. From here flights of stone steps led to the upper stories, outside each of which there was a wide tiled gallery extending completely round the patio. The rooms were entered from these galleries, and some which had no outside windows were lighted by tinted glass panels in the doors. The bedrooms had tiled floors, each was supplied with one or two rugs, and the bedsteads were of iron, a very good plan in a country where fleas and other insect pests are too common. Most of the Mexican hotels are arranged and furnished in this way. The rooms are invariably neat and well-kept, and the bedding, strange to say, in a land where cleanliness is not always regarded as a virtue, is usually clean and fresh.

My Orizaba hotel had another feature which is common to hotels throughout Mexico. Just inside the entrance there was a small office where guests signed the register and arranged for their rooms. Outside the office there was a large blackboard with the numbers of the rooms arranged in rows. As soon as a room was assigned to a new arrival, his name was written with chalk on this blackboard opposite to the number of his room. Any one could thus see at a glance who was stopping at the hotel.

Chambermaids, I discovered, are seldom employed in Mexican hotels, their places being taken by men-of-all-work, sometimes young, sometimes elderly, called mozos (boys). There is a mozo on each floor who acts as bootblack, porter, messenger and chambermaid; he takes away one's linen to some remote laundry and brings it back the next day, clean and snowy white. In the larger towns the mozo often speaks a little English and acts as interpreter for guests who do not understand Spanish. In the American hotels in Mexico he is less in evidence, as these establishments usually employ chambermaids.

The Mexican hotels are comfortable enough for the average traveller, and if they had only been made soundproof they would be still nearer perfection. I thought so, at least, when I was awakened about six o'clock the next morning by a terrible clanging of church bells. This was my first experience of what I afterwards found to be the greatest public nuisance in Mexico. The Mexican churches do not possess sweet chimes, but generally have from one to half a dozen large, harsh-toned bells. Commencing early in the morning, and continuing at frequent intervals during the day, a muscular peon clutching a rope attached to the bell-clapper clangs away with all his strength, making an awful din. Sometimes he wields a sort of sledge-hammer, beating the bell from the outside with all the vigor of a village blacksmith. When all the church bells in a town are kept clanging in this way, the din is deafening.

Unable to enjoy any more sleep on account of these ecclesiastical instruments of torture, I went down to an early breakfast and afterwards took a stroll through the town.

Although the rain had stopped, the sky was still overcast, and the mountains were wreathed with white clouds. Along the streets poured a steady stream of Indian men and women returning from early mass, tramping patiently through the mud, the majority of them being barefooted. The men had their red blankets drawn tightly round them, looking half frozen, although the air was as mild as an early summer morning. Only the poorer classes attend early mass. Later on I saw numbers of white women and a few men walking and driving to the eleven o'clock service. I also noticed several men whom I instinctively recognized as priests despite their dress, which is not what one is accustomed to see in other Catholic countries. The laws having forbidden them to appear in public in their clerical dress, the Mexican priests have adopted the plan of wearing a peculiar black cloak which, while not exactly ecclesiastical, is not worn by men of any other class. With this they wear an ordinary derby or silk hat. The cloak enables them to be distinguished a long way off. Some zealous opponents of the church want to have this cloak declared illegal and various other anti-church laws enforced.

There are some fine old churches in Orizaba dating from the seventeenth and eighteenth centuries; the oldest, called Santa Teresa, was built in 1564. The cathedral, which stands in the main plaza, was built in 1720, and is a large, imposing edifice.

A stroll through Orizaba gives one a very good idea of the arrangement of Mexican towns which, following the Spanish system, were all originally built round a public square or plaza. As the towns have increased in size, similar plazas, which are sometimes called *alamedas*, have been provided, until each quarter eventually has one of these little parks. Orizaba has several of them. On one side of the plaza in the average Mexican small town there is generally the principal church and the municipal building or city hall. The lower story of the latter is usually formed of arcades called *portales*, which are the centre of business, and there the citizens rest and take their liquid refreshment. The plaza serves as the general breathing place, and in the smaller towns the market is held in it. On Sundays and feast-days a band usually plays there; in the larger towns a military band, and in the smaller a municipal or police band. The military bands, as a rule, are excellent, for the Indians have a natural ear for music. It is very interesting to see these swarthy musicians rendering classical compositions, such as selections from "Tannhäuser" and "Lohengrin," for there seems to be so little in common between German legend and song and the descendants of the Aztecs.

Orizaba is a large, straggling place, but clean and well kept, with a population of thirty-five thousand. It lies in a beautiful valley, and towering above the wooded, ever green mountains which look down upon it rises the great snow-capped peak of Mount Orizaba, over eighteen thousand feet above the level of the sea. The surrounding country is wonderfully fertile, and there are numerous sugar and coffee plantations. Through the middle of the town there flows a rushing, foaming stream, spanned by ancient arched bridges of massive stone; and along its banks the Indian women may be seen during the day vigorously washing the clothes which seem to attract dirt so quickly and are so seldom clean.

Although situated in the temperate zone, the town is just on the border of the tropics; it has the moisture of the lowlands, with the cool breezes of the uplands, and is therefore one of the finest winter resorts in Mexico, the climate being always mild. It is very healthy, and has none of the annoying insects or tropical fevers of the hot region. With its soft-tinted, one-storied buildings, with their red-tiled roofs, and its background of green mountains, the old town is wonderfully picturesque. The natives take life easily, in spite of which the place has a cheerful air of prosperity. Like the Spaniards, they seem to possess that happy faculty of postponing disagreeable things until mañana — the morrow. A restful, dreamy atmosphere hangs over the ancient city, and this I afterwards felt in some other Mexican towns.

As it was Sunday morning when I took my walk, the streets were, of course, unusually quiet. At intervals a small street-car, drawn by two mules, passed leisurely along the main street — a remarkably wide thoroughfare— from the railway station to the other end of the town. Nobody seemed to hurry, and that good old maxim, "To save time is to lengthen life," was apparently unknown to the placid Orizabans. I was informed, however, that a great change was in prospect; for in the course of a few months the town was to appear in all the glory of asphalt paving, and the slow-moving mule-car was to be replaced by swift American electric traction. Perhaps this entrance of American progress may prove to be the serpent in the Orizaban Paradise, and will some day replace the ease and quietness of the old town with all the excitement of American hustle.

Founded by the Spaniards and inhabited by their descendants, Orizaba naturally retains many features of the life of old Spain, and the same thing can be said of all the old towns and cities of Mexico. As I strolled along its narrow, cobble-paved streets that Sunday morning, I could easily have imagined myself in Toledo or Granada; and the impression was heightened by the appearance of the Spanish-looking, Spanish-speaking people who passed on their way to church. Many of the women wore the black mantilla gracefully draped round their heads; the men, for the most part, wore clothes of semi-American cut, with soft felt or derby hats, though one occasionally appeared in the national sombrero.

In one of the back streets I witnessed a scene which was even more typically Spanish, when I came to a queer old drinking place filled with peons enjoying their Sunday-morning dram. Attracted by the sound of music, I glanced through the wide open doorway into the vault-like interior, with its grimy, time-stained walls, where numerous barrels stood on the rough stone flagging. A brigandish-looking half-breed, with a bright red handkerchief tied about his head, was strumming a guitar and singing what seemed to be a wild gypsy song. His audience of peons were standing about the place or squatting on the barrels.

A few minutes later, when the song had ended, a half-breed of rather intelligent appearance walked in, carrying a newspaper in his hand. On the back of his head was a new felt sombrero, and he wore a decent suit of clothes, which made him look quite a superior order of being to the scantily dressed Indians in the drinking den. Lifting his hat in salute, the newcomer said, "Señores, with your permission, I will entertain you with the news." The suggestion was evidently received with favor, for several of the peons responded with "Bueno, bueno" (Good, good). With this encouragement, the man with the newspaper leaped on to one of the barrels and commenced reading a news item.

Owing to widespread illiteracy among the poorer classes, public newspaper readers of this sort have become a feature of Mexican life. Very few men of the peon class are able to read or write, though compulsory education has been introduced in recent times. Thus it is that the newspaper reader is enabled to earn a living by making the rounds of the drinking places and reciting the news of the day. A certain amount of literary skill is required to follow this strange calling successfully; the reader is, in fact, a sort of peripatetic news editor, for he selects only two or three items which he knows will please his audience. The Orizaban reader, for instance, started with the most important topic of the day. He commenced upon an article which discussed the financial panic then in progress in the United States, and the hard times it had caused in Mexico through the closing of mines and other enterprises controlled by Americans. Things were improving, said the newspaper, and thousands of Mexicans who had lost employment would soon be going back to work and earning plenty of money to buy food and drink.

Some of the peons in the audience apparently belonged to the great army of unemployed, for they shook their heads and shrugged their shoulders at the mention of "work." They brightened up, however, at the magic word "drink," and applauded by rapping their glasses on the barrel-tops and giving vent to a chorus of "Buenos."

The reader next selected what journalists would call a "human-interest story." In tragic tones, with appropriate gestures, he entertained his audience with a despatch from northern Mexico which related how a drink-crazed peasant had set fire to the hut of a neighbor with whom he had a feud, shooting down his enemy as he attempted to escape, and despatching him with a knife. Pursued by the rurales, the murderer had fallen riddled with bullets after opening fire on his pursuers. This "top of the column" story seemed to excite intense interest, and at its conclusion there was another outburst of "Bravo," "Muy bien," and such comments as "Buen hombre" (Good man), "Hombre valiente" (Brave fellow). Leaping down from his perch, the itinerant editor went round, sombrero in hand, making a collection; then bowing politely, with a "Buenas dias, señores," he sauntered off to the next drinking place.

I had a delightful walk through Orizaba's principal residential quarter, where old Spanish-looking mansions of crumbling stone were set in the midst of large gardens, beautifully shaded with palms, orange trees and other tropical growths. In the Alameda, lined with venerable trees and adorned with statuary and fountains, I found a wealth of flowers — oleanders and lilies and geraniums of all shades, in full bloom. Here, too, there were swarms of blackbirds, hopping about the shady walks and perching in the trees, piping merrily. There were myriads of these birds all over the town, and they seemed to be as prolific as sparrows in our cities.

Lounging about the street corners or squatting along the curb, smoking and gossiping in their quiet way, were numerous Indian men and women, many of whom had evidently come in from the country. Though they all seemed wretchedly poor, their faces bore a look of patient contentment, and occasionally one would actually smile at some choice bit of repartee. Near an old bridge, in the main street, spanning the mountain stream, there sat an old Indian dame, in a much-worn rebosa, placidly puffing a cigarette. Before her was spread a poor little stock consisting of half a dozen bananas, two or three oranges and a few sweets. As I stood there, a small mongrel dog came up and sniffed at her wares. Seizing a stick, the old woman dealt the animal a vicious blow and he ran off yelping down the street.

An ill-tempered, cruel race, these Indians, I thought; but a moment later I gained a different impression, when there came along a small barefooted, grave-looking Indian urchin, scantily dressed in ragged cotton clothing, with a piece of old bagging about his shoulders. He halted near

A VIEW IN ORIZABA.

Showing the main street and old church of Santa Teresa.

the little pile of fruits and sweets and gazed wistfully at them. Catching sight of him, the old woman's face underwent a remarkable change, and actually took on an expression of benevolence. Picking up a bright red stick of candy from her little stock, she held it towards the child. "Here, niño," she said, "this is yours." As he took it with a polite "Gracias, señora," the old dame gave him a kindly pat on his closely cropped head and sent him off overflowing with happiness. This I afterwards discovered to be typical of the Indians of Mexico, — full of the most amazing contrasts of cruelty and kindness, at once hateful and admirable.

The public market is one of the most interesting sights of Orizaba, with its array of tropical fruits and flowers, and their vendors in the bright costumes of a tropical clime. It has probably not materially altered since the days of the Aztecs. In a description of ancient Mexico, Bernal Diaz, one of the followers of Cortés, expresses surprise at the large crowds of people which were seen in the Aztec towns, the order which prevailed and the variety of merchandise displayed. In his account, he says: "The meat market was stocked with fowls, game and dogs. Vegetables, fruits, articles of food ready-dressed, salt, bread, honey and sweet pastry, made in various ways, were also sold here. Other places in the market were appointed to the sale of earthenware, wooden household furniture, such as tables and benches, firewood, pipes, tobacco, copper axes, and working tools and wooden vessels highly painted. The entire square was enclosed in piazzas under which great quantities of grain were stored, and there were also shops for various kinds of goods." The markets in Mexican towns are to-day practically the same. Low piazzas of solid stone enclose the market square and these are occupied by small shops; the central part, open to the sky, is filled with the stalls of the Indian vendors, men and women, who squat on the ground on a rush mat with another suspended above them for protection against the sun, their little stock spread before them.

During the morning hours in the Orizaba market the crowd of natives was so dense that it was almost impossible to push a way through them. Among the fruits on sale I noticed mangos, zapotes, granaditas, sapodillas, bananas, cocoanuts and other tropical fruits. Most of these look much more tempting or interesting than they really taste. The Mexican mango does not compare with the East Indian variety, being smaller and having much more of the peculiar turpentine flavor. The zapote is a small green melon which grows in clusters on trees and contains great quantities of pips resembling black currants; the sapodilla, which looks something like a small round potato, is filled with a dark yellowish pulp of insipid sweetness; the granadita is the fruit of the passion-flower, and contains a slippery, whitish pulp filled with small black seeds.

Everywhere in the market there was a great variety of beans, black, brown and yellow,—beans fried in fat, called frijoles, being the staple food of the poorer classes. There were also great heaps of golden maize, for corn and not wheat is the Mexican "staff of life." This is cooked in various ways, but more especially in the form of unleavened cakes known as tortillas, which are a distinctive feature of humble Mexican life, and are even popular among the wealthier classes.

Considerable labor is necessary to evolve the tortilla, and many women devote their days and a large portion of their nights to its manufacture. The kernels of corn are first soaked in lime-water until they become soft; they are then placed on a flat kneading-stone called a metate, and ground with a rude pestle until they are reduced to

WONDERFUL ENGINEERING.
The Mexican railway scaling mountain heights on terraces hewn in the solid rock.

fine paste. This is shaped into small round cakes, which are worked between the hands and patted until flattened out very thin. They are then baked on an iron pan over a charcoal fire. Having neither salt nor seasoning, they are rather insipid to the unaccustomed palate, although when served hot they are not unpalatable. In many households a special cook is employed to make tortillas and serve them piping hot at mealtimes. When cold, they are rather leathery, but they are said to be very nutritious, and are often carried by Mexicans when making long journeys in unsettled parts of the country.

The meat in the market did not look inviting, some that was dried being as black as ink, and seeming quite unfit for human food. The Spanish word for meat, *carne* (pronounced *carnay*), is not pleasant to the ear, and when you see some of this evil-looking Mexican meat, it somehow reminds you of the English word "carrion." The meat, too, is very carelessly handled. A butcher's boy can often be seen in a Mexican town carrying a string of tough beef-steaks and using it as a whip on any stray dog that he happens to meet.

In addition to the eatables, there were all kinds of native baskets on sale, kitchen utensils, toys, bright red pottery, goat's milk, trinkets and clothing. A peon's cotton suit, by the way, costs about a dollar, his sandals ten cents and his blanket about a dollar and a half, so that he is fully clothed for less than three dollars.

A most interesting part of the market is the pottery department. The shapes of the various vessels have been handed down from Aztec times, and are probably much the same as those seen by Cortés. Many of the pieces are fantastic in shape and ornamentation; some of them have a graceful appearance, resembling old Grecian or Roman pottery. When it is considered that the native potter has no other tools than his wheel, a piece of broken glass and a horsehair, the results are certainly marvellous. With the hair he trims off the top, while the glass is used for smoothing the rough places. Some of the water-bottles and other pieces are ornamented with pieces of china, fragments of broken cups, plates, etc., arranged in tasteful patterns while the clay is soft. Each part of Mexico has its distinctive pottery, that of Cuernavaca being distinguished from that of Guadalupe, Aguas Calientes or Guadalajara by its color and design.

In a quiet corner of the market was the evangelista or public letter-writer, seated at his little table with a pot of ink and a pen, ready to dash off a matter-of-fact business note or an ardent love-letter for natives unable to write. In another place were the cobblers prepared to cut and fit leather sandals in a few minutes. Pushing through the crowd went the picturesque aguadores or water-carriers, with their huge earthen water-coolers strapped to their backs, from which many a refreshing draught was supplied. In towns where there is no public supply of water, the aguadore takes water daily from house to house.

Queer sweets and pastry, called dulces, are sold in the markets. The Mexicans imitate the French in their confectionery, but it is a very poor imitation, their sweets being over-flavored and insipid and their pastry heavy and indigestible.

At various street-corners during my walk, I noticed the policemen of Orizaba, swarthy Indians, most of them, dressed not unlike the policemen of country towns in France; but instead of a sword they have a revolver strapped to the waist by a belt filled with a row of cartridges. They looked stalwart, efficient fellows, and perform their duty well in keeping order.

Later in the morning, in company with several fellow-travellers who had come from Vera Cruz and had stopped at the Hotel de France, I got on the little street-car and rode to the railway station to continue my journey to Mexico City. The waiting-room and the platform of the station were packed with Indian men, women and children, some of whom had come to take the train, and others to see their friends depart. When the train came in at eleven o'clock, we found there was only one first-class car, and that was pretty well filled with passengers, so that we had hard work to find places for ourselves and our portable baggage.

Most of our fellow-passengers were Mexicans of the middle class, chiefly men; and nearly all of them smoked in the car, as there was no compartment for smokers. Mexicans are rarely pleasant travelling companions, as they generally carry a lot of bags, boxes and bundles, which they pile in the seats, and they chatter incessantly. The women, strange to say, are much less talkative than the men. On our train the second-class cars were filled with Mexicans of the lower middle class; the third-class cars were literally packed with Indians, mostly men.

Railway travel in Mexico is very cheap, the third-class fare being less than one cent a mile. The Indians, I afterwards discovered, have a perfect mania for travelling, and when they are not spending their spare cash in gambling or on fiery native drinks, they buy a railway ticket. It apparently matters very little where they go, and they seem to wander off without any definite object in view. The Mexican third-class car is arranged on the American system, has hard wooden benches, and is not inviting; yet it is always packed with Indians, who exchange cigarettes, drink each other's health in pulque and mescal, which they carry, and gossip incessantly. In fact, for the peon, the third-class car is a sort of travelling workingmen's club. He has genial company, and sees the country as he travels.

When the train stops at a station, he gets out and gossips with brother Indians on the platform.

But a pleasure-trip of this kind sweeps away the poor peon's earnings just as the craving for drink does. While we were travelling from Orizaba to Mexico City, I witnessed a pathetic scene at a small railway station which strikingly illustrated this fact. An Indian was on the platform with his wife and several children, and some friends were urging him to take a ride, just as I have seen the companions of a British workman urging a comrade, fighting against temptation, to enter a public house and have "just one more drink." "Don't go, Juan," urged the tearful wife; "we owe for rent, and the grocer hasn't been paid." The children, bellowing loudly, hung on to their father's blanket. "Aw, come along, Juan, old fellow; don't be henpecked," said his swarthy companions in equivalent Spanish, pulling him towards the car. "A few miles won't hurt you or the missus." The engine gave a whistle, the train began to move, the peons jumped on, and poor, weak Juan, unable to resist temptation, sprang in after them. As the train moved off, the poor wife, realizing that the week's wages would be spent in travel, ran after the car, wringing her hands and gesticulating wildly to her husband, who looked stolidly at her from the window. Railway travel in most countries is either a luxury or a necessity, but Mexico is the only land in which it amounts to a positive vice.

From Orizaba the railway runs through fertile fields and wooded hills until it reaches the mountains and enters a deep ravine called the Cañon del Infernillo or Little Hell, a wild spot, filled with numerous cascades and streams of rushing, roaring waters. The train here makes a wonderful ascent, twisting and climbing over twenty-four hundred feet in nine miles. When the train is coming from the other direction, Indians offer fruit and flowers for sale at the summit;

then, while the train is travelling the nine miles, they scamper down the twenty-four hundred feet by a short mountain footpath and meet it again. Climbing steadily upwards, the train crosses numerous iron bridges, spanning deep chasms, passing through many tunnels, sweeping round dizzy, beetling points, the line crossing and recrossing itself, twisting up serpent-like to the mountain heights. Far above, as the train climbs upwards, you see one or two white specks which are stations. Looking backwards, you can see the wonderful twistings of the line. The scenery is often inexpressibly grand, the pink-tinged, treeless mountains rising on all sides from the foliage of the foot-hills.

At Alta Luz, where the engine takes water, the traveller looks down on the village of Maltrata, thousands of feet below in the valley, which is spread out like a toy city on a green carpet, with its white church, its central plaza, its tiled and thatched houses, its little line of streets, and its surrounding green fields and orchards; and high above the valley, and far above where the train is standing, tower the mountains, culminating in the snow-tipped peak of Orizaba, which seems to pierce the skies. From this point there is a steady and continued climb upwards, until Esperanza is reached at an altitude of 8044 feet. As the train travelled upward to this place, the air grew quite sharp, and the rarefied atmosphere caused a noticeable quickening of the action of the lungs.

While travelling slowly up the mountains, we witnessed a novel and pathetic sight. Two natives, carrying a bright blue coffin, trotted down a mountain path, followed by a peon and three weeping children, keeping closely together at the same jog-trot. They were evidently bound for the municipal cemetery outside a little village far below. The Mexican country cemetery is very different from the peaceful God's acres in our own country districts, and is simply a plot of waste land surrounded with a wall of whitewashed brick. A few of the graves are marked with rude wooden crosses; the others are unmarked. The place is usually overgrown with coarse grass and cactus.

At Esperanza, which we reached at half-past one, there was a halt of thirty minutes for luncheon. None of the Mexican railway trains have dining-cars attached, and stops for meals are made at certain stations, the customary price being fifty cents. Passengers of all classes have equal privileges in the dining-room, and unless you are careful, you are apt to find yourself seated with a motley company of unwashed natives whose manners constantly remind you that fingers were invented before forks. The white passengers on the train — that is, the foreigners and best class of Mexicans — usually gather at one table, and it is advisable to wait a few minutes until the company is seated, so as to make sure of getting a place at the right table. Though meals are rather crudely served, the food is generally well cooked and palatable.

At Esperanza, mountain climbers can travel by road to the village of Chalchicamula, whence a trail through the woods leads to the foot of Mount Orizaba. This giant peak of over eighteen thousand feet is, next to Mount McKinley in Alaska, the highest peak in North America. For an experienced mountain climber the ascent is difficult but not dangerous. In making the ascent, one passes through all varieties of climates, from the sub-tropical region of the valley to the pine woods of the north, and then on to the cold, icy, snow-capped Arctic regions. The scenes to be witnessed on every side are magnificent.

Travelling from Esperanza down to Vera Cruz, the descent in many places is so steep that steam-power is not used. The train runs down the mountains by its own weight, brake-power only being necessary to regulate the pace.

WATCHING THE TRAIN.
A familiar scene at a Mexican railway station.

After leaving Esperanza, the line reaches the flat tablelands, bordered with mountains in the distance, dry and dusty in the winter time. The country is dreary and monotonous, with scarcely a tree to be seen. Here and there I noticed a big white hacienda building or ranch-house set in the midst of the plain, where large herds of cattle were browsing on withered grass, the only signs of cultivation being occasional fields where the dry, yellow Indian-corn stalks left from the last harvest were still standing. This dry, dusty appearance of the country was, I found, characteristic of the highlands of Mexico in the winter months. There is then little or no rain, everything gets dry and parched, and only where there is an irrigated patch is there any green vegetation. Sometimes the train passed over a dry watercourse, for in the higher lands most of the streams and rivers dry up during the rainless season. When the rains set in, they soon begin flowing again, and frequently get into a flooded condition. Mexico is very poorly supplied with rivers, excepting along the Gulf coast, where they are very numerous and quite large at the mouth, but not navigable for any distance.

The monotonous country through which we travelled during the afternoon was rendered still more depressing by the weather, the sky which in Mexico is usually a clear, deep blue being still dark and cloudy. Blowing from the coast, the "norther" was making itself felt in the high table-land. There were, however, occasionally a few interesting scenes to relieve the tedium of our journey. At one village there was an encampment of soldiers, infantry and cavalry, and a long line of tents. Everything seemed to be conducted in good military order. At nearly every station where a stop was made the train was besieged by a throng of wild-looking Indian women and children selling boiled eggs, fried chicken, fiery Mexican dishes, such as tamales, and native cakes and drinks. These were eagerly bought by the Mexican passengers, who seemed to be continually eating. Mexican railway stations, especially in the small towns, are always crowded, as the arrival and departure of a passenger train — sometimes there is only one daily — is quite an important event. Poor people with nothing else to do and loafers of every description gather to see the train, smoking and chatting together, staring at the passengers and discussing them with much apparent enjoyment. Beggars of all kinds, the lame, the diseased and the blind, are always on hand, clamoring for centavos, and singing lustily to the accompaniment of their queer old harps, fiddles and mandolins.

We passed very few villages, and these mostly consisted of square, flat-roofed huts of adobe or sun-dried brick. Adobe is an important feature of life in Mexico and is the salvation of the poor Mexican. Wood being very expensive, and stone or manufactured brick out of the question for him, he has to fall back on mother earth for shelter. The soil in many places is a sort of clay which, after being mixed with water and straw, — usually the refuse from stables, — is put in square wooden moulds and baked in the sun. This sun-dried brick is called adobe, and it is wonderful how long it will stand the stress of sun and rain in a country where there are no severe frosts. Not only does the poor man make use of this cheap building material, but many a pretentious wall that is covered with a respectable coating of stucco and finished in imitation of stone, when it eventually falls into decay, shows that within it has relied for strength and support upon adobe.

Later in the day our train steamed across the plains of Apam, relieved only by monotonous rows of maguey plants, from which the national drink, pulque (pronounced *pool-kay*), is made. Apam is, in fact, the most important district in Mexico for the cultivation of this plant — a species of agave which looks a good deal like the "aloe" used for ornamental purposes in American gardens and sometimes called the "century plant," from the fiction that it blooms only once in a hundred years. The Mexican plant, however, is much larger, its dark green spiked leaves sometimes reaching a length of fifteen feet, a foot in breadth and several inches in thickness. From six to ten years are required for the plant to mature in its native soil. It then sends up a tall, stiff spike, which is covered with clusters of small, bell-shaped blossoms as white as bleached cabbage, and then dies. In maguey plantations, however, when the flowering time arrives, the plant is marked with a cross, the stalks being then full of the sap for which it is cultivated. To obtain this, the entire heart is removed, leaving a natural basin in which the sap collects. In this condition the liquor is sweet and perfectly clear, and is called agua miel or honey-water. The sap, which gathers quickly, is removed two or three times a day by an Indian, usually provided with a long, hollow gourd with a hole at each end. He places the small end of the gourd in the sap, and applying his mouth to the opening at the other end, sucks the liquid into the gourd. This primitive method, however, is being supplanted by a long siphon, which enables the sap to be removed more quickly and cleanly.

After its removal, the sap is emptied into a pigskin which the gatherer carries on his back. Each plant yields on an average about six quarts of sap daily for a month or more. It then withers and dies and another is planted in its place. The sap collected each day is put in barrels and fermented, when it is ready for the market. Pulque, after fermentation, tastes a good deal like stale buttermilk diluted with stagnant water — a thin, starchy, evil-smelling liquor. After further fermentation, it acquires a putrid taste. The natives like it best immediately after fermentation, as it is supposed to spoil — if it can spoil — within twenty-four hours afterwards, and there is a law prohibiting its sale after that time. Thus it must be drunk at once, which may account for the energy with which the Indians imbibe it. Very few of the better classes drink pulque; it is the beverage of the poor.

A taste for pulque has to be acquired by strangers. The first experience is always repellent, but familiarity is said to breed contempt for its nauseous qualities. Great virtues are claimed for the drink, especially in the cure of kidney diseases. Some Mexican doctors prescribe it for these ailments, but several physicians who have investigated its alleged curative powers assert that it is of no value whatever.

Pulque was first known in Mexico, so it is said, in 1050 A.D., when a beautiful Indian maiden with the unbeautiful name of Xochitl brought to the Toltec emperor, Teopancaltzin, a large pot of sweet liquid which she had drawn from the maguey plants in her garden. The emperor was so pleased with the drink that he married the girl, and in course of time a son was born who was christened Meconetzin, meaning "The son of the maguey plant." Queen Xochitl did not make pulque, but merely extracted the sweet, sticky juice of the plant, the agua miel. In the northern parts of Mexico the natives drink this, and it has no bad effects.

For a hundred miles and more round Mexico City there are pulque estates where the maguey plant is cultivated, and on some of these over a thousand peons are employed attending to the plants and gathering the sap. Special pulque trains loaded with this vile beverage run into the capital every day from the country districts. It is sold at pulque shops, the lowest class of Mexican saloons, patronized only by Indian peons. A cheap drink, it costs

MEXICO'S NATIONAL DRINK.
Gathering the maguey sap for making pulque.

AN AGUADORE.
The Mexican water-seller. (See page 34.)

only two or three centavos a glass; yet the daily expenditure for pulque in Mexico City is said to exceed twenty thousand dollars.

Indulgence in this drink softens the brain, ruins the digestion and paralyzes the nerves; while its effects on the native population are so destructive that it has been well named "the curse of Mexico." It is principally drunk in Mexico City, where the Indian population is the most degraded in the Republic. Many employers of labor will not hire men from the pulque districts if they can possibly get them from elsewhere. Tequila and mescal, two fiery spirits largely consumed in Mexico, are distilled from a smaller species of maguey. They have some resemblance to cheap brandy, and are equally deadly in their effects on the human system.

CHAPTER III

MEXICO CITY BY NIGHT

HOURS of steaming through bare plains, hemmed in by bare mountains, cone-shaped, the true volcanic type! Hours of dust and rattle, the scenery broken only by the huge, flat-shaped maguey plant, interminable save where a few acres round a lonely village church show the yellowing stalks of last season's harvest of Indian corn! Such are the plains of Apam, through which the heavily loaded train from Vera Cruz panted and jolted as the sun sank and the quick-falling darkness made the weirdly lonely scenery more weird, more lonely and desolate, if that were possible. It is "starved, ignoble nature" in very truth, and the traveller wonders, as he stares through the gathering darkness, where Mexico City can be hidden in the plain's hopeless desert.

Mexico, however, is a land of contrasts, and this the newcomer is not long in learning. Thus the transition from the barbarically wild to the civilized is remarkably sudden. For miles before reaching the Mexican capital we passed through these sandy wastes and fields of maguey; past straggling Indian villages of adobe huts with garden-plots enclosed with cactus, tall and straight, forming natural fence-posts, where Indian men in their red blankets and straw sombreros, and unkempt Indian women in their blue rebosas, squatted about and stolidly watched the train flit by. Suddenly from the desert we entered what appeared to be a suburban district where there were stone houses of Spanish appearance, quite well built, with a few Americanized business buildings mixed with them, decorated with garish advertising signs in Spanish and English. Then electric lights began to twinkle along the highways, and an electric car filled with passengers glided onward to the city. A few minutes later our train ran through some rather squalid streets and then entered a railway station which, though really nothing but a glorified shed, was the terminus in Mexico City. There are no stations in the capital equal in size and appointments to those in even a third-rate American city, and most of them are crude in the extreme. They are arranged in much the same way as are the American stations, without raised platforms, and having only one waiting-room for passengers of all classes.

No sooner had the train come to a standstill than it was besieged by a mob of cargadores, offering to carry our baggage. These men were not in uniform, but wore the ordinary dress of the peon — a dirty linen suit, or just trousers and shirt, and some had a ragged blanket wrapped round their shoulders. As the cargadores are not allowed to enter the railway carriages, the traveller passes his bags to them through the window. I was duly captured by one of these burden-bearers, and following him emerged to find a large crowd of cabs, very much like the Parisian fiacres, in the station yard. The drivers, however, were very different in appearance from the cochers of Paris, for they all wore the heavy felt, steeple-crowned sombrero.

There are first- and second-class cabs in Mexico City, the former bearing a small blue flag and the latter a red flag. The blues charge fifty cents and the reds thirty cents an hour. A local guide-book suggests that tourists can remember the two classes by saying to themselves, "Red cabs for the ordinary red-blooded people, blues for the blue bloods." A year or two ago there was a third class of cabs which sported a yellow flag, and were popularly known as "yellow fevers." This, of course, was a joke, but they certainly were pestilential conveyances, and the city is well rid of them.

As I left the station in one of the red-flag cabs, bound for my hotel, a policeman at the station exit noted down the number and destination of the vehicle. This, I found, is done at all the railway stations in the City, and it is an excellent idea; for if anything happens to a passenger, if he gets lost or robbed, the police are thus able to get some trace of him.

My cab drove quickly through wide asphalted streets, bright with electric lights, and bordered with flat-roofed houses in Spanish style, with their balconies and barred windows. Intermixed with these were a few modern-looking business buildings and stores, and one or two ancient churches with quaint towers and domes. Along most of the streets through which I passed electric street-cars were running, crowded with passengers. As in all Mexican cities, these cars are American-made, and carry passengers inside only. The brilliantly lighted streets, the crowded cars and the passing throngs of well-dressed people all gave me the feeling of being once more in a great metropolis; and this seemed wonderfully strange when I realized that less than half an hour before I had been travelling through Indian villages and a lonely desert.

I had engaged quarters at the Hotel Sanz, which is under American management, and as comfortable as hotels are in the Mexican capital. There are no really fine hotels in the city, most of them being old convents or mansions partly rebuilt.

The Sanz was the usual large, square, flat-roofed building of three stories built round an unroofed patio, encircled by galleries at each story; the office, some reception rooms and the restaurant were on the ground floor. In the centre of the patio there was the usual fountain, with its flowers and shrubbery. All this would have looked very attractive and refreshing on a sultry evening; but the "norther" was still blowing, the sky was overcast, the air was distinctly chilly and there had just been a heavy shower of rain. Everything seemed damp, dark and cold. There was not a stove or open fireplace in the hotel, but in this respect it was no worse off than the other establishments. None of them are heated, and when the weather is cold there is absolutely no way of getting warm unless you go to bed; and even then you are apt to suffer, as the rarefied air is very penetrating. I had a comfortable room, but it made me shiver to look out on the cold, damp patio and hear the chill wind sighing round the open court.

Mexico City certainly needs a good modern hotel, and at first sight such an establishment would seem to be sure of making large profits and well paying its promoters. The servant problem, however, and the extortionate prices which are demanded for ground in eligible districts have thus far prevented capitalists from embarking in such an enterprise. Several well-known American and European hotel lessees have investigated the matter, but none of them have been willing to engage in what they consider would be a losing venture. The present hotels are cheap and clean, but in the majority of them everything is old and dingy, and the service is very inferior. Twenty years ago, I was told, visitors were making the same complaint, but the need for a modern hotel is still a crying one.

With all their faults, the Mexican hotels have one redeeming trait — they are not expensive. Those in the big centres usually make separate charges for rooms and meals, the price of rooms generally ranging from one dollar fifty to three dollars a day, while meals are served à la carte. Some of the hotels, however, serve a regular dinner, which costs, as a rule, about a dollar. In Mexico City, where the cost of living is higher than in small places, one can manage to live very comfortably at a hotel, with room and board, for four or five dollars a day. In the smaller towns the hotels charge so much a day for room and board together, usually from two to three dollars, the price varying according to the size and position of the room.

Good servants are very difficult to get in Mexico, and the domestics, who are chiefly drawn from the Indian population, are seldom long contented with their places. The chambermaids in the Americanized hotels — most of them swarthy Indians or half-breeds — look a good deal like typical gypsy maidens. They wear the usual native costume, a loose skirt and bodice of speckled blue and white and a rebosa draped over the shoulders. Their coarse black hair is generally worn hanging down the back in a long plait, their eyes are very dark, and they are much given to wearing large ear-rings. When not at work, they sit about the stairs in twos and threes, and to a stranger seem very picturesque. Their ideas of housework are also interesting to the stranger who does not have to employ them as domestics, although their method of dusting would drive an American housewife mad in a week. At the end of a stick they tie a cloth and very lackadaisically flick it around in the direction in which they think the dust is. The whole process suggests the indolence with which these folk regard all life's problems.

The district of Mexico City in which the principal hotels are situated is historic ground, for some of the most stirring events of Mexican history have been enacted in this particular quarter. Opposite the Hotel Sanz is the Alameda,

Copyright by Underwood & Underwood, New York.

CALLE DEL RELOJ.
One of the busiest streets in the capital.

a pretty little park about twice as large as City Hall Park, New York, and from this radiate some of the principal streets. Once a piece of waste land, the Alameda is now a long stretch of velvety green lawns and numerous beds of tropical flowers, shaded by fine old trees and graceful palms. In the centre is a handsome fountain, and on one side a quaint Moorish kiosque, in which refreshments are sold. One of the regimental bands plays in the Alameda every day. Until recently, the little park was Mexico City's fashionable promenade, and on Sunday mornings the smart people gathered there much in the same way as they do in Hyde Park during the London season. But the centre of population is moving southwestward, and the Alameda is, as far as I could observe, becoming chiefly the resort of the poorer classes.

This spot has a tragic history, having been the place of execution for the victims of the Inquisition. In 1574 twenty-one "pestilent Lutherans" were burned there. Crowds used to stand on the steps of the old church of San Diego, which still faces the Alameda, to get a good view of the burnings and watch the ashes of the victims thrown into a marsh which then existed behind the church. The Inquisition was not abolished in Mexico until 1812.

In the evening I took a walk through some of the principal streets, and was astonished to find them so deserted. The Mexican capital has a population of over four hundred thousand, and I had read such glowing accounts of the gayety of the place that I confidently expected to find it a sort of transatlantic Paris. I was doomed to disappointment, however, for although it was only nine o'clock when I took my walk abroad, all signs of life had departed from the streets. Only a few stores and restaurants were open, and very few people were to be seen. Nor was this due to the fact that it was Sunday night, for the streets have the same dreary appearance on other nights of the week. There is a reason for this, and it is undoubtedly climatic.

While the day temperature, even in winter, is mild and often hot, the nights in the capital are invariably chilly; in the winter months dangerously so. The whole population are terrified of the night air, and thus it is that after eight o'clock Mexico City is almost a city of the dead, except in some of the important business streets where such night amusements as exist are to be found. A few theatres and cinematograph shows afford amusement to those who will face the night air; but there is no café life as in France, and no sort of out-of-door life. Nobody seems to come to the restaurants, except in the case of a few popular establishments chiefly patronized by foreigners. At some of these good dinners are served, during which excellent music is played; but there is little to attract one in going, on a cold night, through deserted streets to half-deserted restaurants. The theatres do not open until nine o'clock, and unless there is some very good company playing, they do not attract large crowds.

As I wandered along, I noticed a lantern standing in the middle of the street at nearly every crossing. These lights, I found, belonged to policemen, for in all Mexican cities the policemen stand at night at the street corners, placing their lanterns in the middle of the road. The long row of flickering lights, up and down, in every direction, has a curious effect; but to the law-abiding it is a comforting one, indicating as it does that the Argus-eye of the law is on the sleeping city. Unlike Diogenes, the Mexican policeman employs his lantern to find a possible thief, but humorists say that the lantern is really intended to aid the thief in avoiding the guardians of the law.

In dress and appearance the police, who are chiefly recruited from the Indians and half-breeds, are not unlike the Parisian sergeants de ville. On one side of his waist the policeman wears what American policemen call "a night stick," and on the other a revolver is strapped. During the day he walks his beat and takes an occasional rest by leaning against a door-post. At night he wears a long blue cloak, and if the weather is cold you will see him muffled up to the chin, breathing through the cloth. All the Mexican masses seem to dread the night and early morning air. Muffling themselves up in their blankets, the peons breathe through them with heroic disregard of the germs which must lurk in their dirty folds; women cover their mouths with their rebosas, using them as respirators. The popular idea is that unadulterated cold air entering the lungs is likely to cause pneumonia.

Windows in the city are all barred with iron bars; the heavy doors would require dynamite to blow them open, and fires are infrequent. The Mexican policeman's lot is therefore a happy one, for he has little to do, which is what the Mexican likes best. When the streets are deserted, he not infrequently leans against a door and goes to sleep; but if you want him, his lantern enables you to find him and rouse him from his slumbers. The police are very numerous all over Mexico, because the government has found it advisable to keep itself well informed of affairs, in order to check revolutionary movements. Even in the smallest villages there is a uniformed police. The metropolitan police appeared to me to be a very efficient body of men; they are very courteous to strangers, and have made the streets of the capital almost as safe as those of New York.

Just as the London police are affectionately called "Bobbies," so the Mexican guardians of the law have their pet name, "Serenos." The old Spanish watchmen whom they supplanted used to call out the state of the weather just as did the English watchmen in olden times. As

Mexican weather is usually clear, the watchman's cry was simply a reiteration of the words "Tiempo sereno" (weather clear), and thus they came to be called "Serenos." By the way, they have a peculiar custom of arresting all parties in an altercation. If a policeman is called to arrest an offender the complainant will be arrested as well and marched off to the police station. In such cases there is only one thing to do and that is to obey orders, accompany the policeman to the " comiseria," and trust to luck in having the matter settled by the officer on duty there.

During my walk, I not only noticed the sharpness of the air, which every poor man in the street was trying to avoid by breathing through his cloak or blanket, but I also noticed a peculiar atmospheric quality which somehow reminded me of the high mountainous districts of Switzerland. I also felt a queer dizzy sensation in my head and a slight difficulty in breathing. Then I remembered that I was in a region of rarefied air, for Mexico City is nearly 8000 feet above the level of the sea. It is owing to this high altitude that most visitors on their arrival experience a slight headache and shortness of breath, which, however, wears off in a day or two.

The geographical situation of Mexico City is unique among the world's capitals. Lying on a beautiful plain about sixty miles long and thirty broad, the city is encircled by a chain of mountains, some of which have the characteristically pointed volcanic shape, while nearer to the city rises a long range of barren foot-hills. Owing to its altitude, the city usually enjoys an even and moderate temperature, the thermometer showing an average of seventy degrees the year round, and even the summer is pleasantly cool. Its peculiar situation, however, causes some very unpleasant climatic conditions, such as the " norther" which was blowing when I arrived. The sun is always waging war

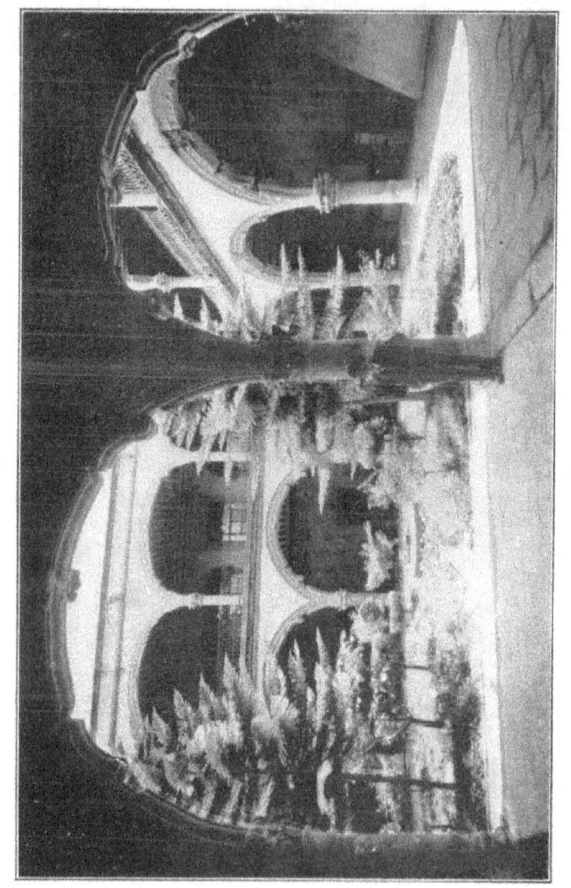

REMINISCENT OF THE PAST
Patio of an old mansion in Mexico City.

with the cloud troops and the mountain air, a combat of nature which gives rise to sudden and trying changes. The city being less sheltered from the north and northwest, the winds blowing over the snow-capped mountains often bring frost and even snow in the winter. On a bright, clear day, too, there is often an extraordinary difference between the temperature on the sunny and shady sides of the streets; for it will be roasting hot on one side, while on the other one feels an unpleasant chill. In fact, the Spanish proverb regarding Madrid is often applicable to the Mexican metropolis, for the wind which on a bright day does not seem strong enough to blow out a candle on the sunny side of the street will almost take a man's life in the shade.

The seasons in Mexico are divided into the dry and the rainy, the former beginning in November and lasting until June. In the highlands during this time of the year little or no rain falls, save a few heavy showers in March or April, and unless a "norther" is blowing, the sun shines with unclouded splendor and the sky is intensely blue. During the rains, from June to November, showers fall every day from two to four, and the dry, sun-baked plains and hills, arid and yellow, then turn to a rich emerald. Thus the climate of these Mexican highlands is no warmer in summer than in winter, and travelling, thanks to the absence of dust, is far more agreeable. It always puzzles the Mexicans why tourists visit their country when it is at its climatic worst.

Around the city lie six shallow lakes, Texcoco, Xochilmilco, San Cristoval, Xaltocan, Zumpalgo and Chalco. The first of these is about three miles from the city. In Aztec times the waters of these lakes entirely surrounded the capital, but since the conquest their shores have gradually receded. Zumpalgo is twenty-five feet higher than the city and drains into Texcoco, which caused a serious flood on three occasions, the city being once inundated to the depth of seven feet, and there being no outlet, the waters remained in possession for years. To prevent such another catastrophe, with all its attendant loss of life and property, the Spaniards, in 1607, began digging a huge drainage tunnel, which cost the lives of thousands of unfortunate Indian slaves. Unaccustomed to hard toil, half starved and overworked, they speedily succumbed to the ill treatment of their Spanish taskmasters. Their labor, after all, was in vain, for when the tunnel was at last completed, a large portion of the roof caved in. Many years later it was decided to turn the tunnel into an open canal, and work on this continued for over a hundred years, the canal being finished in 1789. It was known as the Tajo de Nochistongo, and remained in use until a few years ago, but was never satisfactory. It was then supplanted by a modern scheme of drainage carried out by Pearson & Sons, which has proved a great success not only in draining the overflow of the lakes, but in carrying off the city sewage. The old Tajo is now a dry trench, with an average depth of two hundred feet, from three to seven hundred feet wide at the top and sloping to a few feet in width at the bottom. It is nearly five miles long, and is partly used as a cutting by the Mexican Central Railway.

It is curious that Cortés should have built his city on the site of the ancient one thus placed in the midst of lakes and swamps, with the accumulated débris and filth of ages beneath it. He had plenty of higher ground to choose from near at hand. It is difficult also to understand why he did not select a site nearer either of the coasts. Probably he was tempted by the fact that there was plenty of building material at hand from the Aztec temples and palaces which he destroyed. Thus it was that the site of the modern Mexican capital was most unwisely chosen, and the evil results of it are still experienced. Even to-day, a few feet below the surface the earth is soft and swampy, which has caused many of the buildings to settle unevenly, while it has also made the drainage of the city extremely difficult.

Much has been done to mitigate the unfortunate position of the capital; but the death-rate is still remarkably high, particularly in the winter. The average duration of life is said to be only twenty-six years, which amazing condition is largely due to infant mortality. Typhoid and malarial fevers are prevalent, and pneumonia takes heavy toll. Owing to the effect of the rarefied air on the action of the heart and lungs, diseases of these organs are rarely curable on the spot, and whenever possible patients are transferred for treatment to lower altitudes, such as Cuernavaca and Cuautla, which have altitudes of about five thousand feet.

The hopeless ignorance of hygiene and the entire absence of sanitary conditions of life among the working classes is largely responsible for the heavy death-rate. Their dwellings are mere hovels, their habits are filthy, their clothes are ragged, and the foods they eat are ill-cooked and contain little nourishment. Thus it is no wonder that diseases, especially those associated with dirt, such as smallpox and typhus fever, are terribly common; while skin diseases, scrofula, rheumatism and bone troubles make constant inroads on the national health. No precautions being taken to insure the purity of the drinking water, the typhoid fiend stalks unchecked among the lower quarters of the city. A report of the American consul states that of three hundred and fifty-eight deaths occurring during one week in January, 1908, one hundred and twenty-five were from ailments of the digestive organs, and one hundred and six pulmonary. Bad food, coupled with sudden changes of temperature, were the chief causes of this heavy mortality.

The population of Mexico City is thoroughly cosmopolitan, for it contains representatives from nearly every nation of the earth. The Indians are vastly in the majority; the half-breeds or meztizos, who call themselves *the* Mexicans, ranking next in number, and forming the great middle class. Then there is the richest class, for the most part of pure Spanish descent, "whites," as they like to call themselves, from whose ranks most of the government officials are derived. These people of the upper class are not all dark; still a blonde is very rare among them. Most of them are of olive-brown color, suggesting, in spite of their denial, a mixture of Indian blood; for in the early days it was not considered a mésalliance for a Spanish officer of even high rank to marry an Aztec maiden of the better class, so that Indian blood is, in fact, very widely diffused through the Mexican upper classes.

I had a good opportunity to observe the mixed types of the city's population when I went out on the morning after my arrival, for in marked contrast with their deserted appearance the night before the streets were now crowded, and presented a queer motley of life. Numbers of men and just a few girls (as the custom of employing female clerks, etc., is only beginning to be adopted in Mexico's capital) were hurrying to business. Among these business men and clerks, dressed much as they would be in an American city, were moving typical Mexican Indians in their cotton attire, blankets and straw sombreros. Their women, mostly barefoot, pattered along wrapt in their rebosas. Sometimes one of the Indians would have his whole family with him, a row of ragged children, straggling behind in single file. Filthy little urchins of Indian newsboys, with lank black hair, brown, smiling faces, and merry black eyes, in tattered clothing and battered straw sombreros, hawked their papers at the street corners, shouting lustily, "'El

Im-par-ci-al" and "El Dia-r-io," giving their r's a peculiar long trill. Along the street rode a troop of Mexican cavalry, swarthy, bronzed fellows, mounted on the trim, serviceable Mexican pony, and dressed in blue uniforms and Austrian-shaped kepis of glazed leather, their rifles strapped on their backs. Here and there I passed a soldier on foot dressed in German fashion, a blue uniform with red facings, and a brass-spiked helmet. The scene was full of color and vivid contrasts. Electric street-cars glided by packed with people, many of them compelled to go to business in true strap-hanging fashion. Red and blue cabs were abroad, and now and again an automobile dashed past, its horn tooting merrily; while the quaint old-world country life which lay outside the city boundaries was represented by a chance country wagon drawn by oxen, its wheels clumsy disks cut in a solid piece from some huge tree trunk. The weather was not unpleasant, for although the sky was still overcast, the "norther" was moderating, and the air was slightly milder.

Passing the new opera-house, which was in course of erection, and on which a large gang of workmen were hammering the great steel framework and hoisting stone, I came to the new Post-office, a magnificent structure of white stone and marble of platero or mixed Spanish design. It is one of the most beautiful public buildings in the world, and certainly does credit to Mexico, though its actual construction is due to an Italian architect and American contractors. The interior fittings are very elaborate, fine marbles and bronze being lavishly used. The opera-house is also being built by an American firm.

Mexico City might be described as a sort of Americanized Madrid. The architecture of the older buildings is largely of the antique Spanish style, with a few modifications adopted for domestic and climatic reasons. Many of these old structures are being rebuilt in much the same style as American business buildings; and the Americanizing process is still further evidenced by some large, new office buildings of American design which have been erected in recent years. One peculiarity which is shared by many of the buildings, old and new, is the absence of cellars, which is due to the marshy nature of the soil. Chimneys are also scarce, as fireplaces are seldom used.

The streets of the capital are laid out in blocks of the familiar chess-board pattern, on the same system as that of American cities. Looking down some of the principal streets, one sees a picturesque mixture of ancient, flat-roofed houses of stone or stucco, now used for business purposes, seldom over three stories in height, usually cream white, and having the familiar balconies round the first story. Intermixed with these are modern buildings of various heights and styles. On a clear day, with a bright blue sky overhead, the views down some of the older streets are wonderfully attractive, the long lines of buildings of mixed architecture and varied shades of color ending in a distant vista of reddish-tinted mountains which overlook the city.

Most of the main thoroughfares have an up-to-date and prosperous appearance, but in the residential districts one catches glimpses at the crossways of queer, dingy side streets in which the houses, with their faded, cracked stucco and rusty ironwork, seem to have been painted a hundred years back and forgotten ever since. In many of these old-fashioned streets, houses which were once fashionable mansions are being gradually transformed into business buildings or are used as boarding-houses. In one quarter of the city — quite out of the world — I strolled through some narrow streets so little frequented that blades of grass were sprouting up through the cobble-stone paving. In these streets were some fine old mansions, evidently built in a long-past age and once the homes of wealthy citizens; but the district had become unfashionable, and the ancient mansions, tenanted by a very different class of people, had gradually fallen into decay.

All these old houses had huge double doors, some of them beautifully carved, which opened on to the great stone-paved patio with its fountains, flowers and shrubbery, with wide flights of stone steps leading to the upper galleries. This is the invariable arrangement in the old Mexican houses, which are seldom imposing on the outside, their rows of iron-barred windows giving them rather a prison-like appearance. A peculiar feature of them is that the family usually occupies the upper stories, the ground floor being used for stables, the carriage room, and the servants' quarters. Strange to the American eye is the lack of chimneys, already referred to, which is due to the fact that charcoal is generally used in Mexico for cooking and heating. Very little coal is found in the country, and as most of that used is imported from abroad, it is rather an expensive luxury. All through the city the charcoal sellers can be seen making their rounds with the cry of "Carbosin" (charcoal). Poor families have to content themselves with a few small pieces — just enough to cook their frugal meals of tortillas and frijoles.

Most of the business buildings which have been recently erected or reconstructed have rather an American look, the sign-boards helping to give this impression. I noticed, for instance, such familiar signs as "La Maquina Singer" (Singer Sewing Machine), "Maquina Escribir Remington" (Remington Typewriter), "American Cash Register," "Quaker Oats" and "American Electric Co.," all indications of the great American invasion. There were also some other signs of it.

Americans seemed to swarm everywhere — in the streets,

in stores, in offices, and likewise in the drinking places; for several American bars have lately been started in the central district. These are popular meeting places for a large class of Americans who come down to Mexico in search of employment or to embark in business in a small way. In one short street I saw an Americanized barber's shop, an American grocery store, an American drinking saloon, an American billiard room, an American bootblack's stand, and encountered so many Americans that it was difficult to realize that I was in Mexico City and not in Chicago or New York. As the result of this invasion, the principal shops make a great point of catering for Americans, and display the announcement so often seen abroad, "English spoken here." Some ultra-patriotic Americans object to this frequent use of the word "English," and tell the Mexicans that it should be changed to "United States." While becoming gradually Americanized, Mexico City is, however, still cosmopolitan; for in a short radius one can see a French costumier's, Spanish wines and groceries, a German hardware store and agencies of several important European firms of various nationalities.

Some of the finest buildings in the city are in Calle Cinco de Mayo (Fifth of May Street), a sort of Mexican Wall Street, where there are several new American office buildings — skyscrapers of ten or more stories — most of them being the offices of railway companies. One of the best buildings is occupied by the Mexican Light and Power Company, a Canadian corporation supplying electric power for lighting, running factories, street-cars, etc., from its works at a great waterfall about forty miles out.

Some of the old buildings used to-day for business purposes date perhaps from the sixteen hundreds; but they have lost their antique appearance as far as the outside is concerned. Through their great square doorways, how-

CALLE CINCO DE MAYO.
Mexico City's Wall Street.

ever, can be seen the true old-fashioned patio, with its galleries around each story, its central fountain and shrubbery. Some of these old buildings were once the mansions of Spanish grandees, and fine carved fronts are to be seen. Among the most notable of the older buildings is the former residence of the Escandon family in the Calle San Francisco, which is now cut up into offices, the first floor being the ticket office of the Mexican Central Railway.

Next to the Escandon mansion is the Jockey Club, commonly known as the House of Tiles, built by the Count del Valle in the eighteenth century as a private residence. Its exterior is entirely covered with porcelain tiles of blue and white, imported from China at great cost. The entrance is massive, and the grand stairway is a superb piece of work, practically unaltered from the olden days. A large lamp with an alabaster shade, which hangs on the landing, has a grim association, for it was beneath its light that the Count was assassinated. Throughout the interior the decoration is largely done in porcelain tiles; and tumbago, a valuable composite imported from China, has been used for the balustrading.

The Jockey Club is the most exclusive of all Mexican clubs, very few foreign members being admitted. Mexicans are not clubable in the American or English sense, and instead of being founded in the interests of horse-racing or social intercourse, the original object of the Jockey Club was gambling. This was conducted to such a scandalous extent that, it is said, President Diaz, in his autocratic fashion, had a few years back to put a stop to the ruinously high stakes which were played for. At the present time the Jockey Club is practically a social club, where baccarat is played chiefly as an amusement, and the club now justifies its name by owning a race-track near the city, where meetings are held in the autumn and spring.

One of the most interesting streets in the capital is Calle San Francisco (San Francisco Street), Mexico City's Broadway, which is the most Americanized street of all and a great resort for tourists. The numerous curio stores in this popular thoroughfare are owned principally by Americans, and in their windows are attractive displays of Mexican pottery, feather-work, opals, drawn-work, sarapes and Mexican trinkets — many of the latter suspiciously suggestive of Waltham or Meriden, U. S. A. — and of course quantities of picture postcards. There are also several American bookstores where American and English magazines and newspapers are sold.

In the upper part of the street the shops are not imposing, being much as one would see in a small French town; but farther down are some really fine establishments, jewelers, and others, which would do credit to Fifth Avenue. Here, too, there are several dulcerias (a combination of confectioner's and café) where pastry, tea, coffee, and chocolate are served. At these places, contrary to the usual Mexican custom, there are girl waitresses, most of them dark-skinned, Indian-looking "meztizas," very few of whom would take the first prize in a beauty contest. In this street there are some of the largest hotels, including the Iturbide, and also some of the leading restaurants. Over the Gambrinus, a German restaurant conducted by an enterprising Italian, the British Club has its rooms, where the travelling Briton, with proper credentials, can find an agreeable resting-place. Mexico, Germany, Italy, England — truly a cosmopolis!

In and around San Francisco Street there are a few department stores of the American type, selling a little of everything, and conducted on the American system. These establishments also announce their bargains in true American style. Plastered over the windows are such appeals as "Ojo, gran barata, ojo" (Look at the great bargains; just look at them); "Precios muy reducidos" (Prices greatly reduced); "Gran reduccion" (Great reduction). One worthy shopkeeper, with a limited knowledge of English, announced "Gods at the cut price," evidently a Mexican variation of the popular American expression, "Goods at cut prices." Some shops, in a desperate attempt to Anglicize themselves and appear very up to date, have christened themselves "Fashionable," "Old England," "High Life" (pronounced *hig leef*), "Five o'clock," "Royal Club."

In one restaurant an attempt had been made to "English" the bill of fare, with such lamentable results as "Beefsteati viete" (for sirloin steak) and "Cocteel" (cocktail). One of the dulcerias, too, which caters for English and American patronage and serves American "breakfast foods," had made a brave attempt to translate some of their weird names for the benefit of customers, the menu card being a hotch-potch of Spanish and English. The translator started off with oatmeal, which he transformed into "avena," this word having to do duty in describing various cereals of a totally different character, "Shredded-wheat biscuit," for instance, appearing as "Biscochos de avena." But when at last he came to such terrifying names as "Puffed Rice," "Roasted Pearl Grits" and "Syrup Waffles," he had evidently given up the task in despair, as there was a long series of melancholy blanks. The translated terms were not exactly a success. I ordered some "Biscochos de avena," and the waitress brought me an omelette!

Every shop in the city has a name painted over the door, and sometimes they are very picturesque. It is all much like the old English custom of the sign-board, "At the sign of the Boot," "The Leather Bottle," etc., but the names are not always so appropriate. Thus one drug store calls itself the "Gate to Heaven," and a drinking saloon is "The

Bait of the Devil"; a hat shop is entitled "El Sombrero Rojo" (the red hat), a petty tobacconist's is "El Universo," while a grocer calls his establishment "El Puerto de New York," although it appears to have nothing to do with that city. Other stores were labelled "La Ciudad de Londres" (City of London), "La Suiza" (the Swiss Woman), etc. But the custom is gradually dying out, and the commonplace system of putting up the firm's name is coming into vogue. Mexican shopkeepers are evidently alive to the sweet uses of advertisement. They stock the latest novelties and lavishly advertise in the newspapers, and with wall-posters and street-car signs. Even the drop-curtains of the theatres are adorned with advice to the audience as to the best drinking saloon, the cheapest tailor's or the best cure for corns.

Some of the streets have names as grotesque as those of the stores, which is very bewildering, as there are over nine hundred streets, and each in its length will rechristen itself at almost every street corner. San Francisco Street, for instance, is called First San Francisco, Second San Francisco and Third San Francisco. Some streets bear the names of men honored in Mexican history. Others are of an elaborate religious character, such as "Calle Amor de Dios" (Love of God Street), "Calle Espiritu Santo" (Holy Ghost Street), "Sepulchre of the Holy Ghost Street," "Sabbath Street," etc. Some names are grotesque, such as "Sad Indian Street," "Pass if you can Street," "Lost Child Street," "Street of the Wood Owls," "Bridge of the Raven Street," "Walking Priest Street." Sometimes a street at a special spot is called "Puente," such as "Puente de San Francisco," which means that there was originally a bridge over a canal, but the canal has disappeared ages ago. As in London, some streets belong to certain industries. For instance, there is "Coffin-makers' Street," entirely given over to that lugubrious calling. The narrowness of the sidewalks in the busy streets causes many people to walk in the roadway, and as these thoroughfares are always thronged during the daytime, the city seems to have a much larger population than it really has.

Shopping and shopkeeping in Mexico City have several odd features. In the old-fashioned stores, for example, the salesmen stand in a row behind the counters like a file of soldiers. Smoking is permitted, and the salesman measures off a yard of cloth or fits you with new collars between the puffs of his cigarette. In the smaller establishments the prices quoted are always higher than you are expected to pay, for the Mexican shopkeeper assumes that his customer is a bargain-driver. This is also true of the Mexican stall-keepers in the markets, who always demand about three times the real price of their wares. Some of the goods in the stores are surprisingly cheap, but most of them are dear from the American point of view. This is due to the high protective tariff, which imposes a heavy duty on most imports. American toilet articles and patent medicines are about twice the regular price; furniture, too, is very expensive, and all clothing, hats, shoes, gloves, etc., are very dear. Probably the expensiveness of women's clothing is the reason for the poverty-stricken appearance of so many Mexican women of the lower middle class.

Wherever you walk, ragged Indian men, women and boys badger you with the persistent cry of "Boleto por la loteria, por mañana, señor" (Tickets for to-morrow's lottery, sir). Second-rate shops, too, expose these tickets for sale. There are all kinds of lotteries, for the Mexicans are born gamblers, and people of all classes buy the tickets. Some of the lotteries are conducted by the National and State governments and bring in large revenue. There are also private lotteries of various kinds, and even on the

F

backs of the street-car tickets, and on coupons in cigarette packets are the fateful words entitling you to some kind of drawing. The prizes generally range from fifty cents to $50,000, and the tickets vary in price from twenty-five cents to $25. Men have sometimes founded their fortunes by winning a lottery prize, and thus procuring the capital to embark in business. While I was in Mexico, a poor peon invested all his savings in a ticket and won $10,000, a sum sufficient to keep him in luxury for the rest of his life. Enlightened Mexicans regard these lotteries as a great public evil, and would have them suppressed, but public opinion is too strongly in their favor. An important concession to public morals has, however, been made in recent years by the closing of the public gambling houses which were once common in the city.

One of the worst features of Mexico City is the swarm of beggars, who constitute a serious nuisance. Filthily dirty and truly worthy of the title, "Verminous persons," the lame, the halt, the blind, and able-bodied rogues and vagrants are encountered almost everywhere, demanding centavos. Beggars are common throughout Mexico, but they are seen at their worst in the capital. The city government has made an attempt to check this nuisance by compelling each beggar to take out a license, which, it is true, costs nothing, but is only issued on proof of the beggar's actual want. As elsewhere, these hordes of cadgers have undoubtedly been much encouraged by the public, and especially by American tourists, whose indiscriminate charity, however well intended, has only served to increase the begging nuisance.

CHAPTER IV

MEXICO, PAST AND PRESENT

JUST as in order to understand modern Mexico one must know something of her past, so in order to fully appreciate Mexico's fascinating history, which has been so graphically related in the pages of Prescott, one must stand upon the historical ground where the drama of the country was unfolded. Gazing on the spot where once stood the great temple of the Mexican gods and the palace of Montezuma, upon the identical place where the Spaniards were butchered by the Aztecs during the "sorrowful night" of their flight from the city, upon the tree beneath which Cortés wept over this defeat, the stranger cannot help but feel emotion, however lethargic his interest may previously have been. Fully as thrilling are the events which followed the War of Independence in 1811, when Spanish rule came to an end in Mexico, the series of revolutions which followed, and the incidental wars of invasion; for twice during the past century the Mexican capital has been occupied by foreign armies and its streets have resounded, in turn, to the strains of Yankee Doodle and the Marseillaise. The present is the child of the past, and the influence of all these strange events may be traced in greater or lesser measure in the development of the Mexican people to-day.

Mexico's earliest history is unfortunately shrouded in profound mystery. The native records, which might have thrown some light upon it, were ruthlessly destroyed at the time of the Spanish conquest, when ignorance and bigotry were active in stamping out all traces of native culture.

After the conquest, several Spanish chroniclers collected the oral traditions of the conquered people, while certain native writers who had learned Spanish wrote what purported to be a history of their country. This great mass of material, which has been so fascinatingly condensed and presented by Prescott in his "Conquest of Mexico," is a curious blending of fact and fiction. On one point, however, all narrations agree, namely, that Mexico is a country of great antiquity and has been peopled by a succession of races. Of these early inhabitants almost nothing is known.

Scattered all over Mexico are the ruins of cities, temples and palaces built in remote periods, and which were probably in much the same condition ages before the Spaniards came. The mystery which surrounds their prehistoric builders is deepened by the strange relics of the past which are being constantly unearthed. Jade beads which undoubtedly came from China are found with stone idols and statues of marked Egyptian appearance; while intermixed with pyramids which recall those of early Egypt are ruins of temples and palaces, the architecture of which bears a singular resemblance to that of Japan. Among the Indian races of Mexico to-day certain customs exist which seem to have had their origin in the Far East; and there is much resemblance between the religion of the early inhabitants and that of China and India. These facts have led many historians to believe that some connection was actually established between ancient Mexico and the Orient.

According to native traditions, the whole of Mexico was originally known as Anahuac, and was inhabited by a succession of highly cultured races who built the vast temples and palaces, the ruins of which still exist. The most advanced of these were the Toltecs, who were said to have come from some unknown land. Prescott represents them as having arrived in Anahuac in the seventh century; other authorities believe that they entered the country fully five thousand years earlier. The Toltecs are said to have built a wonderful city called Tula, and an attempt has been made to identify this prehistoric city with a little village of adobe huts and magnificent ruins not far from the capital. This is but one of many instances in which Toltec names of towns and districts still survive.

It was at Tula, according to ancient legends, that Quetzalcoatl, a mysterious messiah, known as the Fair God, made his appearance. He was a white man with a long, flowing beard who taught the Toltecs the arts of civilization, agriculture and war, then sailed away to the west to return to his own country. After his departure he was deified by the Toltecs, who represented him in their sculptures as a winged serpent. He had promised to return after many years, and this pledge was handed down from generation to generation.

All traditions agree that the Toltecs were a people of wonderful culture; that they were peaceful and temperate, had reached a high moral plane, and had a form of religion which was largely nature-worship. Fruit and flowers were offered in their temples, which were never stained with human blood as in later Aztec times. Castes existed among them, and as in the case of some races of the Far East, they had two written languages, one of which was used when addressing superiors, the other for inferiors. Their social classes were divided into priests, warriors, merchants and tillers of the soil. They also had an elaborate feudal system.

The empire of the Toltecs was eventually overthrown by an invasion of fierce tribes who swept down through Mexico from the north, followed in turn by races of higher civilization, perhaps akin to the Toltecs, whose language they appear to have spoken. The Toltecs gradually relinquished possession of the country and retired southwards, while the invaders apparently acquired some of the culture of the people whom they had displaced. Some of them, notably the Tezcucans, eventually made great progress in the arts of civilization. Some of these tribes developed a system of picture-writing resembling somewhat that of the North American Indians.[1]

[1] An interesting specimen of these picture-writings, which is preserved in Mexico, records how the ancestors of the Tarascan Indians inhabiting the State of Michoacan, came down into Anahuac from the far north. A reproduction of this ancient record is given on the opposite page.

According to tradition, the Tarascans were one of nine tribes who wandered down to Mexico, having emerged from seven caves in the west, and passing a narrow arm of the sea on wooden rafts or hurdles made of canoes fastened together. They marched together from this place, and after many days halted at a large tree, in the trunk of which an altar was erected to the god Huitzilolvehtli. While encamped there, the tree suddenly split in the middle. Taking this as a bad omen, the heads of the tribes consulted the god, who advised them to take separate roads, which was done, some of the tribes going in one direction and others in another. The Tarascans eventually took possession of the country around Lake Patzcuaro.

These scenes are all depicted in the record. The square at the upper right-hand corner shows the tribes emerging from the caves, led by their nine high priests; and intersecting the squares are lines showing the road they took. Each square depicts some incident in their long wanderings, a special feature being made of their encampment at the tree of Huitzilolvehtli. Over the squares are inscriptions in the Tarascan and Mexican languages, supposed to have been added by native writers some years after the Spanish conquest. Some of the words have been translated; the meaning of others is unknown. Two colors are used in the drawing — black and red. The latter is used only for the line which indicates the road followed and for the species of shirt or jacket worn by the individuals who appear to be chiefs or priests.

Speaking of these picture-writings, Prescott says: "A Mexican manuscript looks usually like a collection of pictures, each one form-

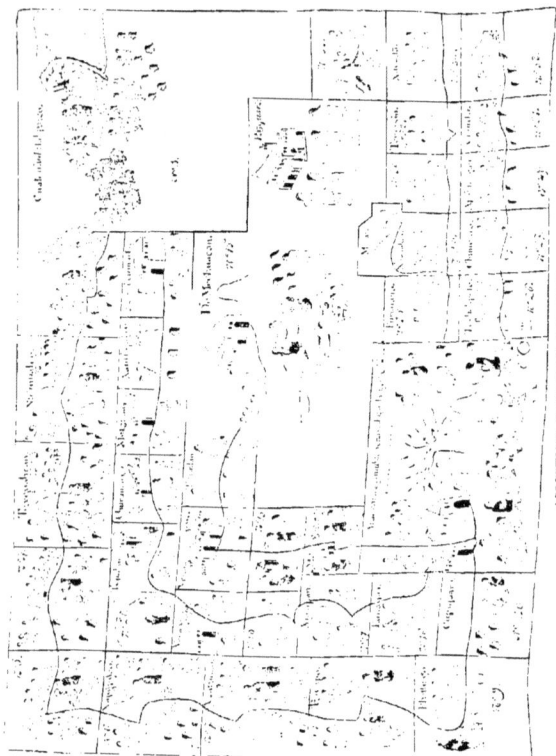

ANCIENT PICTURE RECORD.
Describing the migration of the Tarascans.

Chief among the invading tribes were the Aztecs, who are supposed to have come from northern California and made their way southward. According to Aztec legends, they were told by an oracle that they should build a great city on a site that would be indicated by an eagle perched on the stem of a cactus or prickly pear with a serpent in his talons. In 1325, so tradition says, they arrived in the Valley of Mexico, where the capital now stands, led by their high priest, Tenoch, a sort of Aztec Moses, whose name meant "the stone cactus." As they approached the lake, the site of the present city, they beheld a golden eagle standing on a prickly pear, holding in his talons a serpent, as had been predicted. In obedience to the sign, the Aztecs settled at the lake, built their temple and founded a great city, which they called Tenochtitlan, after

ing the subject of a separate study. The Aztecs had various emblems for expressing such things as from their nature could not be directly represented by the painter. A 'tongue,' for example, denoted speaking; a 'footprint,' travelling; 'man on the ground,' an earthquake. These symbols were often very arbitrary, varying with the caprice of the writer; and it required a nice discrimination to interpret them, as a slight change in the form or position of the figure intimated a very different meaning. They also employed phonetic signs, though these were chiefly confined to the names of persons and places. Lastly, the pictures were colored in gaudy contrasts, so as to produce the most vivid impression, for even colors speak in the Aztec hieroglyphics.

"Clumsy as it was, however, the Aztec picture-writing enabled the people to digest a complete system of chronology and to specify with accuracy the dates of the most important events in their history. Serving as a sort of stenography or collection of notes, these writings were used in the colleges of the priests, where the youth were instructed in astronomy, history, mythology, etc. This combination of the written and oral comprehended what may be called the literature of the Aztecs.

"The manuscripts were made of different materials, cotton cloth or skins nicely prepared; a composition of silk and gum; but for the most part a kind of paper made from the leaves of the maguey. The few Mexican manuscripts which are now preserved in Europe have been reproduced in Lord Kingsborough's magnificent work, 'The Antiquities of Mexico.'"

the holy sign and their priestly guide, the word meaning "the place of the cactus." The legend of the eagle, the serpent and the prickly pear is now preserved in the Mexican arms, and is perpetuated on the coins and the national banner.

In later years the city was called Mexico after Mextili, the Aztec God of War, and this name was eventually given to the entire country.

The ancient city of the Aztecs bore some resemblance to Venice, some of the houses resting on piles, others being built on the numerous islands, with canals intersecting the various parts of the city. Massive stone structures, resembling those of Egypt, were reared, including the great Teocalli or Temple of the Aztec gods, in pyramidal form, over a hundred feet high, with one hundred and fourteen steps, reaching from the ground to the esplanade, broad enough for thirty horsemen to march abreast. Great paved causeways led from the city to the surrounding villages.

The Aztecs, at first, were a fierce, migratory people; but after their arrival in Mexico they seem to have acquired the civilization of the tribes by whom they were surrounded, who had inherited the arts and civilization of the Toltecs or other races whom they had succeeded. Having made great advancement in the arts of war, the Aztecs gradually subjugated the surrounding nations and extended their sway over a large part of Mexico. The empire of their great king, Montezuma I, was established about 1460. Under this monarch their power and prestige greatly increased.

The Aztecs and other races inhabiting Mexico at this time were largely sun-worshippers, their religion being distinguished by the most cruel and terrible ceremonies. Prisoners of war, slaves and other victims were slaughtered by thousands in the temples. When the great temple of Tenochtitlan was dedicated, twenty thousand are said to have been sacrificed in four days. In the centre of this temple stood the sacrificial stone now in the Mexican National Museum. On this the victim was stretched, when his body was cut open by the officiating priest, and his heart being torn out was offered to the sun and the ferocious God of War. The bodies of the sacrificed were afterwards devoured by the populace. Thousands of skulls, the result of this butchery, were formed into a huge pyramid in the temple, the walls and floor of which reeked with blood.

Apart from their terrible religious ceremonies, the Aztecs were a remarkable and cultured race. Even in their religion they recognized a supreme being, and some of their prayers which have been handed down are remarkable for their lofty sentiments and the beauty of their language.[1]

[1] "In contemplating the religious system of the Aztecs," says Prescott, "one is struck by this apparent incongruity, as though some portion of it had emanated from a comparatively refined people open to gentle influences, while the rest breathes a spirit of unmitigated ferocity. It naturally suggests the idea of two distinct sources, and authorizes the belief that the Aztecs had inherited from their predecessors a milder faith on which was afterwards engrafted their own mythology."

The Aztecs recognized the existence of a supreme being, the Lord of the universe. They addressed Him in their prayers as "the God by whom we live," "omnipresent," "that knoweth all thoughts and giveth all gifts," "without whom man is nothing," "the invisible, incorporeal, one God of perfect perfection and purity," "under whose wings we find repose and a sure defence." These sublime attributes infer no inadequate conception of the true God. But the idea of unity was too simple or too vast for their understandings, and they sought relief in a plurality of deities who presided over the elements, the changes of the seasons and the occupations of man. Of these there were thirteen principal deities and more than two hundred inferior. At the head of these stood the terrible Huitzilopochtli, the Mexican Mars, the patron deity of the nation. His temples were the most stately of the public edifices, and his altars reeked with the blood of human hecatombs in every city of the empire. At the dedication of

They were learned in astronomy; were good lapidaries and potters, workers in silver and gold and weavers of cotton and silk. They cultivated the land thoroughly, and had developed elaborate systems of irrigation. Commerce was organized; towns and villages were connected by roadways; and law and order prevailed. They had an ingenious method of picture-writing and a regular system of education for the young.

The doom of the Aztec empire and its neighbors was sealed in 1519, when Hernando Cortés landed in Mexico on his expedition of conquest. He had a fleet of 11 ships carrying 110 sailors, 16 cavalrymen with their horses, 553 foot-soldiers, 200 Cuban natives, a battery of 10 small cannon and 4 falconets. To check mutiny among his Spanish followers and to prevent them from seizing the ships and retreating, Cortés burned his vessels at Vera Cruz, then marched inland to the capital of the Aztecs. Montezuma II then reigned in Tenochtitlan. He had been informed of Cortés' arrival by spies who had been sent down to the coast. By relays of runners it was possible for a message to reach the Aztec capital (265 miles from the coast) in twelve hours. It is said that fish caught at Vera Cruz in the evening was served at the dinner of Montezuma the following day. This would be as fast as the railway train travels to-day. The Spaniards were astonished at the rapidity with which news of their movements was spread. By these runners the Aztec monarchs kept in communication with all parts of their empire.[1]

the great temple in the capital it is said that seventy thousand captives were slaughtered at the shrine of this terrible deity.

[1] Prescott quotes an author who relates how a North-American Indian travelled a hundred miles in twenty-four hours. According to Plutarch, the Greek who brought the news of the battle of Platæa covered one hundred and twenty-five miles in a day. Prescott adds: "The Aztec couriers travelled with such incredible swiftness that

HERNANDO CORTÉS.
From an original portrait in the Mexican National Museum.

Montezuma and his priests were convinced from their official reports that Cortés was none other than the Fair God, Quetzalcoatl, the child of the sun, whose return had been promised ages before. They recalled a prediction that Quetzalcoatl was to overturn the Aztec empire. Montezuma sent the supposed god lavish gifts of gold, and endeavored to dissuade him from coming to the capital; but the gold only whetted the appetite of the Spaniards for more and hastened their march to the interior.

Cortés was greatly aided in his conquest of Mexico by Marina, a beautiful young slave who had been presented to him by a Tabascan chief. She was an Aztec, but having learned various dialects when in Tabasco, she was enabled to communicate indirectly with Cortés, who became infatuated with her beauty and made her his mistress. She eventually learned Spanish, and acted as interpreter between himself and Montezuma. Marina told the Mexicans glowing stories of the greatness and splendor of the Spaniards, and it was undoubtedly through her influence that the natives went in such great awe of these strange beings who had come to them from over the seas.

Soon after his arrival, Cortés invaded the country of the Tlascalans, one of the powerful tribes, who had a republican form of government and were at war with the Aztecs. After conquering them, Cortés gained them as allies, and a large force of Tlascalans accompanied him on his march through the country. He next marched into the kingdom of Cholula, which he subjugated, destroying all the temples and public buildings, and slaughtering thousands of the inhabitants. The natives were terror-stricken by the can-

despatches were carried, by relays of runners, from one to two hundred miles a day. Fresh fish was frequently served at Montezuma's table in twenty-four hours from the time it had been taken in the Gulf of Mexico, over two hundred miles from the capital."

non and firearms of the Spaniards, and as they had never seen a horse, the animal and rider were supposed to be one being, and were regarded as superhuman. Marching over the mountains, Cortés pressed on to Tenochtitlan, passed over the causeways and entered the city on November 8, 1519.

Montezuma came out to meet the conqueror and, under the influence of superstition, regarding the Spaniards as gods, the Aztecs made no attempt to prevent their entry. The Spanish leader took up his residence in the old palace of Montezuma, where much treasure was discovered and divided among the invaders.

Early the next year (1520), owing to the cruelty of a body of Cortés' soldiers, who robbed and murdered a number of Aztec nobles, the people rose in revolt. Montezuma, who had been seized and held prisoner by the Spaniards, was killed while attempting to quell the uprising. On the night of July 1 (afterwards known as "la noche triste" or "sorrowful night") the Spaniards attempted to secretly evacuate the city, but were detected and pursued, many of them were killed or taken prisoners and thousands of their Tlascalan followers were slaughtered. With the remnant of his force, Cortés retreated to Tlascala. In the meantime, Cuautlahuac, brother of Montezuma, was crowned king, but dying four months later, was succeeded by Guatemotzin or Cuauhtemoc, Montezuma's nephew, who proved to be a brave and able leader. Cortés, refusing to acknowledge defeat, recruited his forces at Tlascala, and won the support of all the tribes who had suffered from Aztec oppression. From mountain forests he brought timber sixty miles overland to the shores of Lake Texcoco, built thirteen brigantines, crossed the lake and once more appeared before the walls of Tenochtitlan with two hundred thousand allies.

The siege began on December 3, 1520, and continued until August 13, 1521, when the garrison was starved into submission and the Spaniards entered the city. Before it fell, all the Aztec treasure was destroyed or concealed. Guatemotzin was cruelly tortured by having his feet held over a glowing fire, but he refused to disclose the secret. The lake and canals were dredged several times, but only a small part of the treasure was recovered. The unfortunate young monarch was afterwards compelled by Cortés to go with him on an expedition into Honduras. In the depths of the jungle Cortés had him hanged to the branch of a ceiba tree. Thus perished the last of the Aztec kings.

Cortés destroyed the temples in the city and ordered the erection of churches and convents, the first church — now the cathedral — being built upon the site of the great temple of the Aztecs. The Spanish priests, with fanatical frenzy, destroyed nearly all the Aztec picture records or codices, making huge bonfires of them. Of those which escaped destruction a few are preserved in European museums, notably at the Vatican, and some are in the Mexican National Museum. The Aztec houses and public buildings were gradually torn down and replaced with Spanish houses, but the formation of the city was generally observed. In 1634 there was an earthquake, and the waters of the lake suddenly disappeared and the canals gradually dried up. After the Spanish occupation the native population of the city decreased until in 1600 there were only about ten thousand natives and about the same number of Spaniards. From that time the increase in numbers of Spaniards and mixed population was very rapid, until at the end of the next century there was a population of nearly one hundred and twenty-five thousand.

Cortés became the first governor of Mexico, acquired vast estates, was created Marquis of the Valley of Oaxaca, and subjugated the rest of Mexico. Many of his followers found wives among Aztec women of noble birth.[1]

Warlike enough before the Spaniards came, the Aztec masses seem to have been subdued at one blow, and were soon reduced to the position of mere serfs. The Spanish priests, too, having gained a great influence over the natives, taught them to obey those whom God had sent to conquer their country. Chiefs who would not submit quietly were won by bribery. Thus by means of force, religion and every corrupt means that could be employed, the spirit of the

---

[1] The author of "Picturesque Mexico" (pub. 1897) says: "Many Mexican families of high lineage can point to a family history dating back to the days of the war against the Moors. Some of them are wealthy and still possessed of great estates. Descendants of Cortés still exist, some bearing his name; one of them is living to-day in Tacubaya.

"There are also several descendants of Aztec monarchs, notably Señor Roberto Luis Cuauhtemoc, who is fourteenth in descent from the emperor, Cuautlahuac, brother of Montezuma II. Other descendants of Cuautlahuac are Don Pedro Patino Itzalinque, who lives in Holland, and another, Don Pedro Patino Itzalinque, living in the City of San Luis Potosi, Mexico.

"There are several well-proved descendants of Aztec monarchs now living, who draw pensions from the Mexican government. Some of them reside in Spain and other European countries, and among them is the Duke of Abrantes, the Marquis del Aguilar Fuerte and the Conde de Miravalles.

"The direct descendants of Montezuma are living in Salamanca, Spain, the present head of the family being Señor Don Augustin Maldonado y Carbayal Cano Montezuma, Marquis of Castellanos y Monroy. The Maldonado family is connected by marriage with the English house of Lancaster and also with the house of Abrantes and Medinaceli, which are of the first nobility in Spain.

"Among other descendants of Montezuma is Eugenie, ex-empress of the French. It is therefore apparent that the widow of Napoleon III was of greater imperial stock than her husband, and brought to the alliance more dignity than she acquired by it.

"In Mexico City there is a gentleman named Mercado who is a descendant of Montezuma, who has many relics of his illustrious ancestors, and is extremely well versed in the history of the Montezuma race."

people was crushed and all resistance to Spanish rule was overcome. Then followed a great building period. The cities throughout Mexico were rebuilt according to Spanish ideas; and great churches and cathedrals were erected by Indian workmen on the grandiose designs of Spanish architects.

Thereafter, for three hundred years, Mexico was under the dominion of Spain. During this time there were five governors, two councils of three to five members each, and sixty-two viceroys, the first of whom was appointed in 1535. The rule of some of the viceroys was wise and able, and the country made great progress; but as in all Spanish colonies, there was great corruption, oppression and misgovernment. All public offices were held by Spaniards, while the natives, even those of Spanish descent, received no recognition.

At the beginning of the nineteenth century, when Napoleon had overturned thrones and marched an army into Spain, the spirit of revolution spread to Mexico. The newly acquired independence of the United States of North America also served to arouse a desire for freedom among the Mexicans. Several insurrections started at this period, but were speedily stamped out. The first important uprising took place in September, 1810, when Miguel Hidalgo, curate of the village of Dolores in the State of Guanajuato, began the first great movement for independence by ringing the bell of his church, calling his people together and starting a war for freedom. Raising a sacred banner bearing the figure of the Virgin of Guadalupe, the priest organized a little army of three hundred men, armed with clubs, swords, knives and bows and arrows. At the head of these insurgents, he marched to Guanajuato, the people of the country everywhere flocking to his aid. The Spanish garrison at Guanajuato was defeated and the city captured. After successful battles at Morelia and Valladolid, Hidalgo marched towards Mexico City, but when almost within sight of the capital was defeated, driven back, and his army dispersed. Hidalgo and his chief officers, Allende, Aldama, and Jiminez, were betrayed, captured and executed.

After the death of Hidalgo, a desultory struggle against the Spaniards continued for ten years, and then a new leader, also a priest, Jose Maria Morelos, who had been a student under Hidalgo, entered the field. Organizing a small army, Morelos for two years waged war against the Spaniards, but was at last defeated by an overwhelming force, betrayed and captured. He was tried by an ecclesiastical tribunal and degraded from the priesthood, then handed over to the military authorities, by whom he was condemned to death and shot near the capital in December, 1815. To-day he ranks next to Hidalgo as one of the heroes of Mexico.

The next prominent leader in the fight for freedom was Augustin Iturbide, a Mexican of Spanish descent, and a former royalist officer, who had been largely responsible for the defeat of Morelos. Deserting from the Spanish army, Iturbide gathered all the insurgent leaders around him and issued a proclamation, pledging the support of his party to the establishment of the Roman Catholic Church, to the exclusion of all others; the independence of Mexico, with a monarchical government under a Spanish prince; union and equality of Spaniards and Mexicans. His army thus became known as the Army of the Three Guarantees. A number of Spanish regiments deserted and joined Iturbide, who in 1821 marched through Mexico, capturing city after city, and at last occupied the capital. This practically ended Spanish rule in Mexico, and after a year or two of negotiations, the independence of the country was at last recognized by the Spanish government.

After the revolution, Iturbide forced the Mexican Congress to select an emperor, and by threats and bribes managed to get sufficient votes to secure his own election. He and his wife were crowned in the cathedral as emperor and empress of Mexico. His title was Augustin I. He ruled unwisely, dissolved the Congress in less than four months, sent several members to prison and created so much discord that uprisings were of frequent occurrence. A successful revolution was led by General Santa Ana; the empire was overturned, and a republic established, with Santa Ana as president. Banished from Mexico, Iturbide was given a pension of $25,000 a year for his past services. He went to England for a time, but unwisely returned to Mexico in 1824 to lead a new revolution, when he was arrested, condemned to death and shot. Some of his descendants are still living in Mexico and enjoy a good deal of social distinction.

From 1824 until 1846 there were constant revolutions as the result of disputed elections. In the latter year troubles arose with the United States over Texas, which had formerly belonged to Mexico, but had seceded, and after a few years as an independent republic had been annexed by the Americans. War was forced on Mexico by the United States, and two American armies were marched into Mexican territory, one coming down from Texas southward, the other landing at Vera Cruz. After a series of battles, in which the Mexicans were defeated and sustained heavy losses, the Americans entered the capital. A treaty was then signed which gave the United States a vast territory, including New Mexico, Arizona, and California, the Mexican government receiving fifteen million dollars compensation. General Grant, who was then a lieutenant in the United States army, once declared that the war with Mexico was the most unholy and unjust war ever waged by a strong nation against a weaker one.

Following the American war there were more revolutions, which continued until 1861. Benito Juarez, a full-blood Mexican Indian, called the George Washington of Mexico, then became President. A great struggle between church and state had been in progress for several years, and it came to a climax at that time. The church, which had burdened the Mexican people with such a vast number of priests, friars and nuns, and had acquired most of the wealth of the country, clung tenaciously to its privileges and property. After adopting a new constitution, declaring for separation of church and state, the Mexican Congress passed a law confiscating church property, closing the monasteries and convents and restricting the power of the church. This resulted in civil war between the clerical and liberal parties. Juarez personally commanded the liberal forces, and in 1860 entered the capital. The Liberals, in the meantime, were excommunicated by the church, and in retaliation the Papal Delegate and several bishops were ordered by Juarez to leave Mexico. The country was then in a terrible condition. Bandits committed depredations everywhere, and many foreigners were robbed and murdered.

In 1861 the Mexican Congress passed a law suspending payment of interest on the bonds of the Republic held by foreigners. This gave the European powers an excuse for intervention. The French government claimed $600,000 damages suffered by French subjects during the civil war. No doubt damage had been suffered; but many of the claims were ludicrous, as, for example, one item of $60,000, the value of pies alleged to have been stolen from a French cook by the Mexican soldiers. In 1862, a combined British, French and Spanish fleet arrived at Vera Cruz, and an allied force was landed for the purpose of enforcing payment of Mexican obligations. President Juarez met the representatives of the powers at Orizaba, and signed a treaty ac-

THE EMPEROR MAXIMILIAN.
Mexico's ill-fated ruler, shot at Queretaro in 1867.

knowledging the claims and promising payment. Great Britain and Spain then withdrew their forces. Encouraged by the clerical party, the French remained; and Napoleon III, who was anxious to increase his prestige by establishing a monarchy in the Western Hemisphere, readily entered into a scheme of conquest.

Four thousand French troops eventually landed in Mexico and advanced to Puebla, where they were defeated, on the 5th of May, 1862, by the Mexican troops under General Zaragoza. This date, so important in Mexican history, is annually set aside for national celebration, and nearly every city has a street named Cinco de Mayo (5th of May). On the 17th of May, however, Puebla was captured by the French forces. On June 9 they entered Mexico City. A so-called Assembly of Notables was then called together and a declaration made that Mexico should be governed by a constitutional monarch and that a Catholic prince should be selected. At the suggestion of the French representatives, the throne was offered to Maximilian, Archduke of Austria, who was also a representative of the ruling house of Spain. Maximilian accepted the throne on condition that he should be elected by popular vote, and that the Emperor Napoleon should give him military aid as long as it was necessary. He arrived in Mexico City June 12, 1864, with his wife Carlotta, daughter of Leopold I, King of the Belgians.

After his accession, Maximilian aroused the opposition of the clerical party by enforcing the laws of church reform. Juarez, in the meantime, had crossed the border into Texas, and from there continued to direct the movement for driving out Maximilian and the French. Maximilian, at this time, under the influence of Marshal Bazaine and other evil counsellors, made a fatal mistake. He issued a decree declaring the civil war at an end, and that all persons in arms would be treated as bandits and shot when captured. The execution of the Liberal generals, Arteago, Salazar, Villagomez and Felix Diaz followed. At this time the Civil War in the United States was drawing to a close, and the American government, regarding the French aggression in Mexico as a serious breach of the Monroe doctrine, informed Napoleon III that the United States would not tolerate the establishment of a monarchy on the western continent. On receipt of this note, Napoleon abandoned Maximilian and recalled the French forces in November, 1866. The collapse of the empire speedily followed. As soon as the French left, President Juarez entered Mexico, gathered his forces and marched southward. He defeated Maximilian's general, Miramon, who retreated to Queretaro, where he was joined by the emperor. In the meantime, General Porfirio Diaz, who commanded the republican forces in the south, had captured Puebla, defeated Maximilian's troops in several battles and had commenced the siege of Mexico City. After a siege of several weeks, Juarez captured Queretaro. Maximilian and his generals, Miramon and Mejia, were tried by court-martial on charges of filibustering, of treason and of issuing the decree of October 3, 1865, under which the Liberal generals had been executed. Señor Riva Palacio, the emperor's counsel, and other distinguished lawyers, defended Maximilian, but without success. The emperor and the two generals were found guilty and sentenced to death.

After the trial, Señor Riva Palacio went to the neighboring city of San Luis Potosi to plead with President Juarez for a modification of the sentence, and Princess Salm Salm rode across the country one hundred and twenty miles on the same errand. Although personally inclined to show mercy, Juarez considered it necessary to strike a decisive blow for the maintenance of the Republic. A protest from the United States government was received, but that was of no avail. Maximilian sent in an appeal on behalf of his companions, but this met with no better success. On the morning of June 19, 1867, the emperor and his two generals were shot on the hill outside Queretaro. Carlotta, his unfortunate consort, who was in Europe at the time, had endeavored in vain to get the Emperor Napoleon to send another army to rescue her husband, and had also pleaded with the Pope without success. Grieving over Maximilian's death eventually shattered her mind. The story is one of the most pitiful in modern history.

A few days after Maximilian's execution, General Diaz captured Mexico City, and President Juarez returned to the capital after an absence of five years to reëstablish his government. He died in 1872, and after a brief revolution in 1876, General Diaz became President, and has served almost continuously since that time.

CHAPTER V

THE SIGHTS OF THE CAPITAL

EVERY capital has its great central point from which radiates the life of the city — in London, for example, the Bank of England, in Paris the Opera House, and in Berlin the Unter den Linden. In Mexico City everything starts from the Plaza Mayor or main plaza, a great public space larger than the Capitol square in Washington, which is the true heart of the city. Here it was that the city first began, from it start some of the principal streets, and it is the oldest and in many respects the most interesting part of the Mexican capital. To some extent it resembles the Isle de la Cité in Paris; for in Aztec times it was entirely surrounded by water, and here stood the temples and palaces which the Spaniards destroyed, replacing them with the cathedral and various public buildings. In the great plaza the life of the city had its centre in early Spanish times, the market and the principal shops were here, and it was the public promenade and place of recreation. To-day, with its quaint, time-worn buildings and its memories of the past, it has suffered a modern invasion in the shape of the street-cars which start from it. I felt a curious impression of this juxtaposition of the modern and the mediæval as I stood beneath the giant walls of the sixteenth-century cathedral and listened to the persistent clanging of the street-car gongs.

For there is one feature which dominates the plaza and vividly recalls the days when Spain was a mighty world-

THE HEART OF THE CAPITAL.
Scene in the Plaza fronting the great Cathedral of Mexico.

empire and Queen Elizabeth ruled the destinies of England. That feature is the great cathedral built on the site of the wonderful teocalli or temple, dedicated to Huitzilopochtli, the Aztec War-god and patron deity of the ancient city. Here in the temple centre stood the famous Stone of Sacrifice, upon which tens of thousands of human victims were slaughtered, their breasts sliced open with obsidian knives, their hearts torn out and burned in the holy of holies in honor of the terrible deity. Close at hand were the palaces of the Emperor Montezuma.

It was typical of the splendid arrogance of the Catholic conquerors that Cortés should have seized upon the theatrical idea of building his great stone apotheosis of his faith on a site recking with memories of pagan foulness. It was in 1573, in the reign of Philip II, that the first stone of the great church was laid. The soil was of such a marshy nature that the builders had great difficulties with which to contend. These indeed were so enormous that after nearly fifty years the walls had only been built twenty feet above the ground. Philip III, on hearing of the slowness of the work initiated by his father, had new plans drawn up and lavishly subsidized the undertaking.

The principal sacristy was finished in 1623; the vaults in the middle nave were complete about the middle of the seventeenth century, and in 1667 the interior was so far advanced that an inaugural service was possible. The choir, however, was not complete till 1730, and thus the great church had been building nearly two centuries. The whole cost was nearly three million dollars; but that represents only a fraction of the money lavished on the greatest Catholic fane in the New World, if those who toiled had been paid fair wages and the material had not been commandeered.

From north to south the vast edifice is more than four

hundred feet long, the interior measuring three hundred and eighty-seven feet, while the height from floor to roof is one hundred and seventy-nine feet. The towers are two hundred and forty feet high. The material used is a limestone of a dark cream tint. Over the whole is a superb dome. The architecture in the main is Gothic, with a lavish use of Doric and Corinthian pilasters. But it is in the interior of the cathedral that one realizes the amount of money which has been lavished on the adornment of the great church. The ornamentation of the high altar is said to be worth the almost fabulous sum of a million and a half of dollars. The lamp hanging before the sanctuary is said to have cost $80,000, while the tabernacle of massive silver is valued at over $150,000. The whole place gives one an impression of glittering gold and gems, a treasure-house of an ecclesiastical Crœsus.

There are fourteen chapels in the cathedral, each profusely decorated and gilded. Under the altar of one of them are interred the heads of the patriots Hidalgo, Allende, Aldama and Jiminez, who led the first revolution against Spanish rule and were executed at Guanajuato. After the Spaniards had been finally driven from Mexico, the heads were brought in great state and pomp to the cathedral and buried where they rest to-day. In another chapel lie the remains of Augustin Iturbide, the first emperor of Mexico, known as The Liberator. It is also the tomb of several Spanish viceroys, as also of Gregorio Lopez, the Mexican "Man with the Iron Mask," alleged to have been a son of Philip II of Spain.

The choir is surrounded with a high railing of richly carved woods, and is connected with the nave by a passageway enclosed with balustrading of rich tumbago. In this instance the composite consists of a mixture of gold, silver and copper, and is so valuable that the offer of an American

THE SIGHTS OF THE CAPITAL

to replace the railing with one of solid silver was indignantly refused.

It would seem that Catholic fervor in Mexico is on the decline, for save at the time of the services the devout of the upper classes are rarely seen in the cathedral, the whole building being given over to the poor. Walking through the aisles, one sees the blanketed Indians kneeling, sombrero in hand, at the altars, or on the worn stones of the chapels, often the Indian women at their sides. Here and there a whole Indian family can be seen in their tattered, flimsy clothing, making a touching picture as they remain in reverent contemplation of the figure of the Virgin or saint whose protection they invoke. As in other Latin countries, women form the bulk of the worshippers at all the services. Men of the wealthier class scarcely ever attend. In the early morning the women go to mass dressed in black, with the graceful lace mantilla generally draped over the head, half exposing the olive-brown faces and bright sparkling eyes of the señoritas.

On the east side of the plaza, and facing the cathedral, is the National Palace. This is built on the site of Montezuma's second and greater palace, where Cortés built for himself a mansion. In 1562 this latter building was sold by his descendants to the Spanish government, and for more than a hundred years it was the Viceregal residence, until in 1692 it was destroyed in a great riot. The present building was begun in the same year and finished in 1699. It is the official residence of the President, and contains the state apartments, the offices of some of the chief ministries, the Senate Chamber, the Record Office and the Treasury.

The palace is a long, flat-roofed, gray stone, two-storied building in Spanish style, and while architecturally not remarkable, has a quaint, old-world picturesqueness all its own; and it does not take a great stretch of the imagination to picture the eighteenth-century Spanish caballeros riding in and out of the courtyard. It has a frontage of six hundred and seventy-five feet, extends backwards proportionately and forms a large square. Outside the main entrance, dark-skinned Mexican sentries, with their blue uniforms and glazed leather kepis, march up and down with fixed bayonets on their rifles, and a group of officers and soldiers off duty can generally be seen. All this is in striking contrast for the visitor who comes direct from the United States, where soldiers are never stationed at public buildings, and even the White House at Washington is guarded by only a few policemen.

The presidential apartments are magnificently furnished and decorated. Quite regal in its measurements is the Hall of Ambassadors, stretching the entire length of the palace, and lit by large windows looking out upon the cathedral. Here the President formally welcomes state visitors and receives the accredited representatives of foreign governments on their arrival to take their official posts. At these ceremonies the foreign ministers are presented to the President by an official entitled the Introducer of Ambassadors. At the south end of the chamber is a dais set with chairs in a half circle, where President Diaz sits surrounded by his cabinet ministers. The walls are hung with portraits, including those of George Washington, Benito Juarez, Iturbide, the generals Guerrero and Morelos, and President Diaz.

Over the main entrance to the Palace is hung the Liberty Bell of Mexico, which was rung by Father Hidalgo in 1810 in the village of Dolores, to call the people to arms in the first struggle for independence. This relic was brought to the capital in 1896, and on the night of the fifteenth of September each year is rung with great ceremony by the

THE MEXICAN NATIONAL PALACE.

Copyright by The Detroit Photo Co.

PYRAMID OF THE MOON.

(See page 107.)

President of Mexico, in the presence of an immense gathering. Just above the Liberty Bell is a clock which was exiled from the church of a small Spanish town because it was supposed to be bewitched, having struck the hours out of order. Although the National Palace is the President's official residence, he does not live there, but in a comparatively small house in the Cadena, a thoroughfare running off the Plaza, whence he comes, often on horseback, and always without any escort, to his daily work.

The National Museum has a wing of the Palace devoted to it. Here there is a splendid collection of Mexican antiquities, idols from temples, ornaments from palaces, jewels, arms, shields and utensils of the Toltecs and Aztecs, with some few of the Aztec picture-writings, which were saved from the bigotry of the monks. There are also portraits of the great characters in Mexico's history since the Conquest. Among the most interesting exhibits are the arms and armor of the early Spanish invaders, some of their standards, a fine portrait of Cortés, oil paintings portraying the baptism of Mexican Indians by the first missionaries, and a collection of the weapons, head-dresses and costumes of the Aztec warriors. Near the entrance is the great Stone of Sacrifice which formed the entire altar of the Temple of the Sun, which stood but a few feet from the site of the museum. It is circular, very elaborately carved, the figures on the rim showing the Aztec priests dragging their victims by the hair to the scene of sacrifice to be offered to the Sun-god. At the Conquest the stone was buried by Spanish priests and was not rediscovered until 1791, when some drainage excavations were being made near the cathedral. Near by is a grim and hideous relic of the terrible Huitzilopochtli, the Aztec War-god, an elaborately carved block of stone representing the ferocious face of the deity, with snakes' teeth and a fringe of snakes' heads depending as a breast ornament. At the base of the figure, the feet are in the form of a slab, upon which it is believed the still palpitating hearts of the slaughtered victims were placed as an offering.

In the same gallery is the Aztec Calendar Stone, a stone circle of twelve feet in diameter and weighing 53,790 pounds. This huge monolith, which was originally embedded in the walls of the great Temple, is elaborately carved with what appears to be calendar divisions. Many efforts have been made to decipher the carvings. Perhaps one of the most interesting is that of Mr. W. W. Blake of Mexico City, who sees in the second large circle four parallelograms indicating, in Aztec mythology, that the sun had died four times. These epochs or ages were, Mr. Blake thinks, the Age of Air, the Age of Water, the Age of Fire and the Age of Earth, and he thus interprets them: the Age of Air was the glacial epoch, representing the Aztec traditions of the ice lands to the north, from which their forefathers came; the Age of Water was the time of the submersion of the continent of Atlantis; the Age of Fire was the period marked by the eruptions of the volcanoes and accompanying earthquakes. Finally is the Age of the Earth, which began 4431 years before Christ and ended 1312 A.D. This Calendar Stone, like the Stone of Sacrifice, was buried in the Plaza, and was only unearthed in 1790. According to tradition, both of them were quarried near Coyoacan in 1478, over five thousand men being engaged in the work; they were then dragged over causeways on wooden rollers, crossing the canals on specially constructed bridges, and were thus transported to the great temple. It is said that this event was celebrated by the sacrifice of over seven hundred human beings.

In the museum are many large and terrible Aztec idols from all parts of Mexico, some of them having a very marked likeness to Egyptian figures. This is especially true of the so-called figure of Chac-Mol, which was found by Dr. Le Plongeon at Chichen-Itza in Yucatan, and is supposed to represent the God of Fire. This figure is notable as having an almost perfect Egyptian head-dress. A statue of the Goddess of Water, excavated at Teotihuacan, near the Pyramids of the Sun and Moon, is more than eleven feet high and five feet wide, and weighs forty thousand pounds. The feathered serpent, a mythic figure of great prominence in Aztec carvings, is found all over Mexico. It is called Quetzalcoatl, and represents the Mexican myth of a white man with a long flowing beard, who taught the people religion and civilization, a religion which the early Spanish are said to have found very much like Christianity. According to a Catholic legend, this mysterious teacher was one of the apostles, possibly St. Thomas. The Mexican government now claims all Aztec relics and superintends all excavations, jealously guarding the sites of the ancient cities.

One of the galleries is devoted to pictures, chiefly the portraits of the Spanish viceroys of Mexico from the time of the Conquest to the declaration of independence. They are poor specimens of art for the most part; but they portray a picturesque lot of rulers and give one a very fair idea of those in whose hands the fate of so many human beings once rested. In another gallery are housed the state carriages of the ill-fated Emperor Maximilian and the Empress Carlotta, gorgeously decorated with gold and silver and emblazoned with the imperial arms. The silver-mounted harness is also there, and, in a burst of very unrepublican emperor-worship, is hung on the wall above a picture of a gorgeous footman, inscribed "State footman of the Emperor Maximilian." It is all very pathetic, and the pathos is deepened by the object-lesson in democratic simplicity which is given in the other corner of the room. There, in its cracked, old-fashioned, plain black leather, stands the carriage used by President Juarez, who overturned the empire and authorized the execution of Maximilian.

Strange to say, most of the visitors to the museum are Indians of the working class, who can be seen walking through the galleries, gazing with solemn looks at the relics of the Aztecs, and discussing, in their own language, the achievements of their ancestors. The policemen on duty there, who are also of Indian descent, are very vigilant in enforcing the official regulations, as I found to my astonishment one morning. I had gone to the museum at rather an early hour, when the place was almost deserted, and was strolling through one of the long galleries, when I heard a stern voice far in the rear, commanding me to halt. I turned and saw a policeman who was beckoning to me and saying, "Señor, señor, regrese" (Come back, sir). Returning to the entrance door where he was stationed, I asked him what he wanted, whereupon he simply pointed to a placard inscribed, "A la dereche" (Keep to the right); and it then dawned on me that I had actually been keeping to the left. The rule, of course, was intended for enforcement only when the museum was crowded; but the worthy policeman had evidently been told to keep people to the right, and he was determined to do it whether there was one visitor or ten thousand. Apologizing to him for my disgraceful violation of the rules, I resumed my walk, taking great care to keep to the right.

On the west side of the Plaza is the National Pawn-shop or Monte de Piedad, which was founded as a charity, but which is now managed in much the same way as the French Montes de Piété. Similar establishments exist in most of the larger Mexican cities, enabling the poor to obtain

THE AZTEC CALENDAR STONE.

loans on pledges at a very reasonable rate of interest, and thus rescuing them from the merciless usurers. The Monte opens every afternoon for the sale of unredeemed pledges. Tourists are said to pick up great bargains in jewellery, historical relics and curios of all sorts. While I was in the city, an American bought from a curio dealer what was alleged to be the ivory and gold-mounted cigar case of the Emperor Maximilian, and ten ivory napkin-rings bearing the imperial arms. These were sold for ten dollars. If they were genuine, it is possible that they had come into the bric-a-brac dealer's hands at one of the daily sales at the Monte de Piedad. No Mexican would have bought them, as they are all very superstitious, and believe that anything that belonged to Maximilian brings bad luck.

Not far from the National Palace is the so-called Volador or Thieves' Market, where dishonestly acquired goods of every description are offered for sale by a picturesque crowd of ragged vendors. Most of the things offered are believed to have been stolen, and prices rule low, great bargains being sometimes obtainable. Valuable books, old gold and silverware, relics of all kinds, even old paintings, are displayed for sale. Some years ago a Murillo is said to have been bought here for five dollars. A prettier sight is the Flower Market, which is also close to the cathedral, and in the morning presents a beautiful scene, with its wealth of carnations, violets and roses. The flowers are delightfully cheap, and mammoth bunches of double violets — all you can carry — can be had for fifty cents, and heaps of roses, even in midwinter.

A picturesque row of buildings on one side of the Plaza have their lower stories in the form of arcades or portales, which, as already noted, form a distinctive feature of the plazas in all Mexican towns. Supported by columns, they extend over the sidewalk and furnish a grateful shade on a hot day. Under the portales there are some of the most attractive stores in the city, and they are also a refuge for various itinerant vendors who sell dulces, fruit, trinkets and other small wares. The portales and the two-storied buildings connected with them have a very old look, and date perhaps from the sixteen hundreds.

I imagine that the Plaza has altered very little during the past two hundred years, and to me it seemed to be the most romantic spot in the capital. Spanish officers in doublet and hose and feathered bonnet must once have strolled about there discussing the latest news, perhaps cursing that English terror of the seas, Francis Drake, whose capture of treasure-laden galleons so often caused consternation in Mexico. The very stones that one treads on to-day have probably echoed to the feet of the victims of the Inquisition, as they marched in sad procession from their place of trial (the old Inquisition building erected in 1571, close to the Plaza, and now used as a medical institution) to the bonfires of the auto-da-fe in the Alameda. Threading their pompous way beneath the shadow of the great cathedral, the Spanish viceroys, with silken canopies of state held above them by Indian slaves, have ridden on marvellously caparisoned steeds, surrounded by regal grandeur, into the old palace courtyard.

A large building in the Plaza is the Mexican equivalent of an American city hall, as it is the official residence of the city's administrators, and it also contains the offices of the principal city departments. The government of Mexico City, it may be added, differs entirely from that of other Mexican cities, the capital and various small towns surrounding it being situated in what is called the Federal District, corresponding to our own District of Columbia. It is regarded as neutral ground, as the National Congress is held in the capital; and on this account the government of the district is in the hands of the federal authorities. The government is represented by three officials appointed by the President — the Governor (who is practically the mayor), the President of the Superior Board of Health, and the Director of Public Works. Their power is supreme, and all departments are under their control. The system has worked wonderfully well, and it is perhaps due to the direction of affairs being left entirely to these three officials that public improvements are carried out so quickly in Mexico City. Even the most casual observer cannot fail to be impressed by the fact that the capital is remarkably well governed.

In the centre of the Plaza is a small park called the Zocalo, planted with trees and flowers, where a regimental band plays several times a week. From the Zocalo the electric cars run to all parts of the city and to the principal suburbs. It is strange to see these prosaic American cars labelled with such queer Aztec names as Coyoacan, Tlapan, Tlalnepantla, Atzacapotzalco, all suburban places.

Mexican street-cars, by the way, are divided into first and second class, but they run singly, the first class being painted buff, the second class green. The latter are always crowded with evil-smelling peons.

First-class fares are from three to ten cents, according to the distance travelled. The second class are a few centavos cheaper. Private cars, well fitted up, can be hired for parties, and freight-cars and cattle trucks are also run. One afternoon President Diaz and his cabinet went out to some suburban festival in a sumptuous special car.

Except in the cases of the wealthy, the street-cars are always used for funerals, a special car painted black being employed. Every day, and almost every hour of the day, you can see the funeral cars running out to the suburban cemeteries. The hearse-car, elaborately draped with black cloth, and surmounted by plumes and a cross, with a raised dais for the coffin, goes first; and then come two ordinary cars of solemn black for the mourners. This funeral train is only for the well-to-do. For the poor there is a car completely closed, with doors at the back, and fitted with shelves upon which the coffins are stacked. Attached to this is a second-class car, painted black, and inscribed "Funebre," in which relatives and friends ride to the cemetery.

Mexico City abounds in spots which, like the Plaza, have romantic or historical associations. For instance, a street corner called Salte de Alvarado marks the place where Alvarado, the lieutenant of Cortés, leaped across the canal, using his lance as a leaping-pole, when escaping from the Aztecs on the night of the flight from the city. Close to the Zocalo is the site of the house in which was established the first printing-press of the New World, in 1535, more than a century before one was employed in the English colonies. Prior to 1550, a dozen books or so, chiefly religious, had been printed. The first, bearing date 1536, was called "Escala espiritual para llegar al Cielo, Traducido del Latin en Castellano por el Venerable Padre Fr. Ivan de la Madelina, Religioso Dominico, 1536" (The Spiritual Ladder for Reaching Heaven, Translated from Latin into Spanish by Father Ivan, Dominican). It was here that the first music in the New World was printed in the old illuminated style, as also was the first wood-engraving cut. During the seventeenth century, Mexico City was regarded as a great seat of learning; but even before the spacious times of Queen Elizabeth, literature had its beginnings in the Mexican capital.

In Felipe de Jesus Street there is still standing the house in which the first Mexican saint, San Felipe, was born in 1572. His father was a Spanish merchant, who carried on

SPECIMENS OF ANCIENT AZTEC POTTERY AND STATUE OF HUITZILOPOCHTLI, THE AZTEC GOD OF WAR.

extensive trade between Mexico and the Philippine Islands in slow-sailing galleons. After a wild youth, Felipe was converted, became a Franciscan monk, and for many years was a missionary, until at last he found a martyr's death in Japan. A generation later he was canonized, and became the patron saint of Mexico City. In the patio of the house there is an old fig tree to which a beautiful tradition attaches. Felipe, despite his wild youth, used to tell his mother that he would die a saint. She said that would come to pass when the fig tree in the garden bore figs. The fig tree was then dry and barren. Years afterwards, when Felipe won a martyr's crown, the fig tree became, in a moment, green and healthy, and was loaded with luscious fruit, though it was not the bearing season.

At different points in the city are the ruins of the aqueduct of brick and stone which was completed in 1779. It brought water to the city from a spring at Chapultepec, and ended at a beautiful fountain called el Salto de Agua, still preserved. The water supply of the capital is now so up-to-date that it has almost done away with the necessity for one of the most picturesque street types, namely, the aguadores or water-carriers, bending under the weight of huge earthen pots in which they carried the precious liquid from door to door.

If Mexico City had no other claim to be ranked among the finest cities of the world, she could complacently base her pretensions upon the Paseo de la Reforma, the great drive which leads from the end of the Avenida Juarez for two and a half miles to the park and castle of Chapultepec. It is safe to say that there is no finer thoroughfare than this in the world. Fringed by a double avenue of trees, chiefly eucalyptus, surrounded by trim lawns and flower beds and lined with really fine houses, standing in beautiful grounds, the homes of Mexico's wealthiest families, the whole arrangement, with a double roadway, recalls the beauties of the Champs Elysées. At intervals the Paseo widens into circles, which are called glorietas, and in several of these there are some really fine statues. The bronze equestrian statue of Charles IV, which centres the glorieta at the city end of the Paseo, was set up in 1803, and is a very striking work of art. Its sculptor was Manuel Telsa, a Spaniard. In another glorieta is the Columbus statue by Cordier, a fine piece of carving. On the base are represented historical scenes, beautifully sculptured, and the whole is surmounted by a figure of Columbus drawing aside the veil which hides the New World.

But the most remarkable monument is that by Francisco Jiminez, which honors the memory of Cuauhtemoc or Guatemotzin, the nephew of Montezuma, the last Aztec king. The Indians still revere his memory, and annually honor it by a festival, on which occasion the monument is decorated with wreaths and flowers. Scenes from the life of the prince, and his torture by Cortés, are worked in bronze on the four sides of the base; on the plinth stands an ideal statue of the heroic warrior in war costume, a spear poised in his hand. It is worth noticing that while this worthy memorial has a place of honor in the city which has succeeded the Aztec Tenochtitlan, there is not among the public monuments even a bust of the cruel and bigoted Spaniard, torturer and murderer of the brave Aztec prince.

It was during the empire of Maximilian that the Paseo was laid out, and it at once became the fashionable drive of the capital. Here, in the afternoons, but more particularly on Sundays and feast-days, there is a wonderful display of carriages and horses. The procession passes up one side and down the other, while police duties in directing traffic are performed by the picturesque Republican Guard, mounted on the wiry Mexican ponies, and armed to the teeth with sword, Winchester rifle and revolver. But there is no need for this heavy armament, for the whole scene is one of gayety and good temper. The people have come out to enjoy themselves, and very happily and brightly they do so.

At the end of the Paseo, occupying much the same position as the Arc de Triomphe does in the Champs Elysées, is the Castle of Chapultepec. It stands on a high bluff of volcanic origin, on the scarred face of which are carved some ancient hieroglyphics. In Aztec, Chapultepec means "The Hill of the Grasshopper," and it was on the hill that Montezuma had his summer palace. The castle, which architecturally hardly comes up to its name, having a striking resemblance to some huge sanitarium, is a vast, rambling building which was designed as a viceregal residence and completed in 1785. It has, however, been much enlarged and altered since that date. Maximilian was responsible for the decoration of the castle, and for the planning out of the beautiful gardens in which it stands. With the exception of two chairs, which are traditionally believed to have been used by Cortés, all the old furniture has disappeared, and there is no trace of the short-lived empire, everything bearing the monogram, "R. M." (Republica Mexicana). The President resides at the castle for only a month or two in the summer, and occupies one of the wings, which has been specially furnished for him and his family. Sometimes official visitors of great distinction are entertained there and allotted apartments during their stay in the city.

From the castle terrace, which looks down upon the sweep of the Paseo, and over the tree-tops towards the capital, there is one of the most magnificent views in the world. The eye takes in the marvellous panorama of the vast plain studded with towns and hamlets, centred with the glittering white of church tower and housetop in the city itself, and ringed round with the distant hills shrouded in a purple mist. Beyond these are the great snow-capped volcanic peaks of Popocatepetl and Ixtaccihuatl, which tower above the lesser mountains and dominate the horizon.

In a wing of the castle is the Mexican military college, conducted somewhat after the fashion of West Point. Here the sons of the best Mexican families receive a military education. They are a fine-looking set of young men, wearing a uniform a good deal like that of the French military schools. When the Americans took the castle in the war of 1847, the cadets assisted in the defence, and a large number of them fell. A modest monument to the memory of these young heroes stands at the foot of the hill, and on this fresh flowers are placed every morning.

The castle is surrounded by a beautiful park called the Bosque, very much like the Bois de Boulogne, with miles of shady walks and drives, under semi-tropical groves of tree-ferns and palms, and above them is the foliage of some fine oaks and wonderful cypresses. Of the latter there is an ancient avenue, centuries old, from the boughs of which Spanish moss hangs in graceful fringes. Beneath the shade of these giant trees Montezuma is said to have held his court, and here, too, the news was brought to him of the Spanish invasion. Near the hill is a large stone basin into which a spring drains. This, tradition — probably very inaccurate — declares to have been Montezuma's bath. In later days it has been used as a water supply for the city.

Not far from Chapultepec, on one side of the Paseo, an enterprising American company has started what is called Luna Park, an imitation of the famous New York seaside resort, Coney Island. Here there is a huge Ferris wheel, a switchback railway, shows of every description and a circus. President Diaz, in his apartments in the castle, can probably hear the revels of Luna Park.

Also near the castle is the Chapultepec Café, a fashionable rendezvous, where one can get an excellent meal, served in French style, or if not hungry, can sit outside at a little marble-topped table, and watch the carriages while sipping the ever popular Mexican lager beer. It is here that all the cosmopolitan inhabitants of the capital gather on a fine Sunday afternoon, and almost every European language can then be heard. Almost as many carriages assemble in the Paseo on Sundays as one can see in the Bois, and a visitor can gain a very fair idea of the wealth and beauty of the capital.

For the most part, the carriages are open barouches, landaus and Victorias of the latest European makes, and drawn by the Spanish-Arab type of horse, which, with their curving necks, their glossy silken coats and sweeping tails, make a wonderful picture in the sunshine. The coachmen and footmen are dressed in liveries correct even to the cockades, though many of the old-fashioned Mexican families still favor the native serving dress, tight trousers edged with gold buttons, short bolero coat, heavily braided, and an enormous felt sombrero. Most of the carriages are tenanted by dark-eyed Mexican beauties. The men either drive dog-carts in English style, or ride on a row which runs parallel with the carriage road round the park. There are many smart automobiles to be seen, too, and there is also a large mixture of humbler conveyances, with dozens of blue-flagged cabs filled with men, women and children.

It is said that some Mexicans of good birth but of much straitened means, who find it hard to keep up appearances, send out their carriages with blue flags half the week, and thus earn their keep as cabs. Many poorer citizens, such as clerks, deny themselves every luxury to take this drive with their families on Sunday, and squander all their spare money on it.

The paths of the Paseo are filled with all sorts of people, well-dressed Mexicans, Europeans and Americans, residents and tourists, also people of the poorer classes, including numbers of Indians, men and women, in their blankets and rebosas. Groups of Mexican "mashers" stand on the edge of the walks, criticising the fair occupants of the carriages and seeking to attract their bewitching eyes. The Mexican masher, it may be added, is called a lagartijo (pronounced *lah-ahr-tee-ho*), meaning "little lizard," because he basks lazily in the sun at the street corner to ogle the fair sex.

He usually wears a French morning coat and trousers, American patent leather shoes, with pointed toes, and an English top hat, and in his fingers is the inevitable cigarette.

During the afternoon excellent music is played by the band of the Republican Guard stationed near the Café, where towards the evening hours the scene becomes wonderfully animated, with the moving procession of vehicles and the hundreds of pedestrians. In the far distance are the blue mountains, sharply silhouetted against the clear sky, which in the fading light takes on varied tints under the rays of the setting sun. As the twilight comes, the whole scene suggests a piece of illuminated fairyland; the carriage lights flit, in the growing darkness, among the trees like fireflies; the electric lamps flash out along the Paseo; in the distance the sky glows with the lights of the capital; and as the leaves of the trees idly stir in the evening breeze, the band strikes up the stirring Mexican National Anthem, and the pleasant hours at Chapultepec come to an end.

On week-days, from six to seven, a procession of carriages drives up and down San Francisco Street in an endless chain, going down one side and returning on the other, the occupants sitting up very straight and solemn, looking as if they were taking part in a most serious function. Some of the automobiles are quite imposing. I saw one gorgeous car in which a wealthy Mexican and his family were riding. The chauffeur was dressed in the height of motor style, and in the rear, with folded arms, sat two French footmen, resplendent in black attire, top-hats and white gloves.

Riding and promenading are not the only recreations enjoyed by the people of Mexico City on Sunday afternoons, for thousands flock to the ever popular bull-fights, which are held in the Plaza de Toros or Bull-ring, not far from Chapultepec. On Sundays the street-cars which run in the direction of Chapultepec all bear a great label, "Toros" (Bulls), and are packed with people.

The Plaza de Toros is a huge circular building of stone and wood, with an interior that forms an immense amphitheatre, seating thousands of people. Rising to the top, where the private boxes are situated, are tiers of seats, and as there is no roof except over the outer circle shading the boxes, there is a shady side called "Sombra," and a sunny side, "Sol," with prices varying from ten to twenty-five cents in the sun, and from fifty cents to a dollar and a half in the shade.

Bull-fights or corridas de toros are conducted in much the same way as in Spain, and have been too often described to need repetition. In Mexico, however, the spectators never seem satisfied unless several horses are killed. The picadors, who carry pikes with which they prod and torture the bull, are mounted on old hacks and seem to purposely get in the way of the enraged animal. Their horses get gored terribly, and are kept on their feet as long as they can stand, streaming with blood. Whenever they drop dead, other poor hacks are brought in to take their places, the spectators sometimes shouting, "Otro caballo" (Another horse). The bulls are of Spanish breed, with huge horns, some of them imported from Spain, and some of them bred locally.

I went to the bull-ring one Sunday afternoon and saw six bulls killed. During the fight, several horses were gored and despatched, until the whole place reeked with blood like a shambles. The fight had been well advertised in the newspapers, and the public were invited to see the butchery of "six terrible bulls, unusually fierce — the greatest fight on record." Most of the bulls were very mild specimens, and submitted to being killed without much of a fight. One of them turned tail and fled, leaping over the fence at the entrance to the ring. The spectators were furious, and shouted all sorts of uncomplimentary remarks about the management. One man yelled, "Where are the fierce bulls advertised in the *Imparcial?*" to which the "sol" or the "gallery gods" responded with hooting and groans. All through the fight, the matadors and toreadors were greeted with shouts of praise or denunciation whenever they made a good coup or a bad mistake.

Most of the toreadors come from Spain, and as they get from $1000 to $2500 for each performance many of them are quite wealthy. The toreadors are lionized by the lower classes in much the same way as prize-fighters are in England and America. A popular toreador of Mexican birth is a millionaire amateur who goes into the ring just for the pure love of the sport.

As a rule, the Mexican upper classes do not visit the bull-ring, and the President is never seen at a fight. As a matter of fact, he and Madam Diaz would like to see the sport abolished, but even the all-powerful Diaz cannot carry his point in this instance. The people adore the pastime, and the Mexican small boy plays at bull-fighting as the American boy does at baseball.

Suburban life is yearly becoming more popular with people in Mexico City, and there are several Mexican equivalents of our New Jersey suburban towns, where well-to-do citizens have their homes. Most of these places are old towns and villages adjacent to the city, and easily reached by the electric street-cars. One of the prettiest suburban towns is Tacubaya, which abounds in beautiful parks, gardens and shady streets filled with flowers and fine trees. Tacubaya lies on the hills back of Chapultepec, and was once as infamous for gambling as Monte Carlo. The streets were filled with gambling booths where every sort of game of chance was played, and any one could wager from five cents to a dollar; while in the gambling houses there would sometimes be $20,000 or $30,000 on the table at once. To-day all is changed. Tacubaya is now a model of respectability, and gambling, if indulged in, has to be carried on far more privately.

Twenty minutes' ride in a street-car took me, one afternoon, to Popotla, where still stands the tree of la Noche Triste (the Sorrowful Night), under which Cortés is said to have wept on the night of his defeat by the Aztecs (July 1, 1520). The tree, a cypress, gnarled and withered by the hand of time, is enclosed by a high iron fence to guard it from souvenir hunters. Some years ago, an Indian fanatic lit a fire at the foot of the tree with the purpose of burning it down, but it was fortunately discovered before much damage was done.

The country round Mexico City abounds in mementos of the mysterious races which once inhabited the country, and there is hardly a district that does not contain the remains of once imposing temples, palaces or tombs. Among the most important of these are the Pyramids of the Sun and Moon, which are situated near the village of San Juan Teotihuacan, twenty-seven miles from the city, and reached by the Mexican Central Railway. The village marks the site of a famous Toltec city, and some wonderful structures raised by the Toltecs are said to have been standing there at the time of the Spanish Conquest, but were subsequently reduced to ruins. Teotihuacan means "City of the Gods," and the ancient city may have been a holy place or city of temples. There is a great difference of opinion as to whether the Toltecs or some race that preceded them built the pyramids and erected various great structures near to them, the ruins of which still exist. Some archeologists assert, however, that they are as old as the ancient works of Egypt and India.

In company with an American friend, I went out one day to see the pyramids, which stand in the midst of a great plain. Surrounding them in all directions there are ruins of an ancient city with fortifications and walls, one of the latter measuring 200 feet in width. The Pyramid of the Sun is 216 feet high, the base 751 feet by 721, while the top is 59 by 105; the Moon Pyramid is somewhat smaller. Both are supposed to have served as bases for temples which stood on their summits. In their interior construction a mixture of clay and volcanic pebbles was used, over which was laid a facing of light porous stone, and this, in turn, thickly coated with white stucco. But with the progress of time they have lost their original appearance, and now resemble earthen mounds. At the time of the Conquest, a temple stood on the larger pyramid, having a colossal statue of the sun made of a single block of stone. In a hollow in the centre of this there was a planet of fine gold. The temple and the figure of the sun were destroyed by the Spaniards, who also seized the gold.

There are several smaller pyramids or mounds on the plain, some of which have been excavated, revealing in at least one case chambers with frescoed walls. It has been suggested that they were shrines attached to the greater temples. The frescoes, cornices and walls were colored in ten or twenty different shades or tints. In the Moon Pyramid, some years back, a passage was discovered, the walls of which were of cut stone carefully orientated.

The Indians who live about Teotihuacan have some queer ideas concerning the ruins, and firmly believe that the pyramids were built by giants. Most of them are convinced that treasure is buried somewhere among the crumbling walls; and they can sometimes be seen prowling about the ancient stonework as if in search of this mythical gold. Occasionally, as I discovered, their ideas of wealth are on a much humbler basis. As we were examining the rugged sides of the Moon Pyramid, we suddenly came upon an Indian woman, wrapped in her faded rebosa, seated among the débris of ages, gazing pensively at a large stone on which there was some rude carving. "Musing over the glories of her ancestors, poor soul," suggested my companion, and so it seemed. But the thoughts of this female descendant of the Aztecs were apparently of a different nature; for on catching sight of us, she hurried forward with outstretched palm, and gave utterance to the words so constantly heard in Mexico, "Solo un centavo, señores" (Only one penny, gentlemen).

When contrasted with the present decadence of the Indian races in Mexico, the wonderful skill exhibited by the ancient builders in the construction of their temples and palaces seems all the more remarkable. Charnay, the French archeologist, who made a thorough exploration of the ruins of Tula and Teotihuacan, expresses deep admiration for their architectural designs. In his work, "The Ancient Cities of the New World," he says: "Unlike most primitive nations, they used every material at once. They coated their inner walls with mud and mortar, faced their outer walls with baked bricks and cut stone, had wooden roofs and brick and stone staircases. They were acquainted with pilasters and caryatides, with square and round columns; indeed, they seem to have been familiar with every architectural device. That they were painters and sculptors we had ample indications in a house that we unearthed, where the walls were covered with rosettes, palms, and red, white and gray geometrical figures on a black ground." In several places the remains of irrigation works have been found, showing that the land was carefully cultivated in ancient times.

A curious causeway named Calle de los Muertos (Street of the Dead) connects the Sun Pyramid with the Moon Pyramid; and on either side of this is a terrace of cement and lava faced with mortar of high polish and brightly colored. Along this street many mounds have been opened, revealing chests of cut stone containing bones, ornaments of obsidian, earthen vases and miniature earthen masks. One theory is that these masks were portraits of the dead, buried in the same way as in the Egyptian tombs. Charnay, who collected a number of these masks, says: "Among them are types which do not seem to belong to America; a negro, whose thick lips, flat nose and woolly hair proclaim his African origin; a Chinese head, Caucasian and Japanese specimens; heads with retreating foreheads, and not a few with Greek profiles. The lower jaw is straight or projecting, the faces smooth or bearded; in short, it is a wonderful medley, indicative of the numerous races who succeeded each other and amalgamated on this continent, which until lately was supposed to be so new and is in truth so old."

THE PASEO DE LA REFORMA.
Mexico City's beautiful driveway.

CHAPTER VI

CHURCHES AND MIRACLES

MEXICO CITY, like London, possesses a number of old churches, many of which have been overtaken by the onward march of commerce, and find themselves to-day surrounded by prosaic stores and warehouses. Some of these old structures date from the early days of the Conquest; they give a touch of the picturesque to otherwise unattractive streets; and their history, too, is often full of romantic interest. Few of them are architecturally beautiful, the outside usually being far more imposing than the interior. They are generally built of stone and stucco, painted with kalsomine or distemper, which has long ago faded into soft tints of pink, yellow or cream, giving them an appearance of great antiquity.

One of these old churches, Jesus Nazareno, is famous for having been founded by Cortés shortly after his occupation of the country. Large sums were lavished by him for this building, which was begun in 1575, and took nearly a hundred years to complete. Appropriately enough, the bones of the great Conquistador rested here. He had directed that should he die in Spain his bones were to be taken, after ten years, to Mexico and deposited in the Convent de la Concepcion, which he proposed to erect, but never built.

Cortés died on December 2, 1547, in Castilleja de la Questa, Spain. His body was placed in the tomb of the dukes of Medina Sidonia, and a decade later was removed to Mexico to the Church of San Francisco in Texcoco. There they remained until 1629, when Don Pedro Cortés, his grandson, and the last of the male line, died. The bones of the Conqueror, together with those of the latter, were with great ceremony placed in the Church of San Francisco in Mexico City. But even here they were not allowed to rest longer than 165 years, for in 1734 they were once more exhumed and interred in a splendid marble mausoleum in the church of Jesus Nazareno. This was their home for thirty years; but during the War of Independence, when everything Spanish was hateful to the Mexicans, the coffin was secretly removed and hidden in another part of the church. Later it was sent to Spain, and found eventually a final resting-place in the tomb of the dukes of Monteleone in Italy. Thus the remains of this great Spaniard, after crossing the Atlantic twice and having been entombed once in the country of his birth and thrice in the country he conquered, found, at last, a final resting place in an alien land.

The ancient-looking church of Nuestra Señora de los Angeles, which faces the Plaza de Zaragosa, about a mile from the Alameda, was founded in 1580 as the result of a strange miracle. During that year the city was inundated, and in the course of the flood an Aztec chieftain, Isayoque, discovered a picture of the Virgin floating in the water.

He erected a chapel of adobe, and had a replica of the picture painted on the walls. Fifteen years afterwards a larger church was built over the mud-brick one, keeping intact the wall on which the picture was painted, in the design of which so many angels figured that the shrine was called "Our Lady of the Angels." In 1607 much damage was done to the church by another flood, and the picture was injured, but the face and hands were unhurt, an accident which was superstitiously magnified into a miracle. Two centuries later the present church was built, and the remains of the miraculous painting, covered with glass, are shown within.

Not far from the Alameda there also stands the venerable church of San Hipólito, which marks the spot where the Spaniards were defeated and slaughtered by the Aztecs on the famous "Sorrowful Night" during their retreat from the city. Then the place was occupied by a canal, but this dried up years ago. On the victorious return of the Spaniards on the feast-day of San Hipólito, August 13, 1521, a Spanish soldier, Juan Garrido, built a small chapel of adobe in memory of his fallen comrades. This was called San Hipólito of the Martyrs, and the name is still preserved. In 1599 a much larger church was begun, and completed in 1739. For many years on the 13th of each August the monks made processions to the church, bearing the crimson banner used by Cortés during the wars of the conquest. On the church wall is the "Sorrowful Night" memorial tablet. Cut on the stone is an eagle, with an Indian in his claws, the rest of the design being composed of musical instruments, arrows, spears and trophies of the Aztecs.

Another interesting church is that of Jesus Maria, founded in 1557 by two Spaniards, with the idea that the female descendants of the conquerors should take the veil. The convent was completed in 1580 and removed to its present site in 1582, when there came a nun who was alleged to be a daughter of Philip II of Spain, and a niece of the then Archbishop of Mexico. This story gains corroboration from the fact that the convent benefited largely by grants from the royal treasury of Spain and the viceregal exchequer of Mexico.

Almost all these churches, and in fact most of those found throughout the temperate regions of Mexico, are of similar design, with a central dome and Doric towers.

Some scores of the finer city churches and convents were confiscated by the government after the disestablishment, and are now used as warehouses, hotels, private residences or government offices.

For two centuries after the Conquest there was an epoch of church-building in Mexico. Peon and millionaire subscribed lavishly, and the remarkable feature of this great outburst of building was the way in which Aztec and Spanish art were blended, with a result that, if somewhat barbarically florid, is very impressive. Even in secluded villages and townships you can see towers and domes which rival the best work of Italy and are reminiscent of the triumphs of Moorish art. For the most part, they were the work of the native Indians, who carried out the architectural ideas of their Spanish masters. Many of the intricate designs and elaborate figures doubtless represent the mythology of the Aztecs, blended with the traditions of the victorious church. In some details there is a strong likeness to the strange symbols of the ancient Egyptian and Persian monuments. The ornate façades often exhibit a blending of the two religions, the Christian saints being substituted for the pagan deities.

In some quite small villages the churches astound with their splendor. Here and there is a towering fane with hardly a trace of a human dwelling near it. But this is not the case in the tropical portions of Mexico, where the churches are of a very humble and unadorned nature. Doubtless this is due to the fact that the early conquerors did not penetrate the hot lands, and also to the difficulty which the constant risk of earthquakes presented to the church-builders.

For the most part the beauty of the churches is external, the interiors being often disappointing and garish in their ornamentation. But as you stand outside you feel strangely impressed with the weird beauty of the extravagant and often bizarre sculptures. On this point Charles Dudley Warner says: "There is a touch of decay nearly everywhere, a crumbling and defacement of colors which adds somewhat of pathos to these old Mexican structures, but in nearly every one there is some unexpected fancy, a belfry oddly placed, a figure that surprises with the quaintness of its position, or a rich bit of deep stone carving; and in the humblest and plainest façade there is a note of individual yielding to a whim of expression that is very fascinating. The architects escaped from the commonplace and conventional; they understood proportion without regularity, and the result is perhaps not explainable to those who are only accustomed to English church architecture."

In keeping with the somewhat tawdry ornamentation of the interiors, the organs of most Mexican churches are very inferior, and most of them have too much resemblance to the old-fashioned street organ, lacking both musical qualities and power. The choir-boys rarely have good voices. They are too nasal and harsh.

Most of the old churches were erected as the result of some supposed supernatural occurrence, Mexico, for two centuries after the Conquest, having been a veritable land of miracles. Nearly every town and village has its legend of miraculous appearances of the Virgin, of saints or angels. Almost every church has its wonderworking image or picture, superstitiously guarded through the ages. For example, at Tacubaya, not far from the capital, there is the arbol benito (blessed tree). The story is that an aged monk, weary with his work among the Indians, rested under the shade and gave the tree his benediction, praying that it might be blessed with eternal youth. No sooner had the good man spoken than a choir of sweet angel voices was heard, and a spring of pure water gushed from the roots. You really feel you must believe this, for the tree is standing there, ever green, and the little rivulet flows on forever.

The church of La Piedad, in another suburb, was built by a Dominican in 1562 in fulfilment of a vow. He was commissioned by the brotherhood to bring them from Rome a picture of the Virgin and the dead Christ, painted by a well-known artist. Obliged to come away in a hurry, he brought the picture in an unfinished state. During his journey the vessel was overwhelmed in a terrible storm, and the monk vowed to the Virgin that if the ship came safely to port he would build a church in her honor. The prayer was answered; and more than this, for when the painting was exposed in Mexico, it was found to be finished in all its details. This remarkable picture is hung to-day over the altar.

At Los Remedios, three miles from the city, stands the church of our Lady of Succor, or Señora de los Remedios. During the flight of the "Sorrowful Night" a Spanish soldier, Juan de Villafuente, had on him an image of the Virgin. Wounded and unable to guard it, he hid it under a maguey plant. Twenty years later, an Aztec chief, Cequauhtzin or Juan Aguila, while hunting on the hill of Totaltepec, saw the Virgin in a vision, and she told him to seek the image. The chief searched, found it under a maguey plant and took it home. In the morning it had disappeared, and on returning he found it again under the maguey. Once more he took the image back to his house, where he placed fruit and flowers as offerings before it, but it returned to the plant. Again he brought it back, and this time, being a cautious man, he locked it in a strong-box and all night long slept on the lid. But even these precautions were in vain; for when dawn came, the box was empty, and the image was found under the maguey. The

FIGURES OF CHAC-MOL (GOD OF FIRE) AND EL INDIO TRISTE (THE SAD INDIAN).

The latter, it is believed, once stood in the great Aztec temple.

Indian told his story to the priests, and they, convinced that a miracle had taken place, built a shrine on the spot and placed the image in it. This was afterwards replaced by the present church, begun in 1574, and the restless image, which is of rudely carved wood, much disfigured by time, is now enshrined on the great altar. It measures about eight inches. The gourd in which the Aztec chief placed his offerings before it is also preserved in a silken case.

Greater far than all these miracles, however, is that of our Lady of Guadalupe, the patron saint of Mexico, which is honored by a great national festival on the tenth of every December. The shrine of Mexico's saint is an imposing church at Guadalupe Hidalgo, about three miles from the capital. Thousands of Indians pour into the city to attend this festival, some by train, some on horseback or burro, hundreds more tramping on foot from remote parts of the Republic.

The legend to which these remarkable pilgrimages owe their origin dates from the early days of the Conquest. In the year 1531, so the story goes, an Indian, Juan Diego, a native of Tolpetlac, walking over the hill of Guadalupe to mass, of a sudden heard the singing of angels, and to him appeared the Virgin, who bade him go to the bishop and say that it was her wish that in her honor a temple be built on the spot. Juan hurried to the bishop, Don Juan Zumarraga, who, however, doubted the story. Much disappointed, Juan reclimbed the hill; and again the Virgin appeared to him, bidding him once more convey her commands to the bishop. Juan again returned, but the bishop still discredited the message, and asked the Indian to prove his story in some way. On his departure, the bishop sent two of his servants to follow him, but on approaching the hill he mysteriously disappeared from view. The third time the Virgin appeared, and Juan told her the bishop demanded a proof of her appearance. She bade him come the next day, when she would give him a sign. On his return home, the Indian found his uncle dangerously ill, and during the next day he was busy nursing the sick man.

The following morning Juan started for Tlaltelolco to fetch a confessor. In order to avoid meeting the Virgin, he did not take the usual road, but went by another on the eastern side of the hill, yet, despite this precaution, the Virgin again appeared. Juan told her the reason of his absence the day before and of his errand. She replied that he need have no fear, as his uncle was completely restored. Then she bade him gather flowers from the barren hillside, and to his amazement he saw beautiful flowers growing around. The Virgin ordered him to gather these and take them to the bishop, warning him not to show them to any one until the bishop had seen them. Carefully wrapping the flowers in his blanket or tilma, Juan hurried to the bishop's house. On his arrival, he unfolded his tilma, when upon it there was seen a beautifully painted image of the Virgin. Taking this wonderful picture, the bishop placed it reverently in the chapel of his residence, and when Juan returned home he found his uncle quite well, as the Virgin had declared.

The bishop ordered a chapel to be built on the spot where the Virgin had appeared, and in it was placed the holy painting in February, 1532. It is now kept in a tabernacle in a frame of gold and silver, covered with plate-glass. The tilma is a coarse cloth of ixtl fibre, and of the picture which is painted on it much of the coloring still remains, the blue robe and pink skirt of the Virgin and the surrounding halo being wonderfully well preserved. Ecclesiastics declare that the painting has been examined by many Mexican artists, but the manner of its exact production remains a mystery. Sceptical Mexicans scoff at this and declare the picture is a crude piece of work, while admitting that the coloring is remarkable considering its age.

The present church of Guadalupe was completed in 1836 at a cost of two and a half million dollars. It is a massive stone structure, with a central dome flanked by towers filled with bells. Its height from the floor to the dome is 125 feet. In size the church is quite a cathedral, and its services are so organized. The interior is magnificently adorned, a massive railing of solid silver weighing twenty-six tons enclosing the high altar of Carrara marble. Here is enshrined the sacred tilma. Over the altar are some Latin lines in honor of the Virgin, written specially by Pope Leo XIII. The walls of the basilica are adorned with five frescos portraying the history of Guadalupe. In 1895 a golden crown, richly bejewelled, was presented to the church to be suspended over the painting, the gems having been subscribed by the women of Mexico from their own jewels. It is a glittering mass of diamonds, rubies and sapphires.

To the right of the church is a chapel built over a spring which gushed from the ground where the Virgin stood, and which the superstitious believe has medicinal properties. At the back of the chapel are the tombs of Santa Ana and several other men famous in Mexican history. Beginning at the church is the hill of Guadalupe, ascended by a long flight of stone steps which lead to a shrine at the summit. It is a long, tiring climb, but all the pious who make pilgrimages to the church ascend the hill. Halfway up are the so-called Stone Sails of Guadalupe, an interesting monument of the romantic past. Some two hundred years ago, so the story runs, a crew of sailors caught in a storm prayed to the Virgin of Guadalupe, vowing that if they were brought safely to land they would carry their ship's foremast to the hill of Guadalupe and set the sails up before her shrine. Being saved, the sailors fulfilled their promise, and their curious monument was eventually replaced with sails of stone.

On the day of the great festival, which is kept as a public holiday all over Mexico, I drove with some friends in an automobile to Guadalupe. The electric cars which run out to the city were packed with people, mostly Indians. Hundreds of men, women and children were walking in the road, some coming from Guadalupe, others going there. A large force of the mounted Republican Guard were stationed along the road to keep order. When we arrived within a mile of the church, the crowd became so dense that the police stopped our car. We got out, and making very slow progress, eventually reached the church, where we witnessed a most remarkable scene. The plaza in front of the church was packed with a moving mass of Indians of every tribe and color, wrapped in bright blankets of every hue, the women all wearing the inevitable blue rebosa. There were long lines of booths for the sale of tamales, chili-con-carne, green and red peppers and all the other weird eatables the Indian heart delighteth in, together with gallons of pulque and mescal. There were stalls where crudely colored pictures of the sacred tilma and tilma postcards were on sale, and a roaring trade was being done in candles, beads, charms and trinkets of every kind. The gambling booths were surrounded by excited crowds of Indians intent on losing their last centavos, and a touch of the modern, with its vulgarity, was introduced by the whining screech of a phonograph and the strumming of a piano-organ which ground out tunes for the merry-go-round.

Inside the churchyard, a large stone-paved enclosure, were encamped hundreds of Indian families, some with all their belongings and eatables, a mass of men, women, children and babies. Most of them were filthy and travel-

CHURCH AT TEPOZOTLAN.
A fine specimen of Mexican church architecture.

stained, and the smell of this unwashed humanity was almost intolerable. The encampment of these Indian pilgrims extended for nearly a mile around the church; here and there fires were burning, and repulsive-looking food was being cooked. Pushing our way through the crowd, we managed to enter the church, which was filled with kneeling Indian worshippers, holding tapers in their hands. Almost every tribe in the Republic was represented in this strange assembly, the worshippers all pressing forward in the intensity of their devotion, trying to get still closer to the shrine of their patroness.

Mass was being sung by gorgeously robed priests, among whom was the Archbishop of Mexico, wearing vestments of white and gold. Choir boys in surplices of crimson and white, mostly swarthy young Indians, sang incessantly, their voices being very nasal and harsh. The Indians may sing musically in their own language, but when they speak in Spanish or sing in Latin their voices are almost always unpleasantly nasal. But the scene was one which must live in the memory. The great church, ablaze with candles; the dense throng of devout worshippers in their tattered blankets and worn rebosas; the glittering gold ornaments on the altar, with its wealth of floral decorations, above which hung the sacred tilma with its gorgeous crown; the regal pomp of the clerics standing grouped within the glitter of the solid silver chancel rail; the clouds of incense,—all made such a scene as is scarcely to be described.

While we were viewing the interior of the church, we observed many Indians squirming on the tiled floor, pushing and struggling round small squares of crystal glass. At first they appeared to be searching for something, and I thought they must be scrambling for coins which had been thrown to them by visitors. But on approaching nearer, the small squares of glass proved to contain saintly relics of some kind. The Indians, both men and women, kissed the glass repeatedly, rubbed their hands and faces on it, and some laid their babies on it, all the while uttering pious ejaculations in Spanish and Indian. It was a wild, weird scene. There were several squares of glass set in the tiled floor in different parts of the church, and each had its mass of Indians squirming and struggling around it. Many of the devotees were suffering from bodily ailments for which they sought a miraculous cure. In some parts of the church silver feet, arms and legs of miniature size are displayed on black cloth panels, having been offered by afflicted pilgrims who have been restored.

It is estimated that over forty thousand Indians attend the Guadalupe celebration every year. This means a great harvest for the railways, which run special excursion trains from all parts of Mexico. Pilgrims are coming, however, at all times of the year, for Guadalupe is the Mecca of the poor Indian, and he who has seen the sacred shrine is ever an object of envy.

CHAPTER VII

THE LIFE OF THE PEOPLE

IN Mexico City a visitor sees Mexican social life scarcely at its best, if he is anxious to learn something of the real manners and customs of the people. For the capital is not truly Mexico — at any rate, so far as the richer classes are concerned. It is a city of motley civilizations; and in fashionable circles one finds a great deal of Madrid, a little of Paris and slight infusions of London and New York. Still all this is very superficial, and if the stranger has the good fortune to break through the adamantine barrier of etiquette, prejudice and precedent which stifle social intercourse among well-born Mexicans, he will be surprised to find how thin is the veneer of culture, and how much of seventeenth-century Spanish custom still survives in the daily lives of the owners of twentieth-century motor-cars, and among women who wear the latest Parisian fashions.

Owing her civilization to Spain it is, of course, natural that Mexico should be largely governed by Spanish social ideas; but the curious fact is that many customs long ago discarded in Spain are still observed in Spain's former colony. Women are still kept jealously guarded from the outer world; strangers are rarely admitted to the family circle; and the whole social system is hedged in by as many precautions as a Chinese mandarin adopts to guard his household against the evil influence of the "foreign devils."

High society in the capital is largely a replica of Spanish society, but is far more exclusive and old-fashioned than that of Madrid. It is composed, for the most part, of those families who have been rich for generations, who own huge estates; and besides these are many of the higher government officials, successful lawyers and other professional men. The majority of these people are of pure Spanish descent, or represent French and Italian ancestry.

To any one familiar with the life of London, Paris or New York, society in the Mexican capital appears extremely dull. Dances, musicales and other social entertainments seldom take place, and it is quite unusual for people to dine in parties at fashionable restaurants. Such recreations as golfing and tennis are absolutely unknown to the fashionable Mexican woman. The chief amusements of the upper classes are mostly limited to driving and family dinner parties, which are all very proper, very unexciting and must become very boring. If a stranger is invited to a meal, it is usually to luncheon, a heavy, full-course repast, served at one o'clock, followed by coffee and cigarettes, served in the drawing-room. Chocolate, a favorite beverage, is also often served, being made very thick, and accompanied with rich cakes.

There are some palatial houses in the capital, many of them situated in frowzy residential districts which are being rapidly transformed into business centres. Shabby and unattractive on the outside, they are often richly furnished within, and abound in wonderful old furniture, bric-a-brac and works of art. In recent years some wealthy people have built handsome houses of French design in the new residential quarters, notably in and about the Paseo de la Reforma, these mansions being also decorated and furnished in modern French style. Hardly any of the houses, old or new, are equipped with fireplaces or other systems of heating, and on cold days are far from comfortable. In the old houses there are spacious patios,

CHURCH OF GUADALUPE.
Photographed at the time of the great celebration.

open to the sky, and in these meals are often served, even in the winter time, when the temperature occasionally falls below fifty degrees, and a good blazing fire would be welcome.

Few Mexican women are domesticated, and everything is left to the servants; for the lady of the house would consider it disgraceful to do anything or to see to anything herself. This has a most deplorable result upon domestic arrangements, and even has the effect of deteriorating the value of some of the ancient plate and china, which are treasured possessions of the wealthier families. Left to the tender mercies of untrained and badly managed servants, they get tarnished and broken, lost or stolen. The care which an American or English woman will lavish upon the decoration of her dinner-table is inconceivable to Mexican women. Thus, to save themselves trouble in a land which is one large hothouse, they generally decorate their rooms with artificial flowers.

Many Mexican women of the fashionable class have been educated in French convents, and owing to this, French is very generally spoken in society circles. On the other hand, many of the younger men have been to English schools, and some of them have been at Oxford and Cambridge. They have thus acquired strong British sympathies, which they show by getting their clothes from London, and introducing various English customs, such as afternoon tea, which is popularly known as "5 o'clock." Some of the wealthy families, too, employ English governesses, and it has become quite a fad among fashionable folk to have English coachmen. A knowledge of English is thus becoming much more general among the upper classes. Many members of the Mexican smart set, too, visit New York and Washington during the social season, and have in this way acquired a few American ideas.

Children are brought up in much the same way as in Spain, but are kept somewhat more secluded from the outside world, this being especially so in the case of the girls. In the household, however, as visitors are mostly intimate friends and relations, the youthful members of the family enjoy great freedom, and the system of confining them in nurseries or schoolrooms is not generally common.

Suspicion of strangers, as already remarked, is the invariable rule among the wealthy classes in Mexico, and one must know a Mexican for a long time before being granted the privilege of entering his household as a guest. Once admitted, however, they are found to be the most charming hosts in the world. Nothing is too much trouble for them once they adopt you as a friend. When visiting a country house, your host will think nothing of riding many miles with you over rough roads on your leaving, simply as a mark of esteem.

Mexicans, in fact, are full of Latin enthusiasm; their southern blood is shown by their animated gestures in conversation, and by their flow of complimentary expressions which are never meant. They take sudden fancies for persons and things, gush over them for a time, and then quickly forget them. For this they must be forgiven, as it is simply a matter of racial temperament.

Despite the restrictions of society in the capital, there are many delightful people among the higher classes, who always take a foremost part in entertaining visiting foreigners of any distinction. President Diaz and his charming wife are, of course, the nominal heads of society, and preside at a number of interesting functions during each winter season. Another distinguished member of the official circle is Señor Landa y Escandon, governor of the Federal District and mayor. He is one of the wealthiest men in the Republic, is the principal representative of the aristocratic Escandon family, and has a beautiful house on the outskirts of the city. He speaks English fluently, having been educated in England. Another popular host is Señor Limantour, the Minister of Finance, who is of French descent, and a man of great culture.

An important element in the social life of the city is the diplomatic corps, which is quite large, there being some twenty-seven duly accredited representatives of foreign powers, including even those of Russia and Japan. A great deal of entertaining is done by the diplomats, and especially by the Spanish, German and Russian ministers. The British government is represented, at the present time, by Mr. Reginald T. Tower, whose handsome residence in the Avenida de Paris is one of the finest in the city. Mr. Tower was appointed in 1905, and soon after his arrival in Mexico it was his pleasing duty to present to President Diaz the Grand Cross of the Bath, which had been conferred on the President by his Majesty, King Edward. Among British residents in Mexico Mr. Tower is deservedly popular, and he has done much to assist British commercial interests in all parts of the Republic. The United States has been represented for several years by Mr. David E. Thompson, who ranks first among members of the diplomatic corps, and he alone is an ambassador, the other foreign representatives being simply envoys extraordinary and ministers plenipotentiary.

Among the higher classes art and literature are keenly appreciated, and several painters and authors of Mexican origin are famous outside their own country. Mexico has produced many writers, some of considerable eminence. Perhaps the most interesting of these were the native Indians, Ixtlilxochitli, Tezozomoc and Nitzahualcoyotl, who lived at the time of the Conquest and chronicled the glories of their ancestors in Spanish prose and poetry. Verse has always played an important part in Mexican literature. The chief modern poets are Justo Sierra, Manuel Flores, Juan de Dios Pesa (known as the Mexican Longfellow) and Jose Peon y Contras. Among the novelists are Señor Irenio Paz, editor and novelist, whose stories are valuable for the pen pictures of Mexican life which they present, and Vincent Riva Palacio, whose works are noted for the elegance and purity of their style. Señor Mariscal, Minister of Foreign Affairs, is also a well-known writer, and has translated into Spanish the works of several well-known American writers. Some Mexican plays and books of verse have been widely read in Spanish-speaking countries, but as yet there have been no translations into English. The Mexican government does much to foster literary talent, and a deserving writer is certain of official patronage. Assistance is also given to art students, over two hundred prominent young artists and sculptors having been pensioned and sent abroad to pursue their studies. Among the artists of national repute are Señores Leandro Izaguirre, Ramos Martinez and Alberto Fuster, who studied in Rome and Florence and have produced some notable works. Señor Juan Telles Toledo is the foremost Mexican portrait painter.

While on the subject of literature, a few words about Spanish as spoken in Mexico may be of interest. Most of the Spaniards who colonized the country came from Andalusia, and the Spanish commonly spoken to-day in Mexico is not exactly classical or Castilian. For example, the true Spaniard pronounces the word "cielo" (heaven) as *theaylo*, whereas the Mexican gives the *c* its English value, and never the sound as is given in this and other words in Spain. The Mexicans have another peculiarity of speech. When asking a question, they invariably end the sentence with "no." For instance, a man will ask, "Are you coming out, no?" A shopkeeper says, "Will you buy something to-day, no?" This strikes on the American ear as very strange. Many Spanish words, too, have been altered. Thus, manteca, meaning "butter" in Spain, has been changed in Mexico into mantequilla. A large number of Indian words have also been incorporated in the language, such as sarape, a blanket, for which in Spain the word "manta" is used.

People of wealth in the capital are taking a keen interest in motoring, and large numbers of cars, mostly American makes, are seen in the streets. It is due to the influence of these motor enthusiasts that the suburban roads have of late been greatly improved. While I was in the city, a new motor road was completed to San Angel, a picturesque and beautiful suburb a mile or two out, where many wealthy citizens have their houses standing among gardens of flowers and palms. The inauguration was marked by a military procession, the firing of cannon, a display of fireworks; school children sang hymns and scattered flowers, and the governor of the Federal District, an enthusiastic motorist, made a stirring speech. In San Angel is a popular motoring resort — a beautiful old Spanish mansion — which has been transformed into a luxurious hotel, furnished in a style appropriate to its ancient character and with all its quaintness preserved. On the day of the celebration, I lunched with some motoring friends in the spacious patio, filled with tropical flowers and shrubbery, where a fountain tinkled merrily, and numerous singing birds soothed us into a feeling of mañana.

Another motor road has been laid and opened to Toluca, a curious old town with a population of twenty-five thousand and a reputation for brewing the best beer in Mexico. The principal church there was built in 1585, and is remarkable as containing the first church organ made in the New

World. The trip to Toluca is full of interest, the road commanding views of some fine mountain scenery.

Mexicans of all classes, especially in the country districts, are born horsemen, and are much interested in horse-racing. The races in the capital, however, are very different from those held in the United States. Ladies rarely attend them, and as they are not of a really public character, the crowds of spectators, the bookmakers and other followers of the turf seen at American races are never in evidence. There is a good track near Mexico City owned by the Jockey Club, but owing to the high altitude, which affects the breathing of animals as well as human beings, it is only about half the length of an American track, the horses being unable to cover a greater distance. As a rule, the horses are small and wiry, but wonderfully fast and enduring.

Motoring and horse-racing do something towards relieving the dulness of life in the capital; but dull as it is, the life of the upper classes seems positively gay in comparison with the humdrum existence of people lower down in the social scale. From an American point of view, the social life of the Mexican middle classes certainly seems unbearably monotonous, those recreations upon which the mass of the people in New York, for instance, so largely depend, such as out-door sports, exhibitions and music halls, being altogether unknown, while the cheaper theatres are patronized chiefly by men.

There are, strange to say, no music-halls, in the strict sense, in Mexico City. Latterly, however, there has been an outburst of cinematograph shows which advertise their attractions by electric signs and seem to do a roaring business. About five moving-picture exhibitions are given every hour, each of these being called a *tanda*. At the conclusion of a tanda a collector passes through the hall and

TYPICAL MEXICAN WOMEN OF THE UPPER CLASS.

PUBLIC SCHOOL CHILDREN.
Youthful Mexican Indians whom the government is educating.
(See page 148.)

demands payment for the next. This system is also followed in most Mexican theatres, although it applies more particularly to the cheaper and smaller houses. In these places, people simply pay for an act, and then again for the next if they wish to remain. In all the theatres, between the acts, the men, with their hats on, stand up and survey the audience; and more curiously still, even the fashionable women rise from their seats and glance round the house through their lorgnettes.

The three chief theatres in the capital are the Teatro Principale, chiefly reserved for melodrama and vaudeville performances; the Renacimiento, which holds an audience of two thousand, where are presented Italian and French opera as well as the masterpieces of Mexican and Spanish dramatists; and lastly the Arbeu, reserved for concerts and dramatic performances. The Salon de Conciertos is a concert hall with a fine auditorium, while the Circo Teatro Orrin is a kind of hippodrome. When gala performances are given, the Circo is splendidly adorned with flowers and flags, bouquets and button-holes being presented to the audience. President Diaz has a box, and on state occasions is always present.

Mexicans are very fond of music, and in nearly every house of the wealthy classes you find a good piano, sometimes of excellent make. Many ladies play well and sympathetically, but they do not often sing. The regimental bands are really excellent, and every town has its plaza centred with a bandstand, where music is heard every night. In the interior of Mexico guitars, mandolins and violins are very common, as also crudely formed harps of an ancient pattern. The Indian music is usually of a very melancholy description, which is increased by the fact that the natives chant or rather howl their choruses in a style far from musical. There are, however, several pretty and stirring songs by native composers; while the Mexican national anthem is truly inspiring, and such songs as "La Golondrina" (The Swallow), the Mexican "Home Sweet Home," are irresistibly sweet.

Until recently, it was the custom, even in large cities, for people of the upper class to promenade in the inner circle of the Plaza from half-past seven to half-past eight in the evening, while the band was playing, the ladies walking two or three abreast, strolling round and round in one direction, while the men walked in the other. As they passed, greetings would be exchanged, such as, "Adios, señor" and "Adios, señorita" (adios being a greeting as well as a farewell). Young men and women thus had a chance to see each other and start flirtations. The peons, the blanketed masses, also promenaded in the Plaza; but they always kept to the outer circle, the line between the two classes being distinctly kept. If a peon had dared to trespass in the inner circle, he would have been ejected by the police. Americans and other foreigners walked, of course, on the inner path.

Owing to the enormous influx of foreigners, many of them objectionable characters who haunted the plazas at night, parents and husbands found it undesirable to promenade in this public fashion, and it has been almost discontinued in most of the cities. When the band plays nowadays in the larger towns, people of the wealthy classes ride round the Plaza in their carriages, while the middle-class women stay at home.

In the matter of politeness and ceremonial, all classes of Mexicans are thoroughly Spanish. Imitation of Spain is also noticeable in the habit of procrastination; for Mexico is essentially the land of mañana—to-morrow. Time is idled away, and no man can be depended upon to turn up at an appointed hour, punctuality being regarded as the vice of a bore. Social calls often last hours, and the longer you stretch them out the more polite you are deemed. The foreigners who get on in Mexico are those who have patience with these native customs. Hustling Americans are pre-doomed to failure.

Mexicans of the upper class have a pretty way of telling you that their house is yours — "Su casa es numero," meaning literally, "Your house is number —," giving their address. Of course this is a mere manner of speaking, and must not be regarded as a serious invitation.

A story is told of a "wild Western" American who, visiting the capital, was casually introduced in the street to a Mexican señor who extended to him the formal invitation. Later in the day, when the Mexican returned to his home, he was amazed to find the American seated in his drawing-room in his best chair, his feet perched on another, his portmanteau at his side, puffing a big cigar, and at being greeted with a boisterous, "Wal, Colonel, I've come." History does not relate what the Mexican said or did.

Men of all classes in Mexico lift their hats on meeting, and the laconic American how-d'ye-do is not at all to the taste of the Mexican, who will stop to inquire of his friend as to the health of his wife, children and household, name by name. The poorest Indian is just as polite. I was once fishing in a lake with a poor peon, who rowed my boat and baited my hook. We happened to go ashore and walked along the beach, where we met a tattered, bare-legged Indian hauling in a net, assisted by his wife. Taking off his battered old hat, my boatman said, "Buenas noches, señor" (Good evening, sir). The other Indian solemnly returned his greeting, and then with a sweep of his hat to the woman, he said, "A los pies de usted, señora" (At your feet, lady). The whole act was marked by a grace and ease of manner which would have done honor to a cavalier.

The wrinkled Indian dame, despite her tattered garments, was equal to the emergency, and with the gracious manner of a grande dame replied, "Sus palabras, señor, son agradables" (Your words, sir, are sweet to the ear). It all meant nothing, but it was very wonderful. I asked my Indian companion his name, and with a bow he gave it to me, adding, "Su servidor" (Your servant). Even the lowliest peasant will not fail to say "Con permiso" (With your permission), if he must pass another person, even as lowly.

All Mexicans are the slaves of habit. If anything is not customary, it cannot be right or worth considering. Thus, if a servant were asked to scrub the floor when her usual duty was to cook, she would politely refuse, with the phrase, "No es costumbre" (It is not the custom). Foreigners in Mexico are constantly coming in conflict with their peon servants on this point, and it is quite difficult for the European or American to realize that these humble servants would far rather lose their situations than do anything, however trivial, contrary to their established custom.

It is natural enough that the matter-of-fact, prosaic way of the Anglo-Saxon should jar most unpleasantly on such people. Americans of the crude, "wild Western" type are the people who horrify the Mexicans most. They slap the ceremonious natives on the back after a slight acquaintance and interlard their conversation with strings of oaths. Mexicans look upon men of this kind as we should regard the average New York "tough."

A Canadian business man told me an amusing story illustrating this point. He was calling one day, he said, on the Jefe Politico in a Mexican town, the Jefe (pronounced *hayfay*) being an important government official. This particular Jefe appeared to be laboring under suppressed excitement and said, at last, "You must excuse me this morning, señor, if I am deprived of your delightful company sooner than I wish; but I am expecting a visit from un Americano muy distinguido (a very distinguished American)." The slovenly sentry, marching up and down before the official residence, seemed to think that something important was going to happen; for he straightened himself up, and kept looking down the street as if to catch a glimpse of the distinguished visitor. The Canadian deliberately prolonged his visit, being curious to have a look at this wonderful person, who, he concluded, must be a Pierpont Morgan at least. Suddenly the door was darkened, and a grizzled Western American, with his hat on his head, looked in and drawled out, "Say, which of you fellows is the 'Jeffy'?"

If you express admiration for any article in a house, the polite Mexican will take it up and say, "It is at your disposal, señor," and insist on your accepting it. You are, of course, supposed to refuse, firmly and politely, saying, "No, no, señor, many thanks, but it could not possibly be in better hands." I was told of a Western mining man, however, who took a mean advantage of this venerable custom.

He had done some business with a wealthy Mexican in one of the large towns, and had spent quite a lot of money in entertaining him, giving him dinners, taking him on automobile drives, and giving him a trip in a private railway car. The Mexican, who was extremely parsimonious, did not return any of these little attentions. On the day he was leaving, the American called at the Mexican's house, and there saw a fine collection of golden Aztec relics which had been dug up in that part of the country. He expressed unbounded admiration for them. The Mexican immediately summoned his man-servant and said, "Juan, the American señor has honored me by admiring these things.

Pack them up and send them to his hotel at once." "No, no, señor," exclaimed the Westerner, sweeping the curios into a bag that he carried, "don't put yourself to all that trouble. I'll take 'em along with me right now." Forthwith he said good-by and departed with the whole collection, leaving its late owner wild with rage. A friend of the Westerner, on hearing the story, said, "But didn't you know that you were not supposed to accept those things but politely refuse them?" "Of course I knew," answered the other, "but I wanted to get even, so I simply called his bluff."

With the march of progress the cost of living in Mexico is gradually becoming much higher. Ten years ago a man with a small salary could get a house in the capital, with four rooms and a kitchen, for $12.50 a month; but to-day the rental of such a house ranges from $25 to $75. Nowadays, two small rooms and a kitchen will cost at least $12 a month, while from $60 to $100 must be paid for a small flat or house of the better class. In like manner the price of many foodstuffs has greatly increased. It is true that fruit, vegetables, eggs and milk are, as a rule, about the same price as in New York; but meat is dear,— at any rate, good meat,— and all imported articles are abnormally costly. This, as already observed, is due to the suicidally high protective tariff.

The poor of Mexico City herd together in foul tenements in the slum districts, these dwellings, called viviendas, being usually of one story and built round a central patio. Two, three and even four families are often crowded together in a single room, the cheapest of these — inhabited mostly by working people of the poorest class — costing about a dollar and a half a month. These horrible places, reeking with filth and infested with vermin, look more like pig-pens than the dwelling-places of human beings. With such conditions it is not surprising to find typhus and other diseases extremely prevalent in the capital.

In some of the viviendas women and children sleep on old sacking on narrow boards, which have served for tables during the day, supported by piles of stones. The men sleep under their blankets, which they use as cloaks in the daytime. It is quite common for animals, dogs, cats, chickens and sometimes even a pig or a donkey, to sleep among the tenants of these dreadful abodes. In the centre of the patio is a water-tank, generally filthy, from which water for drinking and cooking is taken. No one living under these conditions could escape typhoid.

The government is doing everything in its power to improve matters, but the work is necessarily slow, as the bulk of the poorer population of the capital are Indians, who greatly resent any sanitary reforms. Some time ago, when there was a serious outbreak of typhus, President Diaz ordered that every peon in the city must take a bath at least once a week. As the Indian masses regard water with aversion and soap with horror, this cruel decree almost led to riots. Police officers were compelled to go from house to house and literally drag the protesting peons to the public wash-houses, their victims the while struggling, kicking and shouting furiously, "No jabon! no jabon!" (No soap! no soap!)

A better class of poor people occupy separate houses, or rather huts, on the city's outskirts. These are usually nothing more than wretched hovels of adobe such as are found in the country districts, and contain hardly any furniture. They are generally surrounded with a broken-down stone wall and a hedge of tall, straight cactus. The tenants spend most of their time outside their doors, and the women can be seen making tortillas and doing the family cooking on a crude stove at the threshold.

The fact that Mexico is a land of startling contrasts can nowhere be seen more perfectly than in the capital, where almost in a street's length there are the strangest transitions from civilization to barbarism. I stood in San Francisco Street one evening, among the brilliantly lighted shops, watching the procession of carriages with their fashionable occupants going by, noticing, on every side, the signs of modern luxury and progress. From this lively scene a walk of less than a mile in the direction of Guadalupe took me to a quiet road lined with adobe huts, with all the characteristics of Indian life, much the same as it was when Cortés landed. Unkempt Indian women were patting tortillas behind the cactus hedge, and half-naked children frolicked among the goats and pigs. Along the road came a train of burros laden with wood, fruit and vegetables for the market, driven by ragged Indians in their red blankets. There was nothing to remind me that I was so near a great modern city until suddenly a big automobile came whizzing along the road, its horn tooting gayly, and I was recalled to the present age.

From Indian huts to city restaurants is a sudden transition, but being typical of life in Mexico, it may serve as an excuse for the devoting of a few words at this point to the all-important subject of eating and drinking. This is a subject, in fact, in which the average man in the Mexican capital is keenly interested, for while there are a legion of restaurants there, very few of them are really good, either in regard to cooking or service. The best are a combination of French, Spanish and Italian establishments, and the charges are not exorbitant. Most of them are housed in dingy buildings, and have no external attractions for the diner. In this respect nothing could be more marked than the difference between Mexican cities and those of other countries, for, with the sole exception of the Chapultepec

Café, there are none of those very ornate establishments which so largely add to the charm of dining out in most lands. The average Mexican restaurant is, in fact, very inferior. A foreign visitor gives first one and then another a trial, returning to the first in despair, after he had sworn never to darken its doors again. Many men of moderate means whom I met appeared to be like de Soto in his vain search for treasure, forever seeking, but never finding, a decent meal.

Of the few restaurants where the cooking can be relied upon, the best are the Café de Paris, the Café de la Paix, Sylvain's and the Café Chapultepec. In all these the cooks are French, and one can order a dish with a quiet mind and the certainty that it will be eatable. The menu cards are usually Spanish, though some restaurant proprietors, as I have said, attempt English translations. In most of the large establishments, too, the head waiters usually speak English.

If a stranger is content to embark on a course of Mexican food and can stomach the highly seasoned dishes, filled with chilis and red peppers, he can get satisfactory meals at the Mexican restaurants, for some of the things which are served are piquant and excellent. But he must beware, for the dishes have a nomenclature all their own, and one can blunder badly. Therefore, unless the head waiter can explain the composition of the various strange dishes, the uninitiated guest is in danger of being served with some very unappetizing messes, reeking with grease and filled with red peppers, chilis and other fiery condiments.

Of the foods most popular among Mexicans mention must be made of chili-con-carne (chilis with minced meat), which is very palatable, although hot. Tamales, another favorite dish, are made of chopped meat, highly seasoned with pepper and chilis, wrapped in a corn husk and boiled quickly. Sometimes a tortilla is used as a wrapping, and the tamale is cooked in boiling fat. Enchiladas are something like tamales, but are seasoned with Mexican cheese and onions and soaked in chili sauce. The native bread, tortilla, has already been described. Frijoles (par excellence the Mexican national dish), a vegetable equivalent to the roast beef of old England, are black beans boiled, then fried in lard and served reeking with grease. As such cooking is quite unsuited for a hot climate, it is not surprising to find that diseases of the stomach and liver are almost universal among Mexicans. At the cost of a few cents, enough frijoles can be bought to feed a family for a day. Few householders furnish their servants with any other food than tortillas and frijoles.

Eggs (huevos) in various forms are served at every meal, a plain omelette being called a tortilla natural or tortilla de huevos. Cocidas are a concoction of potatoes chopped in small pieces, beetroot, carrots, small pieces of meat, maize and cauliflower, all boiled together. A salad of cold sliced tongue, chopped olives, celery and lettuce, with mayonnaise dressing, is very popular. Stewed or roast chicken served with rice, highly seasoned, called arroz con pollo, figures on every bill of fare.

Roast beef is served in every style, always with some highly seasoned sauce, and is sometimes actually smothered with raisins. The meats, as a rule, are fresh, but generally stringy and tough, due to the fact that the grazing is poor, and that meat, on account of the heat, must be eaten very fresh. The same quality is noticeable in the poultry, which is always tough, as it is never allowed to hang long enough. In cutting up meat the butchers never disjoint the carcasses, but cut the flesh off in strips.

Fresh vegetables are not obtainable in Mexican hotels and restaurants as largely as they ought to be, and during the winter season American and French canned vegetables are chiefly used. There is no excuse for this, as vegetables of all kinds can be grown the year round in most parts of Mexico. On the other hand, fresh fruits are plentiful, such as apples and peaches from the temperate zone, and pineapples, oranges and bananas from the hot country. One of the most interesting fruits is the aguacate, which resembles an enormous green pear, the inside of which is like butter, is almost tasteless, and is frequently used as a natural salad dressing.

Bread and rolls are invariably good. The native butter is usually uncolored and unsalted and has very little flavor, but is only served in the best establishments, American butter or oleomargarine being more extensively used. Milk, as a rule, is rather poor and watery, but an excellent cream cheese is made in some parts of the country.

There are very few native drinks which are palatable to foreigners. The ill-tasting pulque is not drunk by the better-class Mexicans or served in the restaurants. French, Italian and Spanish wines and German beers can be had at most of the better-class establishments, and here and there the order "Cerveza de Milwaukee" will be understood. Some very fair light lager beer, brewed by German firms at Monterey and Toluca, is a very popular drink. There are also several native mineral waters, of which the best known is Topo Chico, derived from a spring of the same name near Monterey. The indolence of the Mexicans is solely to blame for their having no native wines, for excellent grapes will grow well all over the country. This is another instance of the Mexican being governed by habit. Wine-making was prohibited by the Spaniards in the interests of the wines imported from the mother country, and as the Mexican has not made wine for four hundred years, he cannot see why he should begin now.

Of course, all Mexicans love coffee, but as a rule the coffee grown and served in Mexico is very strong, with a drug-like bitterness, partly due to the bean being too much roasted.

Service in Mexican restaurants is almost as unsatisfactory as the food. The waiters, mostly swarthy Indians, dressed in the conventional waiting dress, frequently present an amusing resemblance to opera-bouffe brigands, and seem quite out of their element. Very few of them know any English, and unless a person speaks Spanish very well, they do not understand him. From my experiences, I became convinced that most of the Mexican waiters were recruited from institutions for the feeble-minded. If, for instance, I ordered a steak or any other dish which took a little time to cook, and wanted soup to precede it, the waiter, instead of serving the soup just before the steak, would rush off and bring the soup immediately. Twenty minutes later, when my appetite was all destroyed by the soup, he would appear with the rest of the meal. I tried in vain to induce the waiters to do otherwise, or even to serve the two courses together; but they merely shrugged their shoulders and murmured, "No, señor, no es costumbre" (No, sir, it is not the custom).

If you are in a hurry to catch a train, and implore the waiter to be quick, he puts his thumb and forefinger gingerly together and says, "Un momento, señor," as if a moment were a fragile piece of spun-glass and he was afraid of breaking it. Then the swarthy villain strolls off and disappears for nearly an hour. That *is* costumbre.

But vengeance sometimes follows fast on the laggard footsteps of the Mexican waiter and turns his little comedy into an unexpected tragedy. Even while I was in the capital, the always reliable *Mexican Herald* published the following item in its news columns: —

"In the Maison de la Providencia, at Toluca, yesterday, a hungry guest shot Margarito Lopez, a waiter of the establishment, through the hand, because the waiter did not answer his call promptly."

This little gem of journalism is a fitting introduction to the subject of newspaper enterprise in Mexico, which is much older than the stranger visiting the country would at first sight believe. The first newspaper indeed was printed as long ago as 1693, and was known as *El Mercurio Volante* or *Flying Mercury*. Thenceforward other newspapers were founded, but they were always entirely under the thumb of the government, and the numbers of their readers was so small that they had no power in shaping policies for years after Mexican independence had been declared. To-day there are many newspapers and periodicals of all kinds published in Mexico City. There is, however, no Mexican yellow press, as a Mexican journalist would never dream of trespassing upon the privacy of a family to get copy.

When General Diaz became President thirty years ago, such newspapers as flourished then were fairly uncontrolled in their political criticisms. They appealed to the people much as do the French radical newspapers, and many revolutions were due to their turbulent editorials. President Diaz found these journals a considerable obstacle to the establishment of law and order. By his direction, some of the most mischief-making of the editors were arrested and lodged in Belem Prison, a jail reserved for the lowest type of criminals. After a week of solitary confinement and a diet of bread and water, they were brought before the President. "Now, gentlemen," said he, "what do you think of my government?" "Señor Presidente," they replied, "we think it is the finest government on the face of the earth." "Just continue to think so, gentlemen," said the President, "and we shall get along splendidly." As the editors wisely kept on "thinking so," there was no further trouble.

To-day the libel laws are very severe, and the government is keen in suppressing political criticism in the press. The editors, also having a wholesome fear of Belem Prison, restrict their comments to the most respectful choruses of approval. Most of them are subsidized by the government, too, so that President Diaz and his cabinet have little fear that the obsequious gentlemen of the pen will lessen their own incomes by rash words.

The modern Mexican newspapers have a necessarily small circulation, for the amount of illiteracy in the country is appalling. Of the fourteen millions of population, over sixty per cent are still unable to read or write. Chief among the daily papers is *El Imparcial*, which might be called the *Times* of Mexico, but although it is the official organ of the government, its circulation does not exceed a hundred thousand, including the whole of the Republic. It is a fairly good paper, considering the monopoly it has long possessed, its editor being an influential member of Congress. An afternoon edition of *El Imparcial* is published, called *El Heraldo*. Both papers, though printed in Spanish, are in the matter of head-lines and illustrations much Americanized and quite up-to-date. But strangely enough, though copying the methods of the press of the United States, *El Imparcial* is anti-American in tone and vehemently maintains the patriotic doctrine of "Mexico for the Mexicans."

Next to *El Imparcial* in circulation is *El Diario*, a bright Spanish daily recently started by Messrs. Simondetti and Fornaro, able Italian journalists with American training. *El Diario* might be called the *New York Journal* of Mexico, having some tendency to the sensational. It evidently

THE LIFE OF THE PEOPLE 145

pleases the Mexicans, for it already has a large and rapidly increasing circulation. This paper has big head-lines, often in red ink, and its illustrations and cartoons bear some resemblance to those of Mr. Hearst's newspaper.

While I was in Mexico City, *El Diario* was waging war against the local tramway company whose cars were constantly running over unfortunate peons and killing or maiming them. Every morning its front page contained a list of the victims, and articles bitterly denouncing the tramway management. These were accompanied with sensational cartoons with lots of red ink in them, bearing such cheerful titles as "A Vintage of Blood," "A Carnival of Gore."

Other papers published in the capital are *El Pais*, a Catholic journal, *El Popular, La Patria*, and *Los Sucesos* (Events). *La Patria* is a very old Liberal Party paper. *El Tiempo* is the leading Catholic or conservative publication, and circulates all over the Republic. There are also a number of weekly and monthly periodicals issued in Mexico, including magazines, literary reviews and various trade and financial journals.

Two daily papers in English are published in the capital, the *Mexican Herald* and the *Evening Post*, both owned and edited by Americans. They are read by the English-speaking population all over Mexico and by an ever increasing number of Mexicans who understand English. The *Herald* is edited by Mr. Frederick Guernsey, formerly of Boston, a very able journalist, who has lived in Mexico nearly thirty years.

In Guadalajara, Guanajuato, Oaxaca and some other cities with a large English-speaking population, Americans have started weekly newspapers in English. In Monterey there is quite an important American daily. Outside of the capital, however, most of the Spanish-printed newspapers are very insignificant one-sheet affairs. The best paper published in Vera Cruz, for instance, would not bear comparison with some of our American country weeklies.

In the smaller towns the Mexican editors all show a great lack of enterprise, rarely publishing any bright local news, and not hesitating to print intelligence that is at least a week old. An amusing reason for this was given to a friend of mine by the editor of a Mexican weekly. "Good news," he said, "is like good wine; it improves with age. It is always better to hold news over for a week. If it is true, we shall get more facts; and if it proves to be false, why should we print it?"

The Mexican press is much hampered by a high protective duty on paper. Some members of the government are interested in a paper mill, which probably accounts for a policy which forces publishers to use Mexican paper.

Several of the more important American newspapers have correspondents in Mexico City, and one or two English newspapers are represented. The Associated Press of the United States also has an office and a daily telegraphic service.

The growth of the press in Mexico has been greatly assisted by the wonderful railway development which has taken place during the past twenty years. In the old days the circulation of newspapers was almost entirely local, but to-day *El Imparcial*, *El Diario*, the *Mexican Herald* and other city papers, thanks to quick delivery, are read in all parts of the country. Even twenty years ago, Mexicans did a great deal of their travelling in slow, lumbering old stage-coaches, while to-day there are over thirty railways in Mexico, with a total mileage of fourteen thousand.

Most of the Mexican lines have been built with the assistance of government subsidies averaging from ten to fifteen thousand dollars per mile, provisional on the railway becoming the property of the state, at a fair valuation,

THE LIFE OF THE PEOPLE 147

after ninety-nine years. Of the railways now in operation the two most important are the Mexican Central and the Mexican National, which run through the centre of Mexico from the United States boundary and have many branches. Each year new lines are laid down, and the railway communication between ports on the Gulf and Pacific coasts is being constantly increased. The policy of the government being to obtain a controlling interest in all railway undertakings, they have lately purchased control of the Mexican National, and are now to obtain a predominating voice in the Mexican Central, which will be an important step towards the scheme of nationalization of railways at which Mexican statesmen are aiming. It is noteworthy that the lines to which the Mexican authorities are devoting their attention are those which are American-owned, while the two English lines, the Mexican Railway and the Mexican Southern, have so far escaped official attention. No doubt the Mexican government fears that the great trunk railways of the United States would in time absorb the Mexican lines, and by extortionate rates and other trust evils seriously impede Mexican progress.

Heretofore the personnel of the National and Central railways have been almost entirely Americans; but the Mexican government is dismissing the foreigners wherever possible and putting Mexicans in their places. A somewhat tyrannical decree which was recently issued, that every American employee must acquire a working knowledge of Spanish in six months or lose his place, shows pretty clearly what the Mexican policy is. This decree applies to all railway employees except the managers and clerks.

Except in the capital, Mexican railway stations are usually built some distance from the towns, so that cabs or street-cars have to be used to reach homes or hotels. This was done to avoid the purchase of expensive rights of way. The Mexican Central and Mexican National railways run fine vestibule trains between Mexico and the United States, with connections which enable one to make the journey from the Mexican capital to New York in less than five days.

Railway enterprise is doing much to change Mexico. The centres of population have always been on the great plateaus of the interior, the coasts being very sparsely inhabited. Until recent years, communication with the ports, except Vera Cruz and Tampico, was by rough mountain trails. Transportation of goods was slow and expensive and necessitated pack-mules, donkeys and armies of cargadores. Since railway development began, even mining has become of secondary importance compared with the great increase in commerce and manufacture and the impetus which agriculture has received.

Another important fact is that the railway extensions have greatly diminished the chances of successful revolution. In the old days it took so long to travel from the capital to any of the big provincial centres that revolutions might be brought to a successful issue before any considerable body of government troops could arrive. All this is changed now, as with the aid of railways, telegraphs and telephones troops can be concentrated at any place by special train at a few hours' notice. With such a strong government as Mexico at present possesses, there is consequently little chance of a revolution succeeding, even temporarily.

The awakening of Mexico, with the advancement of her press and the development of her railways, has been accompanied by wonderful progress in public education. Much has been done of late under the educational system inaugurated by President Diaz in 1876, and at the present time even the smallest town has its public schools. There are to-day in these schools over eight hundred thousand scholars, while upwards of one hundred thousand pupils are attending private schools, institutions supported by the clergy, or those of a private nature. Education is compulsory, though there are great difficulties in enforcing the law. In the primary schools, where boys and girls are separately educated, the three r's are taught, and in many cases instruction in the English language is given, so that in a few years Mexico will tend to become an English-speaking country. In passing a Mexican public school one hears a strange buzzing like bees, the custom being for the children to sing their lessons in chorus.

In Mexico City the national government maintains the following institutions: Academy of Fine Arts, School of Civil Engineering, School of Medicine, Law School, Academy of Commerce, Academy of Arts and Trades, Conservatory of Music, Military College, School of Mines, and schools for the deaf, dumb, and blind. There are seventy-two public libraries in the country, the National Library in the capital containing over two hundred and sixty-five thousand volumes.

In the army and the prisons there is also a system of compulsory education, strict attendance at the classes being enforced. The soldiers are for the most part Indians, and when they join the ranks are almost without exception illiterate. They are given instruction in reading, writing, arithmetic, natural science, history, drawing and singing. This applies equally to the jails, where, if a prisoner is earnest in his study, he can eventually win his freedom. The Indians, as a rule, are bright and quick to learn. Oppressed and enslaved for centuries, they had little chance to show what was in them; the twentieth century has now given them their opportunity. The supreme importance of education among the masses has been keenly recognized by President Diaz, who, in speaking of the Mexican school system, recently said: "I have started a free school for boys and girls in every community in the Republic. We regard education as the foundation of our prosperity and the basis of our very existence. We have learned from Japan, what indeed we knew before, but did not realize quite clearly, that education is the one thing needful to a people."

The spread of education among the masses of Mexico is destined to have an important effect in shaping the future of the Roman Catholic Church within the borders of the Republic, where it is still a power. A wonderful history is that of the church in Mexico, dating as it does from the Spanish Conquest, when missionary priests marched with the soldiers of Cortés and spread the teachings of Christianity among the conquered race. Once subdued, the Indians took kindly enough to the new religion, their cordial reception of it being strengthened by the shrewdness of the priests in blending the ritual of the new and old faiths. Aztec gods were cleverly metamorphosed into Christian saints, keeping many of their pagan characteristics. Thus the Goddess of the Rains is recognizable in our Lady of the Mists, to whom prayers for rain are often offered in true pagan fashion. Catholic churches were generally built on the sites of Aztec temples. Mexican Catholicism has indeed ever been marked by a strong tendency to idolatry, and Catholic clerics have noticed and denounced this straying from the forms of Holy Church. In some parts of Mexico pagan practices are still kept up, such as the dances in front of the church, while the offerings of fruit and even lambs and chickens at wayside shrines are also fairly common. The priests are unable to stop these survivals of paganism.

Less than a century back the church was all-powerful in Mexico, and its wealth was estimated at close on two hundred million dollars. It has even been estimated as high as five hundred millions. Gifts and bequests were made to it by rich and poor alike, and the best part of the farm lands in the country belonged to it. The church threw all its weight into the scale against progress, and it was the abuse of its power which brought about in 1864 its disestablishment. President Juarez was no man for half measures, and under his government's decree church lands were seized, monasteries and nunneries suppressed, the priests were forbidden to walk in the streets in clerical dress and all religious processions were voted illegal. Marriage was made a civil contract, and in addition to losing this source of its revenue much of the church plate and the interior adornments were looted and sold as old metal.

Even at the present time, though of course looting is out of fashion, church property is still threatened. Quite recently the Mexican government has notified the bishops throughout Mexico that all church property and fittings belong to the state, and that under no circumstances whatever have the priests the right to part with any article. The ostensible ground for this decree is said to have been the purchase of some ancient silver altar candelabra by an American millionaire. The Mexican authorities, hearing of this, prohibited the removal of the candlesticks. But the church sees in this latest move something far more serious than an attempt to restrain globe-trotters from filling their trunks with souvenirs of their travels. The church is probably right.

Still the hold of Catholicism on the bulk of the Mexicans is very firm, and during the past half century it may be said to have regained some of the power lost immediately after the disestablishment. The influence of the priests is almost unlimited, and there are many cases of their grossly violating the laws of the land. Women are the stoutest adherents of the priestly lawbreakers, the Mexican men seldom troubling themselves about church matters.

Though the ringing of church bells is regulated by law, they clang away discordantly all day long; the priests openly appear in distinctive cloaks; and the villagers will often raise money to pay a heavy fine rather than be deprived of their religious processions through the streets.

Slowly the church is once more acquiring much land. When a rich Mexican lies dying, he must restore any church property that he has become possessed of, or the priests will refuse him extreme unction. To defeat the law, the property is placed in the hands of a trustee. In the same way the law regarding marriage is disobeyed, the clergy teaching the people that the ceremony in the church is all that is needed. Thus the church has recaptured one of the most profitable of her sources of revenue, for the priests think nothing of charging the peons five dollars as a marriage fee, and the charge was recently as high as fifteen dollars, a sum entirely beyond the means of the ordinary Indian laborer. In consequence of these heavy charges, thousands of couples remained unmarried. While I was in the Sierras, a Jesuit priest came to a village and married, at greatly reduced rates, a large number of natives who had been living together for years unmarried, as they were too poor to pay the fees. Many of them had grown-up children.

Yet despite all this, one must not condemn Mexican Catholicism too bitterly; for there are many among the priests who are entitled to be called patriotic and progressive men, who struggle to abate existing evils and improve the condition of the masses. The saying in regard to the sins of the fathers is well exemplified in Mexico, where the priests, however well-meaning, do suffer and are likely to go on suffering for the gross sins and abuses of their predecessors.

Under Mexican law there is complete religious toleration, Baptists, Methodists, and other Protestant sects being permitted to carry on an active propaganda throughout the Republic. Still Protestantism makes but little headway, and there are said to be but twenty-five thousand of its followers throughout the country. In Mexico City the Methodists, Baptists and other sects have their own publishing houses and produce a good deal of literature in Spanish. Christian Science is also making some progress. There are in the capital several Protestant churches whose pastors conduct services in Spanish and English, and there are the usual Sunday-schools and mission meetings. The Salvation Army alone is barred by reason of its processions and distinctive dress. In bigoted parts of Mexico Protestant preaching has at times provoked fierce attacks, and native converts have been the victims of terrible and often fatal assaults.

President Diaz has always been keen on religious toleration. His views on this subject were clearly and eloquently expressed in an address to some Protestant missionaries a few years ago, when he said: "I have seen this land as none of you ever saw it, in degradation, with everything in the line of toleration and freedom to learn. I have watched its rise and progress to a better condition. We are not yet all we ought to be and hope to be, but we have risen as a people, and are now rising faster than ever. Do not be discouraged. Keep on with your work, avoiding topics of irritation and preaching the Gospel in its own spirit." Such an utterance from such a man proves that toleration has certainly dawned in Mexico. Official recognition has been freely given to Protestant missionary effort. Vice-President Corral is the honorary president of the Mexican branch of the Y. M. C. A., and President Diaz himself has attended its meetings. He and his cabinet have also been present at special memorial services in the Presbyterian churches. Less than a generation ago this would have been impossible, and such an action by a president would have invited assassination.

The extent of the power still wielded in Mexico by the ancient church is strikingly shown in the burial of the dead, the majority of funerals being conducted with Catholic rites. A number of curious burial customs also exist, some of which are due to racial and climatic reasons, while others have undoubtedly originated in churchly tradition.

In Mexico, as in all other tropical countries, a body must be buried within twenty-four hours after death. This necessarily entails much haste and worry on the part of the bereaved ones, at a time when they are least able to bear it. Haste being thus a prerequisite, coffins are invariably purchased ready-made, and in accordance with the general custom, corpses are dressed in their best clothes, a dress suit in the case of a gentleman, while a lady is arrayed in her finest evening gown. A few of the old families, however, still adhere to a more venerable Mexican custom of dressing the dead as nuns and friars.

In Mexico City, and some of the other large towns, the cemeteries being some distance out, hearses and mourning coaches are not used at funerals, but the coffins of rich and poor are conveyed in funeral street-cars as described in a preceding chapter. The mourners are always men, as ladies in Mexico do not follow funerals. A brief service is therefore read at the house of the bereaved family, a few concluding rites being observed at the cemetery. Instead of being screwed down, the coffin is provided with a lock, and before being lowered into the grave the lid is lifted, so that an official of the cemetery, who is present, can be convinced that the coffin contains a corpse and have it formally identified. The coffin is then locked, deposited in the grave and the key handed to the chief mourner.

In most parts of Mexico burial plots in the cemeteries

are usually leased for a term of years. At the expiration of the time, unless the lease is renewed, the bones are exhumed and thrown into a charnel house. The cemeteries are little visited except on All Saints' Day, when friends and relations flock to them with wreaths, crosses and bouquets of flowers to decorate the graves. Death feasts are also held in the cemetery on this day, tables being arranged near the graves and loaded with eatables which have some ghastly reference to mortality, such as cakes or sweets representing skulls and cross-bones, while a real skull and a bowl of holy water are set in the midst of these grewsome dainties.

Whenever a death occurs among the poor, a kind of Irish wake is held by the family and friends, in which there is much drinking of pulque and singing and dancing. The corpse is never left alone for a moment, for fear that evil spirits might tamper with it. Following the custom of their Aztec ancestors, the Indians still place corn, and sometimes other edibles, in the coffins in order that the dead may have food to sustain them on their long journey to the land of spirits. For poor funerals, coffins are frequently hired for the day, the body being simply conveyed in it to the cemetery, the coffin being afterwards returned to the undertaker.

An interesting religious custom is observed in Mexico in the months of January and February. It is known as the "blessing of the animals," and takes place in connection with the Feast of St. Anthony. On the appointed day, the people congregate in the churchyard, driving with them their household pets and other animals, all of which are decorated for the occasion. At one of these services, which I witnessed near the city, there were cows, burros, sheep and mules, painted and trimmed in various vivid hues. There were green sheep, pink goats and blue pigs, horses covered with scarlet and gold paper stars tied with bands and bows of flaming ribbons. Women brought their parrots and canaries in their cages, while turkeys, geese and old hens were carried in, all adorned with ribbons of gay colors. When the church bell sounded, a priest appeared in the porch, and the people made a rush for the door, driving or holding up their various beasts and birds to catch a drop of the holy water which was sprinkled.

Another remarkable religious celebration takes place on Easter Saturday, when papier-maché effigies of Judas Iscariot are hung along the streets, ranging from little figures to some which are almost life size. Each figure is filled with explosives and has a fuse attached to it. These are exploded in all directions until the noise is deafening. Some of the figures bear such mottos as, "I am the Devil's son," "Blow me to Inferno." Everybody considers it his duty to blow up a Judas.

CHAPTER VIII

THE MEXICAN WOMAN

A GOOD idea of the difference between the status of American and Mexican women could be obtained by comparing a photograph taken at midday in Fifth Avenue, New York, with one taken at the same hour in Calle San Francisco, Mexico City. In the New York view there would perhaps be more women than men, whereas in the Mexican scene, so far as the white element is concerned, there would be comparatively few. This is noticeable, in fact, wherever one goes in Mexico, for among all classes of Mexicans, except the Indians, women are kept more strictly secluded than even in Spain. There is, at present, no strictly defined Mexican middle class; but both the upper class and what would be equivalent to the minor business classes in this country are rather Moorish than European in their treatment of the fair sex.

Girls of the higher class, in taking their walks abroad, are still guarded by watchful duennas, and until recently women of high society rarely took a drive in an open carriage. To such an extent, in fact, was this exclusion carried in former days that some of the grande dames, when shopping, did not leave their carriages, but had the salesmen bring the goods to the door.

These severe restrictions as to women showing themselves in public brought about in Spain and Mexico the use of the windows and balconies so characteristic of the two countries. This is almost the only way in which the señoras and señoritas can, with due regard to propriety, take the air; and thus in the cool of the evening they can be seen sitting like prisoners, peering out through the iron-barred windows at the carriages and passers-by, and perhaps nodding to friends.

With its bolts and bars, real and figurative, the Mexican perhaps cannot claim that the word "home," in the American and English sense, has any real meaning for him; but his house is in very fact his castle, and he guards it from the inquisitive with the precautions of a tyrant. As in Spain, the Mexican father of the upper classes is an absolute lord and master, and to him all are subservient, even the grown-up children being expected to show obedience in matters in which an American father would never dream of interfering. Marriage without the consent of parents is, for instance, quite unknown.

But even with the strong discipline that prevails in the Mexican household, families are not always united; there are the usual quarrels, which in a climate where the blood is hot have led on occasions to serious brawls and duels in which lives have been lost. A disturbing element is perhaps the fact that among the upper classes it is common for a number of kinsfolk to occupy the huge old-fashioned family mansion. An uncle or two, an aunt, a few cousins and sometimes actually two mothers-in-law are added to the family circle and dwell together under the same roof. There is consequently bound to be more or less friction; and that so many families can live peacefully together under such trying conditions is certainly proof of much patience and good nature. Between husband and wife, for whom when they differ there is no divorce, there may exist for years a complete estrangement; but the world will know little of it, for they will go on living in the same house, although they may never exchange a word.

So hide-bound are the rules which govern Mexican home life that even the most cultured and charming foreigners, resident for years in the country, have never penetrated into the houses of the wealthier Mexicans. No foreigner, unless he be associated with diplomacy, is likely to have any chance of studying and judging the Mexican women, so complete is what amounts to a true harem system.

As a rule, the Mexican women are not beautiful. They are generally of medium height and slight build when young; though as they progress in years they tend to obesity. Their skin is of an olive tint and their complexions are usually bad, probably on account of the lack of exercise. They are much addicted to the use of powder, which is laid on very thickly, and their lips are often rouged. Mexican beauties may be divided into two classes: the slight, delicate girl with big, soft black eyes, and features somewhat suggestive of the Madonna type; and a stout, voluptuous young woman, — a sort of Spanish dancing-girl type, — with bold, flashing black eyes.

The free life lived by young American and English women is utterly unknown in Mexico. Girls are watched keenly by their mothers, who scarcely ever allow them out of their sight, save in the custody of some old woman-servant or other trusty retainer. Mexican women have no sympathy with the suffragette movement; they do not want votes, and take no interest whatever in public affairs. The whole question of women's rights is tabooed, and all innovations in the household are looked at askance.

The contrast between the lives of these dark beauties and those of their fairer Northern sisters is perhaps best realized from the fact that no Mexican girl of even the middle class would be permitted to have a young man call to see her or be her escort to the theatre. A Mexican mother would probably have a fit if such an idea were suggested to her. In her estimation, no man is safe until he is married, and even then he will bear close watching. Doubtless this lack of freedom is the reason for the Mexican señoritas gaining the name of coquettes; it is their way of rebelling. But while there is so much outward show of restraint and so much parade of the modest and retiring virgin about the Mexican girl's home life, there is another side to the picture which is apt to jar on the Anglo-Saxon woman. Even Mexican women of the highest classes will permit themselves to talk among their friends or with their servant-girls in a manner which would be regarded as shameful among Americans. If the latter show their astonishment, the Mexican woman, with a laugh, will accuse them of having false modesty.

Mexicans are passionate admirers of the fair sex, and susceptible young fellows who see an attractive girl with her duenna will often follow her, uttering such complimentary phrases as, "Ojos bellos" (Beautiful eyes) or "Bella creatura" ("Beautiful creature"), "Ah, hermosa rubia" ("Ah, lovely blonde"), "Charming brunette." Some of the girls titter and seem to like it. American girls, on the contrary, do not appreciate these Mexican compliments. A lagartijo or "masher," who followed one strong-minded Yankee girl, giving utterance to his expressions of admiration, was rewarded with some swinging blows on his head from the umbrella she carried. In Mexican love affairs, by the way, there is a peculiar slang used. Thus a girl or boy jilted is called a calabaza, meaning the dried, empty gourd; old maids are solteronas; young men are gallinos — young roosters.

A severe critic of Mexico has described it as a land where flowers have no perfume, men no honor and women no virtue. Americans and Englishmen who have lived there generally report that the whole race of Mexicans are grossly immoral. Doubtless there is a great deal of exaggeration in these strictures. Such judgments have been formed largely from appearances, and, where it is so difficult for a foreigner to come into close touch with the intimate life of a people, it is surely only right for him to hesitate before launching general indictments against them. There is no doubt much laxness in morals. The Mexican husband watches his wife as a cat does a mouse, yet very often she deceives him. All Mexican men are said to be unfaithful, and it is almost expected of any one who has the means, to keep two households at least. When an American friend of mine, who lives in Mexico, was recently making his will, his Mexican lawyer asked him if he had any children at home. "No," he replied, "I have none," whereupon the lawyer, with a quizzical look, asked, "Well, don't you have any other household?" putting the question as a matter of course. It is this very different point of view which makes mixed marriages in Mexico almost invariably failures. The American girl or her English cousin who mates with a Mexican generally lives to repent it. In the same way, the marriages of Englishmen or Americans with Mexican women are generally failures.

Under the system of seclusion of which she is the victim, the Mexican girl has but two things in life to occupy her, love and religion. The classical Spanish picture of the maiden at the barred window or leaning, Juliet-like, from a balcony, while her sweetheart thrums music to her on his mandolin or guitar, is reproduced every evening in Mexico. Courtship is a delightfully difficult pursuit. A young man will, by chance, meet a girl in the street or on the plaza. Her languishing black eyes will haunt him and, having followed her home, he must content himself for days and weeks with watching the house. He has reached the stage which is known as "Hacer el oso" (to play the bear), a phrase in comic allusion to his lovesick pacing up and down under the adored one's window as a bear walks backwards and forwards in his cage hour after hour. Now comes the girl's turn. Safe behind her curtain, or in the darkness of her balcony, she can make her coquettish little mind up whether he is quite the kind of bear she wants. If he is, she finds a dozen ways of encouraging him; a smile, a wave of the hand, a suspicion of the blowing of a kiss are enough to make the bear happy. When she goes to mass or walks in the plaza, the faithful bear follows her, and although they cannot exchange a word, they can find happiness in looks.

Sometimes a flirtation of this kind reaches the love-letter stage, servants or tradesmen who call at the house being bribed to deliver the billets-doux, or perhaps the missives are fished up by the amorous young lady with a string from the balcony. This is the moment when fate must decide whether or not the course of true love is to run smooth. If the parents disapprove, the unfortunate bear will soon know; for the girl will be shut up either at home or in a convent to save her from his attentions. If, however, the bear is an eligible party, the parents do not interfere in the rather puerile course the love affair takes. For, having so far advanced, etiquette permits the girl to talk to her bear from the balcony or through the grille of her window; and the moonlight nights are devoted to the pouring of sweet nothings into each other's ear. The patient bears are frequently content that this nonsense should last for years, and even then a bear may lose his prize.

Bears are very jealous creatures, at least these Mexican bears are, and they will disguise themselves as mozos or peons and watch their fair one's window to see if another bear is in the running. An English friend of mine who lives in an old Mexican town witnessed an amusing instance

"PLAYING THE BEAR."
A popular feature of Mexican courtship.

of this not long ago. A young Englishman who happened to be visiting him was very fond of listening to the music in the plaza and watching the people. One evening when he was out with my friend, he remarked, "I've found a ripping place to sit and smoke my pipe and listen to the band. I've been sitting in that old alcove window over there nearly every night. It's just off the plaza, and you can sit there and hear the music without getting in the crowd. Let's go over and sit down." They took a seat on the window ledge, and had been there only a few minutes when a red rose was thrown to them from an upper window. At the same moment they caught sight of a rather shabby-looking Mexican on the opposite side of the street, who looked up at the window, shook his fist and seemed to be in a great rage. He beckoned to another Mexican, who came up and spoke excitedly in Spanish. The Englishmen heard such words as "traidora" (traitress), "falsa" (false one), "corazon duro" (black heart). "Yes," said one of the Mexicans, "and there are actually two of them," pointing at the Britishers. My friend said: "Those fellows seem to object to our sitting here; we had better make a move." So they departed, wondering what connection there was between the red rose and the anger of the Mexicans.

The mystery was solved a few days later when my friend happened to call on an old lady in the neighborhood. He mentioned the red-rose incident, and his hostess became almost hysterical with laughter. "Pardon me, señor," she said, "but it is the best joke I ever heard. It explain a great mystery. My nephew, Don Carlos, is much in love with a young lady, Miss Concepcion, who live in that house and he play the bear. He is very jealous and think perhaps she have another bear, so he disguise himself as a mozo and keep watch with a friend. He see your friend sit by the window every night and believe he is playing bear too.

The señorita see her bear watching in disguise and just for mischief she throw the rose to your friend. Oh, Don Carlos is very angry; he write bitter letters and say he is very much deceived, and Miss Concepcion now repent very much of her joke. I tell him now and everything will be all right." The next evening a very tame, subdued bear might have been seen standing below Miss Concepcion's window, making a very humble apology in choicest Castilian.

But bear rivalries do not always end so innocently. There is very hot blood in the veins of the young Mexicans, and again and again reports will find their way into the papers of fierce conflicts between the suitors for the same girl. Thus, quite recently one of the Mexico City papers reported a fatal encounter at Chihuahua, where two young fellows, members of prominent families, embittered by rivalry, met at night and fought a duel with pistols, both being killed. At Monterey the coquettish desire of a girl to attract attention nearly cost the lives of two men. In the plaza, at night, she mischievously threw a flower from her bouquet towards a young man whose attention she wished to attract. Her lover, furious with jealousy, flew at his rival, and the two left the plaza to fight it out at the back of the town, and one if not both lives would have been lost if friends had not separated the angry young men.

Before a bear can propose marriage he must, of course, interview the girl's parents. After a conventional period, accompanied by a friendly sponsor, he must formally call on the father and propose marriage. If he is eligible, the girl's inclinations are consulted. She will probably say, coquette that she is, that she cannot answer till she has met him. This, too, after months, perhaps years, of evenings on the balcony. When the bear is at last permitted the entrée, every member of the family and even the servants have the right of witnessing his adoption as "son-in-law elect." Thereafter he is the "novis oficial" or accepted lover; but even then he never has the advantage of a tête-à-tête with his fiancée for some one is always playing gooseberry. And this very unamusing courtship also has the disadvantage of being extremely expensive. If, for example, the young fellow would take his sweetheart to the theatre or to a restaurant, he must entertain the whole family as well.

Everything, in fact, falls upon the unfortunate bear; for when the fatal time approaches, not only must he pay for the furniture of the new home, but he is even expected to give the bride her trousseau. Among the wealthier people, it is true, the girl's parents pay for some of the latter, the bridegroom having only to provide the dresses and jewels. There are, in Mexico, two wedding ceremonies, the civil and religious, the latter taking place at the church, while the former is a contract made before the judge of the local court in the presence of six witnesses. After marriage, the wife uses her husband's name as well as her own. Señorita Garcia, who marries Señor Fernandez, thus becomes Señora Garcia de Fernandez.

Religion means a great deal to the Mexican women. Most of them bear the sacred name of Mary, coupled with some incident in the life of the Virgin, such as "Conception," "Sorrows," "Assumption," "Gifts," "Miracles," "Tears," etc. In their own way they are devout enough, and are just as scrupulous in performing their religious duties as they are in the matters of toilet. They are very superstitious, a result of their ignorance, and still believe in signs, omens and other supernatural manifestations. As a rule, they are kind-hearted and charitable. Smoking is very general among them, and this is very often done in quite an open manner and in company with the male members of the family. Mexican women, on meeting one another, kiss each other on both cheeks, but unlike the Frenchmen, the Mexican men do not imitate their wives in their greetings to their friends; they simply embrace and pat each other on the back affectionately, the Mexican equivalent of "good old chap."

The Mexicans have a phrase, "muy simpatica," which literally means "very sympathetic," but really cannot be done justice to in English. It means that charming characteristic of personal attractiveness, the result of a sweet disposition, and this might be truly said to be a terse description of the better Mexican women. They are "muy simpatica," and this the lucky stranger will learn who experiences their kindly hospitality.

Indolence and a lack of domestic training are characteristic of even middle-class Mexican women and girls as well as of their wealthier sisters; but it is more marked in large houses. All the marketing is left to the cook. She has a sum given her each day, and manages to squeeze a commission out of each shopkeeper. No Mexican housewife would dream of getting more than a day's supply of food, — sometimes, indeed, only a meal's supply is kept, — because the servants would steal it, and also because there are no ice safes, and meat and other fresh eatables soon go bad. Such a system prohibits good housekeeping. Servants' wages are very poor. A cook will get about three Mexican dollars a week ($1.50). In a well-to-do household there is a door-keeper (portero), a coachman (cochero), a chambermaid (recamera), an ostler (caballerando), a man of all work (mozo), a cook (cocinera), a woman to grind maize (molendera) and a footman (lacayo). Servants are summoned in true Eastern style by clapping the hands, as in most houses there are no bells. In old-fashioned households the domestics call their mistress niña, literally "little girl." Except in fashionable houses, the servants are always

Indians. Their food costs but little, consisting, as it usually does, of tortillas and frijoles, and they rarely sleep in beds, preferring to spread a mat in the hall and roll themselves in a blanket.

The rigid seclusion of women is a good deal relaxed in the country towns, where girls are seen more in the streets. They have a queer custom of taking a walk apparently after washing the hair, with their long tresses combed out and flowing down their backs. This they do not seem to consider at all strange. Their relations with the store people are equally unconventional. Even well-to-do women will come in and affably shake hands with the shopmen, talk in a friendly way with them, and inquire after their families. But all this freedom stops at the door. In the street the very same women cut their grocer. To do otherwise would be wrong — " no es costumbre."

A great deal of the severity of the old régime is breaking down under the foreign invasion. Rich Mexicans send their girls to schools in France, in England or the United States, and they gain new ideas of woman's sphere. But the change must be necessarily slow, and to all intents and purposes the average Mexican girl is not educated. When she has learned her alphabet and can write a stilted letter in a fulsome Spanish style, can murder a few pieces on the piano, and mangle a few French phrases, use her needle indifferently, and discover that her country is bordered by two oceans, her education is finished. But her greatest deprivation is the fact that she has no share in the happy outdoor life of athletics which has done so much for the present generation of American women.

Still, all this is bound to change. The emancipation of Mexican women is only a question of time, and the day may yet dawn when the suffragette movement will be cordially taken up in the land of the Aztecs. Young women of the middle class are going into business, taking work in the stores and in offices, and moving about freely in the city without chaperones. All this is affecting the prejudiced old Mexican families, who will gradually abandon their Eastern system of seclusion.

Not long ago the *Mexican Herald* published a paragraph about openings for women in Mexico, which was copied by a number of American papers. The editor of the *Herald* subsequently received hundreds of letters from young American women offering to come to Mexico as typewriters, clerks, etc., and demanding absurdly high salaries. But what would most excite the fears of the Mexican maidens was that most of the American girls added a P.S. to their letters, asking what chance there was of their capturing Mexican millionaires on their arrival! It is unlikely that Mexican women will be content with their dreary lives of confinement when they see their country invaded by the ubiquitous Yankee business girl, taking her place in absolute equality by the side of their brothers. A trade invasion is one thing, a matrimonial invasion is quite another. The Mexican girls must look to their orange-blossoms.

One feature of modern progress which is certainly to be regretted is the tendency to abandon the picturesque Mexican dress, the Spanish mantilla type, and to replace it with Parisian gowns and hats. Very few of the bewitching señoritas are now to be seen veiling their charms with those exquisite lace wraps which one associates with sunny Spain. Modish costumes are now generally worn, and owing to the equable climate, there are no such things as winter dresses or furs, summer gowns being worn all the year round.

The Mexicans, like all tropical people, love color, and a strikingly tinted dress wins their admiration much more readily than the most costly of dull-colored silks. But the poorer girls cannot always indulge their taste, having to be content with a flower in the hair or in the dress, while they are usually clothed in a plain black skirt with a black cambric shawl over the shoulders, folded in front in old-fashioned style. This style of girl, whom one is always meeting in the streets, wears no hat. Many of them would be quite good-looking if they were only dressed properly. Ladies whom I interviewed on the subject told me that women's clothing is so expensive in Mexico that it is impossible for people of this class to buy anything better. Some of these meztiza girls, who have far more Indian than white blood in their veins, have rather an unpleasant look. They have dark olive skins, pronounced Indian features, and unnaturally black eyelashes, as if they had been dyed.

CHAPTER IX

THE FOREIGN INVASION

MEXICANS being naturally averse to all business enterprise or energetic action, have for years past left the development of their country to the strangers within their gates. Unless he is a man of wealth, the Mexican usually has one ambition, and that is to become a government employee. With this satisfied, he cares little about banking, trading or mining; at any rate, he does not care enough about them to put himself out and work hard. Thus it is that while the foreigners in Mexico form a comparatively small percentage of the population, yet their importance is not to be reckoned by mere numbers.

The English-speaking population of Mexico City is about six thousand, of which a very large proportion are Americans. What is true of the capital is also true of the country at large, and throughout Mexico there are more Americans than any other foreign nationality. Within the past decade they have been simply swarming in, and with them have come millions of dollars of American money, which Mexico is destined to find a serious factor some day. Formerly, Americans were engaged simply in mining and railway building, but to-day they are to be found in nearly every branch of commerce. In Mexico City one sees American banks, and agencies for all kinds of American goods, such as sewing-machines, typewriters and agricultural machinery; there are American grocers, druggists, booksellers and fancy goods stores, also tailors, hotels and restaurants. So large a number of Americans are collected in the capital that there is an extensive American quarter, where there are modern houses and flats, an American club and several American churches.

During the winter season several of our railway companies advertise Mexico extensively as a winter paradise. They give away tens of thousands of beautifully illustrated booklets describing the wonders of the land. They run cheap excursion trains to Mexico and bring down thousands of sight-seeing tourists, most of whom come from the Western states. The newspapers in Mexico City publish, every day, lists of people stopping at the various hotels. I noticed that the American visitors usually came from such places as Kalamazoo, Mich., Tombstone, Arizona, Cross Roads, Iowa, or Jaytown City, Neb. To most of these people Mexico must certainly seem a land of wonders; they have never been in Europe, and for the first time in their lives they see old churches, cathedrals and ruins, and mingle among people who have a different language and strange customs.

When I first went to Mexico, an old American resident told me that I should find it a triste or melancholy country, and I really believe I should have found it so had it not been for certain of my fellow-citizens that I met. The Mexicans, both the Indians and the whites, are far from lively people, and their often sullen faces are wont to depress you; but many Westerners whom I met were so unconsciously humorous that they kept up my spirits.

There was, however, about these Western people an air of keen mental alertness which one could not help admiring. The men were eager for information concerning the resources of Mexico, the business opportunities of the country and the chances for profitable investment, while the women displayed equal energy in their sight-seeing and quest for general knowledge. Some business women whom I encountered knew much more about Mexico than the average man, and could talk fluently about the status of its railways, its mines and agricultural developments.

Among such a large number of Western tourists as annually invade Mexico and the increasing number of permanent settlers from the Western states, it is not surprising if there are a great many rough diamonds whose crude behavior often disgraces their country. Unfortunately, the world at large often hears far more of the doings of such people than of the praiseworthy demeanor of the majority of Americans who visit Mexico or make their homes there. In the capital, and, in fact, all over Mexico, there are plenty of Americans who would be a credit to any country, — cultured people who respect Mexican prejudices, and take the trouble to learn Spanish thoroughly. They are oftentimes ashamed of their crude countrymen, much resenting their coarse behavior, which reflects so unpleasantly on Americans in general.

An American newspaper man, for instance, told me that, while travelling with a party of his fellow-citizens and walking through the streets of a town, they heard the click of a sewing-machine in a Mexican house. One of the women tourists walked into the patio, looked into the sitting-room and then yelled out to the party, "Why, law me, they've actually got a sewing-machine and an American organ in here. Why, they're quite civilized." The Mexican family sat dumfounded with indignation, but before they had time to express it, the intruder disappeared.

Bad as such cases are, however, there is this to be said, that the unpolished American tripper is rarely so offensive on his travels as the low-class Englishman whom one so often meets in continental Europe. There is usually something extremely amusing about the "bad breaks" of the former, and they are always made with such naïveté and good nature that you half forgive them because of the hearty laugh they occasion. On the other hand, the antics of the English 'Arry abroad are almost always certain to excite wrath.

One very gratifying feature of life in Mexico is the thoroughly good feeling which exists between Englishmen and Americans resident in the Republic. The ties of language and race seem to draw them together. Not only are they associated very closely in business but also in the social life of the country. In most of the American clubs Englishmen and Canadians are also eligible for membership, and the fraternal feeling which exists between the three branches of the English-speaking world shows that no paper treaty is needed to bring them into alliance.

In addition to the American business men and tourists there is a numerous class of Americans in Mexico whom I should call "men with schemes." They hang about the American saloons, which are becoming so general, and are very much in evidence at the cheaper American hotels. Each of them has a scheme with millions in it. Most of them carry a chunk of gold or silver ore in their pockets, taken from some mine with possibilities of enormous wealth. If you enter one of the popular loafing places and listen to the conversation of these men, you will hear "millions of dollars" repeated so often that you might imagine yourself at a convention of the world's plutocrats.

I was seated in the patio of the Iturbide Hotel one day, discussing mining with a friend. He left me for a moment, and a rather seedy-looking individual, with a strong Western accent, sauntered up. "Excuse me, friend," he said, "but I overheard you talking about mines. Now, I've got a little piece of property away down in Guerrero which is worth millions to any man who puts in a few dollars." Here he produced the inevitable piece of silver ore from his pocket. "I suppose," he continued, "you ain't acquainted with no New York capitalists as would like to go in on a good thing. If you could get just a few of your Eastern millionaires interested, there would be something in it for you as well as me." I was obliged shamefacedly to confess to my would-be benefactor that my acquaintance with millionaires was exceedingly limited, and that investors usually required better credentials than a small piece of silver ore.

Most Americans have a firm impression that Mexicans love the United States and that ill-will towards us has practically disappeared. Impartial observers have, however, assured me that a strong anti-American feeling exists in some quarters, for which there are several reasons. In the first place, many Americans in Mexico are much given to boasting that American capital is getting control of all the best mines and otherwise acquiring a great hold on the country. To this is added the bragging of the low-class American — only too common in Mexico — who calls the Mexican "a greaser," and is always asserting that a few hundred Americans could beat the Mexican army and conquer the land.

An American resident told me that while he was lunching one day in a Mexico City restaurant, he heard a party of Westerners discussing the country in very uncomplimentary terms. One of them seemed to be interested in a mining company, which he thought had been unjustly treated by the Mexican government. "If these d—d greasers don't let up on this sort of thing," he said, "we Americans will have to teach them another lesson. Why, man, we could march a few regiments down here from Texas alone, and whip the everlasting stuffing out of them." At a neighboring table sat some young Mexicans, two of them sons of cabinet ministers, and all understanding English perfectly.

From their looks they did not seem to exactly relish the American's remarks.

Mexicans retaliate for this whenever the chance offers. They call Americans "gringos," a term which is said to have arisen during the war with the United States in 1846. Some Mexicans heard the American sailors singing, "Green grow the rashes O," and tried to mock them, "Gringo" being the result. They also get even in more unpleasant ways. A German of my acquaintance was summoned as a witness in a lawsuit to testify to a man's character. The judge said to him, "You are an American, señor." "No," replied the German, stating his nationality. "Oh, that's very different," said the judge. He then apologized for summoning him, put a few questions and told him he was at liberty to go, adding more apologies. A friend of his, an American, was next called. "What is your nationality, señor?" asked the judge. "I am an American," was the reply. The judge put on a very severe look, asked all sorts of unpleasant questions, and kept the poor fellow on the rack for about an hour.

Mexicans, in fact, are becoming so jealous and suspicious of Americans that it is likely that this alone may prevent any serious revolution occurring after the retirement or death of President Diaz. The United States has about $750,000,000 invested in Mexico; Great Britain has probably $500,000,000; France, Germany and other countries also have large sums at stake. If civil war broke out in Mexico, the United States, to protect its capitalists and Americans resident in the country, and to prevent any other power from taking coercive measures in defiance of the Monroe doctrine, would undoubtedly march an army into Mexico to restore order. Intelligent Mexicans realize this very thoroughly, and are anxious that such a thing shall never take place.

All attempts of Mexicans to halt the onward march of progress are, however, certain to end in failure. Whether Mexicans like it or not, every year is witnessing a more pronounced Americanization of Mexico, more American settlers are pouring into the country than ever before, and in two more decades their numbers and influence will be formidable. With the increasing use of the English language among the people, and the education of the masses, old prejudices are gradually disappearing, and the commercial and social ties between Americans and Mexicans are steadily drawing them closer. It is never safe to prophesy unless you know; but it would not be strange if, under these conditions, an Americanized Mexico should some day — perhaps in twenty-five years, or so — become peacefully annexed to the United States.

In France every person who speaks English is called English. I have seen Parisian gamins point at American tourists and heard them remark, "Regardez les Anglais." That is because there are more English than Americans in Paris. In Mexico it is just the reverse. There are more Americans than English, and consequently every person who speaks English is called an American. The natives cannot detect any difference. I was once walking through the Plaza in the capital when I heard an Englishman, who owned an awful Cockney accent, abusing a cabman for overcharging him, and dropping more h's than centavos. One of a party of Mexican loafers standing near by, pointed at the Britisher and remarked, "El Americano no le gusta perder su dinero" (The American doesn't like to lose his money).

Americans are not only gradually Americanizing Mexico, but they are also altering the names of Mexican towns and districts. The Spaniards abbreviated many of the Indian names after the Conquest, and now the Americans are making them still shorter. For example, the City of Mexico is now generally called Mexico City by English-speaking people. The name certainly has the virtue of being more concise. Mexicans simply call the city Mexico. Popocatepetl, a difficult name to pronounce, has been shortened by Americans to "Popo." Ixtaccihuatl is known as "Ixy." Some day Guanajuato and Guadalajara will probably be known as "Wahno" and "Wadly."

The other foreign peoples in Mexico are chiefly Spanish, French, German and English, and in a proportion according to that order. Of course the foreign element is more noticeable in the capital than in the rest of the country. The Spaniards in Mexico are chiefly engaged in the grocery trade; the French confine themselves to drapery, the sale of fancy articles, tailoring and dressmaking; the Germans are bankers, and have almost a monopoly of the hardware trade. The cheap German-made goods are eagerly bought. I myself purchased a pocket-knife which attracted me by the somewhat pretty medallion let into the handle, displaying the face of a dark-eyed señorita. I thought I had captured an example of Mexican industry, but my delusion did not last long. During my travels I happened to meet a German "drummer," and on showing him this knife as a specimen of Mexican skill he burst out laughing. "Vy, mein friendt," he said, "I sold dose knives. Dey vas made by mein firm in Berlin."

The trade of Mexico is to-day chiefly controlled by the United States and Germany, the latter country having of late shown wonderful enterprise. German drummers are encountered almost everywhere, all of them speaking Spanish fluently. The catalogues of German firms, too, are always printed in Spanish, the prices given in Mexican currency, and the goods are specially designed for Mexican trade. British trade was once supreme in Mexico, but owing to lack of proper methods on the part of English firms, this proud position has long been lost.

With decreased business interests the British colony in the capital is naturally a small one, chiefly comprising the managers of several important British companies and their subordinates. But while British influence in Mexico has thus declined, that of Canada, strangely enough, has correspondingly increased. Canada's stake in the country has recently become so large in mines and other enterprises, in fact, that it has been found necessary to appoint a Canadian commercial agent whose duty it is to safeguard Canada's vested interests and to report to the Dominion government on openings for capital, etc. The great Electric Light and Power Company, which supplies Mexico City, is a Canadian corporation. Canadian banks are rapidly extending their business in the country, and Canadians share with Americans the financing of the electric and street railway business. A Canadian company owns the Mexico City street-car lines, and Canadian investors are now taking a leading interest in water-power schemes.

The Mexican is not born to be a business man. He is not possessed of any gifts of invention or initiative, and he detests the hustle and worry of commercial life. Nearly all commerce is, therefore, in the hands of foreigners. All the modern improvements in Mexico have been established by them and with their capital.

In this connection it may be remarked that a fact which impresses most visitors in Mexico is the number of foreign clerks that are employed in American, English and Canadian offices, oftentimes in places where it would seem that Mexicans would do much better. Many of the foreign firms which employ young Mexicans complain, however, that they are lazy and frivolous. Of course there is a great deal in the point of view; and perhaps a Frenchman, an

Italian or a Spaniard of the same Latin race would not find these young fellows so light-headed and inefficient as do Anglo-Saxons. It is also true that many young Mexicans who have been educated in England or the United States are attaining a high position in the professional and business life of the Republic. Nevertheless, the fact remains that most of the younger natives think too much about señoritas, bull-fights and gambling and too little about their work; in short, they do not take life seriously enough. An American railway manager said to me: "It is impossible to get a young Mexican to assume any responsibility or take any initiative. He has to be told the same thing over and over again. I would rather have one bright young American in my office than three average Mexicans."

The exports of Mexico are mainly silver, gold, copper and other minerals; hemp, mahogany, cedar and dye-woods, tobacco, coffee, hides, india-rubber, fruit, vanilla, etc. Those who have not travelled in the country can have no conception of its marvellous richness. Possessing every range of climate, and soils capable of producing every variety of fruit, vegetable and flower; with mineral wealth of amazing extent; and with vast areas peculiarly adapted for sheep and cattle, it is indeed a land of wonders. But although so potentially wealthy, Mexico is still in her infancy as regards the development of her resources. The success of foreign companies and the large and steady dividends they are able to pay are proving that the land of the Aztecs is a profitable field for investment. It must year by year become more so; but a fraction of its wondrous resources have been tapped, and under its present firm government the country is always going forward and must have a magnificent destiny.

An interesting feature of Mexico is the number of children of American and English parentage who are growing up all over the country and are bound to exercise a great influence on its future. Born and educated in Mexico, they are likely to make their homes there; and as they speak both English and Spanish, the Mexican children with whom they play imbibe their ideas of freedom and progress. Many Mexicans holding a high position in the Republic are of British or American descent, notably Señor Creel, the Mexican Ambassador to the United States, and Señor Pankhurst, governor of the State of Zacatecas.

Very few English or Americans marry Mexican women, but a large number of Germans do so. The Germans affiliate with the Mexicans much better than do the English or Americans, one reason for which is that they go to Mexico to establish their permanent residence there, while most Americans and Englishmen wish only to make their fortunes and then to return to their native lands. While travelling in Mexico I frequently heard little Teutons — boys and girls — with flaxen hair and blue eyes, speaking Spanish fluently. They were the children of Germans with Mexican wives. These German-Mexican children usually speak three languages, German, Spanish and English; but they seem to become much more Mexicanized than the American or English children brought up in Mexico. All the European children of whole or half blood reared in Mexico appear to suffer from the climate, having a general look of sickliness, with pale, colorless faces.

Mexico is a tempting land for the business man, as it offers him large profits, for the most part easily made. The salaries, too, for commercial clerks and skilled laborers, engineers, etc., are a great deal higher than those obtainable in Europe. On the other hand, the cost of living is far greater. For the unskilled worker, the mere clerk or the day laborer, Mexico offers no opportunities. The man who has the best chance there is the small capitalist with about ten thousand dollars, who is careful in his investments. At first he must work harder than he would at home; but if he is steady, he will scarcely fail to get on. First of all he must learn the ways of the country and to speak Spanish. Of the easier ways of making money the best are storekeeping, any sound manufacture, cattle-raising, timber, tobacco, sugar and coffee, fruit farms, rubber and mining. The country is so vast and the districts which are being opened up by the railways are so fertile and so rich in minerals that there is an almost unlimited demand for foreign capital throughout Mexico.

During my stay in Mexico I came across some wonderful instances of men of small means having become wealthy. One of the leading bankers of Mexico City, a Canadian, was formerly a railway conductor, and is now one of the richest men in the country. Another Canadian, who is the leading druggist in the capital, and has stores all over Mexico, came down only a few years ago with a small stock of patent medicines and started in a humble way. The proprietor of the biggest hardware establishment — equalling any store of the kind in the United States — is an enterprising German who was a drummer only a short time ago. A clerk who had a salary of a hundred dollars a month and bought a small mining property which proved to be a bonanza is now one of the wealthiest men in southern Mexico.

The Mexican laws affecting investors are generous and, as a rule, are fairly administered, everything possible being done to avoid prejudicing foreign interests. If, therefore, Americans only realized the opportunities Mexico affords for the investment of capital there would soon be so much money forthcoming from this country that our national stake in Mexico's prosperity would be even greater than it already is.

There are several foreign quarters in Mexico City, the

largest of these being the American, already referred to, which is situated in the vicinity of the Paseo de la Reforma. In and about this quarter most of the English and Canadians also reside and fraternize with the Americans. The *Mexican Herald* devotes almost a page every day to the doings of the American colony, its dances, receptions and other social functions. There are also German, Italian and French quarters, but not so much is heard of them. All along the Paseo wide asphalted streets are being laid out, planted with grass-plots and double rows of trees. Three new districts, known as the Colonia Reforma, the Colonia Roma and Colonia Santa Maria, have been built up with American capital, and during the past ten years the value of land has advanced nearly a thousand per cent, many lucky investors having made large fortunes.

Strange to say, very few of the modern houses have fireplaces or any other system of heating. Americans, who always have their houses well heated at home, evidently prefer to follow the Mexican custom and sit about shivering. I heard a good story of a young Englishman who occupied a flat in the American colony, and, determining to be comfortable, installed an American stove. His rooms were so cosey that his friends increased rapidly; men got into the habit of saying, "Let's go round to Smith's place, it's so comfortable." The Briton had only a small income, but he fell in love with a wealthy American's daughter. When she broke the news to her stern parent, to her surprise, he said, "Marry him, my daughter, with my blessing. I like that young fellow. He knows enough to make a comfortable home for himself, and he is bound to make one for his wife." The truth was that the old gentleman had been one of the most frequent callers at Smith's flat on cold nights, and was determined not to lose such a comfortable lounging place.

An outgrowth of American social life in the capital is the Country Club, which has a fine club-house at Cherubusco, a beautiful suburb. It stands in the midst of large grounds and on the borders of a lake, clear as crystal, fed from an artesian well. While the golf links are the chief attraction, cricket, tennis, football and other sports are enjoyed.

American business men have an American business club in the city, and English residents have established the British Club. Football matches between American and English teams formed of members of the two clubs frequently take place during the winter season. The Germans have the finest men's club, a large new building with a splendid gymnasium, a bowling alley, a beer hall, and other Teutonic attractions. The Spaniards and French also have their clubs, the largest Spanish club being the Casino Español, with eight hundred members, which occupies a fine old mansion, rivalling the famous Jockey Club. Even the Chinese have established a club of their own, which has a membership of nearly four hundred.

CHAPTER X

THE WHITE MAN'S BURDEN-BEARER

WHEREVER the traveller goes in Mexico, he finds himself face to face with the Indian peon, the laborer of the country, who is a distinctive feature of Mexican life. One sees him in the cities in his ragged clothing and tattered sarape, bearing heavy burdens through the streets, carrying loads of bricks up among the scaffoldings of new buildings, or, as an itinerant vendor, hawking his fruit, charcoal and other commodities. In the country districts the peon is the farm laborer, and in the mines he can be seen bringing out the heavy loads of gold and silver ore which make dividends for foreign investors.

Although the real natives of Mexico, the great masses, are called Indians, the name gives a very erroneous impression to the average reader. The term "Indian" usually calls up a mental picture of a North American red man with painted face and feathered head-dress; whereas, there is almost as much difference between the Mexican and North American Indians as there is between an Esquimau and an Arab. Instead of being hunters, as were their fiercer neighbors in the North, the Mexican Indians have always been an agricultural people.

At the time of the Conquest, Mexico was inhabited by several Indian nations under separate governments, and all speaking different dialects. The Aztecs, for instance, held the Valley of Mexico under Montezuma; the Tlaxcalans formed a Republic around what is now the City of

Puebla; the Zapotecs were all-powerful in southern Mexico. Even to-day there are no less than forty tribes and their branches, speaking, it is said, some one hundred and fifty different languages; and while most of these people also speak a crude Spanish, there are districts where little if any Spanish is understood. It is said that within a short distance of Mexico City there are still surviving full-blooded descendants of the Aztecs, speaking a language which is almost the pure ancient tongue. All these Indian tribes suffered subjection at the hands of the Spaniards, and were lumped together under the term of "peons," which literally meant slaves. Their descendants, suffering from the evil effects of previous generations of slavery and degradation, form the bulk of the lower classes in modern Mexico. The name " peon " still clings to them, for although Mexico abolished slavery long ago, the peons of to-day are often nothing but bondsmen.

Just as their languages differ, so, too, the physical appearance of the Mexican Indians is often dissimilar. One tribe will have the typical angular face and high cheekbones of the Mongolian peoples, with the small, straight nose which one sees in a Malay. Another Indian, from a different part of the country, will have a round face and a broad, bridgeless nose, and a mouth often large, with full lips. On the other hand, two or three tribes, such as the Yaquis, a wild, unconquered race living in Sonora in northern Mexico, have the dark skin and coarse features of the mulatto. The great mass of the Indians in central Mexico, however, and especially those seen in and about the capital, usually have intensely black hair and eyes, yellowish brown complexions and are slight in stature, bearing a strong resemblance to Japanese peasants, sometimes even having a slight obliquity of the eyes. In some of the tribes one is much impressed with this likeness to the Chinese or Japanese, and it is certainly a fact that if the Orientals were dressed in Mexican style they might easily pass for Indians. It is said that students of languages have found some resemblance between the Mexican tongues and various languages of the Far East. Be that as it may, there is much in Mexico which suggests very close ties with the Orient, and some of the ancient sculptures apparently show distinct Chinese features.

In no part of the Republic is there a more remarkable physical difference among the Indians than is to be found among the Mayans of Yucatan, their appearance being very different from that of the typical Mexican Indian. They are of a red, bricky tint, are much darker than the others, also a good deal shorter, broad-headed, muscular and usually have quite a remarkable development of the chest. They are characterized, too, by a very sunny disposition. Nothing is easier than to make a Mayan laugh, while it would seemingly be a hopeless task to get a smile from the sullen, sad faces of most of the other Mexican Indians one sees at work or at play.

The Mayans had, it is declared, reached quite a high state of civilization when the Spaniards came. It is a historical fact that the conquest of Yucatan cost the Spaniards more in blood and treasure than did the rest of Mexico. To the Mayans are attributed the very remarkable ruins in Yucatan. At the time of the conquest they had a system of writing, had made some advances in literature, and in their temples were great numbers of manuscripts. These were ruthlessly destroyed by the Spaniards in their efforts to stamp out Mayan civilization, and the historical records of the race were thus lost. The Mayan language, however, is still spoken by three hundred thousand people, and many of the white inhabitants of Yucatan use it to a greater extent than Spanish.

THE ANCIENT RACE.
Types of Mexican Indians, young and old.

The various Indian races in Mexico to-day number many millions, those of pure blood constituting one-third of the population, while fully half the Mexicans are those of mixed blood known as meztizos. Many Indians of pure blood and a still greater number of meztizos have played an important part in Mexican history. Several Mexican presidents, among whom were Guerrero and Juarez, were pure Indians, while the majority of the others were half-breeds.

It is from this great Indian population that the peon, the Mexican workingman, has been evolved, and Mexico could not do without him. He not only cultivates the soil, works in the mines and does all the hard labor, but he also acts as servant. Despite his many faults, he has some wonderfully good qualities. Even if he is not naturally cleanly or naturally honest, there is a charm all his own in the simple, whole-hearted way in which he accepts his subordinate position. Always polite, and incapable of taking a liberty, always with his hat in his hand, the Indian has nothing but respect to show you, if you give him the humble wage he claims, a half holiday now and again, and permission to attend any and every fiesta celebrated in his village. Notwithstanding his dirt, his tattered clothes, his battered sombrero and his filthy blanket, the Mexican Indian is one of nature's gentlemen, if he is only treated properly.

But he has his faults, and they are faults which have seriously checked progress in Mexico. He is essential to agriculture, yet his tropical surroundings and his mental characteristics unfit him for energetic work or the adoption of modern improvements. As a farmer the Indian is a rank failure. He brings no intelligence to his work. His ancestors hundreds of years ago scratched the soil with a wooden hoe, and he is content enough to go on with the same implement. If a society were formed for presenting every Indian peon with a modern plough, it would do no good; he wouldn't care to use it, and he wouldn't use it. His ideal of life is to be idle; he does not want to struggle; he does not want to fight; he only desires his little mudbrick hut, his piece of ground, his pig, his tortillas and his frijoles. Furniture he does not need, as his household goods are generally limited to a tin can for boiling water or cooking, a couple of stones for making tortillas, a few picturesque jars made by the native potters and a few old sacks to sleep on. His wants being easily supplied, there is really no incentive for him to be progressive. He cannot read or write, is unable to think, and his mode of life is primeval in its simplicity.

The Indian in the tropical region of Mexico is especially slothful. All he needs is enough to eat, a thatched hut and a little cotton cloth. The hut he can make himself; there are fish in the river and game in the forest. There is plenty of unoccupied land upon which he can raise a little maize for food or to trade for such simple luxuries as coffee, sugar and tobacco. There is no winter to provide against, and though rainy days often come, they only mean more rest. Consequently, the tropical Indian is seldom a hireling.

Mentally and physically lethargic, the peon of central Mexico has been for years little more than a slave, in spite of his very slender wants. The system which is called peonage is very subtle and it is very simple. The peon receives so scant a wage that he has nothing left after his humble wants have been satisfied. He usually earns from fifteen to fifty cents a day, and being very improvident is always without money. On all the haciendas or large estates he is compelled to deal at the hacienda store, being encouraged to be extravagant in his orders. This is deliberate on the part of the proprietors, the haciendados, because, by the law of Mexico, as long as an Indian workman owes his employer a dollar he is the latter's chattel, and must go on working for him till he has paid off his debt.

But the haciendado takes great care that the debt is never paid off, and as very few Indians on big estates are allowed to owe less than twenty dollars, the haciendado may feel quite easy in his mind about his human property. If the estate changes hands, the debt is sold to the new master, the peons passing into his possession just as would the cattle in the farmyard when stock was being sold. As against this tyranny, one must remember that the haciendado has to furnish medical attendance, pay fees on marriages, burials, etc., and that when he is old the peon must be looked after and given the necessities of life. It is therefore as much to the advantage of the employer to keep the peon in good health as it is in the interest of a sheep farmer to keep his flocks from foot-rot, so that, after all is said and done, the easy-going, sweet-mannered peon is little more than a beast of burden.

But if he is cheap, the peon needs humoring. He will only work in one way, the most laborious, old-fashioned and slow way, and he will not work even in that way unless he is watched. Then, too, he is obdurate in the matter of fiestas. The Mexican calendar fairly bristles with fiestas and saints' days, and as the main feature of these celebrations is an indulgence in such cheap spirits as tequila and mescal, the peon insists on knocking off work and taking part in them. Sunday, of course, is also a day of rest, and most peons need Monday to recover from the effects of the libations of the Sabbath. Therefore the average Indian will probably not do more than two hundred days' work in the year.

Although so conscientious in keeping the various holy days of the Catholic church, the religion of the average peon is usually intermixed with the grossest superstition, and amounts to sheer idolatry. Various shrines, pictures and statues are believed by him to possess supernatural powers, and he worships them with a remarkable intensity of devotion. While displaying all this reverence for the emblems of Christianity, it is said that the Indians in some remote villages also worship their ancient idols, and sometimes sacrifice lambs or fowls to win the favor or appease the wrath of these pagan deities. The priests try to put a stop to these practices, but they still continue. Passion plays, flagellation and other mediæval religious customs flourish among the Indian population, to whom the weird and horrible always strongly appeal. As an instance of this, F. Hopkinson Smith thus describes a penitential scene which he witnessed in a Mexican church: "A score of Indian women," he says, "were kneeling upon mats of green rushes spread on the stone floor of the church, their cheeks hollow from fasting, and their eyes glistening with that strange glassy look peculiar to half-starved people. Over their shoulders were twisted black rebosas, and round each head was bound a veritable crown of thorns. In their hands they held a scourge of plaited needles. They had sat there day and night, without moving, for nearly a week. This terrible ceremony occurs once a year in Passion week. The penance lasts eight days. Each penitent pays a sum of money for the privilege, and her name and number is then inscribed upon a sort of tally board which is hung on the cloister wall. Upon this is also kept a record of the punishment. The penitents supply their blankets and pillows and the mats upon which they rest their weary bones. The priest furnishes everything else — a little greasy gruel and the stone pavement."

The greatest inhumanities from which the Mexican Indians suffer are those which result from the transportation of labor to the plantations in the tropical parts of the country. In such tropical places as Tehuantepec, life is very simple and cheap for the local Indian, and he will not work. But work must be done, and therefore hundreds of peons are hoodwinked into signing on as laborers and transported to the tropics from the more temperate parts of Mexico. There are agents at work all over the country picking them up and deporting them. The unfortunate Indians contract to work for six months for twenty-five cents a day, with their food, tortillas, beans, rice and a little meat on Sundays. Of course they at once get into debt at the hacienda store, and they are never allowed to get out again. Armed guards are posted at the hacienda entrances to stop any attempt at escape. Hundreds of these poor creatures, accustomed to cooler climates, die off of fever.

Being utterly without ambition, the Indians have no desire to improve their condition or educate their families. None of them can be trusted with money; in a few hours most of them will drink and gamble away the earnings of months. The great aim of the average peon is to earn a little money, sufficient to supply him with tortillas and frijoles and the opportunity to see an occasional bull-fight or enjoy a little gambling. As long as he has a penny in his pocket he will not work, and even when his money is gone, the word "mañana" (meaning to-morrow, but in fact some more convenient time) springs instinctively to his lips. Untruthfulness is universal among Indians of the lower orders, and in the capital most of them are petty thieves. Very few of them have the slightest conception of morality from the Anglo-Saxon point of view.

Gambling, as already remarked, is one of the Indian's worst vices, and his favorite medium of risking his hard-earned coin is cock-fighting. For this sport he has a passionate love. Fighting cocks are familiar objects everywhere, and can often be seen outside the Indian huts, tied by the leg to a stake. Victorious birds are carried about from village to village, to make up fights upon which the improvident Indians will wager their last pennies. The sport as practised in Mexico is extremely cruel, thin steel blades or spurs, as sharp as a razor, being attached to the birds' claws. One of the combatants will often be despatched at the first stroke; sometimes the birds will fight several rounds, hacked and bleeding, before the fray ends.

In spite of his poverty and his numerous bad traits, the Indian is extremely generous. If he has no tortillas or frijoles, some of his neighbors have, and they will gladly share with him, for conditions may be reversed to-morrow. Although his cruelty to animals is notorious, his love for children is just as marked. It is a common sight to see a peon in the street, with but two pieces of cotton clothing to his back, stop a woman with a baby in her arms, and holding the child's face between both hands, deliver a resounding smack and chuck it under the chin. His politeness is that of a cavalier. In the most unaffected manner the young Indian will take his battered straw sombrero from his head and reverently kiss the hand of some ancient relative, in a tattered dress, when he happens to meet her. To hear these unwashed, ragged folk exchanging graceful compliments in choice Spanish is oftentimes grotesque. Centuries of oppression have degraded the peon, but when given opportunity, he often displays great talent in the arts and crafts, and when educated, many of them are very bright. Among the Indian masses the spread of education is necessarily slow, but it is destined, in time, to put an end to the repulsive aspects of peonage.

The Indian man has a fitting mate in the Indian woman, who is not a wholesome-looking person. Nearly all the women are small, plump and slatternly, with tousled hair, their dresses torn and dirty, their general appearance being reminiscent of gypsies. Some of the girls are handsome enough; but the hardness and monotony of their lives make them old women before their time, and an Indian maiden of thirty is often simply a bent and wrinkled hag. Early marriages are the rule, girls of fourteen in some cases being married to boys of sixteen, after which they become mere household drudges. In many places the immorality which exists is appalling, polygamy being quite general, marriages seldom taking place and kinship being disregarded. The Mexican government, with the aid of the church, is endeavoring to put an end to these deplorable conditions.

Large families are the rule among the Indian population, a childless woman being very rare; but most of the children, through neglect, die in infancy. Like their husbands, the women are invariably dull-witted and unprogressive. Even in those parts where flour is available, they will continue every morning to pound their corn on the metate and bake the tortillas, for they would scorn the American idea of having one big bake and getting it over. They have few virtues save their devotion to their husbands and children; but many of them are not unskilful in fancy work, being able to follow the most elaborate designs, doing also really delicate and pretty work on handkerchiefs and linens.

Whatever his racial weaknesses may be, there is no doubt that the degeneracy of the native and the degrading conditions under which he often lives, especially in the cities, are mainly due to drink. Every centavo the Indian can scrape together is spent on pulque and mescal. To take Mexico City as typical of the drink evil, some idea can be gathered of its extent when one realizes that there are considerably more than a thousand pulque shops in the city, and these sell over seven hundred thousand litres of

o

pulque every day. Four trains loaded with cans of this evil liquid arrive from the country every morning. As it is scarcely ever tasted by Mexicans of the middle or upper classes, practically the whole of this vast quantity of drink is consumed by the Indian population. It acts upon them as a poison, and there is little doubt that by its means their natural laziness and stupidity have been increased a hundred-fold, till they have lost all ambition and have reached a point of animal degradation from which it seems almost hopeless they will ever recover.

Pulque is cheap, a glass of it costing half a cent, a large glass a cent, while the miserable Indian toper can buy a small barrel of it for a quarter of a dollar. The usual method of the drinking Indian is first to take several glasses of pulque and then top off with mescal. This changes him into a madman, and it has constantly happened that an Indian under these conditions has run amuck, drawn his knife and stabbed and slashed at every one he has met. Most of the murders in Mexico City are due to drink. *Pulquerias*, as the drinking shops are called, are for the most part located in the low quarters of the town, and are reeking, foul-smelling dens with earthen floors, the state of which had best not be inquired into. These bar-rooms are decorated and painted in a very strange way, brightly colored tissue paper and flags of all tints adorning them without as well as within. The outside walls of these are usually covered with pictures of warriors, chariots, battles, and even martyrs and saints, daubed over them in gay colors. One pulque shop in Tacubaya is famous for its picturesque appearance, the outer walls being cleverly painted with birds and tropical flowers by a native artist.

The pulque shops all have names, and professional humorists seem to have invented them. There are, for instance, El Serpenton (the Enormous Snake), Hospital de

Crudos (Hospital for Thirsty Men), Hogar Feliz (Abode of Bliss), Amor Fraternal (Brotherly Love) and Paraise Terrestre (Earthly Paradise). I had an impression that the places last named were possibly the resort of saintly minded natives; but one morning I read in the newspaper that a peon had been slashed with knives in the Abode of Bliss, and the police had cracked several skulls in quelling a riot in Brotherly Love.

Some gushing writers assert that the Mexican Indians are miracles of cleanliness, but I regret to say that I saw very few indications of it during my travels. In the tropical regions, where water is plentiful, the Indians do keep clean, and most of them take a dip in some stream or river at least once a day. In the highlands, however, where the water-courses are dry for the greater part of the year, the Indians never take a bath; and you will often see them by the roadside picking vermin from each other as monkeys do. The peons of the temperate zone seem, in fact, to have a deep-rooted horror of soap and water. As a religious duty they must bathe once a year on St. John the Baptist's Day (el dia de San Juan Bautista), on June 24. This is the only bath the poorer classes take during the year, and if they miss it they wait until the next year. Most of them look and smell as if they had missed every year since they were born. In Mexico City the disgusting rags of the peons are oftentimes indecent and expose the body.

Peons, especially in the small towns and country places, are, as I have observed, usually very stupid. When visiting Puebla, I asked several if they could direct me to the post-office, but was unable to make any of them understand, although the policemen whom I asked understood me well enough and directed me correctly. An American afterwards told me that the peons probably called the post-office (Casa de Correos) some such name as "The place where you put letters" or "buy stamps." Many of them had probably never bought a stamp or mailed a letter in their lives, and having no need to go to the post-office, did not even know its name.

In the same way they seldom learn the names of Englishmen or Americans, but when talking among themselves designate the foreigners by some personal peculiarity. Mr. Smith, the Englishman, for instance, may be called "El caballero Ingles con la barba roja" (The English gentleman with the red beard); while Mr. Scroggs, the American, will be known as "El caballero Americano con nariz grande" (The American gentleman with the big nose). Unless you discover these terms, you may inquire in vain among the peons for Messrs. Smith and Scroggs, for you will never find them.

It was this peon peculiarity which led to the very amusing adventure of an Englishman who was travelling in southern Mexico. He went several weary miles out of his way to visit an old acquaintance who was living in a town some distance from the railway. On his arrival, he made inquiries for his friend, but to his surprise found that nobody had ever heard of him. The last place at which he inquired was a large general store, and as it was Saturday, the place was crowded with peons doing their marketing. The proprietor of the store had never heard of the Englishman for whom the traveller was searching. A peon, however, who looked much more intelligent than the other Indians, had overheard the conversation, and he stepped up. "Con permiso, señor — with your permission, sir," he said, "I believe I know the señor you are looking for. He is called Señor Perez." "No," replied the traveller, "that cannot be, unless he has changed his name." He mentioned the name, which was rather a long one. The peon, however, still insisted that Señor Perez was the missing man and pro-

PRESIDENT DIAZ.
A striking portrait of Mexico's great ruler.

ceeded to describe him so accurately that the Englishman was convinced that it must either be his friend or somebody having a wonderful resemblance to him. The peon offered to guide the traveller to the abode of Señor Perez, and they started off, followed by a lot of other Indians who had listened intently to the conversation and seemed to be much interested in the outcome of the affair. When they reached the house of Perez, the Englishman was astonished to see his old friend seated outside.

After they had exchanged greetings, the Englishman asked with some impatience, "How is it that you have changed your name to Perez?" The other laughed heartily. "Well," he said, "it simply happened in this way: One of the storekeepers in the town had a big boxful of Pears' soap, for which there was absolutely no sale, for no peon would touch it with a ten-foot pole. One day, when I was in his place, he offered me the whole lot for about a third of its price, so I bought it. The place was crowded with Indians when I made my purchase. Now, any peon who bought one cake of soap would be regarded as a hero, but here was a man actually buying fifty cakes! Such a man must be almost a supernatural being. The news of the wonderful Englishman spread like wildfire. None of the Indians could pronounce my name, but on the soap-box they saw those famous words, 'Pears' Soap;' and concluding that I must be no less than Mr. Pears himself, they forthwith christened me Señor Perez, their nearest approach to the name."

CHAPTER XI

MEXICO'S GREAT DICTATOR

DURING my travels in Mexico I entered into conversation one day with an old Indian laborer or peon who had once served in the army of the Republic. In the course of our chat I happened to ask him whom he considered the world's greatest man. Raising his tattered straw sombrero, with reverential air, he replied, "Don Porfirio, señor," and added, "Where can you find his equal?" It was in this half-worshipping manner that the old Indian referred to President Porfirio Diaz, affectionately known to millions of his fellow-countrymen by the title of Don Porfirio.

A few weeks after my talk with the peon admirer of President Diaz I was walking across the Plaza in Mexico City one morning when I noticed a distinguished, soldierly looking man riding towards the National Palace. In the well-set, military figure, the strong, handsome face, with bristling gray moustache and searching brown eyes — I at once recognized the President. Hats were raised in respectful salutation as he rode in this democratic fashion from his private residence in the Cadena to his daily work at the palace.

The story of this remarkable man who for thirty years has been the president, but really the dictator, and practically the uncrowned king of Mexico, reads more like a thrilling romance than the actual history that it is.

The son of an innkeeper, Porfirio Diaz was born at Oaxaca in southern Mexico on the fifteenth of September,

1830, and is thus now in his seventy-ninth year. As are the majority of his fellow-citizens, he is of mixed Indian and Spanish descent, his maternal grandmother having belonged to the Mixteca tribe. When the future ruler of Mexico was three years old, his father died, and his mother, with her scanty means, had a hard struggle to bring up her family of six children.

Porfirio was intended for the church, and was sent when a lad to a Roman Catholic school; but there was so little in common between the boy's nature and ecclesiasticism that he soon abandoned the idea of the priestly calling and began to study law. While so engaged, the war between the United States and Mexico broke out in 1847; the young law students promptly formed a battalion for the defence of their city, and Diaz took a prominent part in the movement. At that time the foremost lawyer in Oaxaca was Benito Juarez, afterwards to become President of Mexico. He was much attracted by the intelligence of young Diaz, and gave him work in his office. The youth's progress was so rapid and continuous that in a very short time he was appointed assistant librarian of Oaxaca, and by means of money which he earned as a law tutor, he paid for the completion of his own studies and gained a degree.

Even in those early days, Diaz had shown an interest in politics and some signs of that military genius which was to win him the headship of his country. When twenty-five, he was appointed mayor of the small town of Ixtlan, and during his tenure of that office he organized a company of militia which afterwards rendered Mexico good service. In 1861 he was elected deputy to the Federal Congress. It was in the following year that France invaded Mexico for the purpose of placing the Archduke Maximilian on the throne. Diaz, then thirty-two, had already become a general of brigade. To him was assigned a leading part in the defence of Puebla, and to his courage and foresight was due the great victory of the fifth of May, when a small force of Mexicans under General Zaragoza utterly defeated a large French army.

A year later the French and Austrians captured Puebla, and General Bazaine, with a large army, marched to overwhelm Diaz. The latter was defeated and taken prisoner at Puebla. Refusing to give his parole, he escaped after extraordinary adventures to Oaxaca, where he succeeded in raising a fresh army for the defence of that city. After a short siege he was again compelled to surrender and was taken prisoner once more to Puebla, where he was imprisoned for seven months. He again succeeded in escaping, returned to Oaxaca and collected another army, winning thereafter the succession of victories which led up to the defeat and execution of Maximilian and the end of the empire.

On the second of June, 1867, Diaz was master of Puebla, and later in the month he entered Mexico City at the head of a victorious army. His popularity was unbounded, and had he cared he could have ousted Juarez from the presidential chair. He refused, however, to be untrue to his chief and patron, and Juarez was reëlected. Diaz then resigned his commission and retired to Oaxaca.

In 1871 Juarez's term of office came to an end, and although he was in failing health and had lost much of his popularity, he unwisely obtained reëlection. This time Diaz had allowed himself to be nominated a candidate, and his followers were loud in their complaints that the election had not been honestly conducted, and so high did public feeling run that civil war was declared. Within a few months Juarez died and was succeeded by the president of the Supreme Court, Lerdo de Tejada.

Diaz sold all his property and retired to the United States;

but in 1876 he returned to Mexico, gathered around him an army of four hundred men and captured Matamoras in the northern part of the Republic. Hearing that his enemy, Lerdo, had sent troops to seize him, Diaz fled to New Orleans, but after remaining there a short time he decided to return to Mexico. The steamer on which he sailed for Vera Cruz — an American vessel — put in at Tampico, and there Diaz was recognized by some Mexican officers and soldiers who came aboard as passengers. Fearing arrest at Vera Cruz, he leaped overboard when the steamer was four miles from that port and attempted to swim ashore. He was picked up half dead, and the purser, who admired his pluck, concealed him for several days in a wardrobe, while the Mexican officers, deceived by a story that he had once more attempted escape and had been drowned, unsuspectingly played cards in the cabin each night. On arrival at Vera Cruz, Diaz was smuggled ashore in a launch loaded with cargo, disguised as a Mexican soldier, while a detachment of troops were keeping watch for him.

Returning to Oaxaca, Diaz raised an army and marched on the capital. He won a decided victory, and entering the city on the 24th of November, 1876, assumed the presidency. In a very short time he was at work reforming the country; order was speedily restored, brigandage was put down, trade was fostered, and everything was done to encourage foreign investors. In 1880, in accordance with the provisions of the Mexican constitution, that no man should hold the office of President for two consecutive terms, Diaz was succeeded by his close friend, General Gonzalez. The next year or two made it quite obvious that the Mexicans could be ruled by only one man, and thus when, in 1884, Diaz was again elected President, the constitution was altered to allow of his being continually the chief of the state. From that date to the present day Diaz has been reëlected without a dissentient voice, and although Mexico is a Republic nominally, he wields a power practically as autocratic as that of a czar.

The personal appearance of President Diaz is as remarkable as has been his career. James Creelman, the well-known writer, has recently contributed to *Pearson's Magazine* a vivid pen picture of the Mexican autocrat, whom he was privileged to see at Chapultepec. He writes: "A high, wide forehead that slopes up to crisp white hair and overhangs deep-set, dark brown eyes that search your soul, soften into inexpressible kindliness and then dart quick side looks, — terrible eyes, threatening eyes, loving, confiding, humorous eyes, — a straight, powerful, broad, and somewhat fleshy nose, whose curved nostrils lift and dilate with every emotion; huge, virile jaws that sweep from large, flat, fine ears set close to the head to the tremendous, square, fighting chin; a wide, firm mouth shaded by a white moustache; a full, short, muscular neck; wide shoulders, deep chest; a curiously tense and rigid carriage that gives great distinction to a personality suggestive of singular power and dignity, — that is Porfirio Diaz in his seventy-eighth year, as I saw him a few weeks ago on the spot where forty years before he stood — with his besieging army surrounding the City of Mexico, and the young Emperor Maximilian being shot to death in Queretaro, beyond those blue mountains to the north — waiting grimly for the thrilling end and the last interference of European monarchy with the republics of America."

President Diaz is thoroughly democratic in sympathies, easy of approach and gives one the impression of sincerity. He is rather above the average Mexican height, and his whole appearance suggests the Indian blood in his veins. A man of the simplest habits, he is perpetually at work, going to bed at ten, and at six in the morning at work at his desk. In the matter of diet he is simplicity itself, and rarely drinks any wine or spirits. Disliking ceremony, he resolutely declines to occupy the state apartments in the National Palace, living most of the year in a private house near by. He is never satisfied with second-hand knowledge, and maintains direct touch with the remotest parts of the Republic, almost amazing his cabinet by the fund of information he possesses.

Any man who wants to see the President and has a good reason for so doing will not be disappointed. To all visitors he shows the same patient courtesy, and many a foreigner who has complained to him of some wrong has found him ready to remedy it, and to rebuke those who were guilty in the matter.

Diaz has been twice married, having lost his first wife in 1880. They had a son and two daughters. Three years later he married the daughter of Romero Rubio, whose full name is now Madame Carmen Romero Rubio de Diaz., She is a woman of much beauty, and by her natural charm of manner and the genuine warmth of her heart has won a large place in the affections of the public. She is popularly known as "Carmelita," and the President and she never appear in public without receiving universal marks of affection and esteem. Devoid of all ceremony, they ride and walk together, on Sundays going to church as ordinary citizens. They are both devoted to motoring, and make long journeys in an American car. President Diaz does not understand English, but Madame Diaz, who was educated in the United States, speaks the language fluently.

Under President Diaz Mexico has made wonderful progress. In 1876 the country was bankrupt, a prey to civil war, infested with brigands, almost roadless and quite unsafe for travellers or settlers. He declared instant war upon the bandits, and for the purpose of their extermination organized the mounted police known as rurales. He very adroitly made a proclamation offering positions in this force to those brigands who were willing to surrender and swear allegiance to the government. Many of the miscreants took advantage of this amnesty and became the inveterate pursuers of their former comrades. In a very few years this policy had resulted in brigandage being almost stamped out. With the establishment of a strong central government and a well-organized army, revolutions also came to an end.

Then came the great epoch of railway building. Diaz was wise enough to see that railways were what were needed to secure the stability of his rule. Railway engineering was encouraged, large subsidies were granted, and while in 1875 the Republic had possessed only three hundred and sixty miles of railroad, twenty-six years later there were over ten thousand.

Telegraph and telephone lines all over the country completed the centralizing of the government. With these wires complete, President Diaz, seated in his room in Mexico City, could keep his finger upon the furthest and most turbulent portions of the Republic, and could learn of embryo revolutions while it was possible to put them down with an iron hand. It may be said that the thirty years during which Diaz has been President have been a period of profound peace. There have been outbreaks, but they have been evanescent, and the personal power of Mexico's wonderful ruler, year after year, has borne down all opposition.

That Diaz has been a blessing to Mexico no one who knows her history would venture to deny; but that all Mexicans love him is far from being the case. No doubt there are many who do, but with the majority the love is largely mixed with fear; and recent years have seen the uprise of an anti-Diaz party formed of those who resent

MADAME DIAZ.
The charming and beautiful wife of Mexico's President.

his undoubted autocracy. These discontents form what is known as "the young Mexican party," and quite recently there was reported a serious outbreak in northern Mexico, where two secret agents of the Mexican rebels under the guise of Baptist missionaries were carrying forward the crusade in the Mexican States of Coahuila and San Luis Potosi, holding what were announced as Baptist missionary services, with special love-feasts for the elect at the conclusion — the elect being, of course, those who had joined the proposed rebellion. Much mystery surrounded the outbreak and its suppression, and the Mexican authorities have obviously been most anxious to keep all details to themselves.

The presidential elections since 1880 have been merely a form, the voting, so far as the mass of the people is concerned, being a farce. The President appoints his own cabinet and other important members of the government; the governors of each of the States also owe their appointments directly to him. In this way Diaz has surrounded himself with a band of placemen, each and all rigidly loyal to him personally and entirely identified with his policy. The President is no doubt a man of upright nature, has always shown himself above mere mercenary ends, is a keen judge of men, and has thus been able to gather together a number of very able colleagues.

But able as his cabinet ministers are, it is his word which alone prevails. The iron hand which has piloted Mexico through difficulties which seem almost insuperable is still on her neck. Only recently there occurred an example of the almost ferocious methods which President Diaz still finds necessary for the good of the country. A strike occurred in the cotton-mill districts of Orizaba, when the strikers raised the red flag of anarchy, destroyed a good deal of property and ended by killing several non-striking workmen. A few regiments of soldiers soon quelled the outbreak, and several hundred strikers were arrested and imprisoned. A newspaper man in the capital told me that he had seen over two hundred of them in prison one morning but the next day they had disappeared. He had secured strong circumstantial evidence that they were taken out and shot.

While visiting Oaxaca, I heard of a village in the Sierras which had a very bad name. There were Indians there who had committed many robberies and murdered several white men. One day a company of rurales entered the place, seized the culprits, about thirty in number, and shot them on the spot. Such summary measures as these strike terror into the hearts of the lawless, and that is really the only way in which Mexico can be governed. Diaz knows his country thoroughly. He realizes that foreign capital has developed and is developing the Republic, and that lawlessness will frighten away investors. Therefore crime must be suppressed with an iron hand, and it is better to shoot a few criminals without trial than to have the whole country suffer for their misdeeds. This rule has made Mexico what it is, and it is wholly to Diaz that her present splendid prosperity is due.

Under his stern rule, the progress of Mexico has been marvellous. The old Mexican cities have suddenly become busy places, with new public buildings, fine shops, asphalted streets, electric lights, electric street-cars and other visible evidence of modern progress. Remote parts of Mexico, where it was once unsafe to travel, are now visited by hundreds of tourists during the winter months. Railways are being extended in all parts of the land, new factories are being started, and the resources of the country, agricultural, mineral, commercial, are being developed to a wonderful extent. Foreign capital invested in the country has leaped from $500,000 to the huge total of $1,400,000,000. Welcomed by the government, men with money are swarming into Mexico from all parts of the world to engage in business, particularly mining; for the mineral riches of the country, its gold, silver and copper, have not been half developed. Modern accessories and conveniences are being introduced everywhere; adjuncts to civilization which other countries have taken half a century to acquire have been installed in Mexico within as many months. Electric-light plants, modern drainage systems, waterworks and such schemes are being pushed forward. Above all, the children of the Republic are being educated, and the Mexican of the future will probably be a self-respecting, well-informed type of citizen, thoroughly capable of self-government.

After Diaz, what? That is a question which in these years has been asked again and again in Mexico. The President is now nearly eighty, and must eventually retire or die. From my observations I am convinced that no prolonged revolution will ever undo the good that Diaz has done. For a generation Mexico has had peace, and the former revolutionists have nearly all died. The people have learned the benefits of tranquillity, and they are alive to the most serious danger which would menace them were there to occur any grave civil strife. Under those circumstances it is practically certain that in the interest of American capital and American residents the United States would occupy and possibly ultimately annex Mexico. This forcible destruction of their national integrity patriotic Mexicans are resolved to prevent; and if for no other reason than this, they will bury the hatchet and continue to support the stable government which will be President Diaz's legacy to his country.

Another reason for the continuance of peace is the fact

that Mexico is really governed by a sort of "ring" or trust, with Diaz at the head of it. When he vacates the post, the trust will select one of their number to succeed him. There are several strong men from whom this choice can be made. Chief among them must be mentioned Señor Corral, Vice-President of the Republic, who, unlike most vice-presidents, is by no means a man of straw. He is Minister of the Interior as well as Vice-President, and joined the cabinet in 1904. Another strong man — perhaps the strongest of all — is General Reyes, formerly Minister of War and now governor of the State of Nuevo Leon. Señor Landa y Escandon, governor of the Federal District, is very popular with foreigners in the Republic, and is regarded as one of the most enlightened men in Mexico. A notable member of the Diaz cabinet is Señor J.Y. Limantour, French by descent, who speaks and writes English as fluently as he does French and Spanish, and is one of the most remarkable finance ministers that any country has ever produced. In Señor Fernandez, Minister of Justice, General Cosio, Minister of War, Señor Creel, Ambassador to the United States, and others, Mexico possesses a band of faithful servants whose personalities are in a marked degree a pledge of continued peace.

There has been a certain danger for Mexico in the prolonged rule of Diaz. The tendency has been as the years rolled by to blunt somewhat the wholesome Republican control of the government by means of elections. The President himself realizes this, and in his recent interview, Mr. Creelman reports him as saying: "I received this government from the hands of a victorious army at a time when the people were divided and unprepared for the exercise of the extreme principles of democratic government. . . . Though I got power at first from the army, an election was held as soon as possible, and *then my author-*

ity came from the people. I have tried to leave the Presidency several times, but it has been pressed upon me, and I remained in office for the sake of the nation which trusted me. . . . I have waited patiently for the day when the people of the Mexican Republic would be prepared to choose and change their government at every election without danger of armed revolutions and without injury to the national credit or interference with the national progress. I believe that day has come. . . . The future of Mexico is assured. The principles of democracy have not been planted very deep in our people, I fear, but the nation has grown and it loves liberty. Our difficulty has been that the people do not concern themselves enough about public matters. The individual Mexican, as a rule, thinks much about his own rights, and is always ready to assert them, but he does not think so much about the rights of others. He thinks of his privileges but not of his duties. Capacity for self-restraint is the basis of democratic government, and self-restraint is possible only to those who recognize the rights of their neighbors."

The President referred to education as the greatest lever of civilization. "I want to see education throughout the republic carried on by the national government. I hope to see it before I die. It is important that all citizens of a republic should receive the same training, so that their ideals and methods may be harmonized and the national unity intensified. When men read alike and think alike, they are more likely to act alike."

CHAPTER XII

THE MACHINERY OF GOVERNMENT

FLOATING over the public buildings of Mexico may be seen the national flag of the Republic, a tricolor of red, white and green which in some cases bears the arms of Mexico, the traditional eagle on the cactus, and the letters "E. U. de M." (Estados Unidos de Mexico), meaning the United States of Mexico.

Outside of the Republic this phrase is so seldom heard that one is apt to forget that this is the country's political title. The Mexican Republic is, in fact, a confederation of twenty-seven States, two territories and the Federal District in which the capital stands, formed after the pattern of the United States of America, each State having a governor and a state legislature. There is also a Federal Congress, with its place of assembly in Mexico City, which, like its prototype at Washington, is composed of a Senate and Chamber of Deputies. It meets twice a year; and in it each State is represented by two senators, while deputies are elected for every forty thousand of the population.

All this sounds very democratic, but the truth is that the Mexican representative system is merely a paper one; for the suffrage is so severely limited that only a very small percentage of the population are ever allowed to cast votes. Politics in Mexico are, in fact, an elaborate sham. There is practically no opposition party in the houses, where discussions are academic, and can only end in the fulfilment of those resolutions which have weeks before been made

MEXICAN STATESMEN.
Some of the able men who form the government of Diaz.
1. Señor Corral, Vice-President of Mexico.
2. Señor Mariscal, Secretary of Foreign Affairs.
3. Señor Fernandez, Minister of Justice.
4. Señor Limantour, Minister of Finance.
5. General Bernardo Reyes, Governor of Nuevo Leon.

in the Cadena or Chapultepec Castle by the President. Under these elaborate political fictions President Diaz wisely cloaks his dictatorship.

To these burlesques of legislative chambers every citizen is eligible with the single exception of priests, who are excluded from both houses. Senators and deputies are each paid at the rate of $1500 a year. The President is elected every four years, though, as explained in the preceding chapter, this regulation has fallen into abeyance for more than twenty years.

While Mexico has the usual legislative assemblies, it also has numerous law courts. These are divided into district courts, and at the head of them is the Supreme Court, presided over by fifteen judges. The legal procedure is based on the Roman law. In the criminal courts cases are conducted in a manner very similar to that which prevails in France. There are judges of instruction, who institute proceedings, refer them to the public prosecutor and finally present the case before the jury. The latter consists of nine persons (thirty are summoned), native or foreign, who must have occupations, education or independent means. There are also courts of lesser jurisdiction, like the American police courts, and alcaldes or local magistrates, who administer a summary jurisdiction.

Though all this sounds very well, yet with the possible exception of the unfortunate erring peons, no one in Mexico ever gets quick justice. In the courts the prevailing rule is mañana — to-morrow — and from the judge to the usher they are all faithful to this magic word. But the greatest difficulty which confronts the Mexican courts is that involved in cases which concern foreigners. The whole policy of the Mexican authorities is to be civil to foreigners, and in legal matters this is as obvious as it is in administrative. Sometimes, however, Mexican judges are found too favorable to their fellow-countrymen, and then it requires the interference of the President to tip the scales of justice. Such a case was reported to me. A foreign company, so I was told, ran a cable line through some land belonging to a Mexican, with the understanding that settlement was to be made afterwards. Some ground was also occupied for other purposes. Although no damage was done to the property, the company offered the landowner a generous sum as compensation, but he refused to accept it, and the case was referred to the local judge, his intimate friend. This judge ordered the company to purchase the entire estate for $30,000 as compensation. The company appealed to the Supreme Court, which upheld the decision. The case was then brought to the notice of President Diaz. He summoned the members of the court before him and said in effect: "This won't do. You'll have to reconsider that decision. We are inviting foreign capital to Mexico, and if foreigners discover that they cannot get justice we shall lose millions."

The Supreme Court thereupon ordered the local judge to give the case another hearing. This time he decided that the company must pay $20,000. Again they appealed to the Supreme Court, again that court upheld the decision, and again resort was had to the President, who, however, this time refused to interfere. When the company declined to pay, the court announced that their property would be seized and sold at public auction on a certain date. The company retaliated by pointing out that they were the only corporation rich enough to buy the property if the auction took place; and in any case they would see that the facts of the gross injustice should be published in all the leading newspapers of the world so that foreigners might learn what sort of treatment they might expect in Mexico. This threat reached Señor Limantour, the Minister of Finance, and he hurried off to the President, warning him that something must be done at once. President Diaz thereupon ordered the Supreme Court to fix the damages at $3000, the sum originally offered by the company, and this was paid in final settlement. "But," added my informant, "suppose there had been no Diaz to interfere! What protection should we have had?"

The chief triumph of the Diaz régime has been the policing of the Republic by mounted police, or "rurales," who keep order in the country districts; and an excellent and intelligent body of men are one of the bulwarks of the government. But it is perhaps in the capital that one is best able to gauge the astounding change which has been witnessed during a single generation. Twenty-five years ago Mexico City was the prey of as foul an army of beggars, thieves and cut-throats as could be found in any city in the world. Murders were committed by half dozens every night. In the awful rookeries where the scum of the city — thieves, offal-carriers, rag-pickers, pulque-sellers — congregated, crimes of all kinds were planned and carried out with impunity. The government flooded the city with police, but at first it looked as if the forces of disorder must win. When the electric lights were first installed in the city, the vagabonds cut the wires night after night in the neighborhood of San Lazaro, one of the lowest quarters, that they might carry out their robberies unmolested. Even in the Alameda and the fashionable quarters of the city the foulest murders were committed, and it was even suggested that the police were in league with some of the worst criminals.

But the government was not to be beaten. The arm of the law was stretched out into the worst holes and crannies of Mexico City, policemen were stationed at every corner. Prisons were full to choking, and those criminals caught red-handed were transported to the hot lands in southern Mexico as plantation slaves. The result has been more than good. To-day Mexico City is one of the most orderly places in the world. One can walk from end to end at night, unguarded, with little fear of being even annoyed.

But if the Mexican police are good, they are very often arrogant. In street rows they will arrest everybody within sight, and woe betide the man who resists them. The truth is, the Mexican policeman takes himself very seriously. Just as every French soldier was taught to believe that there was a marshal's baton in his knapsack, so the Mexican "sereno" hoodwinks himself into the hope that he is an embryo Monsieur Lecoq, which self-conceit betrays him into a certain officiousness and anxiety to arrest any and everybody on the slightest provocation.

I heard of an amusing instance which illustrates this. An American visitor to Mexico City was seized with a bad cold and compelled to keep his bed at his hotel. One morning, two policemen marched into his room with a stretcher and told him he must be taken to the hospital. On his demanding why, they replied, "It has been reported that you have typhus, and you must come immediately." They strapped him on the stretcher, took him to the hospital, where he was deprived of his clothes, given a sort of hospital nightgown, and put into a ward with a lot of typhus patients. He did not see any doctor for a day or so. When that official did arrive, he asked, "What are you doing here?" The American replied, "They say I've got typhus." The doctor said, "You've got nothing of the kind, so get out, señor." When the American went to find his clothes, they had been stolen. He borrowed a blanket, and wrapping it round him tried to sneak back to his hotel through the side streets. On his way he was arrested on the charge of "appearing in public in an indecent costume," was taken

THE RURALES.
A squadron of Mexico's famous mounted police.

THE AWKWARD SQUAD.
Country policemen answering the roll call.

to the police station and detained there a day or two more, only being released when the U. S. consul interfered. When he complained to the authorities, they simply laughed at him, seeming to consider it a great joke on the Americano. Indeed, one jovial official remarked, "You came to Mexico to see sights, didn't you? Well, you're seeing them. Then why complain?"

Another case which ended in tragedy was that of a clerk who, buying a revolver from a friend, was putting it in the case when it went off, shooting the latter and inflicting a serious wound. A request to take the deposition of the wounded man was sent to the local magistrate, but he was drunk and could not come. Friends of the wounded man, having procured a stretcher, a journey of seven miles was made to the house of the next magistrate, who took the deposition, which was witnessed by the mayor of the village and the chief of police. The man was then sent to Mexico City for treatment, the clerk and two other friends accompanying him. He was being removed from the train when an officious policeman refused to allow him to be taken to the hospital, arrested the whole party as "suspicious persons" and conducted them to the police station, where they were confined all night. Receiving no medical attention, the victim of the accident died from the effects of the excitement and exposure. The clerk was then taken back to the place where the accident had occurred, and put into prison, charged with murder. It was only after expensive litigation that he was liberated.

Yet another case. A drunken Mexican accosted an American clerk in the main street of a provincial town, demanding money. The young fellow pushed him away, and the man dropped dead, undoubtedly from heart disease, as it was proved afterwards that he had been drinking for days and had some heart ailment. The clerk was immediately arrested. The next proceeding was taken by the local magistrate, who called in a butcher and ordered him to make a post mortem examination. After carving up the body of the dead man, the butcher reported that the internal organs showed signs of a blow; and on this evidence the young American was committed for trial for murder, and kept in solitary confinement. When I heard the story, he had been in prison for more than six months, all efforts to get him out on bail having been in vain. The law's delays in Mexico are very tedious, and many months elapse before even in ordinary cases a trial is held. When the magistrate was asked why he did not call in a doctor to make a proper post-mortem examination, his reply was that the butcher was more convenient and the law allowed him to get a substitute if a doctor was not at hand. "Do you think that a butcher is competent to judge in such a serious case?" asked the defendant's lawyer. The magistrate shrugged his shoulders and replied, "Quien sabe?" (Who knows?).

In Mexico the death penalty is inflicted by shooting, a squad of soldiers being the executioners. This, of course, refers to formal executions, of which many hundreds take place in the course of the year. But there are informal death sentences carried out in any number. Quite a usual way of getting rid of a difficult prisoner is the following: While being taken from one district to another, under armed escort, he is told by his guards to go ahead, and is then shot in the back, the cause of his death being reported as "shot while attempting to escape." This is permissible under the old Spanish Ley de Fuega or Law of Flight. Highwaymen, too, are dealt with summarily, being shot at sight. A year or two ago some desperados robbed a pay-car on the Mexican Central Railway near Cuernavaca. They were caught, taken to the scene of the robbery and without a semblance of a trial shot on the spot. At the time of my visit to the capital there were thirty-one criminals awaiting the death penalty in Belem Prison.

For the rank and file of prisoners, Mexican prisons are not so very bad. They are compelled to work, as are the convicts in an American prison, but the whole system of discipline is lax. Smoking is permitted, talking is winked at, and there is a good feeling existing between the warders and their charges. In fact, the discipline seems to be little if at all more severe than that of an English workhouse. There must, for example, be much worse places than the prison in Oaxaca. One day when I was passing,—it happened to be the afternoon for visitors,— the female friends of the prisoners, with lots of children, were pouring into the prison yard, where a military band was discoursing lively music to the convicts who sat round in easy attitudes, smoking cigarettes, gossiping and having a thoroughly good time.

Next to policemen, soldiers are much in evidence in Mexico, the army being an important national institution. The country is divided into several military districts, and in each of these is a certain quota of troops. Nearly every town of any size has a commandancia or barracks. As mentioned in another chapter, most of the Mexican officers are trained at Chapultepec. Over a third of the commissioned members of the army graduate from that institution. The student binds himself for seven years' service, and should he be discharged or refuse to serve, he must repay the government about ten dollars for each month he has remained in the academy. If there is a war, all retired graduates can be compelled to report for service. There is no conscription in Mexico and the soldier's pay is very small.

The Mexican standing army amounts to between 25,000 and 30,000 men; but this does not represent the total forces of the Republic, which at a time of emergency could summon 86,000 reserves to the colors. Of the standing army 20,000 odd are infantry, 2000 artillery and 5000 cavalry, while there are small corps of engineers and others. Infantry and cavalry are armed with the Spanish Mauser rifles and carbines. The headquarters of the army are in Mexico City, and several battalions of infantry and regiments of cavalry are stationed there at all times.

Mexican soldiers usually wear either a blue cloth or white linen uniform, with a blue or white military cap or glazed leather Austrian-shaped kepi. One of the artillery regiments has a uniform of German appearance, blue with red facings, and a bright, spiked brass helmet. Some regiments wear the national sombrero, and in the country districts the nacionales sometimes wear a pudding-basin-shaped straw hat with a ribbon round it. All the cavalrymen have a carbine strapped to their backs, and carry revolvers as well as swords. The majority of the troops are Indians of half or whole blood.

Some of the crack regiments are presentable enough, but the average Mexican soldier looks somewhat undisciplined and sloppy. As to their fighting qualities there is a great difference of opinion, some authorities declaring them cowardly and untrustworthy, while others assert that they are brave and stubborn fighters. The truth is that there are great differences in the methods of recruiting. While the nacionales, who are equivalent to our militia, are for the most part a well-set-up, loyal body of men, the regulars are quite untrustworthy and have little or no patriotism. The explanation is simple. Most of them are men who as a penalty for some crime have been sentenced to serve in the army, thus forcing them into the service, ill-drilled and with little or no knowledge of the use of firearms, so that it is scarcely to be expected that they will make good soldiers.

CHAPTER XIII

A MEXICAN PARADISE

"Go to Cuernavaca," said an American friend, as I sat by a diminutive oil stove in his office in Mexico City one morning, discussing the cold weather which had lasted through the first weeks of November. "Cuernavaca," he continued, "is a place of orange groves and flowers; it is always warm, and it has the finest climate in the world." This certainly sounded attractive, and as I was determined to get thawed out after my chilly experiences in the capital, I decided to take his advice. The next morning found me on a train bound for the mid-winter paradise.

Cuernavaca is about seventy-four miles from the city, and the journey is one that never loses its charm. Not only is the route of the Mexican Central Railway marvellously rich in scenic attractions, but it also has some historical interest. It follows, in fact, part of the ancient mountain trail by which the looting Spaniards passed to and fro between the oceans in the old romantic days. Loaded with Spanish goods, the galleons would sail from Barcelona or Cadiz for Vera Cruz, where they would discharge their cargoes. A large portion of this freight was taken overland, from the Gulf of Mexico to the Pacific coast, being carried in huge carts drawn by oxen, over rough trails through the wondrous wooded mountains. The port of Acapulco, on the Pacific, was a busy place in those days, and it was there that the galleons from the Philippine Islands and other parts of the East unloaded their precious freights of gold and jewels, the silks of China, pearls, jades and ivory. Packed in the lumbering carts, this treasure was borne over the mountains to Vera Cruz, where it was shipped for Spain.

From the train one sees to-day the long lines of patient burros threading their way up and down the mountainside with loads of fruit and farm produce from the hot lands; and in this sleepy, unprogressive country it is easy to picture those ancient pack-trains commanded by the filibusters of Cortés. The railway has already reached Balsas, the centre of a rich mining district in the mountains; it will some day reach Acapulco, and it is safe to prophesy for the old port a wonderful trade revival.

On leaving Mexico City, the train crosses the plain and then starts an ascent, winding in and out among the mountain peaks, always on an increasing gradient, till before the lucky passengers one of the most wonderful views it is possible to imagine unfolds itself. Stretching to the horizon, which is broken with mountains, lies the Valley of Mexico, as the plain upon which the capital stands is called, dotted over with villages and lakes. At this great height Mexico City looks like a toy city, flashing a silver gray in the sunshine and dominated by the two towers of the cathedral, reduced to pygmy size. As the train climbs higher, the semi-tropical vegetation is left behind and the region of pines is entered. Far away among the ridges occasional patches of snow can be seen, and now and again a glimpse may be caught of the great snow-capped peak of Popocatepetl dwarfing the lesser mountains. The highest point is reached at La Cima (the summit) 9895 feet above sealevel. Then the train passes the stations of Toro (the bull) and Tres Marias (Three Marys), the latter so called in reference to three pine-covered peaks near by.

A road noticeably good in a country where the roads for

the most part are execrable runs from Mexico City to Cuernavaca, crossing the line at Tres Marias and disappearing among the pines. This road was built for motoring; the track of an old road was partly used and miles of new road were made, the money for the undertaking being subscribed by motor enthusiasts, assisted by the government. So excellent is the road and so direct the course it takes that it is actually quicker to motor to Cuernavaca than to take the train.

Even at this great altitude peons may be seen ploughing, and in many places the soil seems to be black and rich. Mosses and flowers of northerly regions are seen growing among the rocks. The air, even in summer, is often quite nipping at Tres Marias.

At the gaunt, gray peak of Ajusco, over thirteen thousand feet high, the train reaches the top of the ridge and begins the descent into the Valley of Cuernavaca. You see then the other panorama of the mountain range stretching westward; a sea of rolling hills and ancient lava-flows miles in length, with here and there small lakes and Indian villages dotted over the valley, almost hidden between the mountains, the grayness of the scene brightened by emerald patches of sugar-cane.

Cuernavaca was called by the old Indians Cuauhnahuac, meaning "Near the trees." The Spaniards — forerunners of American abbreviators—shortened the name to Cuernavaca, meaning "Cow's horn." Running through the town is a deep, rocky ravine covered with trees, which probably gave rise to the ancient name. The pretty Spanish-Moorish looking town, with its cream-colored houses, some flat-roofed, others red-tiled, stands on the side of a vast valley, ringed in by volcanic hills and mountains. Surrounding it are plantations of rice and coffee, orchards of oranges and groves of bananas, mangos and mameys.

It is 4921 feet above the sea and combines a tropic warmth with a mild and temperate climate, making it an almost perfect resort for invalids, particularly for those suffering from lung or bronchial troubles.

When I left Mexico City at half-past seven in the morning, the sky was cloudy, the sun was invisible and the air chill. In Cuernavaca there was a clear blue sky, and the sun was shining with all the warmth of a summer day. Passengers who wore their heavy wraps and overcoats were glad to take them off, and were soon perspiring in this balmy atmosphere. Cuernavaca profits by the great mountain range which lies between it and the capital, effectually guarding it from the northern blasts and the depressing clouds which accompany them.

The town is about half a mile from the station, and being shut in by the hills cannot be seen from the train. Outside the station there were three little street-cars, each drawn by two mules; these take the passengers and their luggage down to the town for eight cents apiece. People who are more exclusive can take a carriage for half a dollar and get their bones well shaken in riding over the cobble-stone streets. I rode in one of the tram-cars with several blanketed Indian señores, some señoras in their rebosas and a few white fellow-travellers. On the way the hotel porter pointed me out a hill commanding a fine view of the valley. This is the site of an American model city for well-to-do Americans and others, which is to be laid out with trees and flowers and equipped with all modern conveniences. Already several picturesque white stone bungalows, with red-tiled roofs, have been built. Fine golf links have also been laid down. The scheme has obtained much support, and there are so many people anxious to join the colony that the spot looks like becoming one of the most popular resorts in Mexico.

A "BIT" OF CUERNAVACA.

Showing the towers, domes, and quaint houses in this beautiful town.

Our car, which took the lead, went merrily on its way for a time, and then through the reckless driving of our Indian Jehu ran off the line. All the passengers got out and lent a hand in lifting the car back on to the metals. Later we crossed a fine stone bridge over the ravine or barranca, and then passed through a pretty little plaza with the inevitable fountain and bright flower beds. Growing all over the rocks in the ravine, I noticed a beautiful convolvulus of sky-blue. This I afterwards saw in other parts of Mexico. Then the car clattered down the main street, paved with rough cobble-stones and lined with picturesque two-storied houses with their flat roofs and barred windows. Through the wide-open doorways there were occasional glimpses to be had of quaint patios, cool fountains and flowers of many colors. Thus we progressed to the main plaza, planted with orange trees, where the car stopped.

There are two hotels in Cuernavaca, both under American management. The one I chose had been an old Spanish mansion, and was to some extent brought up-to-date to serve as a hotel. In the large tile-paved patio, open to the sky, were two pretty little gardens filled with tropical plants and flowers, and in each was a fountain of sparkling water. My room, with cool, tiled floor, seemed quite refreshing, and the heavy lattice to the windows was a welcome protection against the blaze of the sun which would otherwise have poured in. For the first time since reaching Mexico I really felt grateful for shade and a cool breeze. My window commanded a beautiful view of the old cathedral and several other time-worn churches, with their soft red walls and quaint gray towers. Later on, when I walked around the beautiful little town, I could understand why it is the Mecca of kodak fiends and the despair of artists who find its glowing tints and wonderful effects so hard to catch.

Adjoining the main plaza is the market-place, with its

thick stone walls and red-tiled roofs. Here, every morning, the Indian women are found selling their wares,— oranges, bananas, grenadines, mangoes and other tropical fruits, with a varied assortment of dry and fresh beans and other vegetables,— squatting patiently on the ground with their little piles of produce before them. The stalls of the pottery sellers, with their bright red stock-in-trade, give a dash of color to the scene. In the centre of the market-place, which is open to the sky, is the circular stone fountain where the market people get their water. Round the market square, under the massive portales, are some queer, old-fashioned shops or general stores.

In the middle of the town stands the Government Palace, a beautiful little building of white stone, which was once the palace of Cortés, and was finished in 1531. The garden here, although it was December, was ablaze with flowers of many hues — bright red hibiscus, great masses of magenta bougainvillea, geraniums, roses and lilies, set in a velvety green lawn, and over all the orange and grape-fruit trees loaded with fragrant blossoms and golden fruit. From the rear of the palace there is a magnificent view of Popocatepetl and Ixtaccihuatl, towering above the clouds, their snow-caps glistening bright beneath the deep blue sky. In this picturesque old palace meets the legislature of the State of Morelos, of which Cuernavaca is the capital.

Not far from here is the venerable Cathedral of San Francisco, founded by Franciscan monks in 1529. This also owed something to Cortés, having originally been a convent which he liberally endowed; in later years it became the parish church, and has now reached its present dignity. It is really a series of churches and chapels, with connecting roofs and walls. In the main tower there is a clock which was once in the Cathedral of Segovia and was a present to Cortés from Charles the Fifth.

The neighborhood of Cuernavaca is full of reminiscence of the Conqueror. Close to the town is the hacienda of Atlacomulco, once his property, and still owned by his descendants, the present proprietor being the Duke of Terranova and Monteleone of Italy. In the ancient hacienda house, constructed of massive stone after the fashion of the early Spanish builders, there are preserved some great wooden chests which are said to have been brought from Spain by Cortés. Some large brown earthenware jars, which are carefully guarded, are also reputed to have been in use in his time. Most of the estate is still devoted to the cultivation of sugar-cane, and sugar refining is its chief industry.

During his short-lived empire, Maximilian had a pretty home, known as Olindo, near Cuernavaca, and here he used to retire with the Empress Carlotta for a few days' rest from cares of state.

I spent a very pleasant week in Cuernavaca, strolling daily about its cobble-paved streets which wind up and down hill, charmed with its romantic old houses and churches. With its background of rolling mountains, the deep blue sky, its red roofs, sunny gardens and quaint byways, Cuernavaca bears a striking resemblance to one of the old Italian towns; but it is more than picturesque — it is unusually clean and well-kept. The last observation also applies to some of its inhabitants, for even the Indians look clean, and their cotton clothing is more often white than gray-tinted. This may be due to the fact that the town has an excellent water-supply and a fine public bath.

A beautiful spot in the old town is the Borda Garden. Near the cathedral is the mansion built by Jose de la Borda, a Mexican silver king who lived in the good old days when George the Second was king of England. Marvellous tales are told of this Mexican Crœsus, who dug from forty to fifty million dollars in silver from his mines at Tlalpujahua, Taxco and Zacatecas. He was a generous patron to the church, and spent a million dollars or more on the edifice at Taxco, fifty miles from Cuernavaca. Jose was a French Canadian who had wandered into Mexico, and there made three fortunes and lost two because of his devotion to mother church. In the State of Hidalgo he built several churches, and his devoutness was such that after losing his second fortune, the Archbishop of Mexico returned to him a magnificent diamond-studded ornament which he had presented to the church at Taxco. The sale of this altar-jewel brought him a hundred thousand dollars, which proved the foundation of another fortune of many millions.

Long ago the Bordas disappeared from Cuernavaca and the glory of their old mansion has also departed. By paying twenty-five centavos any one may enter the old garden which adjoins the long, rambling house, with its tiled courts and patios. Here are trees and flowers of the tropics, terraced slopes, lakelets, cascades and fountains which in all are said to have cost a million dollars. The whole place is in a state of decay, but there is beauty even in its ruin. The stuccoed walls and palisades are a soft pink tint, streaked with green moss; the stone paving and steps are also softened by the hand of time; the statuary and fountains all show the same signs of neglected age. On the little lake, bordered with mango trees, which were loaded with fruit when I visited the place, was a thriving colony of swans and ducks, but otherwise there was no vestige of life in the old pleasure-ground. At two corners of the walls are quaint stone arbors from which there are magnificent views of the valley and the rugged mountains. One of these nooks overlooks the Indian village of San

A VIEW FROM CUERNAVACA.

A wonderful combination of orange groves, palms, and snow-capped mountains.

Antone, with its crumbling stone church, very much like one of the ancient wayside churches of southern Italy.

I spent many a restful hour in the old Borda Garden, and derived a good deal of amusement from the walls of the shady arbors, which bore hundreds of inscriptions by enthusiastic visitors, chiefly American tourists from such romantic places as "Union City, Neb.," "Grimesville, O.," and "Tin Can, Wash." But such comments as "Hey, fellows, Cuernavaca's all right, and don't you forget it," or "Say, why can't we annex Cuernavaca to Grand Rapids?" however well-meaning, scarcely harmonize with the antique. Some of the Mexican young men and maidens who had visited the place had evidently been aroused to a state of sentimental frenzy, and there were numerous Spanish verses pencilled on the stucco — lovesick outbursts such as, "Ah! mi adorada!" (Oh, my adored one), etc.

I shared the garden's solitude with myriads of bright-eyed lizards, browns and bronzes, greens and yellows, forever darting over the mouldering walls or lurking in the crevices and blinking out at the invader of their haunts. But even here one was not safe from the Mexican beggar. The wall at about three feet from the roadway was pierced with a series of square holes at intervals, and as I sauntered down the path I was startled by a voice crying to me from some unknown place, "Un centavo, señor." A Mexican urchin had spotted the stranger and was serenading me with the cadging cry through each hole!

Cuernavaca has a number of visitors all the year round, and during the tourist season, from February till April, large parties come down from the City. In the main street I noticed the "English Tea Rooms," the "American Curio Store" and the "American Tourist's Supply Depot," the outward and visible signs of the tourist invasion. Motoring trips from Mexico City to the town are very popular, and every Saturday cars make the trip across the mountains, bringing week-end parties.

The deep, rocky ravine called "the barranca," which runs through Cuernavaca, is a favorite ride for visitors, who mount the patient burro or the restless Mexican bronco. There are Indian huts amid groves of oranges and bananas scattered through the ravine, and in its winding depths runs a clear mountain stream. A zigzag rocky path leads into the barranca, where an old stone bridge crosses the stream, and toiling up the other side one reaches the little Indian village of San Antone. Here a fierce battle was fought between the Spaniards under Cortés and the Tlahuica Indians, whose descendants are still living on the spot, probably much in the same way as their forefathers did at the Conquest.

I often crossed the barranca to San Antone in the cool of the afternoon, passing the ancient pink-tinted little church, with its mouldering walls and its neglected churchyard, in which stands a moss-streaked stone cross with a half-obliterated inscription. The village street is bordered with rude adobe huts, embowered in tropical foliage, orange trees, palms and sometimes the gorgeous bougainvillea and poinsettia. Most of the natives of San Antone are potters, producing the famous red Cuernavaca ware; and they can be seen at work in their yards turning out vessels of classic shape that might have been moulded in ancient Greece or Rome. There, too, you may see the potter at his wheel, "thumping his wet clay" in true Oriental style. The squatting earthenware makers are picturesque enough; but here and there by the roadside may be seen even a prettier picture, just a young, dark-eyed Indian lassie sitting on her straw mat, beneath the shade of a red sarape, making some bowl or jar of graceful design, her sole utensils being a piece of broken glass and a horsehair. With the latter in her teeth she will trim the lip of a water-jug, smoothing the edges afterwards with the glass, bending her small black head untiringly over her work.

On one side of the village street runs a mountain stream, and here the Indian women, as the evening shades are falling, can be seen washing their household ware and cleansing the linen; while from the huts comes the sound of the patting of tortillas for the family meal and the low, crooning voices of women singing melancholy Indian songs. The smoke from the wood fires fills the air with pungent fumes. Indian girls with water jars poised gracefully on their heads patter homeward from the village well. Peons swathed in their red blankets trudge wearily back from work. Then from the old church is heard the soft chiming of the angelus, and a hush falls on the village as you wend your way back towards the twinkling electric lights of Cuernavaca, the steep barranca alone separating the ancient from the modern.

A bright young mozo with whom I struck up an acquaintance gave me some interesting information about the Indians of San Antone and their peculiar customs. In his broken English he told me that there were two ancient women in the village who were alleged to be witches and possessed of wonderful powers as fortune-tellers. "They take old Indian figure dug from the ground," he said (meaning one of the old Aztec idols), "and then they put burning flax before it at night, look in fire and tell you all that happens." "Did you ever have your fortune told?" I asked. "No, no, señor," he replied, "I too much fear. Our padre he say if you deal with those people you go to bad place." One could easily imagine that an old wrinkled Indian crone kneeling, on a dark night, and gazing into the smouldering fire before some horrible Aztec idol, would make so weird and terrifying a scene that my friend the mozo might well be excused for hesitating to consult the powers of darkness.

No description of Cuernavaca would be complete without a mention of its exquisite sunsets and evening effects. The height and the mountain air conspire to create some of the most glorious sky pictures that it is possible to imagine; such bewildering masses of scarlets, blues and gold, giving soft hues to the snow-capped peaks, and lighting the domes of the old cathedral and the soft red roofs of the houses nestling below. No one who loves nature could stand unmoved before the spectacle of this sky splendor; and one sympathizes with the stranger of whom the story is told that he would stand hat in hand, in reverent attitude, on the flat roof of a house at Cuernavaca, looking towards the setting sun as if in worship. The distant hills, shaded in exquisite opalescent tints, standing clear against the sky, with groups of the white-trunked royal palms in the foreground, crowned with their glories of dark green, make such a picture as lives in the memory forever.

But one might go on indefinitely in praise of Cuernavaca, its wonderful climate and its lovely views, which remind one of what Mark Twain once said of a New Zealand town: "People stopped here on their way from home to heaven, thinking they had arrived." The sunshine and soft, dry air do much to make the place a veritable subtropical paradise, while the delicious coolness of its streets is due to its fountains and streams, which are fed from the surrounding mountains. But above and beyond all its beauties is the wealth of flowers, each little patio being an oasis of exquisite bloom. One street of half a mile was actually bordered by oleander trees loaded with blossoms of pink and white.

There are plenty of interesting sights to be seen in the country about Cuernavaca, especially the Aztec remains, which are very numerous. I made a trip of eighteen miles

AZTEC ARCHITECTURE.
A section of the vast ruins of Xochicalco near Cuernavaca.

one day to the ruins of Xochicalco, which are believed to represent what was once a fortified post or military colony established by the Aztecs to maintain their authority among the hill tribes of the western slope. The ruins, which are situated on the top of a steep hill, are in the form of a large rectangular pyramid, constructed of well-shaped granite blocks, ranging from four to six feet in width. Sculptured in relief on the upper walls are colossal figures of warriors in feathered head-dress, wearing elaborate earrings, bracelets and breastplates. Most of them are broad-nosed, with sloping foreheads — the peculiar Aztec type. Surrounding these figures are feathered serpents, — the emblem of Quetzalcoatl, — and rabbits, birds and wolves, supposed to represent certain years and events. There are also a variety of other hieroglyphics, the key to which has never been discovered. The carvings are wonderful in execution and exceedingly artistic. Some of the warriors might almost have been copied from the sculptures of Egyptian temples.

Remarkably well selected was the site of this ancient stronghold, for it commands a view of the country for miles round. Beneath it there are several passages faced with cut stone, one of which ends in a square chamber 75 feet long and 68 feet wide, which may have been a temple. The central ruin and some smaller structures which are scattered about are being slowly destroyed by time and the rank vegetation, the roots of trees and huge creeping plants pushing their way between the stones and forcing them from their places.

A day's journey to the westward from Cuernavaca takes one to the caves of Cacahuamilpa, which are among the wonders of the world and surpass even the famous Mammoth Caves of Kentucky. In the village of Cacahuamilpa there is a small hotel, clean and comfortable, the proprietor of which provides guides for visitors. The caves have been explored for over twenty miles, the winding passages leading to a series of natural halls, glittering with enormous stalagmites, which are still in process of formation. Some of these have taken grotesque shapes or formed huge pillars of a hundred feet or more in height. One curious figure, called the camel, from its resemblance to that animal, is said by geologists to have taken from seventy to eighty thousand years to attain its present dimensions. All this wonderful subterranean work has been done by the action of water which once flowed through the caves and is still oozing through the rock. Two rushing rivers still flow beneath the caves, and are probably hollowing out other caverns for completion ages hence.

Among the most wonderful chambers is the Sala del Trono or Throne Room, which is upwards of seven hundred feet in length, two hundred and fifty feet wide and over five hundred feet high. An American writer in attempting to give an idea of the size of this immense cavern, humorously says, "If one of the great New York skyscrapers, three hundred feet in height, were placed inside the Throne Room, a man standing on the top of it would need a feather duster with a handle two hundred feet long to sweep the cobwebs off the cavern ceiling." On one side of this vast chamber are two masses of stalagmites and stalactites, forming two beautiful thrones, from which the cavern derives its name. When lighted with magnesium light, the glittering effects of this hall of crystal are wondrously beautiful. Another majestic chamber is called the Vestibule, the walls being covered with stalactites and stalagmites resembling the purest Parian marble, carved in various graceful forms and beautifully polished. Not far off is El Campanario, so called from a number of stalactites in it which give forth a bell-like sound when struck.

The passages are so winding and confusing that it is dangerous to penetrate even a short distance inside the caverns without an experienced guide. A melancholy reminder of this fact is a gloomy cavern known as El Pedregal del Muerto, where the skeletons of two tourists who endeavored to explore the caves without a guide were found some years ago.

The "hot lands" bordering the Pacific Ocean are reached by railway from Cuernavaca, the present terminus, Balsas, being in the State of Guerrero. This important State, which stretches along the coast for nearly three hundred miles, has nearly half a million inhabitants and approximately covers twenty-two thousand square miles. The climate is very hot the whole year round. In this part of the country there is some wonderful scenery, with mountain ranges clothed with the dense verdure of the tropics, rushing rivers, and precipices thousands of feet high. Until the railway is complete, which has as its eventual goal Acapulco, mule pack-trains carry goods and travellers over the mountain between Balsas and the Pacific coast.

Guerrero abounds in prehistoric ruins which are believed to have been in the same condition when Montezuma reigned in Tenochtitlan, and then, as now, little was known of the builders of these ancient structures. Professor William Niven, an American archeologist, says that tens of thousands of ruins of buildings which had been substantially built of stone are still in existence. During his work of exploration in this part of Mexico, Mr. Niven has unearthed some beautiful objects of gold, including idols, amulets and dress ornaments of artistic design, proving that the prehistoric goldsmiths were workmen of great skill.

Some Mexicans believe that the mysterious region from which Montezuma obtained his supplies of gold — which was never revealed to the Spaniards — is situated somewhere in Guerrero. The country is certainly rich in minerals, and numbers of English and Americans are engaged in mining there. More than five hundred mining properties, with a total area of fourteen thousand acres, are being worked in the State. Copper, gold, lead and silver, with other minerals of less value, are all successfully worked, and from the miner's point of view the district is practically virgin. So far, the difficulty of access has kept prospectors away, but with the extension of the railway a wonderful era of mining development is bound to follow.

CHAPTER XIV

THE CITY OF THE ANGELS

THE difference between the American and his neighbor the Mexican is strikingly illustrated in the names and history of their respective cities. In a past age many a ·shrewd Yankee, with an eye to business, induced his friends to start a town, and while growing rich by speculating in real estate, perpetuated his memory by naming the place after himself. Thus we have our Higgsvilles, Smithburgs and other cities of prosaic name. The Mexican, with his more romantic nature and devotion to the church, usually named his town after some beautiful view near at hand, or some wonderful miracle which was supposed to have happened on the spot. It was a miracle that led to the founding of Puebla, a city with a population of 125,000, which claims to be next in importance to the capital.

The story is that a good friar, Julian Garcia, who lived in the early Spanish days, had a wonderful dream in which he saw a beautiful plain near two great snow-capped mountains. There were also two springs which fed rivers of abundant water. As he beheld this vision, two angels appeared with rod and chain and measured off streets and squares as if planning a city. Then appeared a flight of angels singing a song of praise to the accompaniment of heavenly music. The friar determined to find the place he had seen in his dream, and after journeying many weary miles he eventually reached the site of Puebla, which he at once recognized as the spot he had seen in his vision.

As this was sufficient evidence of a miracle, the good old man persuaded the Spanish settlers to build a town there, and this grew to be the City of Puebla, or as it was originally called, Puebla de los Angeles (The City of the Angels).

With such a miraculous beginning it is not surprising that Puebla should have been much favored by the devout in early times. So lavish were their endowments and so wonderful the amount of building which followed that to-day there is hardly a street in the city that does not have its array of churches, their towers and domes rising in every direction. It is for this reason that Puebla is often referred to as "the City of Churches." In former days pilgrims journeyed thither from afar to worship at the many shrines in the old city. It is still one of the "show places" of Mexico and attracts many visitors; but most of these pilgrims are tourists bent on sight-seeing.

It is a curious fact that pilgrimages to holy places are usually difficult and unpleasant. The devout Mahommedan who travels to Mecca does not find it exactly a pleasure trip; and it is said that the journey to Lhasa has enough misery in it to last two ordinary lifetimes. It is probably on this account that the passenger trains of the Interoceanic Railway take about six hours to run, or rather jog, from Mexico City to Puebla, a distance of one hundred and twenty-nine miles. The passengers, I suppose, are regarded as pilgrims, and as such have no rights that a railway company is bound to respect.

This was the journey I took one bleak morning in December, starting at an unreasonably early hour. In the first-class car in which I travelled the temperature was undeniably frigid, and a little steam heat or a foot-warmer would have been extremely welcome. Some of my Mexican fellow-passengers had come prepared for the cold, and took frequent draughts from black bottles, with grateful ex-

THE CITY OF THE ANGELS 237

clamations of "Bueno." As I was unprovided with a bottle, I sat and shivered. There is, however, a silver lining to the dark clouds of even a pilgrim, for as the day went on the sky became clear and intensely blue, while the sun made itself felt to such a degree that the temperature in our car became almost too sultry — the usual contrast.

The journey to Puebla is not without interest. On leaving the city the train crossed the plain and wound in and out among the sun-baked hills, giving occasional glimpses of the snow-clad peaks of Popocatepetl and Ixtaccihuatl. From the hills there were long stretches of barren country; now and again plantations of maguey; frequent dry watercourses; and sometimes maize fields, where the dry stalks remained from the last harvest. Half the trees along the way were bare of leaves, and when there was any grass it was sere and yellow. This, as I have already observed, is the prevailing appearance of the Mexican highlands during the winter months. The only green vegetation to be seen is on an occasional irrigated field.

In the tropical part of Mexico, where there is moisture and rain even during the winter, the vegetation is always green. But for the lack of rainfall and the difficulties of irrigation, the temperate zone of Mexico would be ideal for the growing of all kinds of grain which flourish in Europe. As it is, the great staple food of the Mexicans is Indian corn, several million bushels of which are raised every year, while little effort is made to grow other crops. Wheat, which was introduced into Mexico by a Spanish monk, is grown extensively in some districts; but as there is only enough for local consumption, a large quantity of flour is imported from the United States. This is used for making bread, cake and all the fancy rolls which are served in the better-class restaurants and hotels.

My pilgrimage to Puebla ended at two in the afternoon,

when I reached the picturesque city of white houses and glittering church domes. Outside the station there was the usual array of heavy, lumbering cabs and also some diminutive tram-cars, drawn by two mules, which ran to all parts of the city. Each car was provided with a big gong which the driver clanged incessantly, as if to awaken any drowsy peons who might be in the way.

I took a cab to drive to my hotel, but soon repented of this rash act, for the street paving of unevenly laid cobblestones was simply execrable. In some places the roadways formed miniature hills and valleys, so that my cab pitched and shook like a storm-tossed vessel. In the middle of the streets were deep gutters — so deep, indeed, that at some of the street crossings they were bridged over. I heard afterwards that the streets of Puebla — like those of Vera Cruz, Orizaba and some other towns — were to be repaved with asphalt in the course of a few months, and that electric cars would take the place of the mule tramway.

The Arcade Hotel, where my coche eventually landed me, is conducted in French style by an enterprising Mexican, and it has the reputation of being one of the best in the Republic. I found that its reputation is well deserved. After luncheon, at the invitation of mine host, I went to the roof, where I had a magnificent view of the city and the towers and domes of its churches, some white, some red, others blue, yellow and pink. Beyond the great plain surrounding the town are rolling hills and mountains of reddish tint, in the foreground the gaunt peak of Malinche; in another direction tower the snow-tipped peaks of Popocatepetl and Ixtaccihuatl; and still further off, in the blue distance, rises the snow-dome of Orizaba.

A wonderfully quaint old city is Puebla, and much more typical of Mexico than is the capital. Its flat-roofed buildings, usually of two or three stories, look a good deal like

IN OLD PUEBLA.
One of the quaint streets in this picturesque city.

THE PYRAMID OF CHOLULA.
In the foreground is a peon using the ancient wooden plough.
(See page 244.)

the older buildings in Mexico City; but there is far less rebuilding, renovating and Americanizing in progress. Most of the houses are painted a cream white, but here and there they are tinted in some soft shade of color which gives a pleasing variety. Beautiful, too, are the fine old Spanish mansions in which Puebla abounds, many of them having their exteriors decorated with tiles of superb glazing and ancient Moorish design. These, in some instances, form mosaics representing figures of saints or birds and animals. The city was once famous for these tiles, which were made by the Indian potters, but the industry is now dead and the art is lost. In almost every street one passes church after church, in various architectural styles, some of them huge edifices large enough for cathedrals. Each is of a different tint; some of the exteriors are beautifully carved; the domes and towers of some are adorned with tiles and many of the domes are gilded. The tiled façades of the old houses and the varied hues and tiles of the churches combine to give the streets a wealth of color that would delight the soul of an artist.

Puebla, however, is not only famous for its churches and picturesque streets; but it is closely associated with those inspiring words, "Cinco de Mayo" (the 5th of May), which mean so much to patriotic Mexicans. For it was at Puebla, on the 5th of May, 1862, that General Zaragoza, with a small force of Mexican troops, defeated a large French army, a brilliant victory which ultimately led to the triumph of the Republic.

Still other claims to distinction has Puebla. It is the capital of the State of Puebla, — the richest of the Mexican States, — which is immensely wealthy in agricultural and mineral products. The city is also an important manufacturing place, particularly for cotton goods, paper, and that article so loathed by the Mexican peon — soap. Iron founding, woodworking and a number of other industries also occupy the busy Pueblans.

Puebla nobly maintains its reputation as the cleanest city in Mexico. Its streets are remarkably well kept, streams of clear water continually run through the deep gutters and the sanitary regulations are carefully enforced. In different quarters there are parks and plazas, with trees, fountains, flowers and some good statuary, which add much to the picturesqueness of the city. Perhaps the most interesting of the public squares is the Plaza Mayor, where stand the cathedral and several fine public buildings, including the new Municipal Palace, designed by an English architect. There are some attractive shops in the plaza, and also in a fine glass-covered arcade leading out of it, which resembles the Burlington Arcade in London, but is on a larger scale. Some of the shop windows contain great displays of paper-weights, inkstands, picture-frames, and various novelties made of Puebla onyx in all shades of color, the most delicate being the red and green. Near the city there are some large quarries of onyx, quantities of which are shipped to all parts of the world to be used for interior decoration.

In Puebla, churches, of course, are among the principal sights, the finest of all being the cathedral, which was completed in 1636 and rivals that of Mexico City in size and grandeur. Onyx, rare woods and gold have been lavishly used in the interior, giving it a wonderfully rich appearance. Inside the choir, a superb specimen of architecture, there hangs a chandelier of solid silver which is said to have cost $75,000. The pulpit is carved from Puebla onyx, and the high altar — the work of a native artist — is a wonderful combination of onyx and almost every Mexican marble. Some fine Flemish tapestries on the walls of the sacristy were presented to the cathedral by Charles the Fifth of

Spain. The churches of San Francisco (1532), La Compania (1557) and San Cristobal, of about the same period, are among the scores of churches which give Puebla its title.

The fact that I was in a city of churches was painfully recalled to me the next morning when I was aroused from my slumbers soon after daybreak by such a banging and clanging of bells that I thought an earthquake was in progress.

Being 7091 feet above sea-level, — somewhat lower than the capital, — Puebla is a little more removed from the "northers," but when one is blowing, the temperature at night is far from tropical. When I reached the city, the day was as warm as a fine June day in New York; but when the sun went down there was a sudden change to November, and a good blazing fire would have been a welcome addition to the comforts of my hotel. To while away the time, I went to a cinematograph show, but the cold pursued me even there. In order to ward off chills and pneumonia, I had to wear my overcoat in the hall, and even then I was unable to sit through the performance without going out now and then to get a hot drink. The Indians in the audience wrapped their blankets tightly about them and sat watching the pictures, grimly defying the cold. It was Christmas week, and a large number of these swarthy natives had come in from the country to do their marketing and see the sights. I witnessed an amusing example of their superstition.

An Indian family sat in front of me, and it was evident that they were seeing a cinematograph show for the first time. The worthy peon, his wife and children, seemed bewildered with amazement, and frequently crossed themselves. At last some French colored pictures were flashed on the screen. The figure of a magician appeared, looking very much like Mephistopheles, and in front of him was a pumpkin. This he touched with his wand, and immediately it was transformed into six sprightly ballet girls. After several transformations the wizard touched the figures, which disappeared in a cloud of smoke and flame. This was too much for the Indians. The man rose, muttering "Diablo, magio, no mas, no mas" (the Devil, magic; no more, no more), crossed himself repeatedly and, followed by his wife and family, all apparently very much terrified, hurried from the hall. It is safe to say that these Indians had a horrible story to tell their padre when they went to confession the next Sunday.

As I strolled about the city that evening, I saw some other interesting sights. . Many of the streets were lined with stalls for the sale of Christmas goods, dulces, toys, mats and baskets of colored straw, the crude earthenware of Puebla, colored clay figures and various knick-knacks. There were also gayly colored piñates, some of them in the form of oval jars, handsomely decorated with tinsel and streams of tissue paper. Others were made up in large, grotesque figures of clowns, ballet girls, monks and animals.

These piñates (pronounced *pin-yah-tay*) are the Christmas trees of Mexico, and take the place of those features of the English Christmas in the affection of the little ones. The jars or figures are stuffed with sweets, crackers, rattles, whistles and other toys, and parents — usually on Christmas Eve — hang them from the ceiling of a room or on a tree in the patio. Armed with a stick and blindfolded, the children are then led some little distance away. What they have to do is to grope their way towards where they think the piñate is and strike out at it. Each child is given three chances. Sometimes they are blindfolded a dozen times before any one of them manages to break the piñate and bring the sweets and toys tumbling to the ground.

Thereupon a great scramble for the dainties takes place. The blindfolded child who has been lucky enough to hit the piñate is sadly handicapped in the struggle, as all the others have been eagerly crowding round to swoop down upon the contents.

Piñates are a source of immense pleasure not only to the little folks but to their elders; and the bigger children are especially keen on this Christmas celebration, for during the excitement which ensues when the jar is broken, precocious lads and lassies find it possible to squeeze into each other's hands ill-written little love-letters or to whisper tender words.

Christmas festivities in Mexico begin on the 16th and last until the 25th of December and are called posadas, a word meaning an inn or abiding place. Posadas are held in the towns and cities only; they are participated in by the richest as well as the poorest classes, and are known in Mexico only of all the countries of Spanish-America. They are a memory of the Gospel story of the Nativity, when Joseph and Mary journeyed to Bethlehem and finding no resting-place in the inn were obliged to shelter in a stable. At the celebration, everybody in the house, the family, guests and servants — each one being provided with a lighted candle — walk together several times round the house, chanting a litany. As each prayer is finished they sing the "Ora pro Nobis." The leader of the procession carries figures of Joseph and Mary, formed of clay or wax, and figures of saints are sometimes borne. A donkey, too, often forms part of the procession to represent the faithful creature in the Bible story. At each door in the house the leader stops and knocks, craving admission, but no answer is given.

When the litany is finished, some of the party go inside a room, while the rest, with the sacred figures, stand outside singing a verse which is a plea for admittance. To this the churlish answer is given that there is no room for the visitors, and that they are regarded as vagrants or thieves. Finally the door is opened, and the figures gain shelter for the night, the closing scene of this ceremony being the depositing of the figures on a roughly improvised altar and a sort of mass being said in front of them.

The sacred side of the celebration over, the family and their guests start feasting and merrymaking, and this is prolonged to a late hour. In wealthy houses these posadas are very elaborate, and at the subsequent feast beautiful presents are given to each guest. At Christmas time all the Mexican cities are ablaze with fireworks and colored lights, which are the invariable conclusion for the posadas, the piñates and all the other festivities.

Puebla, like Mexico City, has no night life, and by nine o'clock most of the streets are deserted. After dark the city seems melancholy and depressing, and even during the daytime it is far from cheerful, which is probably due to the number of old churches with their sombre influence. There are a good many Americans in Puebla, and they do something towards brightening up the place. The city has already been invaded by the American book, curio and grocery stores; the American physician and dentist have arrived; and there are numerous agencies for American goods. There is also a comfortable American club, to which most of the English-speaking residents belong.

During my stay at Puebla I went out one afternoon by the mule-car to the town of Cholula, about eight miles from the city. Cholula was an important city in Aztec times and was the scene of a great battle between Cortés and the treacherous natives. Having been invited to enter the city, he discovered they were preparing to attack and overwhelm his little force. Being in the midst of a powerful and warlike people, he was compelled to attack with his six thousand five hundred men an army of twenty thousand Indians. The result of the battle was the complete rout of the latter, the Spanish cannon and cavalry slaughtering thousands of the defeated Cholulans. After the Conquest, the ancient city soon lost its importance and has since been reduced to a small village.

The ride from Puebla to Cholula is full of interest. Leaving the city, the car wound its way among the maguey fields, passed through several haciendas where cattle were grazing among the dry grass and crossed one or two streams where a fair amount of water was running. On every side was the great plain stretching to the mountains, above which towered the great snowy peaks, against a sky background of the deepest blue.

Cholula, like Puebla, was once a place of pilgrimage; and on a high pyramid just outside the town there stood the great temple dedicated to the mystic deity Quetzalcoatl. It was on this spot that he was supposed to have dwelt. Cholula was also a city of temples; Cortés has recorded that he counted four hundred towers in it, and no temple had more than two. Pilgrims came from all parts of Mexico in pre-Conquest days to worship in the great temple. Whenever the people lacked water or a drought threatened, children, usually from six to ten years of age, were sacrificed with horrible rites. The city swarmed with beggars, and Cortés, much impressed by this, wrote to the king of Spain that "they were as numerous as in the most enlightened capitals of Europe"! Of the great image of Quetzalcoatl, which stood in the great temple, Prescott has given the following interesting description in his "Conquest of Mexico": "He had ebon features, unlike the fair complexion he bore upon earth, wearing a mitre on his head waving with *plumes of fire*, with a resplendent collar of gold around his neck, pendants of mosaic turquoise in his ears, a jewelled sceptre in one hand and a shield, curiously painted, the emblem of his rule over the winds, in the other."

The pyramid now looks like a natural elevation, its sides being overgrown with trees and bushes; its base covers twenty acres, and it is about one hundred and seventy-seven feet in height. Around it have been occasionally unearthed obsidian knives and arrow-heads. Excavations at various points have shown that it is built of adobe bricks, clay and limestone. According to Indian legends, it was the work of giants who wished to reach heaven, but the gods, angered at their presumption, killed them before their work was completed. In attempting to give an idea of the size of this great teocalli, Humboldt has compared it to a mass of bricks covering a square four times as large as the Place Vendome and twice the height of the Louvre.

I climbed to the top of the pyramid by a long flight of rough stone steps, and reached the little church of Nuestra Señora de los Remedios, which marks the site of the Aztec temple, razed to the ground by Cortés. In the vestibule of the church were some modern paintings, presented by persons whose lives were believed to have been spared through the miraculous interposition of the Virgin, to whom the church is dedicated. One painting represented a man falling in front of a railway train which was being stopped by the Virgin. Another man was under the wheels of a large motor-car; but the Virgin's hand was on the chauffeur, and the car was unable to proceed. The knife of an assassin descending on the breast of an unfortunate peon was being stayed by the same guardian influence. In another of these pictures a murderous-looking ruffian is portrayed about to empty the contents of his magazine rifle into the breast of his victim; but the weapon is being pushed aside by the same holy hand. There were over a score of these

A VIEW OF PUEBLA.

In the background is the great snow-capped peak of Popocatepetl.

strange works of art, the execution for the most part being of the crudest. I afterwards saw similar pictures in other Mexican churches.

From the front of the church the view of the valley and surrounding mountains, the many churches with their glazed tile domes, and the numerous villages on the plain, with Puebla in the distance, is superb. Old churches are scattered all over the plain, and it is said that over fifty of them can be counted; most of them are isolated, without any dwellings near them. These churches were erected in the great building age of the Spaniards. Many of them were abandoned after the enactment of the reform laws, and some large, imposing structures, half in ruins, are occupied by peons and their families. Why all these churches were built, nobody seems able to explain. In Cholula alone there are about thirty, though it has but five thousand inhabitants.

The next day I took the train from Puebla to Santa Ana, where a horse tram-car carried me, in forty-five minutes, to Tlaxcala, capital of the State of that name, and the site of a great city visited by Cortés at the beginning of the Conquest. The government of the Tlaxcalans was republican in form; they were a brave race, and had reached a high state of culture. As they were at war with the Aztecs, Cortés gained them as allies, and so was enabled to conquer the latter and thereafter to subdue all the other Indian races.

According to some Spanish historians, Tlaxcala at the time of the Conquest had about three hundred thousand inhabitants; but this is probably an exaggeration. Cortés expressed amazement at the civilization of the Tlaxcalan capital, its shops, market-places, public baths, barbers and police. To-day, Tlaxcala is a small town with a population of barely four thousand.

In the town many relics of the past are still to be seen. The Council Room of the Municipal Palace contains some fine old paintings, including portraits of the Tlaxcalan chiefs who allied themselves with Cortés and who were baptized in 1520. In a glass case is a flag said to have been presented to the chiefs by the Conqueror. There are also robes of silk worn by the chiefs at their baptism and the embroidered vestments of the priests who performed the ceremony. So remarkably fresh is the state of these relics that it is difficult to believe they are almost four hundred years old. The church of San Francisco in Tlaxcala is the oldest in America, its foundations having been laid in 1521. It still possesses the font in which the chiefs were baptized, and also has a pulpit from which the Christian gospel was preached for the first time on the American continent.

CHAPTER XV

A MEXICAN CARLSBAD

WHEN a European is suffering from "liver" or kindred ailments, he betakes himself, if he has the means, to Carlsbad or some other popular and expensive health resort. The Mexican also has his little maladies, and likewise a cure to which he hies, and it is known as Tehuacan.

I first heard of the fame of Tehuacan from a man from Minnesota with whom I struck up an acquaintance in Puebla. He was in search of some place in which to recuperate, and had come across an attractively illustrated pamphlet distributed by the railway company, which described Tehuacan as the Mexican Carlsbad. According to this booklet, if all the virtues of European spas could be combined in one, they would faintly approach the efficacy of Tehuacan water. For Tehuacan also had its spa, in the shape of two or three mineral springs, the waters of which were said to be certain specifics for almost every human ill. Under their influence diseases of the kidneys, calculus and other ailments, more or less serious, disappeared as if by magic.

My Minnesotan acquaintance also produced an article he had cut from a Western newspaper, written by some delighted visitor to Tehuacan. This writer had much to say about the beauties of the place, the fashionable folk who resorted there, and he waxed eloquent in praise of the local hotel. "It is not a hotel," said he, enthusiastically, "but a grand old country house, where the proprietor will receive you with true Mexican hospitality; it is not an inn but a home." "That suits me to the limit," remarked the Minnesotan; "I'm off to Tehuacan, and if the place only comes up to that recommendation, it will be different from any Mexican country hotel that I ever struck; for I'll defy any man to get a square meal and ordinary comforts in any of them."

I had, at that time, decided to continue my travels as far as Oaxaca, the most important city in southern Mexico, and to see something of the gold and silver mines in that part of the country. Oaxaca (pronounced *wah-hack-ah*) is two hundred and twenty-eight miles from Puebla, and as it is a dusty, tiring trip in the winter months, my American acquaintance persuaded me to break the journey at Tehuacan, which is about eighty miles on the way. I was not sorry to do this, as I had great curiosity to see a Mexican Carlsbad.

We left Puebla for Tehuacan the following afternoon, making our journey of four hours in a crude, dusty car, stifling hot and crowded with Mexicans. But the scenery along the way amply compensated for any discomforts of travel. From the city the railway crosses the plain, winds among the hills and mountains and gradually descends to Tehuacan through a succession of rich valleys, dropping from an altitude of 7091 feet to 5408, this change of altitude being marked by a corresponding increase in temperature.

Shortly before our journey ended, the train was boarded at a wayside station by a Mexican serving man or mozo, resplendent in a sort of German infantryman's uniform. This gorgeous being represented the hotel at the springs. He condescended to distribute among us humble passengers illustrated pamphlets describing the establishment in the following eloquent language. —

"The table service is unexcelled, even in the most expensive hotels in the capital of the Republic. The dining hall is probably the largest in the country, and is particularly noticeable for the elegance of its furnishings and the scrupulous neatness of all its appointments. Travellers who have stayed at the most famous hostelries of foreign capitals are loud in their praises of the tempting, wholesome, daintily prepared meals served by the artistic chef and his able staff of assistants."

The pamphlet went on to point out that you could not be unhappy or bored at Tehuacan. There was tennis, golf, hunting, and riding in plenty for visitors, the recreations even including a bowling-alley and a church. My companion, with a look of great joy exclaimed, "We seem to be in luck. This place is evidently a sort of Mexican paradise."

When we arrived at Tehuacan, we got on a little streetcar standing outside the station, drawn by two mules, which took us and our baggage to the hotel, some two miles distant. We travelled at a good pace through the dark country roads, and at our journey's end found ourselves outside a picturesque, long rambling stone building bearing very little resemblance to a hotel. In fact, it was what in Mexico is called an old hacienda building, a sort of large country house and farmhouse combined, in which the proprietors of haciendas or estates make their homes. Passing through the main doorway, we entered a large, old-fashioned, cloistered patio, filled with flowers, orange trees and tall banana plants; in the middle was a fountain playing from a wide, moss-covered basin. Adjoining the hotel was a long shady avenue of orange trees and palms. In Puebla or Mexico City the open patio would have been uncomfortably cool, but in Tehuacan, at a much lower altitude, the night air was deliciously balmy; the sky was perfectly clear, the stars wonderfully brilliant; and there was not the faintest suspicion of a "norther."

No one came forward to receive us or show us our rooms; but at last we met a drowsy-looking mozo who spoke no English. When we asked him about rooms, he shook his head in a bewildered manner — probably the effect of our bad Spanish — and walked away. My companion said, "We must evidently help ourselves"; so we opened door after door until, finding two that seemed to be unoccupied, we took possession of them. We then wandered about in quest of the proprietor or his representative, whom we had expected to receive us with "true Mexican hospitality."

A jolly looking, bearded Spaniard was sitting outside the house, puffing a big cigar, talking to the mozo we had encountered, and apparently very much amused about something, possibly our arrival. As the mozo strolled by, my companion asked him who the Spaniard was. "Este el patron, señor" (He is the proprietor), replied the man. Alas for Mexican hospitality!

The hotel was crude in the extreme. The bedrooms, it is true, were comfortably furnished and scrupulously clean; but the dining-room was certainly not what you would expect at a Carlsbad. It was a long room, paved with stone flagging and furnished with an array of small deal tables; at the end of it there was a bar where guests could take a drink between the courses. The waiters were unkempt Mexican mozos with their coats off and clad in dirty vests. The cutlery and linen were of the coarsest description, and as for the food, only a robust constitution and a good appetite engendered by the healthy climate of Tehuacan could have made it endurable. No invalid could have eaten it and lived.

The proprietor was, I discovered, one of the largest landowners in the neighborhood of Tehuacan, having an estate of many thousands of acres. People told me that he conducted the hotel simply to oblige the public and as a recreation for himself. I suppose he had done this on the principle that "what is death to you is fun to me."

My illusions about the dining-room had been shattered, but worse was to follow. I ordered a horse the next day that I might enjoy the wonderful riding the neighborhood was said to afford. The horse produced looked as if it had come over with Cortés and taken part in the famous march on Tenochtitlan. He was far too old to be interested in me or my plans. He stood motionless while I mounted. But then the worm turned. I was the last straw that broke the faithful steed's back. He did not kick, he did not plunge; for he could not have done either if he had tried — he simply foundered, sank to the earth and stretched his weary, ancient limbs upon it. He was lifted to his feet and two mozos pushed him back into his stable. My American friend, as eager for shooting as I was for riding, started out with a gun, but after tramping about the country for half a day, came back with one small quail as a trophy of the chase.

The morning after my arrival I was standing at the entrance to the hotel when I was startled by a voice which said in a strong Western accent: "Good morning, neighbor; I suppose you ain't got such a thing as a kidney about you?" Turning, I found myself confronted by a wiry, wizened Westerner, with a face like a dried apple. There was a look of inquiry and a knowing twinkle in his eye. In answer to his question, I hinted that my anatomy did include a kidney or two, and that I was occasionally reminded of it when I had dined unwisely. "Wal, then," continued my Western friend, "you ain't got no business with that kidney when there's Tehuacan water near by."

He then proceeded to relate how he had suffered mortal agonies for I don't know how many years from acute kidney disease. "I took that durned kidney on trips all over creation," he said, speaking of the offending organ as if it had been some evil sprite with whom he had been doomed to keep company. "I took him to San Antonio, Texas — my native state — and dosed him with sulphur water, but, Lord, it wasn't no good. He kept the upper hand. Then I took him off to Topo Chico Springs near Monterey, and poured down buckets of water, but he only laughed at it. I tried a score of other places that the doctors sent me to, but none of them wasn't any good, and he just thrived on the water. Well, sir, finally I was advised to try Tehuacan, and I came down here with very little faith in it. Wal, I wasn't here twenty-four hours before that durned cuss realized that his time had come. I had him where the wool was short. He squirmed and kicked and didn't exactly like the water, but I fixed him with it and, by Gum, he's kept quiet ever since."

"But," said I, "when you leave Tehuacan, how do you manage; doesn't he break loose again?" "No, siree," replied the gentleman from Texas; "Tehuacan water is bottled and sent all over Mexico, and I drink nothing else." Here he looked around with a mysterious air as if afraid that he might be overheard. "There's only one gen-ew-ine Tehuacan water," he said, "and the stuff they give you here ain't fit to dose a dog with." "It comes from the spring, doesn't it?" I asked. "Yes, it does come from *a* spring," he answered, "but not from *the* spring, the gen-ew-ine one, and that's why I'm just a-going to walk two miles to the right place to fill my little jug." Here he tapped affectionately a wicker-covered demijohn which he carried. "If you like," he added, "I'll pilot you to the place." I accepted the invitation, and along the dusty road, under the blazing sun, off we trudged to the spring.

On our way my companion informed me that there were three springs. The original spring, he said, had belonged to the hacienda, but the proprietor had sold it to a company called La Cruz Roja or Red Cross Company, which bottled the water, the trade-mark being a red cross. In the meantime he had dug a well which supplied Tehuacan water, it is true, but this my companion insisted did not have the curative properties of the original spring. Then a second well was dug in the neighborhood by another company, which also bottled water, and this, too, my Western friend insisted was less efficacious. For that reason he walked every day to the Red Cross Spring to fill his demijohn.

The country about Tehuacan abounds in high, rolling hills of grayish limestone rock, covered with scrubby trees and cactus of every description. On the way my guide pointed out numerous holes in the hillside where attempts had been made to find water. As we crossed some fields, he called my attention to the remains of some Aztec irrigation works, little aqueducts of crumbling stone, extending for long distances, which had been supplanted by the much cruder work of the Spaniards. A great deal of irrigation is still done about Tehuacan, a plentiful supply of water being obtainable when wells are sunk. The gray soil in this district is wonderfully fertile, and there were many green fields of sugar-cane and maize.

When we reached the bottling works, we went to the ancient spring to which the Aztecs once resorted as a cure for their ailments. It has been enclosed with stonework in the form of a well, and adjoining it are the bottling and carbonating rooms. When we had quenched our thirst with copious draughts of the water, which had only a slight mineral flavor and is quite pleasant to the taste, my companion filled his jug. The manager of the bottling works showed us some grayish powder which remains when the water is evaporated. A geologist who knows the district well afterwards told me that all the water comes from an underground stream, and there is no difference between one well and another, despite my Texan friend's assertion to the contrary.

As we returned to the hotel, my companion confided to me that his business was selling kitchen appliances, stoves and so on, to hotels. He knew all the dark secrets of the hotel kitchens in Mexico, and gave me the benefit of his long experience. He warned me against certain establishments in the capital. "Don't go to Blank's," he said, "if you want good vittles. That there place is inch deep in grease, and they have the dirtiest mozos in the city." "How about Dash's?" I asked, referring to a well-known establishment. "Clean outside, dirty in the back," he replied sententiously, with a deprecating shake of his head. "They use canned goods, too, and buy the cheapest stuff in the market." After listening to some of his horrible recitals, I was more than ever impressed with the truth of the familiar saying that ignorance is sometimes bliss.

During my stay at Tehuacan I took a walk over the hills near the hotel, which were thickly covered with cactus of every shape and size. One was a straight specimen, as tall as a lamp-post, covered with ugly prickles. There were round cacti looking like colossal hedgehogs. Others resembled the huge, straight-leaved aloe, but were armed with formidable spikes. Then there was another with a gnarled trunk, like that of a small oak tree, with great extending branches arranged like the pipes of an organ and called the organ cactus. There was also a species which had great flat leaves, and when these were shaken there seemed to be quantities of liquid swishing about inside them. Some of the cacti bore a sort of prickly pear fruit; some had white and others flaming red blossoms. These cactus-covered hills would have delighted the heart of a botanist. Sickly, diminutive specimens of these plants are sometimes

THE PLAZA, OAXACA.
A scene characteristic of life in the average Mexican town.

seen in northern hothouses bearing long Latin names and labelled "Native of Mexico." Here they were growing on their native heath in magnificent perfection.

The town of Tehuacan is more than ordinarily attractive, with its pretty plazas and its wide streets which have rows of trees in the centre of them. Outside some of the old-fashioned Spanish mansions are curiously curled iron brackets for holding the street-lamps. Tehuacan was an Indian town long before the Conquest. The present town, which has a population of ten thousand, was founded by the Spaniards in 1524. Its business is still largely in the hands of Spaniards, some of whom are direct descendants of the families that came over from Spain four hundred years ago. It is a quiet, sleepy place, and was rarely heard of until the advent of the railway transformed it into a health resort.

With a really good, up-to-date hotel, Tehuacan, with its mineral springs, its fine climate and its beautiful scenery, would become a resort well worth visiting, and one where many classes of visitors could regain health and strength. Under present conditions, however, there are too many hardships to be endured to make it attractive to people accustomed to comfortable living. Mexicans do not seem to mind discomforts so much as Europeans and Americans do; and they patronize the place all the year round, some of them coming from long distances. From Tehuacan there was until recently a horse tramway line of thirty miles to Esperanza on the Mexican Railway (the line from Vera Cruz to Mexico City). This has just been converted into a steam railway.

CHAPTER XVI

THE VALLEY OF OAXACA

IN the matter of scenic attractions there are few railways in the world which can equal that from Tehuacan to Oaxaca. As a feat of engineering the line is also wonderful; for in the one hundred and fifty miles between the two places it ascends and descends thousands of feet, passing through deep valleys, threading narrow gorges, winding upwards among the mountain heights, and taking the traveller through the heart of the hot lands and the sub-tropics. It is true that it takes fully eight hours to make this journey, and the dust, in the dry season, is appalling; but there is so much to interest one on the way that the dust is forgotten and the hours slip by unnoticed.

On this fascinating trip I started early one morning when the gray hills of Tehuacan were gleaming in the brilliant sunshine beneath the wonderful blue Mexican sky. It was a fair specimen of the delightful weather I had enjoyed during my stay at the springs, and it made the "northers" of my first Mexican experiences seem like some fantastic dream.

My Texas friend — he of the kidney — came down to the station to see me depart, and he had a parting word of advice to give me. As the train was moving off, he remarked solemnly: "Keep yourself filled with Tehuacan water, and you'll fool all the doctors and undertakers." With this lugubrious farewell I started for Oaxaca.

The first, second, and third class cars of the train were

all well filled with passengers, the latter being literally packed with peons, chatting, drinking, smoking and enjoying themselves as they always seem to do on their aimless wanderings. In the car in which I travelled there were three American passengers; the others were all Mexicans. The railway men — the conductor, engineer and brakemen — were also Mexican and spoke no English. This is not customary in Mexico, for many of the lines, particularly those built with American capital, employ English-speaking conductors at least.

The weather was warm in Tehuacan, but in a few hours it was still warmer, for the train made a steady descent into the hot country. Passing through a wide valley, it skirted a range of towering limestone hills which at times reach the height of mountains; it ran through immense fields of sugar-cane of vivid green; and at last clumps of date-palms could be seen, a usual indication of a warm climate and lower altitude. At Tecomovaca the line enters a great amphitheatre of lofty mountains, far up on the sides of which nestle clusters of adobe huts, marking the spots where Indian villages have been built almost at the level of the clouds. Rocks of varied tints that have been worn into all sorts of strange shapes by the action of water attract the eye, while the views on every side are wild and grand, greatly resembling those in some of the most picturesque parts of Colorado.

Through a deep cañon, bordered by a rushing, roaring, foam-covered river the train ran onward, skirting mountains which towered thousands of feet skyward, with peaks and crags of fantastic shape. Through cañon after cañon, and through more rocky valleys, and the line at last reached its lowest altitude of 1767 feet and the little wayside station of Tomellin, a veritable oasis in the rocky desert, where our train stopped for luncheon. This place is in the true hot country, which well maintained its reputation, for the heat was sweltering. The scene, however, was charming, the station being set in the midst of tropical trees covered with strange fruits, and in the branches of which chattered bright-plumaged birds. But more inviting even than these to the dusty, weary travellers was the railway restaurant where luncheon was served, its thick stone walls and tiled floor furnishing a welcome retreat from the roasting atmosphere outside. Bustling about, superintending the waiters and exchanging greetings in Spanish and English with his guests, was the manager of the establishment, "Dick, the Chinaman," quite a well-known character. He furnishes hungry travellers with excellent meals which are long and gratefully remembered.

After leaving Tomellin, the train began to ascend, winding round curve after curve, between mountains of impressive height and grandeur ùntil it reached the summit at Las Sedas (6304 feet). Here a fine panorama unfolds, the mountain ranges rising one above the other and fading in the distance, the setting sun tingeing each with a different hue. Later on, the country assumed a more cultivated appearance, a few green, irrigated fields were occasionally to be seen, while here and there were masses of magenta bougainvillea and varied tints of crimson and pink flowers. In this part of the country there are many haciendas, with their great houses, granaries, churches and hosts of peons, reminding one of the baronial domains of feudal times.

A Mexican who had been travelling in our train — a very unimposing person — got off at a small station where there was waiting a sort of old-fashioned, lumbering stage-coach drawn by six mules, and about a dozen horsemen in the Mexican national costume, — tight trousers, bolero coats and sombreros, — each with a rifle strapped to his back. This Mexican, it transpired, was the owner of a large haci-

THE VALLEY OF OAXACA 261

enda in the neighborhood, and these were his retainers who had come to escort him home. After an exchange of salutations, the magnate entered the coach, the cavalcade fell in at the rear and off they galloped amidst a cloud of dust.

Towards evening the journey drew to a close, and I witnessed another of those strange contrasts which are so characteristic of Mexican travel. One moment we were passing through what seemed to be a wild country without a habitation in sight; then suddenly electric lights shone out along the roads and a city appeared. It was half-past six, and we had reached Oaxaca.

The journey had been very trying, for the heat had been almost unbearable until the sun went down, and the dust came through the windows in perfect clouds. These discomforts are, of course, experienced to a much less extent by those fortunate tourists who can charter a special train composed of Pullman cars. Travelling in this way, they can escape a good deal of the dust, have iced drinks to cool their parched throats, and cover the distance far more quickly than in the ordinary train. Many of the large excursion parties that come down from the United States during the winter months travel in this, the proper, way to "do" Mexico. Rather a strong constitution is required to enjoy such a trip as that from Puebla to Oaxaca in an ordinary train. At the same time one must needs feel grateful to the railway company, when comparing the present with the past; for it is not so many years ago that people who travelled to Oaxaca were obliged to make the journey in jolting stage-coaches over terrible roads. Nor is the railway company responsible for the discomforts of travel, which are mostly due to climatic conditions.

It is of interest to add that the Mexican Southern Railway, which connects Puebla with Oaxaca, is owned by an

English company and was opened in 1893. The company received a bonus of ten million dollars from the Mexican government, and if it had not received this subsidy it is certain that the line could not have paid its way. There are so few places of any importance between the two terminal points that the receipts must be very small. But it has opened up a rich agricultural and mineral district in the Valley of Oaxaca, and it will probably develop into a profitable property in the future.

A mule-car takes passengers from the railway station in the outskirts of Oaxaca to the centre of the city in ten minutes. I got into one of the cars and made the trip through the narrow streets. The houses along the way were much lower than those at Puebla, being mostly of one story; they were of the same flat-roofed style, but everything seemed to be on a much more primitive scale. As in Puebla also the streets had a wide central gutter and were paved with cobble-stones. On the way the car passed a little market-place where Indians squatted beside their wares, their "pitches" lighted with flickering oil lamps. It was Christmas week, and large numbers of these dark-skinned, blanketed folk had come in from the country to do their shopping. There were many of them in the streets walking, sitting along the curb, hanging about the street corners and passing in and out of the drinking places.

The car stopped at a large plaza in which stands the cathedral and several public buildings; and not far distant was a hotel where I found quarters. It was the usual Spanish mansion, partly rebuilt and changed into a hotel, rather crudely furnished and conducted in a slightly wild-western fashion. Several mining men — Western Americans — were staying here, some alone and some with their families. Among these Americans was one of a type rather too common in Mexico. He spent his time loafing about the place discussing "schemes" and mines with anybody who would talk with him, posing as a mining expert. By some of his friends he was called "Professor ——." His wife — such is the faith of womankind — seemed to regard him as a great genius. Some time afterwards, while talking with a mine-owner of the district, an American, I happened to mention the professor as a mining authority. The mining man shook his head dubiously. "I never heard of the professor," he said. When I told him that I referred to the man at the hotel, and mentioned his name, he exclaimed, "Well, well, calls himself a mining expert, does he? Why, he used to be my carpenter, and a d—d bad carpenter too."

I took my evening meal in the hotel dining-room, a rather unattractive apartment paved with tiles and furnished with the usual small tables and hard wooden chairs. Two Indian criadors (waitresses) who served the guests were swarthy and black-eyed, had long plaits of hair hanging down their backs and wore the popular speckled-blue dress and rebosa. They were picturesque but unkempt. An American mining man sat at my table and I chatted with him. One of the waitresses sauntered up and some pleasantries in Spanish passed between them. The bold criador playfully tapped him on the head with a plate, he made a movement as if to snatch it, and she went off giggling. "You have to jolly 'em along to get good vittles in this place," he said to me, half apologetically, seeing that I was shocked at such goings-on. A Chinaman, who acted as both cook and waiter, took a hand at waiting occasionally, cracking jokes with the criadors in Spanish with a Chinese accent. It was all very amusing.

After my frugal meal I went out for a stroll about the town; the evening was fine and balmy, much milder, in fact, than our average May evening in the Eastern States.

There was a full moon and the stars were sparkling in the clear tropical sky.

Oaxaca stands 5067 feet above sea-level, and at this height in Mexico one always get a mild, healthful temperature.

The old triple-towered cathedral, founded in 1563, is an ancient, imposing and picturesque pile. It stands on one side of a large stone-paved plaza, on the other side of which is a row of shops or stores, rather gloomy and cavernous, such as are seen in old Spanish towns. On another side is the Municipal Palace, and further on the Post-office and Courts of Justice, all fine buildings of white stone with the usual patios. Adjoining the cathedral square is the Plaza Mayor, centred by the usual band-stand and planted with fine old shady trees and bright-hued flowers, such as hibiscus and poinsettia, all in full bloom. There were also several orange trees bearing their golden fruit.

The seats in the plaza were filled with Mexicans of all shades, and there were also a good many Americans — Western mining men, from their appearance. As I strolled past them I occasionally heard such remarks as, "Richest ore in the whole —— country." "Millions in sight," "The biggest bonanza ever struck," and so on. There, too, was my old friend the "man with the scheme," showing his companions a chunk of ore supposed to represent fabulous wealth.

On one side of the plaza, beneath the portales or arcades, were several drinking saloons. Outside some of them were small tables at which more Americans were seated, imbibing the national rye whiskey, and discussing American politics in loud tones. Blanketed Indians lounged against the stone columns, regarding the Americans with lethargic curiosity; Indian women in their blue rebosas squatted against the walls, selling cakes and dulces. At another end of the plaza some enterprising citizen had started an American boot-polishing stand, with a row of chairs on a low platform, with foot-rests before them. Several ragged young Indians accosted passers-by with "Shine, boss, diez centavos," and wiled away the time by romping about the pavement, indulging in all kinds of horseplay.

Facing the plaza stands the Government Palace, the residence of the governor and the meeting place of the State Legislature, Oaxaca being the capital of the State of the same name. A sentry in a white linen uniform, with a rifle and fixed bayonet over his shoulder, marched back and forth in front of the principal entrance. There is, in this respect, a great difference between a Mexican and an American city. In the smallest town in Mexico there is always the armed sentinel on guard outside the official building — the emblem of governmental authority. In an American country town, as we all know, there is not even a policeman, and half a dozen old citizens may perhaps be seen, sitting outside the courthouse or city hall, whittling wood with their pocket-knives and talking politics. Such easy-going ways would not do in Mexico; for there the sight of the armed sentry, typical of force and the iron hand, is needed to impress the natives with the dignity of the government. What is suitable for the Anglo-Saxon is not suitable for the still semi-civilized Indian and the treacherous, half-bred Latin.

With a population of forty thousand, Oaxaca is quite a large place. It has several pretty parks and public squares in various quarters, and many of the stores and other business houses would do credit to a much larger city. Among the public buildings are a scientific institute, a seminary, an historical museum and a public library. Branching off from the plaza are some of the principal streets, full of shops and other business places, several of the largest owned by Germans. There, too, one sees the usual signs of the American invasion—the "American Grocery Co.," the American druggist, the doctors, the dentists and two American banks. The town also has a weekly American newspaper, the *Oaxaca Herald*. An American club has also been started and to this most of the English-speaking residents belong. The members are chiefly men interested in mining, the majority Americans, the others being Englishmen and Welshmen. This club has some very comfortable rooms in the Casino Building near the main plaza, where I afterwards met a number of pleasant fellows and heard many a weird and wonderful story about the mineral wealth of southern Mexico.

Oaxaca is a progressive place, and many improvements are being made. In the course of another year, so I was informed, the rough cobble-stone streets were to be repaved with asphalt, and the mule-cars, which already run out into the country for several miles, were to be replaced with electric traction.

Although it was hardly nine o'clock when I took my evening stroll, nearly all the shops were closed; for all Mexican cities believe strongly in early closing. A street-car occasionally jingled by and gave a touch of life to the quiet streets, but very few people were to be seen. In the residential part of the town, where there were quaint, low houses, with balconies and heavily barred windows, I suddenly came upon a more animated scene. Hearing the strains of music, I wandered up one of the streets, where I found an excellent military band serenading the house of some prominent citizen. The Indian musicians, in blue uniforms, were playing the Pilgrims' March from Tannhäuser in wonderfully good style. A large crowd of peons in their red blankets and great sombreros had gathered in the street and were squatting along the pavement and on the door-steps. Indian women stood in groups, enjoying a bit of gossip. Señoritas leaned from the upper balconies of the houses, while their faithful bears stood below, looking upwards at their divinities and chattering away so continuously that they must have had terrible cricks in their necks. The moonlight, the music and the tender passion probably made them oblivious to such a material thing. Altogether, in its strange contrasts of blanketed Indians and Tannhäuser, tattered Indian women and charming señoritas, it was a wonderfully picturesque and typical Mexican scene.

The next day being Saturday and market-day, I first of all paid a visit to the local market. Along the roads leading into the city from the country came droves of burros, loaded with fruit and vegetables, butter and other merchandise, driven by blanketed Indians. Queer old carts with wheels cut out of solid sections of trees, went lumbering by, drawn by a couple of oxen, to the accompaniment of loud cracks of the whip and constant "arres" (*ah-rays*) shouted by the drivers, the r's being sounded with the long-drawn trill. The Mexican custom of yoking the cattle by the horns seems very cruel, as the heads of the animals are dragged down almost to the ground.

Indians on foot and burro and horseback — men and women — went by in a swarthy procession. Some of them had come over a hundred miles to the market and had been travelling for days. From the hot lands, still farther south, the goods brought to market were chiefly fruits, — oranges, bananas, cocoanuts, limes, pomegranates, aguacates, guanabanas and a variety of luscious, fruity nuts. There was also farm produce, — chickens, turkeys and ducks, eggs and cheese and what not. Women balanced on their heads huge baskets loaded with such wares, sometimes carrying by the legs, in the usual Mexican fashion, a brace of live chickens. On the backs of some were slung brown-skinned, tangle-haired babies, staring out from the dirty wraps which enfolded them, with blinking eyes, upon the world which was so strange to them. The Indian families brought all their household essentials with them, a tin pot for drinking and cooking, a few tortillas, some firewood, and a little coffee; the whole stock of provisions and utensils probably does not exceed in value one or two dollars; but the peon's travelling needs are few. His lodging costs nothing, for he sleeps under the stars, and he will have to buy nothing but a little fruit, a few beans and some spirits. His children often, and his wife always, accompany the peon on his travels, for she fears desertion if he once goes away alone.

The procession of Indians constantly reminded me of scenes in the East, particularly those Biblical pictures of desert travelling, the donkeys, the ox-carts, the women balancing their loads on their shapely heads like the daughters of the Nile, and in the background the white walls, red tiled-roofs and domes of Oaxaca almost like a bit of Bagdad or Cairo.

The objective of all these processions was, of course, the market-place — a great walled enclosure on the outskirts of the town. This was packed with a motley crowd of Indian men and women, wandering about intent on making hard bargains, and the air was filled with the constant hum and buzz of their voices. No one seemed to be disturbed by the dogs, pigs and donkeys in the market, whose barks, grunts and brays added their quota to the general din. Near the entrance were the stands of the butchers, where small pieces of very dark-looking and rather high-smelling meat were being hacked and torn to the size desired by the purchasers. Dealers in fried meats were doing a roaring business, slices of pork and beef being served smoking hot to hungry peons by old dames who did their cooking over small braziers filled with glowing charcoal. The food was amazingly cheap: for five cents a peon could relieve the pangs of hunger; while for a dime he could enjoy a veritable gorge.

Although it was Christmas time, Oaxaca was ablaze with sunshine, the weather being more balmy and much more delightful than the fairest day in an English midsummer. The stalls of the fruit and vegetable sellers were loaded with a tempting array of new potatoes, luscious tomatoes, large radishes, peas, beans and cabbages. There were oranges, bananas, pineapples, limes and plantains fresh from the hot lands as well as aguacates (the vegetable salad), granaditas, mangoes, granadas, cocoanuts and prickly pears. The fruit and vegetables were attractively arranged in little piles on large banana leaves, while such things as dried beans, Indian corn, chilis and eggs were spread on clean cloths. In gayly painted gourds there were sweets, rich preserves and cakes, while here and there was a barefooted Indian girl selling cream cheese and lumps of unrefined brown sugar. There were also stalls where thirsty souls could quaff the freshly extracted juice of the pineapple, lime or tamarind, or imbibe mugsful of the evil-smelling pulque. The stall-keepers sat behind their little piles of merchandise smoking cigarettes, these booths with the jostling crowds which surrounded them making the place almost impassable.

In one corner of the market were pigs and other live stock, chickens, ducks, turkeys and brightly colored parrots. Next to these were stalls where sarapes, sombreros, cotton suits, rebosas and other articles of clothing were on sale. Baskets, mats and bright red pottery of fantastic shapes were sold in another quarter. But the flower stalls, with their fragrant and many-colored blossoms, formed the most attractive sight of all. Here, in this December week, were great masses of sweet-smelling carnations and violets, with a wealth of crimson and white roses, heliotrope, sweet-peas, pansies and wild orchids. An immense bouquet of these — all that you could carry — costs but a few cents.

Oaxaca, like most Mexican cities, contains a number of fine old churches built in the days of Spanish domination, seven of them dating from the sixteenth century. Of these the most interesting is the Church of Santo Domingo, which is not only the most imposing of them all, but is one of the most important in Mexico. After it was built, the great gold-mining millionaires of the district lavished their wealth upon it. The life-size figures of saints, which are in relief, were literally covered with gold, and so rich and so heavy was the precious metal on the walls in former days that it could be easily removed. During revolutionary periods, when soldiers were quartered in Oaxaca, the men frequently clamored for their pay, and as there were usually no funds, it was quite customary for the commanding officers to say, "Go to Santo Domingo, boys, and help yourselves." Having recently been restored at enormous cost, the church is one of the most richly decorated edifices on the American continent. Its interior is a blaze of gold decoration and presents a magnificent sight.

The restoration of Santo Domingo, the cathedral, and most of the other churches in and about Oaxaca is due to the energy of the archbishop, Dr. Gillow, one of the most popular ecclesiastics in Mexico. Archbishop Gillow, who is the son of an Englishman, was educated at Stonyhurst College, and afterwards spent some years in Rome. He has been at the head of the diocese of Oaxaca for over twenty years.

Despite the renovating and modernizing which are in progress, Oaxaca has still an old-world appearance. It is situated in a broad valley surrounded by lofty hills and rocky, barren mountains of reddish tint, which form a striking background to the white city. Viewed from a distance, under a cloudless blue sky, the effect is wonderfully beautiful. On one side of the city, lying close to the hills, the streets have a slight ascent, and streams of clear water flow down their central gutters from the waterworks which are out in that direction.

Over three hundred years ago a Spanish traveller described Oaxaca as "a not very big yet a fair and beautiful city." It was a place of some importance before the Spaniards came. The native inhabitants called it Huaxyacca, meaning "the place of the guages," because the guage tree, useful for its wood and fruit, abounds in the Oaxaca valley. The Spaniards who colonized the place in 1521 abbreviated the name to Oaxaca. The Zapotecs inhabited Oaxaca and the surrounding country when the Spaniards came, and their descendants, the Zapotec Indians, still living there, speak the Zapotec dialect as well as Spanish. Cortés owned vast properties in this part of Mexico, and Charles the Fifth of Spain bestowed on him the title of Marquis of the Valley of Oaxaca, for which reason he was generally called "the Marquis." Oaxaca has a still more important part in Mexican history; for it was here in 1806 that Benito Juarez was born, and in 1830 the city had the further honor of being the birthplace of the present great ruler of Mexico, General Porfirio Diaz.

Oaxaca played a very important part in the revolutionary wars and in 1865 was taken by the French army under General Bazaine. The garrison was then commanded by General Diaz, who was captured, but afterwards escaped. A year later, at the head of a victorious Mexican army, he defeated the French, recaptured the city with all the French cannon, ammunition and stores, then marched on to Puebla and Mexico City. The remains of the old forts are still to be seen on the heights overlooking the town.

CHAPTER XVII

LUXURIOUS LIFE AT A GOLD-MINE

ALTHOUGH Mexico is the greatest silver-producing country in the world and is also rich in gold and other minerals, the average tourist sees very little of the great mining industry. Nor is this surprising, for very few of the mines can be reached by railway, and to get to them one must oftentimes make long, tiring journeys on burro or horseback over rough mountain trails. In this respect the city of Oaxaca is much more favorably situated, as a number of mines can be reached from there by a short railway journey or a day's horseback ride over fairly good roads.

In Ocotlan, Taviche, Ejutla, and other adjacent districts there are numerous mines producing gold, silver, copper and lead, the precious metals being invariably combined with other minerals. Some of these mines were worked in the early Spanish days and even in prehistoric times. One of the best known of them is the Natividad in the Ixtlan district, which is one of the oldest and richest in Mexico. It produces both silver and gold, and from an original capital of $25,000 has yielded many millions in dividends. Most of these mines are controlled by foreigners, chiefly Americans, some being operated by stock companies, others by individual owners. This has brought a number of American mining men into Oaxaca and also a few English, Welsh and Canadian mining engineers.

During my stay in Oaxaca I was introduced to Mr. W. H. Baird of Pittsburg, manager of the Zavaleta gold

TORTILLA MAKING.
Indian women grinding corn on the metate.

MEXICAN REBECCAS.
Indian maidens at the village spring.

mine, some twenty miles out. Upon learning that I wished to see something of the mining industry, he invited me to spend a few days at Zavaleta, which invitation I gladly accepted.

It was arranged that we should start for the mine the same afternoon, and forthwith a horse was found for me, equipped with an American saddle, a great luxury for an unhardened rider, as the heavy Mexican saddle is usually very uncomfortable on first acquaintance. Just as we were starting on our journey we were joined by another American known as Don Carlos,—his name was Charles,—who had been employed at the mine, but was now prospecting on his own account and was going out to Zavaleta to spend Christmas with his friends.

It was about one o'clock when we mounted our horses and rode off through the cobble-paved streets; and as it was market day, we had to pick our way among a procession of burros, ox-carts and Indians, some still straggling in from the country and others already leaving for their homes. The road that we took led down to a wide, shallow river with a long stretch of sandy bed on each side of it. Although the stream was spanned by a bridge, we crossed by a ford lower down, thus saving about half a mile. Most of the Indians took the same short cut, some removing their sandals and wading through the water, others splashing through on their horses and burros. Most of them had two or three ugly looking curs trotting at their heels; for however poor an Indian may be, he is never too poor to keep a hungry pack of mongrel dogs. After crossing the river, a gallop along a very dusty road soon brought us to the open country.

The road after a short distance became a mere trail, and at times when we left it to take a short cut our horses had to climb up steep, rocky paths among brush and cactus, performing the feat with wonderful agility. For mountain-climbing the Mexican horses are unexcelled.

All around us were the towering, barren mountains, bordering a rocky plain, occasionally planted with maguey, and here and there was a bright green patch of sugar-cane or vegetables where irrigation was in progress. Occasionally we passed the crumbling stonework which marks the ancient irrigation conduits which were in use long before the Spaniards came to Mexico. The pre-Conquest natives of these valleys were an industrious race, and there is hardly a hill or hollow where it was possible to collect a little soil that has not been cultivated at some time. These plains, most of which are now arid in the dry months, were then kept fresh and luxuriant.

Among the bright green patches which here and there we passed would be seen a square adobe hut with a few shady trees, a perfectly Oriental picture. Sometimes there would be a herd of goats watched by a solitary shepherd with his crook, in the truly Biblical way. Once we passed a bare-legged ploughman in his white linen suit and big straw sombrero, ploughing with a yoke of oxen, using an ancient one-bladed wooden plough such as is seen in Eastern lands. Above was a cloudless sky, and the sun streamed down with tropical intensity. We were glad to take a rest at a wayside spring where the Indian Rebeccas from a neighboring pueblo (village) were filling their cantaros or tall red water-pitchers and going off with them balanced on their heads.

An American clergyman whom I met in Puebla told me that during a long residence in Mexico he had been greatly impressed with the numerous illustrations of Biblical customs that he found in the life of the people. Some of these had been introduced by the Spaniards, who, at the time of the Conquest, had retained many of the usages of the Moors, who had only recently been driven from Spain. Many of the customs, however, were in common use already when the Spaniards came to Mexico, and have been supposed by some authorities to point to the Oriental origin of the Aztecs or their predecessors.

On our way we passed a hill with a picturesque ruin, an old domed church, built by the Spaniards early in the sixteenth century. Tradition says that it was built by Cortés, and that he immured one of his numerous wives in the convent adjoining it. Mexico is full of legends of the great Conqueror and his wives; at one place you are shown the house where he is said to have strangled one of them; at another, a well where he drowned one; and another, where he is said to have poisoned one.

Zavaleta is about fifteen hundred feet higher than Oaxaca, so that our ride was a gradual ascent. About halfway the country changed, the barren, sun-baked mountains giving place to towering heights of three and four thousand feet, covered with trees, most of them beautifully green. The air also grew much cooler. Onward we rode, up hill and down dale, along rocky roads, some of them so steep that our horses in descending almost slid down, their haunches being so much higher than their forelegs. Sometimes we forded a brawling stream which dashed along its rocky bed, winding in and out among the mountains. At last, about four o'clock, our journey came to an end and we entered the valley of Zavaleta, as wild as any glen in the remote Scottish Highlands.

A foaming stream, rushing down from the mountains, wound through the middle of the valley, leaping through a succession of beautiful cascades. Our road was about a hundred feet above this, and on the opposite side of the valley was a small group of huts of adobe, each standing in a small cultivated patch. Outside these the Indian women were squatting, busily patting their tortillas, preparing the evening meal; the Indian children were playing about in their solemn way; and the pungent smoke of the village fires was slowly rising in the air.

We passed the crushing works or stamp-mill, where the ore is ground, the mountain stream furnishing the power for this and also for the electric-light plant. A short distance beyond we reached a veritable oasis in the desert, a spot of marvellous beauty. Two picturesque stone houses, which furnished quarters for the manager of the mine and his assistants, were surrounded by beautiful irrigated gardens filled with trees and flowering plants in wonderful variety. The houses themselves were covered with magenta bougainvillea in full bloom; the gardens were bright with red and white roses, pansies, violets, camellias, scarlet hibiscus, red poinsettia and jasmine, filling the air with exquisite perfume. Through the gardens ran streams of clear water, irrigating them and keeping them perpetually green.

Baird told me that the houses were built and the gardens laid out by an Englishman interested in archeology who had formerly owned the mine. He had lived in the valley for several years, and while looking after the mine had explored the prehistoric ruins in that part of the country. He eventually sold the property to an American syndicate. Baird added: "If we had started the mine, you wouldn't have found a place like this. American mining men always work first and play afterwards, living in any kind of an old shanty until the mine has been developed and is paying. Englishmen usually do just the reverse. There is a mine in this district," he continued, "which belonged to an English company, and they sent out some young Englishmen to run it. The first thing they did was to build comfortable houses and make a good road to the town, so that they could gallop in there occasionally on their fast horses. Then they laid in a fine stock of provisions, all kinds of canned things, lots of wine, and lived like fighting-cocks. It wasn't surprising that the company couldn't pay dividends. Finally they sacked the Englishmen and employed some rough-and-ready, hard-working Americans, and are now getting a fair profit on the investment."

In point of solid comfort Zavaleta was far ahead of anything I had experienced in Puebla or even Mexico City. Not only were the houses at the mine cosily furnished and electric lighted, but they had — joyful sight! — open fireplaces; and when the sun sank behind the mountains, crackling wood fires were started, and one could sit down and positively enjoy life. Being nearly seven thousand feet above sea-level, with cool streams running through it, the valley has the usual characteristics of a mountain place. During the winter months it usually loses sight of the sun before five o'clock in the evening, and when the long shadows fall the air soon grows chilly; by night it is quite sharp.

The view from the porch of Baird's house was superb; all around were towering mountains covered with dense woods; and there were varied tints in the foliage which strongly reminded me of autumn scenes in our White Mountains. Each of the houses had an Indian woman acting as housekeeper, and during my stay we had very good meals, plain food but well cooked, and the keen mountain air was a great stimulus to the appetite.

On the following day, which was Sunday, I inspected the mine, which was about half a mile from the houses, and consisted of several tunnels driven into the side of a neighboring mountain. Along these tunnels tramway rails were laid, small trucks taking the ore from the mine down the line to the stamp-mill below, where it was put in the crusher. The tunnels were lit with electric light, and as most of them were quite dry, the miner's work was not unhealthy. About twenty peons were employed.

While I was in the mine Baird called my attention to a rude shrine near the entrance, consisting of a small hollow in the rock which held a rough wooden cross. Before commencing work, he said, it was the custom of the miners to pause at the shrine and say an Ave Maria, which was supposed to preserve them from accidents and bring them good luck in striking rich ore. The same custom is followed by Mexican bricklayers, who when erecting a building always set up their crosses in the scaffolding, firmly believing that these will protect them against falls. In factories, too, small shrines are usually set into the walls of the various work-rooms.

Baird's mining foreman was a very intelligent German called Gus, who came from a small town near Bingen on the Rhine. Having been apprenticed to a florist in his youthful days, he was something of a botanist, and when he was not at work in the mine he was always pottering about the gardens looking after the flowers. Another member of the staff was an American named Green, hailing from Boston, who superintended the stamp-mill and made assays of the ores, being a skilled metallurgist.

The gold in the Zavaleta rock is mixed with a certain proportion of silver, iron and copper. During my stay I saw the whole process of gold extraction. The ore, on being taken down to the mill, passed under six heavy iron stampers, which were continually stamping down like steam hammers, hence the name — stamp-mill. These pulverized the ore into powder, which was then passed over a long, slanting metal table coated with quicksilver. Water was kept flowing over this table at the same time, and the powdered ore was thus converted into a sort of thin mud. All the free gold in it — that is, gold unmixed with any other mineral — amalgamated with the quicksilver. The rest of the mud, containing gold combined with other minerals, ran into a box called the "concentration box." There it was dried, eventually made into bricquettes and sent to a smelter where the gold was extracted. The mud containing no mineral runs off in a different direction and is called "the tailings." For over half a mile along the stream below the mill the bank was covered with tailings, and the stream itself was milky white from the waste running into it. Every day or so the quicksilver is scraped from the table and taken to the laboratory and there, with the aid of a furnace, a crucible and other apparatus, Green separated the gold from the quicksilver, the gold remaining in the shape of a small disc varying in size according to the richness of the ore taken from the mine.

Oaxaca is one of the richest mining States in Mexico, and quite near to the city Baird pointed out to me some rocks which he said contained a percentage of copper. The country between Sonora, on the borders of the United States, and Oaxaca is the richest in minerals of all Mexico. It is as yet but half realized by foreign capitalists what vast wealth still lies hidden there. Cecil Rhodes is said to have once declared, "I am not blind to the union of opinion as expressed by scientists and experts that Mexico will one day furnish the gold, silver, copper and precious stones that will build the empires of to-morrow and make future cities of the world veritable New Jerusalems."

Enterprise and capital, particularly the latter, are the essentials necessary for the great mining developments in the Republic, which a few years will probably witness. Good properties are not to be obtained for nothing, and the carpet-bag exploiter must ever meet with disappointments. The Mexican government is thoroughly alive to the value of the land, and good mining concessions are not in the gift of the "man with a scheme" and a piece of ore in his pocket. Many of the richest of the old Spanish workings will yield sooner or later, in return for a generous outlay of capital, fortunes for companies willing and able to take up concessions seriously and install machinery which will make possible what could not be effected by the antiquated methods of the seventeenth century.

The Spaniards overlooked very little of the best yielding properties; but here and there are districts which are almost virgin. For example, southwest of Oaxaca, and not far from the wonderful ruins of Mitla, are to be found free milling gold ores on which work has only just begun. Close at hand are the copper mines of San Baltazar, believed to be the place from which the ancient inhabitants obtained the copper used in the manufacture of the axes and other tools employed in the hewing and shaping of the great stones of which the Mitla palaces are built.

The Mexican mining laws, which are very liberal, give foreigners the same rights as Mexicans. Boards are established in every mining community to look after mining interests. Any one who discovers mineral can take up a claim by what is called "denouncing" it before the board. The ordinary claim is called a pertencia and is a hundred metres square, containing therefore ten thousand square metres. A tax of ten dollars must be paid annually to protect the claim from forfeiture. According to the government reports, over twelve thousand claims have been recorded. The Mexican government claims only a twenty-fifth part of the proceeds of a mine; a fifth was exacted by the Spanish viceroys in the good old days.

Possession of a claim gives no right to the surface ground within its boundaries, and all parts occupied have to be settled for separately. There is, however, never any difficulty about this, as the surface ground can be expropriated

LUXURIOUS LIFE AT A GOLD-MINE 281

from the owner if any trouble is experienced, and as a rule no compensation whatever is demanded. According to law, the owner of land can demand compensation only for the ground on the surface actually occupied by the miners and their buildings. The ownership of the land does not extend more than a certain number of feet under the soil, so that only the surface land actually occupied has to be paid for. After a miner has once settled for the entrance to the mine, he can drive his tunnels for miles beneath the ground without paying anything further. I may add that there is little or no placer mining in Mexico; nuggets do not lie about in the mountains or in the streams as in Klondike and other gold-fields. Nearly all the gold is mixed with other minerals and must be extracted by the process already described or by what is called the "cyanide process," which is much more complicated and expensive. The ore in the Zavaleta mine was blasted out with dynamite and also removed with drills and other miner's tools, and then broken into convenient size with sledgehammers for the stamp-mill.

Hundreds of American adventurers in Mexico go out prospecting for gold and silver, and if they discover a rich deposit they can start a gold or silver mine, provided they have enough money to pay the small government tax, settle with the native under whose land the mineral is situated and do a little preliminary work. In cases where mineral is found on public lands, no charge is made by the government for the surface land occupied, and only the tax has to be paid. Sometimes a prospector will strike something rich and manage to sell out to capitalists and thus make a fortune.

Green and Gus were both practical mining men, and had worked in gold and silver mines in Colorado. They had been prospecting round Zavaleta, and having discovered that the vein of Baird's mine extended to a mountain still farther on, they obtained a concession for mining there and had driven a tunnel into the mountain side. Some good ore had already been found, and they expected to find eventually a purchaser for the property and so become rich. I rode out with them to see their mine the day after my arrival. The way was rough and rocky, and our horses had to climb up nearly a thousand feet to reach the place, the trail winding round the side of a ravine, where a false step would have sent horse and rider down an awful precipice. While crossing the stream which runs through the Zavaleta valley I noticed beautifully cool, placid pools where trout might lie, but there was not even a minnow. I was told that there are no trout in any of these mountain streams. A few of the rivers in Oaxaca have fish in them, but they are not prolific, which is probably due to the lawless methods of the Indians, who use fine nets, poison the water and even blow up the fish with dynamite.

Up in the mountains above the valley the air was delightfully cool even at midday. The mountain sides were thickly wooded, the rocky soil was covered with fine green grass, and beautiful ferns, from the delicate maiden-hair to the large, broad-leaved species, were growing luxuriantly. It was indeed almost impossible to realize that I was in the wilds of southern Mexico. I might have been in the woods of New England in early summer time or amid the Scottish Highlands, except that there were very few pine trees. Birds, too, seemed to be scarce in these woods, and save for an occasional whistle or chirp, silence reigned. There is, in fact, very little animal life in this part of the country. There are a few small gray deer in the mountains, but they are very rarely seen. I also noticed that there were very few insects at this season, no mosquitoes or other troublesome pests usually found in warm countries.

A VALLEY IN THE SIERRAS.
One of the charming scenes in Southern Mexico.

WITHIN THE RUINS OF MITLA.
The wonderful Hall of Mosaics. (See page 306.)

The State of Oaxaca is famous for its scenery and is exceedingly mountainous. Its southern boundary reaches almost to the Isthmus of Tehuantepec in the extreme south of Mexico. It is traversed through its entire length by a majestic chain of mountains (Las Sierras Madre del Sur), rising at some points to eleven thousand feet above the level of the sea. The State is surprisingly rich in its forests and valuable woods, of which there are a wonderful variety, including mahogany, ebony, rosewood, maple, walnut, acacia, cedar, pine, oak, holly, olive, poplar, apricot, lignum vitæ, veneering woods of all kinds and a number of costly dyewoods. Oaxaca abundantly produces Indian corn, wheat, beans, cotton, barley, coffee, cacao, sugar-cane, rice, vanilla, pepper, tobacco, hemp and india-rubber, oranges, lemons, bananas, mangoes; in fact, every known fruit and vegetable will yield abundant and profitable harvests.

The climatic range of Oaxaca is of a most charming character, varying from the cool, fresh, invigorating temperature found in the mountainous districts to that of tropical heat. In the uplands, from five to six thousand feet, the climate is the most genial and temperate on earth, from day to day and from season to season the weather changing only sufficiently to provide a gentle variety without violent transitions. A day's ride from the city of Oaxaca will take you to an elevation of ten thousand feet, where you can kick about among the pine cones and oak apples, experiencing the coolness of a northern October, or down to the hot lands to revel among the pineapples, strange orchids and rank vegetation characteristic of a tropical climate near the sea-coast.

The scenic beauties of the State are unrivalled. Majestic mountains whose peaks seem to melt into the clear blue sky form the background of scenery full of charming peacefulness, of beautiful valleys enriched with nature's bounty of tropical verdure; whilst ravines, cascades and swift-flowing rivers and streams give a touch of the wild and romantic to every view.

The days of Zavaleta were like midsummer, but the nights were cool and bracing. There was a beautifully clear sky, and the stars shone with that dazzling brightness peculiar to the tropics.

If Zavaleta had been in any country less remote it would, by this time, have been transformed into a popular winter resort. A fine large hotel would have been established there, equipped with all modern luxuries; several miles of the surrounding lands would have been laid out as a great park; the streams would have been preserved and stocked with trout. These attractions, combined with its superb climate and magnificent scenery, would make it an earthly paradise in the winter-time.

The country about Zavaleta is very scantily settled, with only an occasional Indian village of adobe huts. Only a fraction of it is cultivated, although its agricultural possibilities are unlimited. What a country it would be if, instead of the dirty, lazy Indians, it was inhabited by, say, the sturdy, industrious peasants of northern Italy! Its barren hills and valleys would then be covered with vineyards and fruit trees of every description. Peopled by an industrious, progressive race there would be no end to its possibilities.

It is pitiful to think of such a wonderful land remaining in the hands of the shiftless Indians. In a country where nearly every description of fruit, cereal and vegetable can be raised, they are content to live on tortillas and beans; their little farms are rudely cultivated; they reap one large crop of Indian corn and then let the ground lie idle for the rest of the year, whereas they might gather two or three crops. Fruit trees might be easily planted or even raised from seed; but that is too much trouble. Nor have they any idea of beautifying their huts. I do not remember seeing one that had any flowers planted about it unless they were wild creepers planted by the hand of nature. The idle peon dawdles at home, smoking his cigarettes and living from hand to mouth. Give him enough tortillas and beans, a little sugar, coffee and tobacco, his wants are satisfied, and he cares not a jot about the world and its progress. Even if his contentment and his preference for the simple life are suggestive of a latter-day Arcady, he is undoubtedly an obstacle to progress and to the best interests of his lovely land.

As I rode through this fair country I thought how topsy-turvy the world often seems to be. Thousands of wretched, half-starved people herding in the great cities of Europe, their minds and bodies dwarfed by their surroundings, knowing nothing of the beauties of nature; and here a great district capable of supporting a hundred times as many is literally going to waste.

I had a good opportunity of studying the indolent habits of the peon's life, for just across the valley the little group of huts was inhabited by typical Indian families. Most of the men worked in the mine when they were not celebrating feast-days; the women, when not engaged in making tortillas, spent most of their time in washing the household clothing in the stream. I often wondered why it is that with all this washing the peon generally appears to be so dirty. By some queer law of gravitation dirt seems to actually fly to him. Here, too, was another of those remarkable Mexican contrasts. On one side of the valley were the Indians living their simple, primeval life; on our side were the comfortable electric-lighted houses with all the conditions of civilization.

Looking across the valley one afternoon, I witnessed a touching little scene. It was a day or two before Christmas, and the children were gathered outside the Indian huts to celebrate the festive season. Suspended from the branches of a tree was a piñate, gorgeous with its colored tissue paper, tinsel and ribbons. The mothers stood in a group affectionately watching the children as they strove to knock it down, one after another being blindfolded, until one grave little maiden managed to strike and break it, when there was a general scramble for its sugary contents. They had probably been looking forward to this little festivity for weeks, and it was all conducted in such a quiet, subdued way, as if generations of oppression and squalor had crushed all the joy from their hearts. With their poverty and pitiful surroundings there was to me something extremely pathetic in this little scene. I forgot their dirt, their indolence and all their other bad traits, for this one touch of a common nature had made us akin.

CHAPTER XVIII

CHRISTMAS AT LOS REYES

To spend Christmas in the wilds of the Mexican Sierras would seem attractive to any one in search of novel experiences. And it was thus that the idea impressed me when I accepted an invitation to accompany my friends at Zavaleta on a holiday-making trip of twenty miles across the mountains. Our destination was the little village of San Miguel Peras in the beautiful Peñoles district, near which place is situated the famous Los Reyes gold-mine, owned by an American company. Its superintendent, a hospitable Canadian, had invited us to spend Christmas there.

Early in the afternoon of the previous day we started on our expedition, my companions being Green, Gus and Don Carlos. "What would your friends in New York think of this for Christmas weather?" asked Green, as we mounted our horses and rode off. I wondered; for, unlike the weather of the average northern Christmas, the sun was blazing down from an unclouded sky with an intensity more in keeping with a tropical midsummer.

We took a rough trail winding up the mountain side, climbing higher and higher, our path at times bordering deep gorges of a thousand feet or more. As we gained the summit of the range, a magnificent view unrolled before us, with miles upon miles of wooded mountains and valleys, and the great plain of Oaxaca backed in the far distance by the towering peaks of the Sierras. The trail at last joined a rough, rocky road, with occasional level stretches where we could indulge in the luxury of a gallop.

On our way we passed through two or three Indian pueblos or villages, always of the same type, a collection of adobe huts, most of them surrounded with a cactus hedge, and one more pretentious than the others serving as a sort of general store. From these pueblos and from some of the scattered huts a pack of yelping curs sallied forth, snapping at our horses' heels. One of my companions was for shooting some of them with his revolver; but the others dissuaded him, as the peons, they said, would follow us for miles, demanding compensation. Some Americans in Mexico arm themselves with small air-guns loaded with ammonia with which to keep off these dogs, which are certainly one of the curses of the country.

Occasionally we passed rude wooden crosses set up in piles of stones, mute reminders of an age that has almost passed away. Each marks the spot where a murder has been committed, and it is the duty of a good Catholic to mutter a prayer for the soul of the victim as he passes, and perchance to add a stone to the pile. In some parts of Mexico there are so many of these crosses that a stranger would suppose that they marked the graves in a wayside cemetery. The Mexican bandit in former times not only robbed, but more often than not killed his victims; and even to this day men do not travel in the remoter districts without a revolver and plenty of ammunition. The mining men who went into the Sierras from Oaxaca, I noticed, always had their revolvers strapped to their belts.

By a continuous ascent we eventually reached an altitude of nearly ten thousand feet and entered one of the most charming bits of country that I had seen in Mexico. It was, in fact, very hard for me to realize that I was actually in Mexico and not in the midst of some peaceful English park in the early summer-time. We trotted through green woodland paths shaded by fine old oaks and other trees common in temperate climes; through deep glades where the earth was carpeted with green, luscious grass, the air cooled by limpid streams which dashed over mossy rocks. All the features of an English June were here save that the woods were silent; there were no signs of animal life and scarcely the chirp of a bird to be heard.

Farther on we came to a long stretch of well-laid road, probably made in the old Spanish days. On one side of this road was a deep, wooded glen; the other was bordered by a high bank which had been faced with rocks, now covered with thick moss and fern. We were now making a descent, and over the tree-tops below us we caught occasional glimpses of a broad valley and wild stretches of forest. Down the road we galloped, and after crossing the valley, a few more miles brought us to San Miguel Peras, the end of our journey.

Entering the village, we passed the casa municipal or town hall, a neat little building of white stone, the parish church and then the usual collection of peon huts. Strung along the village street were telephone wires, which we had also noticed during our journey, connecting the district with Oaxaca and other places. The government at Mexico City is thus kept in direct touch with the remotest parts of the Sierras.

At the fonda or village store, Don Ignacio, the bookkeeper of the mine, was waiting to greet us. He spoke with such a strong Scotch accent that at first I thought he was a real Scot, and wondered how he had contrived to translate Duncan or Sandy into Ignacio. He informed me, however, that he was of Portuguese parentage and having been born in Scotland had acquired his accent there. The Don spoke Spanish fluently, and was of great service in acting as mediator between the mining people and the natives.

A few minutes' ride beyond the village brought us to the headquarters of the mine. Here we met the superintendent, Mr. Alexander Smith, and his Canadian assistant, who gave us a cordial welcome. We had rooms assigned to us over the company's store, a long stone building where all sorts of things were sold, provisions, clothing, tools, etc., many of the miners taking their pay in goods instead of money. A second story of wood had been added to this building, also a large wooden veranda its entire length. In this part of the building were rooms for the superintendent and his staff, including the sitting-room where we gathered and had our Scotch and soda. There were eight of us altogether, a Mexican friend of Smith's having arrived.

The mining property formed quite a little village itself. In addition to the building already mentioned, there was a large, old-fashioned stone house, used as kitchen and dining-room, and adjoining this were various huts occupied by the menservants, no women being employed, and some of the mining hands. Beyond these were the stamp-mill and other structures connected with the mine works. The mine itself was about a mile away, the ore being brought down on the backs of burros.

San Miguel Peras is about seven thousand feet up, so that the night air was much colder than at Zavaleta. At night some of us had five blankets, and even then found it hard to keep warm, the thin, rarefied air being so penetrating. I nearly froze before the morning.

An attempt was made the next day to celebrate Christmas in good, old-fashioned English style. A yule log drawn by two burros was dragged into the big stone-paved dining-room, where it soon blazed in the open fireplace. The weather was fine and warm, although it had been so unpleasantly cold at night.

After breakfast a turkey that had been fattening for weeks was taken to a level piece of ground near the mine and put in a box with its head protruding. Each man then took a shot at it with a rifle, until one of our number managed to hit it. The bird was then carried off by Tom, the Chinese cook, to serve as the pièce de résistance of our Christmas dinner.

Later on, we went to an enclosed field where sports were to take place during the day. The fence-posts were gayly decorated with Mexican, English and American flags. In a tent near by was placed a Victor talking-machine, and there it ground out Spanish and American songs and music all day long for the edification of a large crowd of peons and peonesses. When the talking-machine was first started, Smith remarked to his assistant, who was managing it: "Give them La Paloma and plenty of other Spanish music; that's the sort of thing they appreciate." But he soon realized that the musical taste of the modern Mexican Indian has suffered from the American invasion; for a peon came up, sombrero in hand, and addressing him, said: "Señor, la gente prefiere 'rag-time' Americano; no mas musica Española" (Sir, the people all want American "rag-time" (he pronounced it "rahg teem"); no more Spanish music).

In the field some of the young men of the village were solemnly playing pelota (the national ball game of Mexico), empty gourds having been fashioned into catchers for the ball and tied to their arms. Quite a crowd of natives had gathered in the field, and the padre, a good-looking Mexican priest, came down to give ecclesiastical approval to the festivities. The Presidente, or Lord Mayor of San Miguel Peras, was absent, however, having had, it appeared, some dispute with the mining people, and to show his displeasure had kept away. I told Don Ignacio that I was very much disappointed, as I wished very much to see what a Mexican lord mayor looked like. "Ye havena missed ower much, I'm thinking," replied the Don. "Ye see yon disreputable-looking Indian squatting by the fence. Well, he was the present Presidente's predecessor, so ye can get a vera guid idea of what a village Presidente is like." The old gentleman in question wore the usual white cotton suit, red blanket and straw sombrero, and I rather think that he was barefooted. Don Ignacio further told me that the alcalde or magistrate of the village had been chosen because he was the only man in the place who could read and write! He was therefore regarded as a gente de razon or reasoning man, literally "one who has a mind." It is in this humble way that the peon refers to any man who has an infusion of white blood or is possessed of superior knowledge.

The natives squatted about the field and swarmed around the talking-machine, the boys and girls seeming to be much more interested in this than in the games. Later on, some Indian women came down with baskets of fruit and dulces to sell, so that the place took on quite a public-holiday appearance. During the morning we had football and cricket, the competing teams being composed of swarthy, barefooted Indians.

Later in the day there were a number of sports, such as blindfold and obstacle races, a burro race and finally the great concluding spectacle — a chase for a greased pig. When the pig was turned loose, a host of men and boys gave chase, the squeaking animal scurrying amongst the spectators, knocking down some of them; then it turned and fled back to the field again, where three peons who headed the pursuit fell in a heap on top of it, catching it in their blankets. This, of course, was not according to the rules of the sport as played in England. Each peon insisted that he alone had caught the pig, and each was determined to have it. Two of them drew ugly looking knives and swore by all the saints that they would defend their rights. Bloodshed seemed impending, when Smith plunged into the mêlée, and vowed that none of them should have the pig, as they had not played fair. To prevent hostilities he compromised matters by offering each man two dollars. The pig, the innocent cause of the whole disturbance, was then taken back to its pen. After some argument, the peons came to terms and peace was restored.

We sat round the long table in the stone-paved dining-room that evening and ate our Christmas dinner, warmed by the welcome blaze of the yule log. There was roast turkey, Christmas pudding, mince pie and numerous other good things, and some excellent wine. Afterwards we adjourned to the veranda where a large company of peons and their wives and young men and maidens had assembled for a dance.

The festivities were opened with a dance called the Danza de Sombrero. A sombrero being placed on the floor, a girl and boy danced round it, in and out, drawing near and gliding away without touching it. Then there was the bottle dance, a young Indian deftly balancing a wine-bottle on his head as he danced with his dark-skinned partner. The music was furnished by three natives playing queer old mandolins. Then followed dancing by the entire company to the music of the talking-machine, alternating with that of the mandolins. This dancing was interminable and monotonous, both men and women moving round with expressionless faces, their whole demeanor melancholy and funereal. But they seemed to enjoy it in their solemn way and kept up their gloomy revels until long after midnight.

The air was rather chilly outside, so after watching the dancing for a time we adjourned to the sitting-room to play cards. Later on I went on the veranda to have another look at the peon festivity, and to avoid catching cold swathed myself in a red blanket and put on a sombrero. An Indian seated near me apparently thought that I was one of his own race and spoke to me in his native tongue; but one of his companions, glancing at me, interrupted him. "No es Indio," he remarked; "es un señor; un gente de razon." (He is no Indian; he's a gentleman; one who can reason.) I felt very much complimented. My swarthy friend spoke in Spanish, I presume, that I might see that he, too, had some pretensions to being a gente de razon.

During my stay at the Los Reyes mine I examined some of the workings, which are very extensive. In some parts of them there are traces of excavations made by the aboriginal miners in prehistoric times, and also those of Spanish gold-seekers. Spaniards mined in the Peñoles district for over a hundred years, and were followed by the Mexicans and lastly by the Americans. The earlier mining operations, however, were conducted in a very superficial manner, and it is only within recent years that modern methods have been introduced. Large quantities of paying ore are now taken from the Los Reyes mine; some of it is wonderfully rich, and I was shown several specimens in which almost virgin gold was embedded in the glittering quartz.

Our festivities at Los Reyes ended with Christmas night. At eight o'clock the next morning we mounted our horses, bade farewell to our hosts and rode back over the mountains to Zavaleta. After resting there for a day or two, I returned to Oaxaca.

During my absence large numbers of American mining men and others had come into the town from the country districts to spend Christmas. My hotel was quite well filled. Among the newcomers were various "men with schemes," with some of whom I formed a speaking acquaintance. They had much to tell me of the enormous deposits of gold and silver which were tucked away in remote corners of the Sierras, the whereabouts of which had been revealed to them alone. This mineral wealth simply needed removal, but mining unfortunately requires some money, and my friends with the schemes were short of cash. With true generosity, however, they were ready and willing to share their prospective millions with any lucky mortal who would back them to the extent of a few thousand American dollars.

Cynical, sneering people have sometimes been heard to suggest that the man with the scheme is not a philanthropist, but a shrewd individual, keenly alive to the interests of number one, who has some worthless piece of property and is ready to unload it on some guileless victim. This may be true, but there are cases when the man with the scheme is a well-meaning person who is sometimes victimized by a still shrewder schemer. Of this I had actual demonstration during my stay in Oaxaca. At the American Club I was one day buttonholed by a Greek who, having been born in Wales, called himself a Welshman. He told me that he had struck some wonderfully rich silver ore about twenty-five miles out in the Sierras and that the assay showed I know not how many thousands of dollars per ton. On the strength of a wonderful report drawn up by a firm of assayers who were interested in the property, he had paid down quite a sum to secure an option on it.

One evening my friend, the silver king, insisted upon my going to his quarters to look at the ore and the diagram of the mine. A Welsh mining engineer with whom I had become acquainted at the club was with me, and he was also invited. We went and looked at the ore, which seemed to contain some kind of mineral, and also examined the blue-prints of the mine workings. The engineer, who was a practical mining man, studied the report closely and made some notes. My Greek Welshman, who I could see was an unpractical, visionary sort of person, was wild with excitement, talking incessantly of the millions that he expected to make. The next day I met my friend the engineer and he said: "I have been making an estimate from ——'s own report, and I find that the poor fellow will actually lose ten dollars on every ton of ore that he takes from the mine, the percentage of mineral being insufficient to even cover the cost of working it. His assayer's report is absolute rubbish." He added that many of the assayers in Mexico were grossly incompetent, and for this and occasionally for other reasons every mine that they reported on was, according to their estimates, certain to make its owner a multi-millionaire.

There has been, for some years, quite a boom in mining around Oaxaca, and some Americans have made large fortunes. Each year a larger number of prospectors are at work seeking new deposits, and I heard many amazing stories of finds of rich ores. One mine-owner told me that an Indian had brought him some specimens which assayed nearly a thousand dollars per ton, and offered for a small sum to tell him where the deposit could be found. "Of course," he added, "this piece of ore may have been exceptionally rich, but if the rest only pans out a tenth part as well, I shall soon be a millionaire." Stories like this are responsible for the increasing number of prospectors who prowl about Mexico, spending their days in searching for the gold or silver which is to make them wealthy. A few succeed; but the majority, for a number of reasons, are doomed to failure.

Some of the stories of sudden wealth won by prospectors

are marvellous. I heard of an American who spent several years and all his money in searching for silver near Oaxaca, at last securing a claim which seemed to promise paying ore. He invested his last few dollars in dynamite and blew up the rocks in sheer desperation. The blast revealed a wonderfully rich vein, and he eventually sold the property for two hundred thousand dollars.

There are many other mines than those of silver and gold in the vicinity of Oaxaca, for some of them, notably in the Ocotlan and Taviche districts, are rich in copper and lead. Americans, as already remarked, have been most keen in getting control of these properties, and during the past few years have invested fully ten million dollars in mines and smelting plants.

When I was not occupied in listening to stories of mineral wealth at the club, I found a great deal of amusement at night in strolling about the plaza and watching a line of booths where all kinds of gambling games were in progress. These booths are set up in the plazas of most Mexican towns during the Christmas season, gambling of any sort being dear to the Mexican heart.

In Oaxaca the most popular game, patronized by the richer plungers, was played on a large table divided into squares containing colored pictures of animals, such as a horse, a donkey, tiger, lion, serpent, and over each was a certain number. Players bought chips or counters for ten cents each and staked them on whichever of the animals they selected. A man at the table turned a wheel containing as many balls as there were animals, and each bearing a number corresponding to that marked on the animal. Whichever ball eventually dropped out of the wheel was the winning number. This table was usually surrounded by a large crowd of both sexes. When the wheel was turned and the winning number dropped out, the dealer would shout, "Burro," "Tigre" or "Elephante," as the case might be. A certain number of the losing counters were subtracted by the proprietor as his percentage and the remainder, divided among the winners, were exchangeable for money at their face value. There were also tables for faro, monte (the three-card game), roulette, etc., the betting being for any amount from a centavo to a dollar. There were even booths where little boys and girls sat gambling away their pennies at a simple sort of game with picture-cards, on which were rude pictures of a cow, a boy, a man or a horse.

In these street festivities many Americans were showing keen interest, especially those who had come in from the mines for the fiesta week. Groups of them usually stood around the gambling booths. There is quite a large American colony in Oaxaca, and one of the districts where most of the Americans have their homes is becoming gradually Americanized. The colony has built two churches, and I believe that an American school has also been established. Most of the American women whose husbands are engaged in mining prefer to live in the town, where they can have some recreation, meet other Americans and escape the discomforts of the mining camps. There are quite a number of American children in Oaxaca, and these Yankee boys and girls astonish the Mexicans by their free and independent ways.

In Oaxaca the home life of the Mexicans can be studied to even better advantage than in the capital, and this is especially true of the shopping arrangements. The grocers' stores, for instance, are extremely interesting; they have a strange, old-world appearance, and are conducted in a manner which gives a very good insight into the domestic customs of the people.

Almost every large grocery store in Mexico is owned by Spaniards, just as many dry-goods establishments are owned by Frenchmen, and hardware stores by Germans, and all of them are alike. Behind an unpolished zinc counter are arranged the shelves and pyramids of dust-covered bottles of liquor. At one side is a small bar-room. The salesmen are always Spanish or Mexican youths in their shirt-sleeves, with grimy hands, and they slam each piece of silver on the counter to test its metal with an almost vindictive motion. A big business is done each day, although it takes a hundred sales to aggregate a dollar; for, as already mentioned, everything in Mexico is bought by the day's supply or even for one meal. At a grocer's store you can buy a cent's worth of sugar, tea or coffee. The grocer will not permit a customer with one cent to escape, and he will break a package of cigarettes to sell a pennyworth with the same apparent alacrity as he pours out a centavo glass of Mexican fire-water. When not engaged in waiting on customers, the shop hands employ their time weighing out small one- and two-cent packages of various classes of staple articles, deftly doubling and fastening the old newspaper wrapper without a sign of a string. When the rush comes, just before the meal hours, these boys hop from one side of the store to the other, grabbing the ready-made packages with the greatest swiftness, supplying the many wants of the cooks in short order.

Oaxaca saw the old year out in a very noisy fashion. At half-past eleven, on the night of December 31, a military band paraded the streets, playing stirring music, and shortly before midnight stationed itself in the plaza and played the Mexican National Anthem. Then all the church bells in the city commenced banging and clanging, excited citizens leaned from their windows and fired off rifles and pistols or exploded fireworks till the din was deafening. With this uproar the new year was ushered in.

CHAPTER XIX

PREHISTORIC MEXICO

THE more one travels in Mexico the more does one become impressed with the fact that it is a country of old races of ancient civilizations and a wonderful past. Scattered all over the land are the ruins of cities, palaces, temples and fortresses, the architecture and extent of which are amazing to even the present age. Of their builders little or nothing is known. They may have lived thousands of years ago and may even have been contemporary with the people of Nineveh.

The traces of these ancient races are especially numerous in the Valley of Oaxaca, where the plains and hills abound in the remains of their wonderful works. Notable among these are the ruins on the summit of Monte Alban, about five miles from Oaxaca. Monte Alban and other mountains near Oaxaca rise abruptly from the plain like huge pyramids to a height of four thousand feet or more. On most of them there are traces of prehistoric dwellings or temples. Some scientific men have a theory that the plain in the early days of the world was under water, and that the mountains were then islands inhabited by various semi-civilized tribes.

Early in January, in company with an American friend, I went out to Monte Alban, the foot of which we reached after a hot and dusty ride. Here we took a rough, winding trail which led to the summit, and so steep that our panting horses had to make frequent stops to get their breath. Halfway up the mountain side we noticed what seemed to be the remains of former fortress walls almost completely buried in the earth.

On the summit of the mountain, many acres in extent, were a number of mounds of earth about twenty-five feet high, with steep sides. In all directions were great masses of stones which had formed temples or forts, and below some of these were narrow subterranean passages and immense sculptured blocks. One of these mounds had been excavated, revealing a massively constructed court nine hundred feet long and two hundred feet wide. It is of rectangular shape, is built of huge square stones and faces the west. During the excavations at this point some necklaces of agate, fragments of worked obsidian (volcanic glass) and golden ornaments of fine workmanship were found.

A peon and his boy, who joined us while we were examining the ruins, volunteered to show us the sights. They took us to another mound which had, by the law which has recently come into force, been partly excavated by the government archæologists, who alone are permitted to explore any of the Mexican ruins. Their investigations had disclosed four large, rudely sculptured stone figures in bas relief of more than life size, seated in a row like the figures found in Egyptian temples. Some of them resemble the Aztec figures in the National Museum of Mexico, but one has pronounced Mongolian features and what looks like a Chinaman's pigtail. "Who are these fellows?" my companion asked the peon. Pointing to them, one after another, he replied, "San Miguel, San Jose, San Pedro and King Montezuma," the last being the figure with the pigtail. That is how the peon had solved the problem which perplexes scientific men.

All theories as to the age of these ruins are mere guesswork. Some archæologists declare them to be thousands of years old — perhaps older than Nineveh. Nobody knows. They are traditionally stated to have existed when the Aztecs came to Mexico; but Aztec traditions are quite untrustworthy.

Guided by our peon, we crawled through an opening in one of the mounds. The entrance was built in a perfect square, the builders of Alban not knowing anything of the building of arches with keystones. In the cavernous interior of the mound, lined with solid square stones, we disturbed a number of bats which came whizzing about our heads until we emerged through another square door at the other side.

Nearly all the ruins on Monte Alban are covered with mounds of earth which has collected and covered them in the course of ages. From their position it is surmised that they formed part of an ancient stronghold or place of refuge for the ancient inhabitants in time of war. The fact that a number of stone idols have been found among the ruins seems also to prove that some of the structures were used as temples.

Still more wonderful in size, extent and architecture are the famous ruins of Mitla, a great city of prehistoric times and now the site of a small Indian village. The journey of twenty-five miles from Oaxaca to Mitla is not without its discomforts and, like many other Mexican sight-seeing trips, requires a great deal of time, patience and physical endurance. The first stage of the journey is generally accomplished in a little street-car drawn by two mules, which runs to the village of Tula, six miles distant; and it was in this queer little conveyance that I started off on my expedition to Mitla early one morning.

Leaving the cobble-paved streets of Oaxaca, the car went along a country road between fields of sugar-cane and the ubiquitous maguey. Then it crossed a treeless, sun-baked plain which extends to the mountains, relieved only by an occasional green, irrigated field. In the midst of this plain is situated the little village of Tula, a place of adobe huts, cactus hedges and Indians. Rising from among the rather squalid dwellings are the towers of a large, ancient church, brightly tinted and picturesque, embowered in a mass of tropical verdure.

In the churchyard, which is unusually well kept, stands the famous "big tree of Tula," one of the tree-monarchs of the world. It is an ahuetl or species of cypress, and its age is unknown, but when Cortés came with his army and rested under it, the natives of the district had traditions that it had stood there when their forefathers came to the Valley of Oaxaca. It may have given shade to the builders of Mitla. Truly impressive in size and appearance is the "big tree." Six feet from the ground it is over one hundred and fifty-four feet round the trunk, and twenty-eight people with outstretched arms touching each other's finger-tips can barely complete the circuit. The trunk is a group of compact sections something like that of the cottonwood trees, and towers up to a great height. Standing under the sombre, wide-spreading foliage, one gains an impression of awe and solemnity, a feeling such as might be experienced in the dim cloisters of some ancient cathedral. On one side of this giant of the forest is a tablet with an inscription by Humboldt, the German traveller and scientist, who visited Tula and Mitla in 1806. It has been there so long that the bark has grown over it, obliterating part of the inscription.

A light American buggy, drawn by two mules, and driven by a taciturn peon, took me from Tula to Mitla, a distance of some twenty miles. Our road led over the plain, dotted here and there with Indian pueblos and haciendas; then on to the quaint old town of Tlacolula, with its cactus-hedged lanes, and pretty little plaza, its beautiful domed church, picturesque old inn and casa municipal. A short stop was made here, and it gave me an opportunity to see the interior of the parish church, which is famous for its altar, the front of which is covered with plates of solid silver, ornamented with elaborate repoussé work; the altar candelabra, which are over five feet high, and the exquisite lamps are also of silver.

On leaving Tlacolula we entered a broad valley where hundreds of huge boulders, weighing thousands of tons, were scattered about; all around was an arid, rocky country. A few miles of this, across the wide, rocky bed of a stream, then dried to a brooklet, but a large river in the rainy season, led to our journey's end at the hospitable hacienda of Don Felix Quero.

The owner of a typical Mexican hacienda, Don Felix provides accommodation for travellers who visit Mitla; and connected with his house is the general store of the district, of which he is sole proprietor. Here the Indians come to trade for provisions and the luxuries of life and spend their meagre centavos. Don Felix and his swarthy son are kept busy every evening selling such things as a centavo's worth of coffee or two centavos' worth of cigarettes and mescal, or half a cent's worth of lard, sugar, salt or matches. Some of the wealthier Indians — the peon millionaires — will actually buy five or ten cents' worth of aguardiente (fire-water) or such an almost unheard-of luxury as a five-cent cigar.

The next morning, in sunshine which was positively grilling, I went out to see the ruins, which are but a short distance from the hacienda. Passing through the village, with its thatched huts almost hidden behind hedges of tall cactus, a few minutes' walk along the dusty road brought me to the wonderful structures of prehistoric Mexico.

Extending for some distance were mounds of earth, masses of fallen masonry, huge blocks and piles of débris; in the midst of all this was a series of long, low buildings of massive stone bearing a striking resemblance to the temples of ancient Egypt. Some were almost demolished; others were in a fairly good state of preservation.

The Mitla ruins consist of four distinct groups facing the four points of the compass, and which were originally of the same general style, the north group being the best preserved. In both the north and south groups are four-walled courts built round a central patio and also having their lines agreeing with the compass points. Along the entire front of each of these buildings is a broad, stone-paved terrace broken by wide flights of steps which lead to square Egyptian doorways. But in marked contrast to the structures of early Egypt the outer walls of the edifices at Mitla are composed of oblong panels decorated with typical Grecques and arabesques, about fifteen geometrical designs being employed. When viewed at a distance, these seem to be carved in the stonework; but a closer inspection reveals that the effect has been produced by thousands of small pieces of stone let into the face of the building and fitted together so accurately that no cement was required. In some cases the lower parts of the walls are faced with rows of stones so finely polished that they have the appearance of having been made in a mould.

Wonderfully impressive is the simple dignity of these prehistoric structures, the architecture and construction of which have won the admiration of every archæologist who has visited Mitla. "The walls," says an American technical writer, "present the appearance of preserving the most absolutely pure lines, and one is filled with astonishment when it is considered what a number of centuries have passed since these pretentious palaces or temples were built. The excellent workmanship shown in these structures is such that, with the remarkable precision displayed in the cutting of the stones and their elaborate ornamentation, they must in their prime have presented a wonderful aspect."

One of the most impressive features of the ruins is the Hall of Monoliths, a great corridor extending through the entire length of the north court, a vast structure which covers eight thousand square feet. Standing in a row in the centre of this hall are six massive monolithic columns, each over eleven feet high and about eight feet round, each of them quite plain and without any pedestal or capital. From here a dark passage leads into a second hall surrounded by four smaller rooms, one of which, known as the Audience Chamber, is beautifully decorated in stone mosaic and is in almost perfect condition. In each of these rooms are square niches faced with heavy stone, somewhat of the piscina type, and believed to have been shrines in which were placed small figures of gods. In one of the rooms, called the Hall of Mosaics, which has inlaid ornamentation of exquisite design, the walls in some places show signs of having been covered with a hard plaster and richly colored, some traces of dark red paint still remaining.

The ancient builders not only used stone but bricks composed of adobe and pulverized rock, possessing wonderful durability. All the structures are decorated in the same intricate manner; all are without windows; and each is entered by three large square doorways side by side, the lintels being formed of huge monoliths eighteen feet long, five feet wide and four feet high. In architecture and general appearance the ruins of Mitla differ entirely from those in other parts of Mexico, and are also distinct in being unadorned by any human or animal figures. As in other Mexican ruins, however, there are no arches; for the architects of Mitla had not reached the stage of arch designing, and were therefore obliged to avoid curves.

The work of the Mitla builders seems amazing when it is borne in mind that it was done without machinery and with the crudest implements; for the only tools that have been found on the spot are chisels and axes of untempered copper. Under these circumstances the shaping and hoisting of the huge blocks into position and the fitting of the stone mosaics were really marvellous achievements. So wonderfully, too, were these huge stones put together that all the earthquakes that have taken place in Mexico in even historic times have not sufficed to move them from their position.

Not far from the Hall of Monoliths is a large, dilapidated structure, adjoining which is a comparatively modern church, obviously built from the ancient materials. This ruin was once the largest of all, and has been estimated as covering a space of nearly three hundred feet in length and six hundred in width. The enclosing walls were six feet thick. One portion of this temple, if such it were, was formerly used as a stable, its beautiful frescoed walls being whitewashed. A few faint vestiges of the decorations still remain, mostly undecipherable hieroglyphics in conventional life-forms, apparently painted with the same red pigment as is noticeable in the Audience Chamber. These are the only inscriptions at Mitla.

In 1902 an entrance which had been blocked up was discovered in the south court, which, being opened, was found to lead into a subterranean cruciform chamber some thirty or forty feet below the floor of the main building. This crypt has the same style of decoration as in the upper chambers, except that in this instance the Grecque pattern, instead of being formed by mosaic, is carved in the solid stone. This cross-shaped chamber and several others which exist at Mitla were used as tombs, and in each instance their entrances face the west, the idea of the ancient people having probably been that the souls of the dead journeyed to the regions of the setting sun. In some of the tombs entire skeletons or charred bones were found, also stone or clay idols, funereal urns which had contained incense and various other relics; but the chamber last discovered had evidently been rifled of its contents at some early period.

Until recent years the ruins at Mitla were treated in much the same way as were many old English castles a few generations ago. Beautiful structures were demolished by vandal hands to provide building material for the modern village of Mitla, and some of the stonework was even carted into the City of Oaxaca. The Mexican government at last took charge of the ruins and put a stop to the work of destruction. Government archæologists are now engaged in restoring some of the ancient buildings and superintending the excavations which are taking place in their vicinity.

The origin of the great structures at Mitla is shrouded in mystery. Nobody knows or is ever likely to know who the builders were or at what period these mighty edifices were raised. Their massive walls are to-day in much the same condition as when first visited by the Spaniards in the sixteenth century; the Aztecs at that time could tell practically nothing concerning the ancient builders. The resemblance of the ruins to those of Egypt has, however, led many savants to believe that the Western world was visited centuries before its discovery by Columbus. Prescott has declared the structures to be "the work of a people who passed away under the assaults of barbarism at a period prior to all traditions, leaving no name or trace of their existence save these monuments which have become the riddle of later generations." According to some authorities, the builders were the earliest races of Mexico, the

Nahuas or Toltecs, and the age of the ruins has been variously estimated at from two to five thousand years. The name Mitla is said to be a Mitlan-Nahuan word meaning "the place of the dead."

Several recent investigators are of the opinion, however, that the structures were raised at a much later date by the Zapotecan race, from whom the present natives of the country, the Zapotec Indians, are descended. The Zapotecs, who were there when the Spaniards came, have always called Mitla in their dialect Zyaboa, meaning "the centre of rest." They certainly have much the same type of features as those found in the stone figures and pottery which are unearthed among the ruins, but there the resemblance ends; for the modern Zapotecs of Oaxaca are typical Indian peons, while the ancient builders of Mitla had evidently made great advances in the arts of civilization.

Fully as mysterious as the identity of the builders is the purport of the structures themselves. Whether they were temples, palaces or fortresses is never likely to be known with any degree of certainty. The general opinion, however, is that they were temples, and this gains support from the fact that tombs have been discovered beneath several of the buildings. The ruins are also supposed to mark the site of a great city of prehistoric times, the entire valley being strewn with the remains of walls and columns. Idols of clay and jars of terra-cotta are found everywhere, and earthenware drain-pipes have also been dug up. There is every evidence, too, that the now arid valley once supported an immense population.

I spent the entire day in the midst of these mighty ruins, and would gladly have journeyed twice the distance from Mexico City to see them; for the famous Palace of the Alhambra, with all its glories, is scarcely more imposing. As I stood in the great Hall of Monoliths on the evening of my visit, its mysterious walls touched by the rays of the setting sun, I re-created, in fancy, the great structures. I could imagine the stately march of princes and warriors through the long corridors or the wild chants of priests engaged in their sacred rites. What a vista of the days when the world was young, mystic primeval times when —

"Wal, I've seen Mitla, and I'll admit it's quite a place; but if some of our young men from the Tec' couldn't have taught them Toltecs a few things, then I've lost my reckoning."

I turned and found myself confronted by an elderly American woman, thin, wiry and determined, who stood, umbrella in hand, regarding the line of ancient monoliths with a defiant air, as if challenging all the past races of Mitla to dispute her word.

"Yes, sir, I rather guess that some of our young men from the Tec' could have given 'em a few wrinkles."

"What is the Tec'?" I ventured to ask.

The old lady gave me a withering look which said as plain as words, "Well, you're about as ignorant as a Toltec."

"Of course I mean the Technological Institoot of Chicago," she replied. "Why, some of our young men from that institootion are simply astonishing the world, and if they couldn't turn out a better column than that, well, then they ain't got no business a-getting their diplomas as architects." Here she gave the offending column a resounding whack with her umbrella, as if to show her disapproval of its primitive lines.

"They knew how to build, them Toltecs did," she continued, a little more leniently, "but, law me, the world has been a-moving since their time. They couldn't have built a skyscraper to save their necks. Why, our young men learn all about building them big twenty-story buildings, and I reckon them Toltecs would just open their eyes if they could see some of 'em." With this parting shot at the past, the tourist lady disappeared through the ancient doorway. Alas, poor builders of Mitla, how little did you imagine that your efforts would one day be eclipsed by the young men from the Chicago Tec'.

On returning to the hacienda, I found that the old lady had just arrived with her son, a gloomy, morose youth who wore spectacles, and was probably a graduate of the famous institution. I have frequently met tourists of this type in my wanderings. None of them seem to enjoy travelling or the sights that they see, and why they ever travel I have never been able to discover.

After viewing the wonders of ancient Mitla, it seems impossible to believe that the Zapotec Indians now inhabiting the valley are in any way related to the builders of old whose works astonish the present age. Living in small huts of adobe, the men follow the usual peon occupations of farm laboring, and the herding of cattle, sheep and goats; the women are kept busy with their everlasting tortilla-making and clothes-washing. The Zapotecs are of short, stocky, muscular build, but are not bad looking, and do not have the flat noses which distinguish so many of the Indians further north. In some districts they speak very little Spanish, the use of the Zapotec dialect being very general.

A number of pagan superstitions and practices still survive among them, a belief in witchcraft being very general; they also have some peculiar medical customs. Once in the market-place at Oaxaca two aged and wrinkled Indian dames were pointed out to me as great curanderas or wise women. Most of the Indian communities have no other doctors.

These curanderas usually claim to have a great knowledge of medical science and make use of some very queer remedies. According to their superstitions, air can enter the human system through blows or unusually vigorous sneezing, and will then cause nervous tremblings, sore eyes and swellings. To effect a cure, lotions, plasters and bandages are employed. When the alimentary canal is obstructed, it is because undigested food has adhered to the stomach or has formed into little balls which rattle about in the intestines. Heroic treatment is needed for this condition, and a drop of quicksilver is usually prescribed, which, swallowed at a gulp, will generally effect a cure or kill the patient. Tiricia, the word used for homesickness, melancholia or insomnia, is caused by a subtle vapor produced by the action of the moon and dew, and is absorbed through the pores. A sensible prescription — change of scene, good company and tonics — is usually given for this. Mal de ojo or evil eye causes the sufferer to fade away or die of inanition, and is a disease common among children. To draw away the attention of the "evil eye," bright, attractive objects are hung near the patient. For a child who is slow in learning to talk, a diet of boiled swallows is often prescribed. Certain colors are supposed to work wonderful cures, and in cases of paralysis blue and red beads ground fine are sometimes administered. The curandera is also called upon to prepare love potions and to supply poisons, which will cause delirium, insanity and even death.

The Zapotecs have a number of strange dances, including the Devil Dance, which usually takes place on the feastdays of the saints to whom their villages are dedicated. On these occasions some of the dancers have their bodies painted to represent skeletons, and also wear strange feathered head-dresses. An American acquaintance who had come from a mining camp some thirty miles from Oaxaca told me that he attended one of these dances, which took place in an Indian pueblo. The Zapotec ball-room was an open space near the village, and here the dance went

RUINS OF MITLA.
South front of the great Hall of Monoliths.

on by the light of a blazing fire, the dancers, men and women, being arrayed in all kinds of fantastic garb. "But what astonished me," said the American, "were three Indians dressed in old-fashioned French zouave uniforms. One had evidently belonged to an officer, and was covered with gold lace. To my surprise, I learned that the fathers of these Indians had stripped the uniforms from the bodies of French soldiers after one of the battles near Oaxaca in 1865. The uniforms had been carefully preserved, and the cloth must have been wonderfully good to have been in such sound condition after so many years.

"The Indian who wore the officer's uniform said to me: 'When my father took it, there were big gold pieces like American gold coins on it. My father sold these at the pawnshop. There was also a gold cross, and that he gave to our padre.'" A strange ending for the uniform and decorations of a gallant officer of Napoleon the Third!

CHAPTER XX

LIFE IN AN OLD MEXICAN TOWN

"INFLUENZA epidemic in Mexico." Thus read the heading of a special article which appeared in one of the American-Mexican newspapers during my stay in Oaxaca. The news was not at all surprising; for it does not require a long residence in Mexico to realize that the unwashed, filthy living peon is a ready catcher and transmitter of any infectious disease. From Mexico City the malady soon reached Puebla, and in a short time it had invaded Oaxaca, where, despite the mild climate, it had numerous victims. I contracted a bad case of it myself, and did not improve matters by returning to Puebla, the inhaling of dust in large quantities on the long railway journey not being exactly a specific for the complaint.

"Try Cuautla," said the doctor whom I consulted at Puebla; "there's nothing like it in a case of influenza with bronchial complications." My first thought was that Cuautla was some strange Mexican drug, and was wondering whether it would be a nauseous dose, when the doctor proceeded to enlighten me. "Cuautla," said he, "is the name of a popular health resort between Puebla and Mexico City, the climate of which does wonders for sufferers from lung and bronchial troubles."

Upon making inquiries at the railway office about trains to Cuautla, the clerk handed me an illustrated pamphlet with a fine colored picture on the cover representing a Mexican tropical scene. It bore the title, "Cuautla,

Mexico's Carlsbad." What! I thought, another Carlsbad? In glowing language the booklet described Cuautla as an earthly paradise with a magnificent climate, beautiful scenery, splendidly equipped hotels and a warm sulphur spring whose waters were a certain specific for almost every human ailment. What more could one desire? But with a keen memory of another Mexican Carlsbad and its primitive surroundings I was determined not to be caught a second time nor to allow my hopes to be raised too high.

Cuautla is about a hundred miles or so from Puebla, and the speedy trains of the Interoceanic Railway take about ten hours to make the journey. The train which I took left about seven o'clock in the morning; it was not timed to reach Cuautla until five in the evening; and as there was not any restaurant at any intermediate station, a somewhat terrifying prospect of starvation faced travellers. How were they to get their luncheon? A little pamphlet given away by an American tourist agency and evidently written by an accomplished press-agent gave me the desired information: —

"At a certain station on the road," said my traveller's guide, "your train will stop for some twenty minutes. Here you will be greeted by graceful Indian women, — beauties, many of them, — with their olive skins and dark, flashing eyes, bearing themselves with queenly grace in their dainty rebosas and flowing garments, white as the driven snow. They will offer you such dainties as tamales, chili-con-carne and tortillas, piping hot from their little stoves, and prepared with all the scrupulous cleanliness of a Parisian chef. They will bring you dainty refrescos of freshly gathered pineapple or orange to quench your thirst, and pastry such as your mother may have made when her cooking was at its prime."

Now, what more could any reasonable traveller demand? What need was there for a restaurant when there were all these good things to be enjoyed? I showed my guide to an American friend before I started. He chuckled, gave a knowing wink and remarked, "Great is the faith of man, for after all your experiences you can still believe in a Mexican guide-book." "But," I said, "here it is in black and white, the dainty cooking, the clean Indians—" "That settles it," he interrupted. "When you come across a clean Indian in this part of the country, telegraph me at my expense." He added, "If I were in your place, I would be on the safe side and take some provisions along." I took his advice, and was afterwards profoundly thankful that I did so.

Between Puebla and Cuautla the railway descends to the hot lands, the descent being marked by a decided increase in temperature. On this account the weather towards midday became uncomfortably warm. About one o'clock, in dazzling sunlight, we stopped at the station where, according to the guide-book, the Indian beauties were to greet us. There certainly were a lot of women waiting, and they came rushing forward to meet the train; but what I saw completely took away my appetite. There were the usual Indian women food-sellers in their faded blue rebosas and dusty skirts, most of them old, withered and uncleanly, having been born, I fear, with a rooted aversion to soap and water. Some of these beldames were squatting outside the station, cooking various queer foods on crude charcoal stoves. I watched the process of tamale-making, not exactly an appetizing sight. An old lady thrust her rather dirty hand into a jar containing chopped meat and other ingredients, took out a handful and slapped it on a piece of tortilla dough which she deftly wrapped round it until it formed a sort of roll. This she plunged into some boiling fat, and in a few minutes it was cooked. "Oh, what delicious tamales they're a-making. Mercy! I'm going to have some." The speaker was a Western young lady who was travelling with her father, mother and two brothers. Some Westerners apparently have strong nerves as well as appetites, at least these did; for they called to the Indian woman, who brought them her greasy delicacies, of which the whole family partook with great relish. A solemn young man who accompanied the party insisted on having the Mexican equivalent of a jam tart, and managed to make one of the women understand him by means of dumb signs. The old lady rammed her dirty and rather greasy hand into a jar of jam, took out a handful, slapped it on a piece of pastry, and presto! there was the jam tart.

The Mexican passengers were, of course, even less fastidious. They bought the Indian dainties recklessly, loading themselves with them externally and internally. I was content to appease my hunger with some biscuits and cheese and to quench my thirst with some Tehuacan water. I expect, in common with my fellow-men, to eat a peck of dirt in my lifetime, but I positively decline to take it all at one dose. So much for the guide-book. I was now ready for Cuautla.

On my arrival there, I crossed a pretty little plaza opposite the station and reached the Hotel Morelos, an establishment under American management where I had arranged to stay. It was the usual old mansion that had been turned into a hotel and very little altered. There was a large interior patio, with fountain, trees and flowers; a large garden adjoined this filled with orange trees, banana plants and palms, with great masses of bougainvillea growing everywhere. All the rooms opened into the patio, and on one side of it there was a long, rustic dining-room.

The place looked very old-fashioned and crude, but was interesting and picturesque, and in the mild climate of Cuautla, where outdoor life is so pleasant, many luxuries indispensable elsewhere could be dispensed with. The rooms were furnished in the usual Mexican style, with tiled floors and one or two rugs, but were clean and comfortable.

The attractions of the hotel were hardly up to those of a Carlsbad establishment, for it had neither a writing nor a smoking room; but the terms were rather more attractive than the usual Carlsbad tariff, being about two dollars a day inclusive. It is true there was a good deal of Mexican about the cooking, but the meals were not at all bad and the service very fair. There were many visitors at the hotel, chiefly Americans, most of whom had fled from the capital to escape influenza or to recover from it. But for the tropical surroundings, one could easily have imagined one's self at an American resort.

Situated at an altitude of about five thousand feet, Cuautla has a splendid winter climate, fully rivalling that of Cuernavaca, the mean temperature averaging seventy degrees the year round. It is a quaint, old-fashioned place, with narrow, cobble-paved streets, and houses of the usual low, flat-roofed type. As I strolled about the town the next morning, I noticed some unusually amusing signs of Americanization. An enterprising barber, for example, displayed a big signboard with the English inscription, "Hygienic, non-cutting barber shop," as a tempting inducement to tourists, and one or two other establishments displayed in their windows the interesting announcement, "American spoke here."

Before the Conquest, Cuautla was an Indian settlement of some importance; and in 1600 the present town was founded by the Spaniards. In 1812, during the War of

Independence, it was the scene of some fierce fighting. It was in that year that General Morelos, the Mexican patriot, with a small force, was shut up in the town and besieged by a large Spanish army under General Calleja. After a siege of three months, Morelos was enabled to evacuate the place, but not until he was starved out. During the siege food became so scarce that cats were sold for six dollars, and rats and lizards for one and two dollars. One street in the town is called "Armaguras de Calleja," which means "Bitterness of Calleja," the forces of the Spanish general having suffered terribly in this particular thoroughfare. Another street, called "Las Victimes," is so called because the Spaniards, after entering the town, are said to have cut the throats of all the women and children in its houses.

Cuautla is also famous for having the oldest railway station in the world, the crumbling, ancient structure which is now used for this purpose having been the Church of San Diego built in 1657. Near it was a convent now also used for business purposes. When the law appropriating church property was enforced in 1856, the Franciscan fathers who then occupied the church and adjacent buildings vacated the place, and in 1881 the railway company purchased it for its present use.

The day after my arrival I went into the old church, the body of which is now used as a warehouse, while one side of it bordering the railway line provides accommodation for the waiting-room and various offices. A quantity of wine-barrels were piled up at the spot where the high altar had formerly stood, and all kinds of merchandise were stored in other parts of the building. Over the door was an inscription, the first words of which seem appropriate enough to the present condition of the once sacred edifice: "Terribilis est iste hic domus dei et porta coeli" (How dreadful is this place. This is none other but the house of God and this is the gate of heaven).

The warm sulphur spring — the great attraction of Cuautla, and its only claim to be reckoned a spa — is some three miles out of the town, and visitors go out there on horseback, or in a wagonette which makes the trip several times a day. In the daytime the roads are too dusty, and it is too hot, for walking.

In a blaze of sunshine which was worthy of the subtropics, I started for the springs the morning after my arrival, riding in one of the wagonettes, which was well filled with passengers. Rumbling through the cobble-paved streets and almost dislocating our bones, the vehicle at last reached the white, dusty highroad which led out into the country. For most of the way it is bordered with large banana plantations, and the tall plants were loaded with green fruit. These plantations are artificially irrigated, and even in what was now the dry season streams were running through them. There are several rivers round Cuautla, and in the hottest weather the country is well watered. It is, in fact, one of Cuautla's great charms that everywhere there is running water, through the streets and roads, in the gardens and plazas and through the fields. Irrigation has made the land to blossom like the rose, and after seeing so much of the dry, arid districts, the green trees and fields, the miles of fruit trees, the graceful palms and wealth of flowers were a welcome sight.

Later on the road passed over some barren, rocky hills, from the summit of which there were some magnificent views. All around, in the distance, were rolling, reddish mountains, and far beyond these could be seen the snow-covered peaks of Popocatepetl and Ixtaccihuatl. The air was wonderfully clear and the sky the never changing, cloudless blue. By the roadside were occasional Indian huts, not of the usual square, flat-roofed type, but circular, and looking something like round English haystacks. They are built partly of adobe and partly of bamboo, interwoven with reeds and rushes, the roofs being thatched with grass. Most of them were embowered in a jungle of tropical vegetation and oftentimes in a dense thicket of green bamboo. The peons here seemed to look a shade cleaner than elsewhere, probably because there was plenty of water in the neighborhood; their clothing of homespun cotton, too, looked almost white.

My fellow-travellers in the wagonette were two French families, men, women, boys and girls, and they talked incessantly of the wonderful sulphur bath they were going to enjoy; but when we reached the spring I could see no signs of a bath-house. Flowing through a narrow ravine was a small stream which at one point formed a waterfall, pouring over a high bluff into a large rocky basin. This basin was divided into two parts by a low brick wall built through the centre.

On our arrival, the ladies and girls wandered off in one direction, and I followed the men and boys in another. They went under some trees near by, took off their clothes and donned bathing-suits. The ladies and girls, who had retired to other trees at a respectful distance, also appeared in their bathing costumes. They went into the water on one side of the brick wall, while the men and boys took possession of that on the other side. That is how this Mexican Carlsbad is conducted. I did not take a bath, but I put my hand in the water, finding it tepid, and as the day was quite hot, I have no doubt that the bathing was very pleasant. The water is strongly impregnated with sulphur, and is said to be extremely beneficial in cases of rheumatism and various other diseases.

The drive or ride out to the springs is about the only

amusement at Cuautla, so people contrive to pass away the time by getting up late and going to bed early. It is, however, a pretty spot, a midwinter paradise; and if it only had a good, up-to-date hotel, with organized recreation, it could be made into a very fine resort. Even as things are, the place is always crowded during the winter season.

There is another spring of a different kind less than a mile from Cuautla. It is reached by a beautiful lane, bordered by a low, moss-grown wall of rough stones and shaded by an occasional group of banana plants or palms. From this tropical by-path there was a view over miles of bright green sugar-cane to the horizon of reddish mountains, and towering above them all were the two great snow-covered peaks, standing out sharply against the deep blue sky. The scene was always magnificent, and in the evenings, when the sun was setting, the color effects were exquisite beyond description. At the end of the lane was a wide, clear brook dashing over the rocks and bordering some cool woods, full of fine old trees, green as the trees of New England in early June; beneath them was a carpeting of long, lush grass and a myriad of bright flowers. Crossing the brook by some stepping-stones, one could enter the wood and reach a deep, sandy basin, where several springs forever bubbled up beneath the water which flowed off in wide streams, branching in every direction. The only visitors to this charming spot seemed to be a few Indians who came down to bathe.

In the vicinity of Cuautla there are several great haciendas or farming estates, some of them as extensive as counties. One which employs thousands of men is over three hundred thousand acres in extent, and within its limits are several Indian villages with their big churches. This part of Mexico is a sugar-cane country, and here can be seen great mills which convert the chopped stalk into sugar, the capacity of each mill being estimated by the hundred tons instead of the pound. From the sugar-mills you can see the glistening peaks of Popocatepetl and Ixtaccihuatl — sugar-making within the sight of snow! Is there any other place on earth revealing such a contrast?

An idea of the size of Mexican haciendas can be gained from the fact that one of the largest estates near Cuautla has two railway stations within its limits and its own line of railway. Such a thing, however, is not at all uncommon in Mexico.

In the seventeenth century these great estates were to Mexico what the feudal castles were to Europe in earlier times. The hacienda house — the great stone mansion where the haciendado and his family lived — was then surrounded with farm buildings and the homes of the workmen. From early morn until night, trains of burros were constantly going in and out loaded with wood, maize, vegetables, poultry, baskets of fruit; the great house having a life of its own, self-supporting, quite apart from the State. In the tower of the hacienda chapel, or if there was no chapel, then from an arch over the main entrance to the hacienda house, there was usually a bell which had been blessed. This was rung to call in the field-hands whenever danger threatened; and as soon as the alarm sounded they would drop plough and sickle and run to the great house, where the women and children gathered in the patio while the señor armed the men with rifles from the storeroom. Then from the port-holes of the heavy stone walls, from the corner turrets and from the protected roof the hacienda's defenders were able to offer stout resistance against wandering marauders or bands of soldiery in search of plunder. In these peaceful times the bell is now rung only when rain or hail threatens in harvest time, as its blessed voice is supposed to be a charm against the elements.

In the daily life of these great haciendas many picturesque and beautiful customs still survive. An interesting description of some of these was given by the author of an article which recently appeared in one of the Mexican magazines. "When the day's work is done," says this writer, "and the last red gleam has faded from the mountains, the field-hands gather together to sing the evening song of praise. A deep bass begins the chant: —

> 'Dios te salve Maria.'

A shrill, childish voice joins in: —

> 'Dios te salve Maria.'

Then from the long line of men and women rises the chorus: —

> 'Dios te salve Maria
> Llena eres de gracia.'

The Indian voices vary in pitch from a shriek to a roar. When the whole company joins in, each singing or yelling: —

> 'Bendita tu eres
> Entre todas las mujeres,'

one might imagine it to be the fierce war-song of the Aztec legions defending their royal city on the lakes. But it is only the 'Ave Maria' sung to the gentle Mother."

In harvesting grain, short-bladed hand sickles are very commonly used. Whenever a reaper straightens up to rest from his work, he raises his hat and shouts in a high, monotonous key, "Ave Maria, Santissima!" Some fellow-worker in a neighboring field answers back, and so round all the wide fields a continuous cry of rejoicing goes up. If a field is fruitful, a cross, hung with wisps of grain and stiff decorations made from the maguey flower, is set up in a corner of it as a sign of thankfulness. Even the noxious pulque has its peculiar religious rites. As the peon pours the agua miel, freshly gathered from the maguey, into the evil-smelling cowhide vats of the tinacal, he calls out in a loud tone: "In the name of the holy sacrament on the altar! Hail to the most pure Virgin Mary! May the pulque turn out well." Every man in the building raises his hat.

On many of the larger haciendas the baronial magnificence which was once common is still kept up. Some of the great estates include villages with a population of peons, all laborers employed by the haciendado. It would take days to ride from one end to the other of these vast domains. Years ago, when there were no inns, any traveller could stop at the hacienda, sure of hospitality and a hearty welcome. In northern Mexico there is one immense hacienda which formerly controlled twenty thousand peons. Some of the great estates still remain in the hands of the original families, to whom they were granted at the Conquest. The owners of these properties enjoy princely incomes, and most of them keep elaborate houses in the capital, where they spend their wealth with a lavish hand.

Many of the hacienda houses are comfortably furnished; but even the richest Mexicans are more or less barbaric in their household ideas, and know very little of those luxuries which go to make up the delight of an American home. The cooking is usually atrocious, there are rarely bathrooms and other requisites, and so primitive are the arrangements that very few people accustomed to modern civilized life would care to visit them.

The great hacienda system has been a serious obstacle to progress in Mexico; and if these huge estates were divided up among smaller proprietors and properly cultivated, the country would be much richer. As it is, half the land is lying idle, going to waste, or is only half tilled.

The agricultural methods in vogue on many of the old

estates are still very primitive, and there is oftentimes a curious mingling of the ancient and modern. The latest improved harvesting and threshing machines can sometimes be seen in operation, while not far off peons are ploughing with the old wooden ploughs and driving along the lumbering ox carts. Grain is still threshed in some places by driving teams of horses or mules over it every day for hours at a time, and is winnowed by being tossed in the air. While accepting a few modern improvements, the average haciendado clings tenaciously to many of the old ways and is strongly opposed to giving them up.

A wonderful variety of grains, fruits and vegetables are grown on the haciendas of Mexico. In the north the chief products are wheat, barley, maize, and other cereals, and in the south, sugar-cane, coffee, cocoa, vanilla, tobacco, pineapples, bananas and india-rubber. All over the country there is a great cultivation of fibre plants. Some haciendas, too, are exclusively devoted to the breeding of horses, cattle, and other live stock.

Visits to the haciendas in the surrounding country form a very interesting diversion to life at Cuautla, and there are many interesting scenes to be witnessed in the old town itself. For, like many of the smaller Mexican towns, Cuautla still retains much of the romance and manners of sunny Spain. At night in the plaza there is Spain in miniature. One evening I passed an old fonda, open to the street, in which were gathered a number of peons, in their blankets and sombreros, drinking their aguardiente and playing their favorite game of picture-cards. Three picturesque natives twanged away merrily on old-fashioned mandolins and occasionally burst into song. In the neighboring plaza, beneath a sky brilliant with tropical stars and an unclouded moon, there strolled a few dark-eyed señoritas with their duennas, regarded with languishing looks by the young señores who stood in groups beneath the old trees, greeting the fair ones with an occasional "adios." In a side street I caught a glimpse of one or two faithful "bears" standing below the balconies, chatting in low tones with the Juliets above. Evidently romance had not yet passed away in old Cuautla.

CHAPTER XXI

IN THE CRATER OF POPOCATEPETL

As almost every tourist who gazes upon Mont Blanc is seized with the ambition to make an ascent, so there are few travellers who can behold Popocatepetl without feeling an overwhelming desire to scale this king of Mexican mountains. To do this was once regarded as a wonderful feat, and the adventurous traveller who performed it was acclaimed as a hero. But nowadays, so prosaic has the world become, that scores of American tourists climb to the snowy heights of "Popo" every year, including the expedition as part of their "round-trip" excursions to Mexico.

Popocatepetl had fascinated me from the time I had first seen its wondrous outline standing sharply against the blue Mexican sky, its snow-clad tip glistening beneath the dazzling Mexican sun. Viewing Popocatepetl daily across the green fields of Cuautla, I became possessed of a keen desire to emulate the American tripper by including a climb to the summit as part of my own itinerary. I was given an unexpected opportunity to realize this desire when I received an invitation one day to meet some friends at Amecameca and join them in making an ascent of the great mountain.

Amecameca is about halfway between Cuautla and Mexico City, or a distance of forty miles. The train which I took one morning made this journey in something like four hours! It was a hot, dusty ride; but as in other Mexican railway journeys that I had made the interesting sights to be seen on the way served to alleviate the discomforts and slowness of travel.

Between Cuautla and Amecameca there is some wonderful scenery. Leaving the cultivated valley, the railway passes between a succession of lofty, treeless, sun-baked hills; then, gradually climbing higher, opens up a splendid view of the surrounding mountains, with the great peaks of Popocatepetl and Ixtaccihuatl rising above them all. Many of these hills show unmistakable signs of volcanic action and the effects of the lava which once flowed from the two volcanos when they were active.

A great deal of maguey is cultivated in this district, and there are several large plantations along the line. A number of fibrous plants are also grown which are extensively employed in the manufacture of hemp. There are in Mexico about one hundred and fifty species of agave of various sizes, all fibre-producing plants, some of them having leaves as much as six or eight feet long. They thrive best in the semi-arid districts and in a thin, rocky limestone soil. All that is necessary is that the soil around the plant should be kept clear of weeds.

Most important of these fibrous plants is henequen, which is extensively cultivated in Yucatan, the dry climate and sandy soil of that part of Mexico being peculiarly adapted to its cultivation. The fibre produced is used very largely in the manufacture of carpets, rugs, twines, ropes and bagging. Owing to the check that Manila hemp crops received from the Spanish-American War, Yucatan in recent years has acquired almost a monopoly of the hemp trade. Formerly one of the poorest States of Mexico, it has now become one of the richest. Enormous fortunes have been made by the henequen growers in the last ten years, many poor men having suddenly acquired great wealth. The value of the fibres exported from Mexico every year now amounts to nearly $40,000,000.

Some species of cactus are also valuable for their fibre-producing qualities, notably the ixtle, which was used extensively by the Aztecs for weaving blankets. The famous tilma in the shrine of Guadalupe is made of this material. It is said that some cacti will produce an excellent quality of paper pulp, and experiments are being made with them. If the project is successful, it may do something towards relieving the situation in the paper trade caused by the decreasing area of forests available for paper-making purposes.

The maguey, which supplies the national beverage, pulque, was found useful in other ways by the ancient races of Mexico. Its thorns were used for needles and pins, while the leaves made a good thatch for the roofs of their huts, and when properly prepared, furnished as good a material for their writing as the Egyptian papyrus.

As in the trip from Mexico City to Cuernavaca, the line from Cuautla runs over the mountains, and at one point it reaches the altitude of nearly eight thousand feet. It passes through miles of cool pine woods with all the characteristics of a northern forest, and occasionally there are glimpses of the great wooded valley leading to Popocatepetl, whose pointed snow peak towers above the clouds. Comparisons are always odious, but to my mind the magnificent distances to be seen here, the glorious blue sky, the thin, clear air, and the wonderful tints of the mountains and trees combine to form scenic beauties which rival even those of the valley of Chamounix and Mont Blanc. At three in the afternoon I reached Amecameca, met my friends and had a good night's rest at the comfortable little hotel in this picturesque town, preparatory to making the ascent of the mountain the following day.

ASCENT OF POPOCATEPETL.
View of the snow-clad summit from the Half-way House.

THE JOURNEY'S END.
Mountain-climbers on the summit of Popocatepetl.

IN THE CRATER OF POPOCATEPETL 331

Not far from Amecameca is a new winter and summer resort under American management, known as "Popo Park" — that is how the Americans have abbreviated "Popocatepetl Park." A large, comfortable hotel has been started at this place, which has become quite a popular week-end resort for people in the capital, especially during the winter months. Before long a motor road will be completed between Popo Park and the city, the distance being about forty miles. The hotel is situated in the midst of the pine woods, and although the air is cool during the day and sharp at night and in the morning, blazing wood fires enable the guests to be very comfortable. A number of wealthy people are building bungalows in the park, which is destined to become, in time, one of the most popular resorts in Mexico.

This is the place from which tourists usually make the ascent of Popocatepetl (17,782 feet). The hotel management arranges all the details of the ascent, the cost for each person being $25. This includes a return ticket from Mexico City, room and board at the hotel, a guide, pack-mule, and complete outfit of bed, clothing and food for the trip. For $10 extra the visitor can be carried up the most difficult part of the route after the animals are left behind, making the ascent possible to those who are too much affected by the high altitude to exert their strength. Visitors who come from Mexico City can make the trip to the summit and return to town in three days.

Our party for the ascent consisted of three, each of us mounted on a sturdy mule. At midday we stopped for luncheon at the ranch of El Paraje, a point where many who set out to scale the mountain often turn back, either losing courage or finding the strain on the heart and lungs too great. As we left the ranch and rode onward, the scenery and vegetation began to change until only a few stunted oyamal trees and patches of withered grass were to be seen.

When we reached the ranch of Tlamacas at four in the afternoon, a freezing, bitter wind was blowing, there was a light fall of snow and we were glad to get inside the hut and warm ourselves at a wood fire. It was agreed that we should continue our journey to the summit at three o'clock in the morning. In spite of the fire and plenty of blankets, we spent the early hours of the night very uncomfortably, as it was impossible to keep out the intense cold. At two in the morning, after refreshing ourselves with some hot tea, we commenced the ascent by the light of the full moon, its brilliant rays reflected by the white field of snow. As we mounted upwards, the path became more and more steep, the mules being compelled to stop frequently to gain their breath. We were forced at last to dismount and proceed on foot. In the far distance the City of Puebla, with its twinkling lights, could now be seen, backed by the towering peak of Orizaba.

As we climbed steadily on, the moon sank behind the mountain heights and the sky was diffused with the first rosy flush of the coming dawn, a most beautiful sight. The green mountain looked so majestic that one could not wonder that it had taken its place with its companion, Ixtaccihuatl, in the mythology of the Aztecs. Legend says that Popocatepetl (the smoking mountain) and Ixtaccihuatl (the woman in white) were once giants who, having displeased the gods, were transformed into mountains. The appearance of the smaller mountain strikingly illustrates this story, for the outline of its summit bears a close resemblance to the form of a woman shrouded in snow. After being changed into mountains, the legend adds, the woman died, but the man was doomed to live on and to gaze on his beloved forever. At times, in his deep grief, he trembles and moans, while tears of fire course down his furrowed cheek. Both mountains are extinct volcanoes, Popocatepetl having been active within historical times. The fires of Ixtaccihuatl were probably the first to cease, thus giving rise to the beautiful legend.

People who climb Popocatepetl are warned not to eat much, which advice is not altogether sound, as the great strain upon the system is weakening enough without the exhaustion necessarily caused by the lack of food. Before we had reached the summit we were all tired out, and our breathing became so labored that we were obliged to call a halt. Then we made a final struggle, pushing forward with a grim determination which was soon rewarded. A few minutes more of hard climbing brought us to the crater, and before our eyes was unfolded a magnificent scene. Around us were the rugged mountain heights, half shrouded with clouds of varied and beautiful tints, which in the course of an hour or two drifted away, enabling us to see into the depths of the vast crater. Here the scene vividly recalled the descriptions of the infernal regions in Dante's great poem. The rugged sides of the crater, glistening with yellow sulphurous incrustations, intermingled with masses of black volcanic earth and white patches of snow, assumed a thousand weird shadows and variegated colors; and on one side was a large pool of intensely green water. As a fitting accompaniment to this scene the air was filled with pungent fumes, and a strange noise was heard like the escaping of steam, combined with another sound which closely resembled the rapid firing of musketry. One of these noises is caused by the rush of sulphurous vapor from great fissures in the crater, called "respiratorios"; the other is made by stones which are continually being detached from the sides of the crater and fall into its depths. The smoke which issues from the fissures can only be seen at close range, but it was formerly visible from a distance, thus giving rise to the name Popocatepetl or "smoking mountain."

After inspecting the bottom of the crater and being half choked by the sulphurous fumes which issued from its depths, we were glad to climb back to the outer edge. The rarefied air was so oppressive that we were constantly obliged to rest. Shortly afterwards the mists again surrounded us and we seemed to be standing on a rocky island in the midst of a boundless sea. We afterward learned that a storm was raging in the neighboring valley. Before long, however, the sun's rays pierced the mist, and it grew so warm that we were obliged to discard our blankets.

Popocatepetl is to-day owned by a company, and until recently a large force of peons were employed in mining the sulphur, of which there are enormous quantities visible; but the work of mining is extremely difficult, because the miners suffer greatly from exposure and the strain resulting from the high altitude. Work was abandoned a short time ago owing to these conditions and the difficulties of transportation. When Cortés invaded Mexico, he obtained the sulphur for making his gunpowder from the crater of Popocatepetl, some of his adventurous followers scaling the mountain and bringing down a large supply.

The sulphur miners, after work, used to seat themselves on mats of rushes, give themselves a push and whiz down over the snow-field in a couple of minutes. There is said to be no danger in this feat, and many tourists have undertaken it. But the snow at the time of our visit was frozen into hummocks like the waves of a choppy sea, so we had to trudge down on foot. Having lunched on the summit, we commenced our descent, reaching Tlamacas a little after three o'clock, and after a brief rest mounted our mules and resumed our journey downwards to El Paraje, where we spent the night. Next day we were back in Amecameca again. All our faces were reddened and burned by the glare from the snow-fields, and our bodies ached from the fatigue we had undergone, but otherwise we felt none the worse for our climb.

Before leaving Amecameca I visited the famous sacred mountain, which is on the outskirts of the town. Here, in a deep cave which served as a hermitage, once lived the good friar Martin de Valencia, one of the "twelve apostles of Mexico," who was sent by Pope Adrian the Sixth as a missionary to the Indians, with the title of "Vicar of New Spain." After many years of faithful service he died, deeply revered by his flock, and was buried at Tlalmanalco; but it is said that the Indians secretly removed his body and buried it in the cave. A legend says that, years after his death, a mule, bearing an image of the Virgin intended for the parish church, stopped at the cave and refused to budge. This was regarded as a miraculous sign that the image was to be deposited there, and there it has remained ever since. It is removed once a year, on Ash Wednesday, when it is taken down, with great pomp, to the church and placed on the high altar. On Good Friday it is carried back to the cave. This is the occasion of a great fiesta at Amecameca, and visitors from all parts of Mexico come to see the passion play which is enacted in the town shortly before the image is taken back to the shrine. The representation of the Crucifixion by Indian actors is a wonderful sight.

The play is opened by a body of horsemen enacting the rôle of centurions, who call upon the people to attend the sacred ceremony; whereupon the vast multitude of Indian spectators makes a general movement to a hill near the church, supposed to represent Calvary, preceded by the various characters in the mystic drama. On the way to the hill a continuous roar goes up from the excited mob, and the representative of Judas is unmercifully pummelled and kicked. At the head of this strange procession walks the Indian representing the Saviour, staggering under the weight of a heavy cross, scourged and reviled by a number of other Indians representing the Jews. When, at last, the cross has been erected, and he has been raised and lashed to it, the air is rent with shrieks and yells, and a general fight often follows between the representatives of the Christians and Jews, the latter barely escaping with their lives.

Another weird scene is enacted at night when the sacred image is conveyed up the mountain side, escorted by a great multitude with torches, joining at intervals in a wild chant, while many of the devout crawl on their knees up the rocky path.

Upon my return to Mexico City, where I arrived in the evening, I went to the Hotel Sanz. I was surprised to find this place in festal array, with its patio decorated with American and Mexican flags, and a large floral shield bearing the words, "Welcome, Shriners." On inquiry I learned there was another American invasion in progress, five hundred members of the masonic order, the Mystic Shriners, having come down to Mexico from the States to make a tour through the country and arouse interest in "shrining." The local newspapers were full of their doings. They were headed by the officers of the order, who were called "The Nobles of the Mystic Shrine," while the chief officer bore the imposing title of "The High Imperial Potentate." Many of the members had brought their wives and daughters, so that there was a very large party. The wives of some of the Shriners seemed to take great delight in their husbands' titles and the pomp and paraphernalia of the order. On the other hand, I heard one irreverent Shriner, possessed of the Western craze for abbreviation, remark to an acquaintance, "Say, old man, where's the Imp. Pot. stopping?"

O, great and imperial potentate, to think that a Shriner should have dared to brave the awful curses of the mystic shrine by dubbing you " Imp. Pot."

At their meetings the Shriners wore a sort of Turkish costume with a red fez, and they greeted each other with the word "Salaam." Next day, President Diaz gave them audience at the National Palace, receiving what the Shriners called a "grand salaam," and being presented with a jewelled fez. He was also enrolled as a member of the organization. During their stay in the city the ladies of the Shriner party conducted a bazaar, which, for some reason unknown to ordinary mortals, was called a "Jamaica" — probably some mystic term only to be understood by the initiated.

The Shriners not only saw the sights of the capital, but went in special trains to Cuernavaca and other places. With this swarm of American tourists in the city, San Francisco Street seemed more like the main street of an American town than the leading thoroughfare of the Mexican capital. The curio shops, the dulcerias, and the big department stores all did a rushing business. My admiration for President Diaz greatly increased, too, at this time. Half the American tourists wanted to see the President and grasp his hand in the same way as they treat their own President when they go to Washington. Some of them, with an eye to business, sought special interviews with the President to interest him in some gold-mining project, a meat-canning factory, an automobile, or even to reveal to him the wonders of a new patent medicine or hair-restorer. That so many of them succeeded certainly showed a wonderful amount of good nature on the part of Mexico's great ruler.

Before I left the city, nearly fifty women from the Western States, mostly widows, came down in a body to see Mexico, led by a very determined-looking female who had organized them into a sort of women's travel club. All of them wanted to see the President. I overheard one lady remark, "Say, if that President Dye-az doesn't see us ladies, well, there's going to be trouble, that's all." The President must have considered it unsafe to refuse, for he received them all at the palace the next day. Hero as well as statesman, I say; for a man brave enough to face fifty determined women, mostly widows, is surely well fitted to rule a nation!

One afternoon a young woman belonging to this party entered the hotel writing-room in which I was sitting; a giddy-looking girl with light, fluffy hair, and rather overdressed. She seemed to be quite excited. "Oh, say," she remarked to one of the older women of somewhat prim and old-maidish appearance, "I had such a funny experience on San Francisco Street just now. A young Mexican with big black eyes followed me and another girl. He was one of them Mexican dudes — lagerteegys they call 'em. He kept a-saying all sorts of things like 'hermosy' and 'dulcy.' The girl I was with understood Spanish, and she said he was a-saying 'beautiful girl,' 'lovely eyes,' 'sweetness.' Say, wasn't it funny?" The elderly lady gave a snort of contempt and disapproval. "*I* should just like to see one of those lagerteegys follow me and say such things," she retorted. The girl went off giggling, and commenced singing, "Oh, take me back to New York town." A few minutes later I heard her remark to a friend out in the patio, "Say, did you hear what she said? Why, she said she'd like to see one of them lagerteegys follow her. Well, I guess if a lagerteegy ever did he'd never escape."

CHAPTER XXII

GUADALAJARA THE WONDERFUL

"GIVE me a ticket to that place, please," said an American tourist to the booking-clerk at the Mexican Central Railway office. The man from the States held out a railway guide in which he had marked the name of the place to which he wished to travel; for he had serious doubts about the correct pronunciation of it.

"You want a ticket to Guadalajara," replied the clerk, but he pronounced it something like "Wahda-la-hara."

This beautiful city with the perplexing name has a population of over a hundred thousand, is three hundred and eighty miles northwest of Mexico City and is not far from the Pacific coast. It has the distinction of being the handsomest, the cleanest, and most cheerful of Mexican cities; it is also acknowledged to be next in importance to the capital, although Puebla has long claimed that honor.

The wonderful progress that Mexico has made within recent years is strikingly exemplified in the case of Guadalajara, which, less than twenty years ago, was a sleepy, backward, place but little known to the outside world. The nearest railway was then some distance away, and travellers from the capital were obliged to make a large part of the journey in slow, uncomfortable stage-coaches. To-day, Guadalajara has become a busy, cosmopolitan city and an important railway centre; while on account of its great manufacturing industries it might be appropriately called the Manchester of Mexico.

The Mexican Central Railway maintains a good service of trains between Mexico City and Guadalajara, so that the journey can be made in absolute comfort if not with excessive speed. I left the capital at eight o'clock one evening and reached Guadalajara at one the next afternoon, making the journey in a comfortable Pullman car.

For most of the distance the railway traverses the great central plateau, and the country, as seen from the train, presented the usual vista of arid lands, dry, yellow grass and occasional green, irrigated fields. Forming a distant background to these typical highland scenes were the outlines of a range of reddish, barren mountains which sometimes assumed fantastic shapes and were evidently of volcanic origin. Most of the watercourses were dry, but once or twice we crossed small streams and one winding, shallow river of fair size. Very few towns or villages are to be seen on the way, the majority of those along the route being hidden among the hills a little distance from the line. Sometimes there would be a mule-car at the wayside stations to take travellers to some invisible town.

This part of Mexico, including the State of Jalisco, of which Guadalajara is the capital, was originally called Nueva Galicia by the Spanish colonists who settled there in 1530. Most of these colonists came from Andalusia, and the pleasant manners and light-hearted ways of their descendants are still typical of sunny Spain. The women, too, have the reputation of being the most beautiful in Mexico. Guadalajara was founded in 1540, and was called Espiritu Santo, but was afterwards given its present name, after Wadal-il-harah, the Moorish capital. In this part of the country there are many delightful towns and villages, with fine old churches and other substantial buildings left as mementos of Spanish domination.

Guadalajara certainly merits its reputation of being the

most beautiful city in Mexico. It is a bright, clean town with wide asphalted streets and handsome white stone buildings, which, in the principal thoroughfares, are mostly in the modern Spanish style. Looking down the broad streets, one sees a distant vista of mountains; for Guadalajara lies in the midst of a plain with mountains rising around it. The streets run at right angles, intersecting a number of parks and plazas filled with shady tropical trees and resplendent with flowers. If there are any slum streets in the city, they are very carefully concealed. I saw none. The peons whom I encountered in the highways and byways also seemed to partake of the general cleanliness of the place; they looked much more intelligent than any I had seen before.

Not only is Guadalajara a beautiful city, but it is a busy commercial place. In the principal streets there are good shops of all kinds, numerous banks and commercial agencies, and other outward signs of wealth and prosperity.

From its appearance no one would imagine Guadalajara to be an important manufacturing place; there are no huge chimneys belching forth black smoke such as are seen in our manufacturing towns. The fact is that all the machinery in the local factories is driven by the same electrical power which lights the streets and runs the street cars, this power being generated by the great falls of the Lerma River a few miles distant. Here, again, is evidence of the wonderful progress that is being made in Mexico in the utilization of water-power.

In addition to all these advantages, Guadalajara is blessed with one of the finest climates in the world. Like Cuautla and some other favored places, it is situated at an altitude of five thousand feet, which gives it an average temperature of about seventy degrees the year round — a perennial June. During the winter months the city has probably the driest air on the American continent, which, with its balmy climate, makes it a favored resort for invalids suffering from bronchial or lung affections. The early mornings and late evenings are never cold, as in the higher altitudes, but occasionally a light overcoat can be worn with comfort.

As in most Mexican cities, the life of Guadalajara centres about its main plaza, which is famed for its beauty, its palms, orange trees, and tropical flowers being forever green. Beneath the portales, which border two of its sides, are a number of fine shops and cafés, and also facing it is the Governor's Palace, a magnificent building of white stone which would command attention in any European capital. All over the city there are imposing old churches dating from early Spanish times, tinted in beautiful soft colors and having wonderful towers and domes. Adjoining the plaza is the cathedral, a beautiful edifice commenced in 1561 and completed in 1618, with two tall Gothic towers, wholly unlike any others in Mexico, which can be seen from a long distance. The interior is rich in decorations and paintings, and in the sacristy is preserved Murillo's "Assumption," for which $75,000 has been refused.

This picture is one of the twenty-seven versions of the theme painted by Murillo. When Napoleon invaded Spain, the clergy of Guadalajara, in testimony of patriotic devotion, sent King Carlos the Fourth a large sum of money to aid in the defence of the country. In recognition of this the king presented the cathedral with Murillo's masterpiece from his collection in the Escurial. When the French were in Mexico in 1864, and captured Guadalajara during Maximilian's short reign, they endeavored to seize the painting as a trophy for the Louvre, but it was concealed, and even an offer of $25,000 did not lead to a revelation of its hiding-place.

In one of the buildings overlooking the main plaza is

IN GUADALAJARA.
View of the cathedral and beautiful main plaza.

the American Club, where visiting Americans and Englishmen are welcomed. There are quite a number of Americans in the city; they have started several churches and a school, and there is an enterprising weekly newspaper, the *Jalisco Times*. The well-to-do Americans have established themselves in a beautiful quarter where the wide streets are lined with shady trees and the houses are embowered in tropical foliage. This district, which is rapidly assuming an Americanized appearance, is popularly known as the American Colony.

On several evenings during the week a fine military band plays in the main plaza, and it is now the fashion for the élite of the city to ride round and round while the concert is in progress, the promenading, which was formerly in vogue, having been practically discontinued. Even in these prosaic days a wonderfully picturesque sight is presented when the band is playing. The music, the balmy tropical evening, the plaza illuminated with its many electric lights, the palms, flowers and orange trees, the peons in their red sarapes and sombreros, the lines of carriages passing round, filled with dark-eyed beauties daintily attired as in summer-time, — all, under a clear sky, dazzling stars and a glorious moon, combine to make a scene of enchantment.

There is, in fact, a good deal of life in Guadalajara, and the atmosphere of the place is far more cheerful than that of Mexico City. The climate, too, is much more favorable for outdoor life; and you can sit outside a café enjoying your refresco while listening to the music in the plaza without having the chilly sensation and dread of pneumonia that are too often experienced in the capital.

Guadalajara has five theatres, one of them, the Degollado, being the largest on the American continent, excepting, perhaps, the Metropolitan Opera House in New York. It is a handsome building much larger and finer externally than any theatre in the United States. In the city there are twenty-eight hotels and twenty-five public baths, and when it is remembered that Guadalajara did not have a railway to it seventeen years ago, these statistics are interesting.

The day after my arrival the city was en fête, celebrating one of the numerous Mexican public holidays. The business buildings were gayly decorated with the national colors of red, white and green, there was a civic and military procession and the streets resounded with the strains of music. Itinerant vendors of all kinds had gathered round the plaza, giving the place quite a festive appearance. The streets were thronged with sight-seers, and the smart American electric cars which run through the city and out to the suburbs were crowded with passengers.

In the midst of this holiday-making a large party of Mystic Shriners arrived from Mexico City and found quarters at one of the large hotels. They were given a luncheon by their compatriots residing in the city, and while this was in progress, some good music was furnished by one of the local military bands. In honor of their American visitors, the Mexican musicians played a selection of American national airs, such as the Star-Spangled Banner, Hail Columbia, and Yankee Doodle. Most of the Shriners had a very limited knowledge of Spanish, and at the conclusion of this complimentary pot-pourri some of them shouted such appreciative American phrases as "Good, good; bully for the Mexicans," while several enthusiasts yelled "Adios, adios" (good-by), evidently thinking that the word was synonymous with "Bravo." The bandsmen naturally understood it to mean that the Americans wanted them to go, having had enough of their music, so they commenced to pack up their instruments preparatory to marching off.

It was only when the High Imperial Potentate himself hurried to the bandmaster and explained matters with the aid of an interpreter that the irate musicians were pacified and smilingly resumed their playing.

The Shriners were afterwards given a reception at the American Club, all the members and their wives being present to meet the visitors and the ladies of their party. It was there that I had an opportunity of meeting the "Imp. Pot.," who, throwing off his imperial dignity for the time being, was very convivial, told funny stories in the smoking-room, and indeed was quite the life of the party.

Leaving the club later on to return to my hotel, I strolled across the plaza, with its throngs of fashionably dressed people, and went along one of the quieter streets. Here I witnessed a scene which furnished a delightful contrast to the rush of prosaic modern progress which is rapidly transforming the ancient City of Guadalajara. A drowsy peon and his boy were slowly driving a large flock of turkeys along the street, keeping them in motion with the aid of long sticks with which they occasionally prodded the birds. This is one of the olden customs of Guadalajara which still survives, in spite of the city's wonderful up-to-dateness. Instead of going to a poultry shop, the housekeepers of Guadalajara buy their turkeys from these vendors as they pass through the streets. Sometimes the purchaser has the bird despatched on the spot, but, in most cases, the turkey is kept for a week and fattened until it is in prime condition for the highly seasoned stew into which it is made.

During my stay in the city I paid a visit to the Hospicio, one of Guadalajara's public institutions which is unique in its way. Instead of being a hospital, as its name would indicate, it is an asylum for the poor of all ages. It is a series of great stone buildings covering an entire square, contains twenty-three patios with fountains and flowers, and shelters a strange assortment of humanity, — aged men and women, boys and girls and even babies. The inmates all looked well-fed and cheerful, everything was scrupulously clean and the appointments of the place would have done credit to any American institution. The children in the Hospicio are given a good education, and when they grow older are taught some useful occupation. In one of the departments which I visited, the girls, mostly Indians, were making some beautiful embroideries.

Electric traction, which has done so much in developing the suburbs of some American towns, is having the same effect on the growth of Guadalajara, the laying of suburban street-railway lines having caused the city to extend in every direction. There are few rides in the world which in point of picturesqueness can equal those about Guadalajara; the swift-moving cars, passing through fields of tropical vegetation and between hedges of cactus and palms, reach the plain from which there are superb views of the lofty mountains and distant glimpses of the beautiful white city.

In the village of San Pedro, to which the cars run, many of the wealthy citizens of Guadalajara have their country houses, and some of these are very charming. The famous Guadalajara ware comes from the potteries in this village, which turn out all sorts of water-jars and bottles in various beautiful shapes. They also make little figures representing almost every phase of Mexican life, such as water-carriers, cargadores, mule-drivers, vaqueros or cowboys, colored most cleverly and wonderfully modelled. An interesting collection of these can be bought for a few dollars. San Pedro is the home of two Indian sculptors, the Panduros, father and son, and at their studio a visitor who wishes to carry away a souvenir of Guadalajara can have

THE OLD AND NEW.

Street-car lines and electric-light posts are here shown in one of the old streets of Guadalajara.

his bust or statuette modelled in clay while he waits. These statuettes are wonderfully lifelike and are colored with great accuracy.

One morning I went out to see the most wonderful of Guadalajara's local sights, a deep gorge called the barranca, about six miles from the city. This, at some points, has a depth of nearly three thousand feet, and as climate in Mexico depends entirely upon altitude, this freak of nature enables Guadalajara, situated in the temperate zone, to have the climate and fruits of the tropics only six miles away, large quantities of bananas, cocoanuts and other hot-land fruits being grown in the depths of the barranca. In the higher lands adjacent to the city the fruits and vegetables of temperate lands are grown the year round, so that the people of Guadalajara are provided with a bountiful supply of good things for the table.

A small tram-car drawn by two sturdy mules took me to the beginning of the barranca, the line ending at the edge of this great chasm, where the scenery is magnificent, somewhat resembling that of the Grand Cañon of Arizona — a series of great castellated rocks, frowning precipices and deep abysses. Mounting a horse, I rode for miles down a winding road to the depths of the rocky gorge, experiencing a wonderful change of climate. At the top of the barranca the air was fresh and balmy; at the bottom of this natural hot-house the heat was tropical in its intensity. The ride, however, was delightful, my rocky path bordering the narrow Lerma River which flows through the depths of the barranca, dashing over the rocks amidst the tropical verdure of banana plants, orange trees and cocoanut palms; on either side the towering walls of the gorge rear themselves in perpendicular cliffs.

From Guadalajara the Mexican Central Railway has been extended westward between one hundred and fifty and two hundred miles to Manzanillo, an important port on the Pacific coast. With the completion of this line Guadalajara will now become still more important as a commercial centre, as the new ports of the Pacific coast will give access to the trade of the interior. The line opens up a vast mining region, rich in gold, silver, copper and lead. It runs through a fertile, picturesque country of high mountains, small lakes, rolling hills and broad valleys. The only active volcano in North America is a few miles from the line, — Colima, twelve thousand feet high, — twice as high as Vesuvius and higher than Mount Etna. From Manzanillo steamers run regularly to San Francisco and other American ports as well as to ports in southern Mexico. Thousands of cattle are raised on the plains west of Guadalajara, and in the hot lands along the coast all kinds of tropical fruits are grown. In the State of Colima, through which the railway passes, there are a large number of coffee plantations.

The State of Jalisco, in which Guadalajara is situated, is one of the most important in the Mexican union in point of population, and it is also one of the richest. It is a wonderfully fertile country, and having an abundance of running streams, irrigation is carried on extensively; it is also well wooded, some of the mountain ranges being covered with forests of timber suitable for all purposes. While manufacturing, agriculture and cattle-raising have hitherto been the main industries of Jalisco, mining now bids fair to take a foremost place. In recent years some rich mines of copper and other minerals have been developed in the western part of the State, on the route of the new railway extension.

Many of the members of the American Club whom I met in Guadalajara were engaged in mining in the mountains west of the city, and were enthusiastic concerning the mineral-producing possibilities of the country. The future development of these great states of Jalisco and Colima offer wonderful opportunities for the investment of capital, and undoubtedly this part of Mexico is destined to be one of the richest countries on the face of the earth.

Mining developments in the neighborhood of Guadalajara have brought there the usual number of "men with schemes." Strolling round the plaza one evening, I noticed some Americans of the Western "schemer" type seated together talking very excitedly. As I passed them, I caught such remarks as "The biggest —— thing in Mexico; millions in it." One of the prospective millionaires produced the usual piece of ore from his pocket and I heard him say, "Well, gentlemen, I've got the golderndest richest proposition here that you ever heard of. This little chunk of metal came from over Colima way and — wal, there's just simply millions in the little hole it came out of." I waited to hear no more, but fled. Was I never to escape from these men of millions?

What the men of schemes probably did not know is the astounding fact that some of the streets of Guadalajara are actually paved with gold. A few years ago, when the asphalt company repaved the city streets, the asphaltum was mixed with tailings from the old Spanish and Mexican reduction works in the Etzatlan district of Jalisco. After the paving had been done, the company's manager, out of curiosity, had a number of assays made of the old tailings. To his surprise, these assays revealed the fact that the tailings contained about fifteen dollars' worth of gold and silver in each ton. About four hundred tons of tailings were used in paving, so the net amount of gold and silver laid in the streets represented over $6000.

On leaving Guadalajara, I took the train to Atequiza, a village about forty miles from the city, the nearest station to Lake Chapala, where I had arranged to spend a week-end.

There are few important rivers and lakes in Mexico, but two of the latter, Chapala and Patzcuaro, are famous for their great size and beauty. Chapala is becoming a popular resort for visitors from all parts of Mexico. From Atequiza an old-fashioned stage-coach drawn by eight mules takes travellers to the village of Chapala on the shores of the lake.

Between Atequiza and Guadalajara there is a large hacienda through which the railway runs for several miles, and being so close to the city, this property has become extremely valuable. It employs an army of peons, and on its farms are grown all kinds of fruits and vegetables. There are broad fields of grain and large grazing grounds for herds of sheep and cattle. The stage-coach runs through one of the hacienda villages, with its church, schoolhouse, several modern mills, ancient granaries, massive dwellings and adobe huts.

The road from Atequiza to Chapala, like most Mexican country roads, is not macadamized, but is full of rocks and ruts which toss the old coaches about like ships in a stormy sea. Lucky are those passengers who get outside seats, for those who ride inside are almost choked with dust before the journey is over. Recently some steps have been taken to improve the public highway from Guadalajara to Chapala, and although the road would stagger most American motorists, several cars come over it every week from the city to the lake.

I sat beside the stage-coach driver, and was very much amused at the way in which he kept his eight animals on the move with constant cracks of his long whip and frequent trilling a-r-r-es, which he would vary with shouts of "mula, macho" — mula being the female, and macho the male, mule. How they ever managed to drag the great lumbering stage-coach, with its load of passengers and luggage,

I could not understand. A German mechanical engineer who was my fellow-passenger, remarked to me, "This coach is typical of old Mexico. They use it simply because their forefathers used a coach of this kind. It's a big load in itself without any extra weight. A light American coach would get over the ground in half the time and stand the wear and tear just as well; but these fellows wouldn't think of using one because 'no es costumbre,' it isn't the custom." The only redeeming trait that I could see about the old vehicle was that it was picturesque. It was unwieldy and uncomfortable, being hung upon leather bands instead of steel springs, and jolting so much that the unfortunate passengers inside had to be strapped in their seats to keep them in their places.

So we swayed and jolted over the rough road, bordered with low stone walls dividing the cultivated fields from the highway, winding up and down hill amongst rocky mountains until, in the distance, we saw the glistening waters of Chapala melting away to the horizon; by the side of the lake was nestling the village of Chapala, set in a little oasis of green verdure, and towering above the housetops were the two beautiful spires of the parish church. A few miles more and we clattered down the main street, over the rough cobble-stones, to the door of the hotel.

There are three hotels at Chapala, all very much alike. I found quarters at the Arzapalo, a rambling stone building of two stories, a few feet from the lake and commanding some beautiful views. Although somewhat crude in a few minor particulars, the place was comfortable and, for a Mexican hotel at least, unusually well managed.

Very few Americans have ever heard of Lake Chapala, although it is one of the largest lakes in the world. It is seventy miles long, east and west, and twenty miles across at some points, covering a superficial area of a thousand square miles. It has an altitude of about five thousand feet and is surrounded by mountains, some of which are over ten thousand feet. They are covered with scrubby trees and vegetation of various hues that add much to the beauty of the scenery.

All along the shores of the lake, and in the Lerma River which runs into it, hundreds of peons are employed in gathering and burning yellow water-lily which has invaded the waters. A few years ago some imbecile planted a quantity of the lily in the river, thinking it would look pretty. In an incredibly short time it spread like wildfire; some of the streams were completely choked with it, and when I visited Chapala the river was covered in places with green masses of the plant. It had spread all along the lake when the Mexican government took the matter in hand and appropriated a large sum of money for its destruction. At night, fires can be seen blazing along the shores of the lake where the peons have collected and are burning large piles of the noxious weed.

The village of Chapala is built on the northern shore of the lake, where a sloping, sandy beach makes a capital bathing place. The narrow streets centre at a tiny plaza adorned with orange trees and other tropical vegetation. Here on Sundays the market is held, and picturesque natives from the surrounding country pour into the little town and gather there. A number of pretty villas are dotted along the lake's side, embowered in bougainvillea and hibiscus, palms and orange trees. On a hill a short distance from the shore some land has been divided into building lots for villas, with the idea of starting a model American summer village; but the price of the ground is so high — about $1000 per lot — that very few purchasers had been found.

A rude pier of rough stones extends into the water, and here one can embark in a rowing or sailing boat or a naphtha launch and take trips up and down the lake. There are one or two old-fashioned steamers on it, but they do not make regular runs and have to be chartered for special trips. There are also a number of small fishing schooners. The little village, with its big white church and mountainous background, bears a wonderful resemblance to some of the lake villages in northern Italy, and makes a most beautiful picture. This little bit of the lake might be taken for a scene on Como; but the waters of Chapala are slightly yellowish instead of blue. The lake, too, is very shallow, and for this reason the government has prohibited its waters being used for irrigation.

In the lake there are some small white fish (pescados blancos) which are caught with nets, but there is nothing to tempt the angler. The Mexican government is now stocking the waters with trout, bass, perch and other game fish, which may eventually make the lake more attractive to lovers of the rod and reel; but the Indians along the shore are such inveterate netters that it will be very difficult to breed the fish.

For the sportsman Chapala is far more attractive. Lying along some parts of the lake are extensive flats that are overflowed at high water. During the winter months these swamps are favorite resorts for myriads of feathered visitors from the north, ducks of all kinds and sizes, snipe, plover, geese, swans, and in fact all varieties of birds that like muddy creeks and shallow waters here congregate and fatten. While I was in Chapala a retired English naval officer, who had been cruising about the lake, brought in thirty geese one evening, the result of only one day's shooting. He said that Chapala afforded the finest wild-fowl shooting that he had ever enjoyed in his travels.

Chapala is beautiful at all times, but is particularly charming as the day wanes; in fact, it is famous for its sunsets. The great expanse of waters with its mountainous background then becomes a thing of wondrous beauty. As night falls a stiff breeze generally springs up, which makes the air very fresh and invigorating. Then the waters of the lake dash on the shore and break over the pier in marked contrast to their placid appearance in the daytime.

A short distance along the shore, within sight of the beautiful electric-lighted villas, there is another of those queer contrasts so often met with in Mexico. Here is a little village of Indian fishermen who live in huts or wigwams of rushes and adobe, some of the fishing houses being built on piles in the lake like those of the prehistoric lake-dwellers in Switzerland. These Indians are the descendants of the fierce Chapaltecos, one of the last tribes subdued by the Spaniards. At sunset these wild-looking creatures, in very scanty raiment, can be seen casting their nets in the lake and catching the small white fish, which they sell in the neighborhood. To visit this place when the sun is setting, and see the weird figures flitting about beneath the semitropical foliage, conversing in low tones in their ancient dialect, living the most primitive of lives, makes it almost impossible to realize that hardly a mile away are comfortable hotels, newspapers, the telegraph, the telephone, a railway, Pullman cars and other adjuncts of latter-day civilization.

QUAINT OLD GUANAJUATO.
Where much foreign capital is invested in silver-mining.

CHAPTER XXIII

"THE SILVER CITY"

FROM the days of the Spanish Conquest, Mexico has taken the lead as a silver-producing country; it is preëminently the land of silver, and it has furnished fully one-third of the world's supply of this precious metal. Silver is found almost everywhere in the country, but the richest mines are those in the vicinity of the ancient city of Guanajuato. From these wonderful mines came a large part of the treasure which helped to build up the great Spanish empire; and much of the glittering white metal was coined into those huge pieces of eight which figure so prominently in pirate stories. It is to its great mining industry that Guanajuato owes its existence and its prosperity, and to-day it is popularly known as "the silver city."

It was to this interesting place that I set out on leaving Lake Chapala. Jolting back to Atequiza in the old stagecoach one morning, I took the train southward 136 miles to the junction of Iripuato, which I reached late in the afternoon. Iripuato, a pretty little town with a population of twenty thousand, is situated in the midst of a rich farming country, wheat, maize, fruit, vegetables and various other products of the temperate zone being grown on the haciendas. To Mexicans the name of Iripuato is synonymous with strawberries, as that delicious fruit is grown there all the year round and sold every day in the year. Swarms of peons with large basketfuls of luscious berries surround the trains when they arrive, offering their wares for sale.

On changing at Iripuato, a train of the Mexican National Railway took me to Silao in about an hour, where there was a change to another train and a ride of about half an hour to Marfil. It was late in the evening when I left the train there. A cargador piloted me to the outside of the station, where there were three little street-cars, one first-class and two second-class, each drawn by two mules. The first-class car was already packed with passengers, and I had to stand on the rear platform, which was also crowded. We started off at a good pace, rattling down an unlighted country road. Occasionally, in the semi-darkness, I could catch a glimpse of rolling hills on each side of the road, quaint stone bridges over a rushing stream, and square, massive stone buildings which a fellow-passenger informed me were silver-reduction works.

Although Guanajuato has a population of over forty thousand, and is an important city, the railway when I arrived there was still three miles distant, and this little street-car was the only means of getting passengers and their baggage into the place. A large force of men were at work, however, extending the line into the city, where a station was being built.

The unlighted, dusty road eventually gave place to the narrow, cobble-paved, electric-lighted streets of the city. Along the way were houses and business buildings of the usual Mexican type, built of stone or stucco, with barred windows, balconies and flat roofs, but looking much more dingy and ancient than any I had yet seen. The streets were thronged with blanketed natives, and there seemed to be an unusually large number of street vendors squatting beside their little stalls, selling fruit, dulces and other articles. At first sight Guanajuato seemed to be a typical city of the past. Unlike Guadalajara, there were no smart modern buildings in the principal streets, no swift-moving electric cars, no asphalt paving; and the whole place seemed to be enveloped in a drowsy, old-world atmosphere.

I went to an American hotel, which was the usual old Spanish mansion slightly transformed. In its palmy days it must have been quite a palatial residence, this rambling old building, with all sorts of queer corridors and a large central patio where there was a moss-covered fountain and bright flowers. It was quaint and rather crude in its appointments, but comfortable enough, and the meals were well cooked and served.

Guanajuato is two hundred and fifty miles from Mexico City, and is the capital of the State of the same name. It has an altitude of nearly seven thousand feet, so that its climate is not so uniform as that of Guadalajara, the days being usually warmer, while the nights and mornings are much colder. Built in a deep, narrow valley or gulch between the mountains, the situation of the city bears some resemblance to that of the lower town of Carlsbad; but the surrounding mountains, unlike those at Carlsbad, are sun-baked, treeless and overgrown with cactus.

The city derives its name from the word " Quanashuato," meaning the Hill of the Frogs, which was given to it by the Tarascan Indians, whose descendants still inhabit this part of Mexico. After the Conquest, the Spaniards altered it to Guanajuato (pronounced *Wah-nah-wahto*). There is no extant tradition throwing any light on why this place was called the Hill of the Frogs, unless it was so named in honor of some Indian deity. This theory has gained some support from the fact that a huge frog cut in stone was found during some excavations in the city a few years ago. Silver mining, the industry for which Guanajuato is famous, was commenced by the Spaniards in 1548, and the first settlement was started in 1557.

Owing to the peculiar situation of the city, very few of

the streets are level. Craggy mountains rise above the housetops, and the side streets run up hill, oftentimes having cobble-stone steps. Perched on the hillsides that rise almost perpendicularly above the city are huts of adobe and low, flat-roofed, stucco houses, tinted pale blue, cream and pink, in such out-of-the-way spots that you wonder how even a goat could ever reach them. The whole place, with its houses of antique mould, has an appearance that strongly reminds one of some city in the East, in Egypt or the Holy Land. Guanajuato is admitted by travellers to be one of the most picturesque cities in the world, and it is unlike any other in Mexico. Many of its streets are irregular, precipitous, rock-paved paths upon which wheeled vehicles are seldom seen, and down whose steep inclines half-dressed, picturesque men, women and children of the peon class contest the right of way with dashing horsemen and droves of patient burros.

A stone's throw from the hotel and right in the centre of the city is the principal plaza, the Jardin de la Union, a pretty square with shady trees and ever blooming flowers. Here, three or four times a week, good music is played by the local regimental band. Here, too, are some good shops, one or two fine old churches and a magnificent theatre (el Teatro Juarez) which would be a credit to London or Paris. This beautiful structure of pale green stone and marble, with a grand portico surmounted with statues, took twenty years to build and cost over a million dollars. Its internal decorations are magnificent, being unsurpassed by those in any other theatre of its class in North America. Near the plaza is the Mint, the Governor's Palace, and other fine public buildings. Some of the old churches have elaborately carved fronts, and the cathedral, a beautiful structure in early Spanish style, has a fine chime of bells, a rarity in Mexico.

One of the most interesting old buildings in the city is the Alhondiga or Castilla de Granaditas, erected in 1785 as a chamber of commerce and now used as a prison. When the first War of Independence broke out in 1810, the followers of the Mexican patriot priest, Hidalgo, forced their way into the city, and after a fierce battle captured the Spanish garrison, which had taken refuge in the Alhondiga. While the attack was in progress, Hidalgo called for a volunteer to go under the walls and set fire to the massive doors. A stalwart peon came forward, and with a large flat stone on his back as a shield against the Spaniard's shots, rushed in, torch in hand, and burned down the doors, giving admittance to Hidalgo and his followers. Breaking into the patio, the patriots met the Spaniards there and drove them up the grand staircase to the roof, where they surrendered. There are stains still shown which are said to be those of blood spilt in this fight. In one of the halls there is a statue of the Indian hero with the stone on his shoulders and the torch uplifted. After the suppression of the revolt, Hidalgo and his lieutenants, Allende, Aldama and Jimenez, were executed at Chihuahua, when their heads were brought to Guanajuato and hung on hooks outside the walls of the Alhondiga. These hooks are still to be seen outside the old building.

From the plaza the narrow streets wind up hill, revealing many artistic "bits" that recall scenes in one of the old cities in southern Italy. As I strolled in this direction early in the morning, there came down the cobble-paved highway a constant procession of barefooted Indians from the country, and clattering burros loaded with all sorts of merchandise — a wonderful picture of movement and color.

At the plaza I afterwards took a mule tram-car up the steep, winding street to the extreme end of the city, where there is a beautiful little park called the Presa de la Olla, in the middle of which are some large reservoirs supplying the city with water. In this district there are some charming houses, and here is situated the foreign colony, where a number of well-to-do Americans and some English, French and Germans have established their homes.

I must award Guanajuato the palm for having one of the prettiest parks in Mexico. The Presa de la Olla is surrounded with bare, towering mountains of pinkish hue, along the steep sides of which narrow trails run out into the country. Through the centre of the park, which abounds in green, well-kept lawns, runs a stream which comes down from the upper hills, falling from one reservoir into another and forming little lakelets crossed by bridges. The walls of the reservoirs and the bridges are covered with vines and flowers, while the surrounding houses are completely embowered in them. Altogether it is one of the most beautiful spots in all Mexico. From this end of the town, which is perched on the top of a hill, there is a splendid view of the city, with its quaint churches, narrow streets and the queer houses on the hillsides.

Returning to the other end of the town, I visited another of the sights of Guanajuato, a most grewsome one. This is an underground catacomb, such as is found in some parts of the Old World, which is situated in the Panteon or municipal cemetery on the outskirts of the town. Under a broiling sun I climbed up a steep hill in the afternoon and reached this burial-ground, a small square surrounded with a high stone wall. In the middle were a few humble graves with simple headstones, and some fine monuments. On two sides, built in the walls, were rows of vaults under porticos, the compartments for bodies rising in tiers. According to Mexican burial customs, graves or vaults are leased, a certain stipulated sum being paid for the first five years with the privilege of renewal. If at the end of that time the mourners' grief has cooled and further payment is not made, the remains are taken from the vault or grave. If only bones remain, they are thrown into a heap at the end of an arch under the pavement. Sometimes, however, a body is preserved and mummified by the peculiar soil and the dry air of the climate. In that case it is wrapped in a shroud and placed standing in a vault with similar mummies.

The gate-keeper of the Panteon acted as my guide and revealed to me the horrors of this underground charnel-house. Lifting up a flagstone in the pavement, he disclosed a flight of stone steps by which we descended to a large underground vault, lighted by some windows somewhere above. In one corner of the vault was an enormous pile of skulls and bones, and the stench was almost overpowering. At the end of the vault was a glass door. I looked through this and saw about forty mummies standing on their feet, wrapped in white shrouds. They were, until recently, left naked, but the authorities have now had them draped in this manner. In two or three instances the clothing in which the bodies had been buried was preserved. These awful relics of humanity were standing in all kinds of attitudes, and their distorted features presented various grotesque expressions: the laughing lady, the weeping lady and the toothless old coquette with ghastly leer from under her thin gray hair. A scraggy gentleman with black beard and hair leaned against the wall, meditating on the vanity of flesh, while a young woman with composedly folded hands stood in what Delsarte would have called the attitude of subjective reflection with a half-suppressed yawn. It was a horrible and ghastly sight. It seemed such a terrible desecration to disinter the poor dead and to make them a cheap exhibition for tourists.

One of the ghastly company was dressed as a vaquero in full riding-dress of ancient pattern. I afterwards observed to an American acquaintance that this mummy in life might have been a cavalier of old Spain in pre-republican days. "Pre-republican nothing," he retorted. "Why, that's the mummy of old man Smith, the saloon-keeper who got killed in a fight a few years ago. His widow is still doing business at the old stand." It is thus that our prosaic countrymen destroy romance. I was glad to leave the evil-smelling vault, registering a vow then and there never to enter another catacomb.

There are many grisly stories of adventures in the house of the dead. One is of an American from Texas who was suspected of being in the pay of the French during Maximilian's ill-fated attempt to found an empire. He was caught and robbed by bandits near Guanajuato. His captors then decided to punish him for being a traitor to Mexico; and in order to bring about his death through horrible torture, they conceived the idea of shutting him up in the mummy vault, where, after some days, he was discovered raving mad.

Like all Mexican cities, Guanajuato is a place of contrasts. On the main street there are some very fair shops and several American agencies for such goods as typewriters and phonographs. While you are contemplating these evidences of progress, you hear a clatter of hoofs, and a train of burros comes along the street driven by swarthy Indians in their picturesque garb, bringing in fruit and vegetables, or perhaps loads of silver ore from the neighboring mines. But these interesting scenes will soon have passed away; for Guanajuato before long will have asphalted streets and electric tram-cars, while electric trains will bring in the market commodities and carry down the ore from the mountains.

A CHAMBER OF HORRORS.
Mummies in the vault of the Panteon at Guanajuato.

The increasing number of Americans, too, cannot fail to have some effect on the manners and customs of the people. I was very much amused at overhearing a conversation between the son of my hotel proprietor, who acted as clerk, and another youthful American. They were just at the age when young men devote a good deal of thought to the fair sex, and were discussing one of their friends who was very sweet on a Mexican girl. "Well," observed my young friend, the clerk, "Mexican girls will wait a long time before they'll catch me playing bear outside a window. If I'm not good enough to go inside the house, I'm not going to play the fool outside."

"That's just what I say, and I was telling Bob the same thing," remarked the other young man. "If he plays the bear for a girl, he ought to be ashamed of himself. That's a thing no decent American would ever do." Evidently, if the young ladies of Guanajuato wish to marry Americans, they will have to modify the popular Mexican bear-playing custom.

As in other Mexican towns, the citizens of Guanajuato have abandoned their promenading in the plaza, which formerly gave a touch of life to the old city after dark. When the band played in the evening, I noticed very few women in the plaza, and certainly none of the higher classes. Plenty of Mexican men and a good many Americans were to be seen there. As I strolled round one evening, I passed a group of Americans seated together, talking rather excitedly, and at once recognized them as my old friends, "the men with schemes." "Yes," said one of the party, as I passed, "it's the biggest —— proposition in the whole of Mexico. Why, man, there's millions in it." I hurried away to the seclusion of a quiet, dimly lighted street — anywhere to escape from those omnipresent Western men of schemes and visionary wealth.

But Guanajuato is par excellence the place for schemes connected with precious metal, and to describe the place without giving a few details of the great silver-mining industry, which is the backbone of its prosperity, would be like the play of Hamlet with the melancholy Dane left out. For without the silver mines there would be no Guanajuato.

The first important silver mining there was commenced by the Spaniards in 1548, when the San Bernabe vein of the famous La Luz mine was discovered. These mines, however, had been worked by the Aztecs long before the Spaniards came. The fame of Guanajuato as a silver-mining region grew apace after the first operations of the Spaniards; other mines were discovered, and from 1548 to the present time it is said that fully 1,500,000,000 dollars' worth of silver has been produced there. It is undoubtedly the richest mineralized district in the whole of Mexico.

In the old Spanish times the wealthy mine-owners lived like princes, spending their money lavishly. Fortunes were constantly made and lost. Early in the last century two mines alone, in the La Luz district, yielded about four million ounces of silver every year. The stories of the Mexican silver kings of the past read more like Monte Cristo romances than the hard facts of lives actually lived. Money was made so fast in those days that it was impossible to spend it except in gambling, for the refinements of luxury on which millionaires now lavish their wealth were then undreamed of.

A shrewd prospector in the early days, named Zambrano, discovered a mine which brought him immense wealth. He spent most of his time at the capitals of Europe, living as extravagantly as possible, squandering vast sums at the gaming table, but he managed to leave a snug little fortune of $60,000,000. One of his whims was to lay a silver pavement in front of his house, but this the authorities forbade. In those days, too, it must be remembered that silver was on a parity with gold. The Conde de Valenciana, who discovered one of the richest mines in Guanajuato, derived so much wealth from it that he is said to have got rid of $100,000,000 in a few years. Another silver king sent the king of Spain $2,000,000 as a Christmas present, and asked to be allowed to build galleries and portales of silver around his mansion. This request was refused, the Spanish authorities declaring that such magnificence was the privilege of royalty only.

The Guanajuato millionaires eventually became so wildly extravagant that one of the viceroys prohibited their scattering handfuls of silver coins as they rode through the streets, because it increased the number of beggars in the city and constituted a public nuisance! It is said that at the present day there is a Mexican who owns a mine of such wonderfully rich ore that the entrance to it is guarded by thick stone walls and steel doors. He is an inveterate gambler and when his available funds have disappeared, he simply hires a few miners to take out $50,000 or $100,000 worth of silver, which is very soon lost.

One of the famous Mexican mining kings of the present day is Pedro Alvarado, an Indian, known as the peon millionaire. A few years ago some wonderfully rich ore was struck in the Palmillo mine that he owned, and he became one of the wealthiest men in the world. Although he and his wife still dress in peon clothes, he has built a magnificent house, and being fond of music, has filled it with musical instruments of almost every description, including a number of costly pianos. Alvarado is very charitable and recently distributed $2,000,000 among the poor of Mexico. He has given away several fortunes in this manner, and during the past eight years has built fifty churches and a hundred schools. Not long ago he offered to pay off the Mexican national debt, but altered his mind when he found it was a little too big for even a silver king to settle.

Until recently, when foreign capital began to develop so many of the Mexican mines, the processes of extracting gold and silver were very slow and wasteful. To-day the tailings of many of the old Spanish mines are being worked over, and the precious metal extracted at a good profit. A few years ago, some Americans discovered that the adobe bricks used in constructing some peon huts in Guanajuato had been made from tailings containing a large percentage of gold and silver. They bought the huts, tore them down and extracted the precious metals, clearing a large sum by their enterprise.

The patio process of silver extraction, discovered by Bartolome de Medina in 1557, is still in use in Guanajuato, although it is being gradually supplanted by more improved methods. In this process the ore is first crushed into powder by great stone rollers turned by droves of mules. It is then conveyed to a paved court by a stream of water until the mass, which resembles thin mortar, is about two feet deep. Into this patio mud, as it is called, quicksilver salt and blue vitriol are thrown. A number of mules are then driven round it for hours at a time until everything is well mixed, several weeks being usually required to complete this process. The resulting mass is next deposited in troughs of water, where the amalgam of silver and quicksilver sinks to the bottom, the metals being afterwards separated by a method of distillation. By the patio process it is asserted that not more than ten per cent of silver is lost. Terrible suffering, however, is inflicted on the poor mules by the action of the vitriolic liquid, which eats into their legs and soon disables them. All along the road, from Marfil to Guanajuato, there are large silver haciendas or

SILVER MINING.
Burros bringing the ore from the mine to the smelter.

reduction works, to which the ore from the neighboring mines is brought for extraction.

Next to Guanajuato, the richest silver-mining district in Mexico, is in the neighborhood of Pachuca, eighty-four miles from the capital. This town has a population of nearly forty thousand, and its altitude is nearly eight thousand feet, even higher than Mexico City. Pachuca is a very windy place; at times roasting hot, at others freezing cold, so that it is not exactly a health resort. It is the only town in Mexico where there are houses with stoves and chimneys. In the surrounding districts there are nearly three hundred mines. Silver ore was first discovered there by a poor shepherd nearly four hundred years ago, since which time the mines have been worked constantly and have yielded fabulous sums. One of them, La Trinidad, produced nearly fifty million dollars' worth of silver in ten years. There is a large American population in Pachuca and a good many Englishmen and Canadians.

The Spaniards, in the early days, worked only the richest mines, thinking little of ore that did not yield at least a hundred ounces to the ton. Their mining operations were conducted in a very primitive manner. In working the mines, they constructed great shafts down which ran ladders, and peons brought up the ore in sacks on their backs. The same method is still followed in most of the mines, the "poor Indian" toiling up the long ladders several times a day without a rest, carrying a leather sack on his back, sometimes containing over two hundred pounds of ore. In the early Spanish times thousands of Indians were enslaved and compelled by their cruel taskmasters to work in the mines early and late, being flogged if they refused. When a mine was flooded, the peons cleared it by carrying up bucketfuls of water. Several rich mines which were abandoned in those days on account of flooding have now been cleared out and are again in operation. Improved extracting processes and transportation are also making many old mines profitable. The trains of burros still bring down ore from the mines, but are being gradually supplanted by tramways.

The Spaniards, in describing the wealth of the Aztec land, did not mention the silver, but spoke much of the gold, of which all the ornaments of the chiefs were made. It is narrated that Montezuma gave presents of gold ornaments to Cortés to the value of more than seven million dollars. Where these great quantities of gold came from has never been discovered; for while gold in paying amounts is found in many places combined with silver and other minerals, still the quantity mined has ever proved very small in comparison with the value of the silver. It is believed that many of the Indians know where gold exists in enormous quantities in Mexico, the traditions having been handed down from their forefathers; but for some unaccountable reason they keep the whereabouts of these deposits a profound secret.

In the land of the Tlapanecos there is said to be a gold deposit of fabulous richness, tradition relating that the Indians paid tribute to their Spanish conquerors in gold nuggets. All attempts to discover the source of this gold supply have been in vain. It is related that the Indians once agreed to take a Spanish priest to the place on condition that he made the journey blindfolded. The wily old padre consented to this, but before starting tied a small bag of Indian corn to his belt under his cloak, and after every few steps of his horse dropped a grain to the ground, with the object of marking the way. After travelling some distance, the bandage was taken from the priest's eyes and he was allowed to look around, when he beheld tons of quartz glistening with rich yellow gold. As he stood spellbound, contemplating the vast wealth that was soon to be his, an Indian stepped up and handed him a bag, saying: "Padre, you lost your corn on the way; but here it is, every grain." Thus he was never able to find his way back to this wonderful region, and the cunning Spaniards were again outwitted by the simple natives.

With the introduction of railways, improved machinery and extracting processes, large quantities of low-grade ores are now being profitably worked in Mexico. Smelters and works for the cyanide process are being started in all the important mining districts, and at the present time the mining industry gives employment to nearly two hundred thousand men. Wages are still very low, the native miners rarely earning more than fifty cents a day, while common labor is paid only half that amount. In the production of silver, Mexico is unsurpassed by any other country, the annual output of the mines ranging from thirty to forty million dollars. As a gold-producing country it now holds the fifth place, the total output for 1908 having been valued at over $18,000,000.

Among the other valuable minerals found in Mexico are copper, iron, lead and graphite. There are a number of rich copper mines in the country, and the total production for 1908 was about 70,000 tons. There are some important iron deposits in northern Mexico, especially in the vicinity of Durango and Monterey. Lead exists in great quantities, and most of the graphite used in the United States comes from Mexico. An abundant supply of petroleum is being obtained in Tehuantepec and Tampico. Coal has been found, but only in small quantities, most of that used in Mexico being brought from England and the United States. In some of the mining districts it costs fifteen dollars per ton, and its high price has been a serious obstacle to the introduction of modern machinery requiring steam power.

CHAPTER XXIV

THE TITIAN AT TZINTZUNTZAN

THE charm of Mexico is the variety of its scenery — the majestic snow-capped mountains; the rolling prairies; tropical forests jewelled with gorgeous orchids amidst which flutter spangled blue butterflies; rivers embowered in the densest shade; fields yellowing to harvest; and the steaming, miasmic marsh lands waving with green sugar-cane. You can see all these facets of the earth's beauty in a journey of twenty-four hours.

Mexico can even rival the picturesqueness of Switzerland and the Italian lakes. For at Lake Patzcuaro one has scenery which is not surpassed by that of Interlaken or Como. This lake is certainly one of the most beautiful in the world.

A railway journey of a few hours took me from Guanajuato to the little town of Patzcuaro on the borders of the lake, which is one of the most picturesque places in all Mexico. The town is about three miles from the station, and travellers journey thither in an old-fashioned stage-coach similar to that which runs between Atequiza and Chapala. I found it a dusty, jolting ride, but Patzcuaro proved a sufficient recompense for all the discomforts experienced in getting there. It is a wonderful old town and, in some respects, is Toledo in miniature. Lining its narrow, crooked streets are quaint old houses, with overhanging eaves supported by roof rafters similar to those which are seen in the towns of southern Spain. Many of these old mansions have large shady verandas overgrown with creeping plants and masses of bright tropical flowers. In some parts of the town iron chains stretched from house to house support wonderful old lanterns, formerly the only method of street lighting. Patzcuaro has some fine old churches dating from early Spanish times, and crumbling stone shrines are set in the walls at almost every street corner. In the middle of the town is a wide plaza shaded with venerable trees, and here on market nights swarms of Indian vendors sell their fish, fruit and vegetables by the light of little fires, making a scene that is wildly picturesque. Although seven thousand feet above sea-level, the town is so close to the hot lands that the market is always filled with tropical fruits and flowers, and the streets are thronged with natives in costumes of warmer altitudes.

Viewed from the shore, the lake presents a scene of surpassing beauty. It is rather narrow but of great length, and from its very edge rise lofty cliffs or pine-clad mountains, round the base of which its waters are often lost to view; while dotted over its surface are numerous little islands, on some of which are primitive Indian villages of grass-thatched bamboo huts. Queer flat-bottomed sailing boats, for freight and passengers, are navigated by Indian mariners on the blue waters.

A voyage of three hours in one of these craft took me from the town of Patzcuaro to ancient Tzintzuntzan, now a straggling Indian village, but which before the Spaniards came was a great city and the capital of the Tarascan kings. In the vicinity of the place there are a number of prehistoric ruins. After the Conquest, Tzintzuntzan again became a place of importance, but in the course of time its greatness once more departed and it fell into decay. Bordering the narrow streets of the village, which run at right angles, are crumbling walls of stuccoed adobe, behind which are the houses. Through gaping holes in the walls occasional glimpses can be caught of once pretentious mansions, now in ruins and overgrown with a tangle of vines.

The dilapidated parish church which stands in the middle of the village was once the chapel of the powerful Convent of San Francisco, which was closed in 1740, and since then has gradually fallen into ruins. In the convent garden there are still to be seen some venerable olive trees whose gnarled trunks have weathered the storms of 350 years. Beneath the shade of some of these were buried some of the great dignitaries of the church and several of the chiefs who sided with Cortés in the days of the Spanish Conquest. The Indians of Tzintzuntzan are industrious folk, mostly engaged in farming and fishing, and are intensely devout.

My principal object in visiting Tzintzuntzan was to see one of the most important paintings in the world, which hangs in the old church, and is no less than a Titian which was presented to the Convent of San Francisco by Philip II of Spain. Its authenticity is beyond dispute. The subject is the "Entombment of Christ."

Escorted by the padre and the sacristan, I was led through the patio and along a dark corridor which ended at a massive door, barred, chained and padlocked. After much clanking of chains and creaking of rusty hinges, the key turned in the padlock and the door was opened. The sacristan carried a lighted taper, for the room was quite dark. Stepping forward, the padre pulled back the shutters from an unglazed window protected by iron bars, and a flood of sunshine revealed the picture. The coloring was magnificent, with all the superb tints for which Titian is famous.

Strangely out of place the great picture looked, in the midst of its tawdry surroundings, gleaming from a wide carved white frame which had once been gilt. But its

MEXICO'S ART TREASURE.
The famous Titian at Tzintzuntzan.

preservation is marvellous, probably due in a great measure to the climate and to the clear air which circulates through the church. Large sums of money have been offered for the painting, the Archbishop of Mexico, among others, having offered, it is said, $50,000 for it; but the devout Indians of Tzintzuntzan steadfastly refused to part with their masterpiece. They worship it with a blind idolatry, even refusing to allow it to be photographed.

F. Hopkinson Smith, the well-known artist and author, visited Tzintzuntzan some years ago, when tourists were seldom seen in that region, and the painting was far more rigorously guarded than it is to-day. In his book, "A White Umbrella in Mexico," he has given an interesting account of his expedition and a technical description of the famous painting, which, he says, is undoubtedly the work of Titian.

In giving a brief history of the painting, Mr. Smith adds: "In 1533 Charles V of Spain appointed Vasco de Queroga to the Bishopric of Michoacan to restore peace to that part of Mexico which had been almost depopulated through the misgovernment of the Spanish officials. Queroga established his see in the church of San Francisco at Tzintzuntzan in 1538; he founded schools, developed agriculture, conciliated the natives and restored prosperity. When Philip II ascended the throne, the good deeds of the bishop reached him. During this period the royal palace at Madrid was filled with Titian's finest pictures. Titian was living at this period, and visited Spain in 1550. Remembering these dates, the religious zeal of Philip and his interest in the distant church, it is quite possible that he either ordered this very picture from the master himself or selected it from the royal collection. It is quite improbable that the royal donor would have sent the work of an inferior painter or a copy by one of Titian's pupils.

Another distinguishing feature, and by far the most conclusive, is its handling. Without strong contrasting tones of color, Titian worked out a peculiar golden mellow tone — divided it into innumerable small but effective shades, producing thereby a most complete illusion of life. This Titianesque quality is particularly marked in the nude body of the Christ, the flesh appearing to glow with a hidden light."

Mr. Smith made a close inspection of the picture and examined it with the aid of a powerful magnifying glass. "In the eagerness of my search," he says, "I unconsciously bent forward and laid my hand on the Christ.

"'Ciudado! Estrangero, es muerte' (Beware, stranger, it is death), came a quick, angry voice behind me. I started back in alarm, and noticed two Indians in the room. One advanced threateningly, and the other rushed out, shouting for the padre. In an instant the place was crowded with natives, clamoring wildly and pointing to me with angry looks and gestures. The padre arrived, breathlessly followed by Moon (the author's travelling companion). 'You have put your foot in it,' said Moon in English, in great agitation. 'Now, do exactly what I tell you, and perhaps we may get away from here with a whole skin. Turn your face to the picture!' I did so. 'Now, walk backwards, drop on your knees and bow three times, you lunatic.'

"I had sense enough left to do this reverently and with some show of ceremony. Then, without moving a muscle of his face, and with the deepest solemnity, Moon turned to the padre and said to him: 'This distinguished painter is a true believer, holy father. His hand had lost its cunning, and he could no longer paint. He was told in a dream to journey to this place, where he would find this sacred treasure, upon touching which his hand would regain its power. See, here is the proof.' Here he pointed to a sketch I had made which was resting on an easel. The padre examined it, and repeated the miracle to the Indians in their own tongue. The change in their demeanor was instantaneous. The noise ceased; a silence fell upon the group and they crowded about the drawing, wonder-stricken. Moon bowed low to the padre, caught up the easel, pushed me ahead of him, — an opening was made, — the people standing back humbly, and we passed through the group and out into the village and thence to the lake, where we regained our boat and set sail."

From Patzcuaro I went to Queretaro, a town on the Mexican National Railway, which almost rivals Puebla in the number and size of its churches. It is a thriving place, with a population of forty thousand, and is rapidly coming to the front as a commercial centre.

In the early Spanish days Queretaro was not only one of the greatest strongholds of Catholicism in Mexico but was also the scene of a famous miracle. One of the Indian chiefs baptized by the priests who accompanied Cortés was Fernando, Chief of the Otomites. Soon after his conversion he marched an army to Queretaro, then an Indian town, with the intention of conquering the inhabitants and compelling them to accept Christianity. During the battle which ensued, an angel is said to have appeared in the heavens with a fiery cross, whereupon the fighting ceased and the baptizing began. The old church of Santa Cruz marks the site of the conflict and surrender. Of another of the old Queretaro churches — Santa Rosa — Charles Dudley Warner said: "It is one of the finest chapels in the world, rich in wood carving and overlaid with thick gold-leaf, almost gold plate. In some places the gold is covered with transparent tortoise-shell. The French, in 1866, tore down the great altar and burned it to get the gold, securing, it is said, the value of $1,500,000."

In 1867 Queretaro was the scene of the surrender of the unfortunate Emperor Maximilian and his little force of imperialists to the victorious Republican army. In the old convent of La Cruz, which served as the emperor's headquarters, the formal surrender took place on May 15, an event which sealed the fate of the short-lived Mexican Empire. The Republicans, it is said, were enabled to enter the town through the treachery of Colonel Lopez, Maximilian's chief-of-staff, who received a bribe of twenty thousand pesos.

Under the title of "Fernando Maximiliano of Hapsburg, Archduke of Austria," the emperor was summoned to appear before a court-martial on charges of filibustering and treason. He refused to attend, but his two generals, Miramon and Mejia, who were indicted on the same charges, were present during the proceedings. Although ably defended, the emperor and his generals were found guilty and sentenced to be shot the next day, but were granted a reprieve for five days. All appeals for mercy, including one from the United States government, were in vain, President Juarez firmly refusing to interfere.

On the morning of June 19 the three victims were taken to the Cerro de los Campañas, a hill near the town, and placed against a low wall. An officer with seven riflemen — the firing squad — were stationed a short distance away. Maximilian went up to the soldiers, shook hands with them and gave to each a gold coin. He then said, "Aim well, muchachos" (boys), and pointing to his heart, added, "Aim right here." Returning to his place, he addressed a few words to the soldiers, expressing the hope that his blood might be the last shed in the Mexican civil war. He then shouted, "Viva Independencia, viva Mexico." Miramon and Mejia cried, "Viva Mexico, viva el Emperador." The command to fire was then given, and the Mexican Empire came to an end. The two generals fell at the first volley, but it required a second volley before the emperor was dead. He had requested that he should be shot on the body, so that his mother might look upon his face. His body was interred in the old convent of the Capuchins, but was afterwards taken to Austria and buried at Miramar.

In 1869, with the permission of President Diaz, admirers of Maximilian erected a *chapelle expiatoire* on the spot where the execution took place, the project having been approved by the House of Hapsburg. Diplomatic relations between Austria and Mexico were then resumed. The beautiful little chapel of white stone has three slabs near the altar marking the positions occupied by Maximilian and the two generals at their execution.

CHAPTER XXV

THE ISTHMUS OF TEHUANTEPEC

WHEN President Diaz, in 1905, formally opened the Tehuantepec National Railway, he gave official recognition to one of the most wonderful enterprises that the world has witnessed in recent years. This railway, a magnificent piece of engineering, runs across the Isthmus of Tehuantepec from the Atlantic to the Pacific coast, and is now doing on an important scale what it is intended the Panama Canal shall eventually do, to a larger extent, in transporting freight between the two oceans.

From the early days of the Spanish Conquest the Isthmus of Tehuantepec was recognized as an important highway from the Atlantic to the Pacific. Situated at the extreme southern boundary of Mexico, the Isthmus, with the exception of Panama, is the narrowest neck of land on the American continent. Cortés, it is said, conceived the idea of building a canal across it; but as this was not feasible, a carriage road was constructed by the Spaniards. Engineers in later times recommended this route for a canal in preference to Panama, the distance in a straight line being only one hundred and twenty-five miles from the Atlantic to the Pacific.

When the Panama project under French management proved a failure, President Diaz, with his customary foresight, proposed a railway across the Isthmus of Tehuantepec, the idea being to unload vessels on the Atlantic or Pacific side and take the cargoes across the Isthmus for reshipment.

The plan was formally carried out, and the railway was completed in 1894. When opened to traffic, however, it proved to be imperfect, so in 1899 the Mexican government entered into an agreement with the English firm of S. Pearson & Sons, whereby they and the government were to be joint owners of the railway for fifty-one years and to share the net earnings. Although the construction was extremely difficult, owing to the nature of the country traversed by the line, which included some deep cañons, numerous rocky cuttings and miles of swampy land, the work was eventually finished, and the line, which is one hundred and ninety miles in length, was opened to traffic. The work was well done, and to-day the railway is one of the best in Mexico and excellently managed. It is also one of the few railways in the world which uses oil for fuel.

Fine harbors have been constructed at the ports of Salina Cruz on the Pacific, and Puerto Mexico, formerly called Coatzacoalcos, on the Atlantic coast, large warehouses having also been erected for the storage of freight. At both places the trains run right up to the ships' sides, where there are various modern devices for unloading cargoes quickly and economically and transferring them to the railway cars or *vice versa*. At Salina Cruz one of the finest dry-docks in the world is being built.

The Tehuantepec route will not only benefit Mexico by building up its ports on the two coasts but is already proving of great importance to international trade. A large amount of traffic which formerly went round Cape Horn or across the Panama Railway is now going *via* Tehuantepec. Another important fact is that this route is twelve hundred miles shorter between New York and San Francisco than the Panama Canal route. The average freight steamer would require four or five days to cover this distance, the expenses of the vessel for that period and the tolls for passing through the canal representing a far greater outlay than the charges incurred by the Tehuantepec route. It will probably be possible for the average cargo to be unloaded and carried across the Isthmus and reloaded in two days, and considering the amount of labor involved, the charges are reasonably low.

Tehuantepec is not only a much shorter route to the Pacific ports of the United States but to the Orient and Australia as well. American commercial interests are already recognizing this, and are using it extensively for the shipment of freight between the Atlantic and Pacific. A contract has recently been entered into with the American-Hawaiian Steamship Company for the carrying of sugar from Hawaii to New York *via* Tehuantepec, these great sugar cargoes having formerly gone round Cape Horn. The distance from Hawaii to New York *via* Tehuantepec is only 5305 miles, while by Cape Horn it is over 12,000.

It is a long journey from Mexico City to Tehuantepec, but it is one that is well worth taking, for the route is through those wonderful "hot lands" bordering the coast, the veritable heart of the tropics. To reach Tehuantepec from the capital, one has to take the Mexican Railway to Cordoba, a distance of one hundred and ninety eight miles, where connection is made with the Vera Cruz and Pacific Railroad, which runs two hundred and two miles to Santa Lucrezia in the extreme southern end of Mexico.

One evening at the beginning of March I started from the capital for Tehuantepec, travelling to Cordoba in a comfortable Pullman sleeping-car, and arriving there early the next morning, with ample time to catch the train for Santa Lucrezia, which left at nine o'clock. This train, which was the most comfortable one that I had thus far seen in Mexico, included Pullman sleeping- and drawing-room cars, and a well-arranged restaurant. In the sleeping

THE MEXICAN TROPICS.
An Indian Village on the Isthmus of Tehuantepec.

compartments the berths were specially designed for service in the tropics, and were provided with mosquito netting, an important requisite in the insect-infested "hot lands."

The railway journey from Cordoba southward is full of interest, the line running for nearly fifty miles through plantations of sugar-cane, coffee, bananas, oranges, pineapples and other tropical and semitropical fruits. Then comes a long stretch of fine grazing and agricultural lands, with wide prairies, where can be seen the picturesque Mexican cowboys or vaqueros mounted on swift ponies with heavy saddles and cruel bits, carrying the ever present lasso. There are many villages along the line but no cities. At Tierra Blanca, fifty-seven miles from Cordoba, there is a branch line to Vera Cruz; and at Los Narajos the railway crosses the Papaloapam River, the bridge and its approaches being over a mile long, the largest in Mexico. Passing through a dense jungle for several miles, the line again enters a prairie country, which continues for another fifty miles.

At San Marcos (one hundred and fifty seven miles) the prairie gives place to jungle and swamps, which in turn are replaced by a dense tropical forest, largely unexplored, of giant mahogany, ebony, dyewood and rosewood trees, palms of all varieties, medicinal woods, vines, plants and flowers. It is alive with chattering monkeys, green parrots and flocks of other gaudily colored birds seen only in the tropics. This is indeed the forest primeval, vast and impenetrable! Coiling about the tree-trunks like green great snakes are creepers and other parasites, which hang from the boughs and replant themselves in the moist earth. Among these are growing a variety of beautiful orchids, while forming a dense undergrowth is a tangled mass of wonderful ferns and flowering plants. In these dense woods there lurks the fierce jaguar, called by the

Mexicans the *tigre*, and in their sombre depths crawl the python and other tropical snakes.

This district would seem to promise a happy hunting-ground for the sportsman, who could stalk the jaguar and puma or the great river-hog, the tapir, floundering in its marshy haunts, or bring down a good-sized deer or a fierce wild bull; or spear the ever game peccary. Birds — quail and plover on the prairies, pheasants and turkeys in the forest — are there in plenty. But so great are the difficulties of traversing these tropical forests and so terribly unhealthy are they that for the most part they are virgin ground as far as sport is concerned. The Indians alone can enjoy the chase in such solitudes; and for the greater part of the year they live upon the game which is so plentiful and the wild fruits with which the woodlands abound.

From Cordoba to Santa Lucrezia the railway runs through the "hot lands" again. Here are seen the hot-land habitations, constructed of bamboo and light poles and thatched with palm-leaves, affording shade from the sun, but allowing the air to circulate freely; for the only shelter needed is protection from the rains. In this part of the country there are none of the imposing stone buildings found in the temperate regions of Mexico, and there are very few towns of any size. The tropical villages are not unlike those in central Africa. They swarm with naked babies, and boys and girls past childhood almost as simply clad. The population in the hot country is much smaller than that of the temperate zones, though it could easily support an immense number of inhabitants. So wonderfully rich is the soil that all kinds of tropical fruits, coffee, tobacco, the vanilla bean and many drug-producing plants grow luxuriantly. A large number of india rubber plantations have been started of late years, and bid fair to make a great success.

But farming in the hot lands requires a great amount of capital, and to be successful it must be conducted on a big scale, with a large force of laborers. The land can be bought cheaply enough, but that is only the preliminary expense, for it has to be cleared and planted; and as a rule it is only after years of careful cultivation that profitable returns can be obtained from such things as rubber, coffee and cacao. Conducted by experienced men with sufficient capital, however, coffee and banana culture are proving extremely profitable in Mexico, and some large fortunes are being made. Everything considered, there are few richer countries in the world than these lands in southern Mexico, in the States of Vera Cruz, Campeche and Tabasco. With forests yielding mahogany and numerous other valuable woods, with a prolific soil and a wonderful climate, making it possible in some cases to raise three crops in a single year, these hot lands must have a marvellous future.

The dense forests and numerous swamps of the hot lands would not seem to make this part of Mexico a very inviting place in which to live; but strange to say, these tropical regions are not so very unhealthful, if a careful system of living is followed. Intemperance in eating and drinking has, of course, to be avoided, and fevers and malaria are certain to result from exposure to rains or the intense heat of the midday sun.

We reached Santa Lucrezia at half-past nine in the evening. It is only a small village, with one wretched hotel. Fortunately, passengers are not obliged to pass a night there but can remain comfortably asleep in the Pullman car.[1]

The day had been baking hot, and even summer clothing

[1] The trains now run direct to Salina Cruz, the service of late having been much improved.

seemed unbearable, but at night the air was deliciously cool. Swarms of mosquitoes and other insect pests buzzed outside the car, some managing to find their way inside, but safely behind the mosquito curtains we could ignore them. Poets who rave about the "stilly night" could never have visited the tropics of Mexico. There is no stilly night there. From the neighboring woods came the incessant croaking of frogs and the loud buzzing, whistling and chirping of innumerable insects, — a combined volley of sound not unlike that made by a cotton mill at high pressure. Strangely enough, nearly all these noises cease in the daytime.

Near Santa Lucrezia are many plantations of tropical fruits, coffee, cacao and rubber. Some groves of cultivated rubber contain from one hundred thousand to one million trees. Of the fifteen hundred species of rubber plants and trees which exist, very few are found in Mexico. A tree known as castilloa elastica, which is indigenous to the soil, gives the best results and is chiefly grown in the plantations. It begins to yield rubber when six or seven years old, but the growers rarely tap it until it has reached the age of nine or ten.

In extracting the caoutchouc or rubber, one or two V-shaped incisions are cut in the trunk, penetrating the bark, but not so deeply as to reach the wood of the tree, and always leaving behind some of the cambium or growing layer of the stem, so that the wound may rapidly heal and the tree eventually be suitable for tapping again. As soon as the cuts are made, the milk-white latex begins to flow and is caught in a galvanized-iron cup placed at the base of the trunk. As much as half a pint of this fluid may run into the cup, after which the flow ceases. Tree-tapping is usually carried out once a year, either in October, November or December, and each tree usually lasts twenty-five years, producing one pound of rubber per annum when ten years old. The latex, after being collected, is deposited in barrels of water mixed with the juice of a wild vine or convolvulus (*ipomœa bona nox*) which hastens coagulation and transforms it into a spongy white mass — the crude rubber of commerce.

Over $25,000,000 has been invested in Mexican rubber plantations, but very few of them have ever yielded satisfactory dividends. In some instances this has been due to incompetent management, coupled with the difficulty of getting the proper kind of labor. Under the most satisfactory conditions, however, it is doubtful whether Mexico will ever be able to compete with Brazil, the Malay Peninsula or Ceylon, or even with Central America as a rubber-producing country.

The growth of Indian corn in these hot lands of Mexico is marvellous, attaining as it does a height of fifteen to eighteen feet, with ears that will mature within sixty days from planting. Similarly, sugar-cane in ten months will have stalks twenty feet high and ten inches in circumference. Bananas make a growth of twenty feet in a few months. There are about twenty varieties, and when properly cultivated, each stalk usually bears from seventy-five to one hundred pounds of fruit. On some plantations, where the plants are set about twelve feet apart, each acre of land will produce from six hundred to nine hundred large bunches a year. Under these favorable conditions, banana-growing is proving wonderfully profitable. The growth of fruit trees is just as wonderful. Peach trees two years old attain a height of twelve feet and bear fruit; oranges bear at four years of age. The soil is rich, indeed practically inexhaustible; the climate is summer all the year round, and the rainfall is from one hundred to two hundred inches per annum. With these advantages, tropical agriculture is certainly destined to become one of the greatest wealth-producers on the American continent.

After spending the night at Santa Lucrezia, our train was switched to the Tehuantepec National Railway the next morning, and went on to Salina Cruz, which was reached in the afternoon. At Rincon Antonio, a small place on the way, which is the highest point on the line, the railway company's general offices, workshops and hospital have been established. The climate here is pleasant and salubrious, the heat being tempered by the winds that are constantly blowing across the isthmus.

The workshops at Rincon Antonio are equipped with the most modern machinery and appliances for every possible repair to the rolling-stock and engines in use on the line. Here, as at Salina Cruz and Puerto Mexico, all the machinery is driven by electricity generated by a steam plant, crude oil being used for fuel. As at all other places where Messrs. Pearson have large works, every care has been taken here to make life as agreeable and homelike as possible for managers and employees. Comfortable modern houses have been erected for the various heads of departments, while the subordinate employees are lodged in excellent staff houses. A club-house has been built and quarters provided for a Catholic chapel and a masonic lodge. Special attention has been given to a pure and abundant water-supply. The general officers of the railway and the head men at the ports of Salina Cruz and Puerto Mexico are Englishmen and Americans, the latter being in the majority.

From Santa Lucrezia to the Pacific coast the line is fairly level, passing through a succession of dense forests, among low, rocky hills, across wide swamps and skirting some good grazing lands. The soil here, as in other parts of the Mexican tropics, is wonderfully fertile, and the growth of vegetation is marvellous. This bountiful aspect of nature constitutes, in fact, one of the many difficulties which confront the managers of the railway. So rapid is the growth of the wild plants along the line that, if left to themselves, they would soon overgrow the track. Laborers have to be constantly employed in cutting down these rapid growths, and the expenditure on this amounts to a large sum in the course of the year.

I was surprised to find Salina Cruz so remarkably progressive and up-to-date, with smart new buildings, modern houses and a comfortable hotel. When the railway was first started, the site of the present town was occupied by a squalid Indian village. A new town has since been laid out, in accordance with modern ideas and sanitary principles, the dwellings being erected on higher and more healthy ground. The port is destined to become one of the most important on the Pacific coast, and is an interesting example of the progress that is taking place in this remote part of Mexico. At the back of the town is a range of hills which furnish some protection against the northers which occasionally blow from the Atlantic side of the Isthmus. One of the features of the harbor is a massive stone breakwater nearly a mile in length and a dock fifty acres in extent. In former days, owing to the numerous sand-bars and the shallowness of the water, large vessels were unable to enter the port, and there was no protection against the stormy seas which occasionally sweep along the Pacific coast. Ample protection is now afforded by the great breakwater, and as the result of recent improvements the harbor now has a draught of over thirty-five feet at low tide.

Salina Cruz is becoming a very busy place. In the harbor, at the time of my arrival, were two large American steamers discharging cargoes of sugar for transportation across the Isthmus, while an English "tramp" was taking on a quantity of freight which had come across the Atlantic. Three lines of steamers touch at this port, the Kosmos Line (German) running between Hamburg and Pacific coast points of Mexico, Central, South and North America; the Pacific Steam Navigation Company (American) whose vessels call at the principal Mexican Pacific coast ports; and the new Canadian line from Vancouver. By the Kosmos line one can travel from Salina Cruz to various ports in South America, — in Chili, Peru and the Argentine, — and many travellers from the United States who wish to avoid a long sea journey to the Pacific coast of South America are now going by this route.

The wonderful improvements made at Salina Cruz have been repeated on a similar scale at Puerto Mexico on the Atlantic side of the Isthmus, where the old town has been thoroughly renovated and put in good sanitary condition. Some pestilential swamps which made the place a hot-bed of yellow fever have been almost entirely filled in, and the terrible scourge is now practically obliterated. The town is situated at the mouth of a river of the same name, which is navigable for seventy miles. Great stone jetties have been constructed in the harbor, insuring an ample depth of water; extensive wharves have been built, and some good business buildings erected. Puerto Mexico is rapidly becoming a place of importance; two lines of steamers are now making regular calls there, and others are arranging to make it a port of entry.

Enormous sums have been expended in rebuilding the Tehuantepec Railway and in carrying out the improvements at the two ports. It is estimated that since the work was begun the sum of $50,000,000 has been expended, and before the harbor works are perfected about $5,000,000 more will have to be disbursed. In addition to this, $10,000,000 has been appropriated by the Mexican government, making a total expenditure on the railway and ports of about $65,000,000.

The opening up of the country, which has resulted from the successful operation of the Tehuantepec Railway, is likely to be followed by further important developments in southern Mexico. In the course of a few years it is quite possible that a line will be built to Tehuantepec from Oaxaca, less than one hundred and fifty miles distant, thus tapping one of the richest parts of the country; another line may possibly be built in an easterly direction through the States of Campeche and Yucatan. Merida, the capital of the latter State, is a busy city, with a population of over a hundred thousand, and is only a few miles from Progreso on the Gulf of Mexico, the nearest port to Havana and New York.

One of the great projects of American statesmen has been a Pan-American railway or direct railway route from the United States to the southernmost republics of South America. At various conferences between representatives of the United States and the South American republics this matter has been fully discussed. It is not generally known that the idea is being gradually carried out. At San Geronimo, on the Tehuantepec Railway, there is a branch line called the Pan-American Railroad which runs along the Pacific coast to Tapachula on the borders of Guatemala. This line is to be gradually extended through Guatemala, Salvador, Nicaragua, Costa Rica and Panama to South America, where it will connect with the lines already in operation there. While at present this is rather a visionary prospect, still the world is moving rapidly, and not so many years hence it may perhaps be possible to take a train in New York for Chili and Peru *via* Mexico and Central America.

The Pan-American line already built has opened up the rich coffee lands in the State of Chiapas, and is gradually developing several new ports along the Pacific coast. The railway was built by an American company subsidized by the Mexican government. The completion of the line to Guatemala will probably tend to render that little republic more peaceful by bringing it under the civilizing influences of Mexico.

There is fine scenery along the Pan-American Railroad, some of the mountain peaks in that part of the country rising from eight to nine thousand feet. Near Tomala, and some eight miles from the line, are the remains of an ancient city, with temples and fortresses of cut stone, in the midst of an almost impenetrable forest. The whole State of Chiapas, through which the line runs, is filled with these prehistoric relics. Greatest of all the ruins are those of the city of Palenque, its wonderful temples and palaces being overgrown by the luxuriant tropical woodlands. There is an Indian tradition that Palenque covered an area of sixty miles; but the American traveller, J. L. Stephens, proved this to be a ridiculous exaggeration. The city was about two miles round. Several archæologists who have visited Palenque since Stephens have fully confirmed his estimate.

Before leaving the Isthmus, I visited the city of Tehuantepec, a short trip by railway from Salina Cruz. It is a queer, straggling, ramshackle sort of place, with a population of some twenty thousand. Although it is always hot and sunny there, the heat is generally tempered by a good breeze blowing from the Pacific. It rains but seldom. Most of the low, one-story buildings in the town show the effects of earthquakes, which are not infrequent. As in all the Mexican tropical lands, none of the buildings have the solid, imposing appearance of those to be seen in the temperate zones.

Until the railway was opened, Tehuantepec was shut off from the outside world, strangers seldom going there. For this reason many quaint customs and costumes still survive, unaltered by the prosaic march of progress. The natives belong to the Zapotec tribe of Indians, and are remarkably clean. Groups of them are constantly bathing in the broad river which runs through the town, and they do not seem to share the strong antipathy for soap found elsewhere among Mexican Indians. The clothing of both sexes is generally immaculate. These Indians are very closely akin to the cleanly Mayas of Yucatan, and are believed by some authorities to be one of the remnants of the Mayan race which probably once held all Mexico before the wild, fighting tribes of Aztec type broke in from the north, driving them southward to Yucatan and Guatemala.

Nothing else betrays so quickly the social condition of a race as the status of its womankind. The difference between the Zapotec women and their uncomely, unkempt sisters of northern Mexico is almost the difference between savagery and civilization. A Tehuantepec woman is a being who has rights and can enforce them. In the market-place women conduct most of the business, as in France, while the poor, henpecked men keep in the background. The women usually hold the family purse, and it is even impossible for a man to get credit unless his wife vouches for him. They are not only shrewder and brighter but more intelligent than the men, whose position is manifestly inferior. Under these circumstances, Tehuantepec would be a blissful abiding place for the suffragettes.

Of the docility of the men I saw a most amusing instance during my visit. I stopped in the market-place to buy some fruit at one of the stands, which was presided over by a buxom young woman with keen dark eyes. She was gossiping energetically with a neighbor, while her husband was seated near by placidly smoking a cigarette. Catching sight of me, the comely Zapoteca called out sharply, "Pedro, Pedro, attend to the señor." Pedro, a big, burly fellow, came forward rather sheepishly and supplied my wants, while his wife kept an Argus eye on him. He was about to pocket the money I handed to him, but Mrs. Pedro was ready for the emergency. "Pedro," she remarked severely, "I want that cash," and the lamblike Pedro surrendered it without a word of protest. He noticed my amused expression, however, and when his better half was not looking, returned a covert smile which seemed to say, "I'm only doing this for fun; I'm not really henpecked."

The Zapotec women are famous for their beauty, cleanliness and their devotion to their homes. They are copper-colored, with smooth, coarse black hair, small brown eyes, aquiline features and fine white teeth, the face being characterized by a gentle, pleasant expression. They are rather short, well-proportioned and possess a natural grace of carriage, probably because of their habit of bearing loads on their heads. Besides being the housekeepers, they weave cloth, mats, baskets and hammocks. Their costume is very quaint and attractive. They wear a little jacket with extremely short sleeves, sometimes richly embroidered and cut rather low at the neck; then comes a short upper skirt, generally of soft linen or cotton material, and from the knees downward a second skirt of embroidery or thick lace starched very stiffly. The jacket and upper skirt are generally some shade of red or blue. They have a peculiar head-dress of coarse lace, which is arranged in several ways. On festive occasions they wind it round their necks so that it spreads out something like a sixteenth-century ruff; while for church wear it is worn somewhat in the fashion of a French fishwife's cap.

The wealthy ladies of Tehuantepec do not wear diamonds,

but adorn themselves with necklaces of gold coins, usually the large five, ten or twenty dollar gold pieces of the United States. English, French and German coins are sometimes worn, but are not considered so fashionable. The women save all their money to buy these gold pieces, which, when worn by them, present a rather beautiful appearance. Their wealth and social standing are indicated by the amount of gold they wear, and some members of the Tehuantepec smart set are said to possess necklaces worth fifteen hundred dollars and more. Even when arrayed in all this finery, very few of the Tehuantepec women ever wear shoes, most of the poor going barefooted and the better class finding sandals more comfortable.

These gentle, orderly Zapotecs might well serve as models for Mexicans farther north. They live quiet, peaceful lives, enjoying the simplest diversions, their clean, temperate habits producing the health, happiness and longevity which characterize them. Quarrels are rare, and murder is unknown. They are extremely kind to animals, and the burro or ox which serves the Zapotec is treated as a pet. Bull or cock fights are not held because public opinion is strongly against cruelty in any form. These people are passionately fond of music, and the concerts of their local band would do credit to any city.

CHAPTER XXVI

TARPON FISHING AT TAMPICO

ALTHOUGH the streams and rivers of Mexico have little to tempt the angler, the Gulf coast has become famous the world over as the place of places for tarpon fishing. This wonderful fish, which sometimes attains a weight of over two hundred pounds, and is as gamy as a brook trout, is found in its perfection in the waters round Tampico, and the delights of the sport have brought fishermen there from all parts of the world.

Tampico, which has become almost synonymous with tarpon, is about three hundred miles north of Vera Cruz; and it was to Tampico in quest of tarpon that I journeyed after my visit to the Isthmus of Tehuantepec.

From the Isthmus I returned direct to Vera Cruz, which, on this occasion, fully merited its reputation as a city of the tropics. Instead of the gloomy weather and depressing "norther" which I had encountered on my arrival some four months before, there was a cloudless sky, the sun was blazing with tropical intensity and people who walked the streets all kept to the shady sides. The principal streets had already been asphalted, and the work on others was proceeding rapidly. When I first landed, there were no carriages to be seen, owing to the bad paving, but now I noticed several as I strolled through the town; and before I had been in the place half an hour I saw two automobiles whizzing along the main street. The old mule-cars were still running, but electric wires were being installed for the new American electric cars. Wonderful indeed is the march, or I should say the rush, of progress in modern Mexico.

There is no railway between Vera Cruz and Tampico, and as the country along the coast is very swampy and there are no important towns there, it would be very expensive to build a line. But some day a railway is certain to be built between the two places. At the present time the only way to get from Vera Cruz to Tampico by railway is to return to Mexico City and make a détour of several hundred miles. For this reason travellers have to go by steamer. There are two lines running between the two ports — the Hamburg American and the Mexican Steamship lines. The German liners are splendid vessels, several of the large Atlantic steamers being used for the Mexican service during the winter months. These steamers run from Bremen, Havre and Plymouth to Havana and thence to Vera Cruz and Tampico, returning to Europe by the same route.

I had to wait three days at Vera Cruz for the *Kronprinzessin Cecilie*, on which I booked my passage to Tampico, but managed to pass the time very pleasantly. The Hotel Diligencia, where I found comfortable quarters, was a typical Mexican hotel, facing the plaza, with a large, open, tiled dining-room through which the breezes circulated refreshingly in the hot daytime. In the shade it was quite comfortable, no matter how baking hot it might be in the sun. Under the clear blue sky Vera Cruz was completely changed; the soft-tinted houses, the palm trees and the flowers in the plaza were all transformed into things of beauty, proving how essential is the bright sun to life in the tropics.

Having three days to spare before the steamer left for Tampico, I took a trip to the famous city of Jalapa (pronounced *Hahlappa*), eighty-two miles from Vera Cruz, on the Inter-oceanic branch of the Mexican National Railway. It is situated at about the same altitude as Orizaba, but in point of picturesqueness far excels that city. Like Orizaba, however, it lies at the foot of lofty mountains which encircle it, the great snow-covered peak of Orizaba being visible on clear days. The women of Jalapa, many of whom are quite fair, are famed for their beauty, and judging by the many attractive faces I saw in a short walk, it would seem this reputation is well deserved. The Mexicans, in fact, have a saying that Jalapa is a part of heaven let down to earth, and the proverb "Las Jalapenas son lalguenas" (Bewitching, alluring are the women of Jalapa).

A less pleasing characteristic of the town are its frequent days of mist and rain, a very serious drawback to the enjoyment of its great loveliness, which has given rise to another saying in Jalapa. During these melancholy days, the Jalapeno, muffled in his sarape, dismally mutters, "Ave Maria purisima, que venga el sol" (Holy Virgin, let the sun shine).

Jalapa means "a place of water and sand." It was an Indian town at the time of the Spanish Conquest, and, because of its position on what for a long time was the main road between Vera Cruz and Mexico City, early became a place of importance. After the establishment of the Republic, it was made the capital of the State of Vera Cruz. The medicinal plant from which that nauseous old family medicine, jalap, is extracted is grown all around Jalapa.

The city is curious and old-fashioned, with houses of crumbling stucco; their red-tiled roofs project over the eaves so far that they seem to cover the sidewalks like a shade, and extending from these are the spouts to carry the rainfall from the roofs to the centre of the street. Jalapa has an abundant supply of water and a perfect drainage

THE ROCKY ROAD.
A train of burros toiling up one of the steep streets in ancient Jalapa.

system. Its streets slope gently to the middle of the roadway, thus forming deep troughs or gutters, and all refuse is soon washed beyond the city limits by the frequent rains. This probably accounts for the scrupulously clean appearance of the place. So steep are the streets that carts or carriages cannot be used for the transportation of goods or persons, all the carrying being done by cargadores or pack-mules. A car runs from the railway station through part of the main thoroughfare, and is the only wheeled vehicle found in Jalapa, but even this requires six mules to haul it up the steep grades.

There is a very pretty plaza in the centre of the town, and some fine old churches, notably the cathedral, which was founded in the sixteenth century, and the Church of San Francisco, built in 1555. These and other sights may be enjoyed by the visitor to Jalapa, and when the weather is clear, a day may be delightfully spent in and about the little city. But perhaps the most interesting sight of all is to be witnessed in the cool of the evening, when the fair Jalapenas stroll in the plaza to listen to the band, their dark, flashing eyes reminding the susceptible Jalapenos of the truth of their local proverb.

Upon my return to Vera Cruz from Jalapa, the weather was still clear and warm, and I looked forward with pleasure to my trip up the coast. The *Kronprinzessin Cecilie* was advertised to sail for Tampico at six in the evening, the journey taking about sixteen hours. When I went down to the steamer, about four o'clock, I was greatly impressed with German enterprise. A large crowd had assembled on the wharf, listening to a brass band stationed on the promenade deck, which was playing "Die Wacht am Rhein," the German ensign was flying from the steamer's foremast; and it was all like a little piece of Germany dropped down in Mexico. From the remarks of the Mexicans which I overheard, they evidently seemed to think that Germany, next to Mexico, must be the greatest country in the world.

I had not been aboard the ship many minutes before I noticed a sudden change in the weather; some dark clouds on the horizon increased and spread with wonderful rapidity; before long, the sky began to take on an ominous leaden tinge, and the sun's rays shone only at intervals through the drifting clouds. The breeze, which had been quite light, began to increase in force, and the sea, which had been as smooth as glass, was very soon covered with whitecaps. I heard cries of "Norte" everywhere. Some fishing boats came dashing into the harbor for safety, with the spray flying over them; a steam launch followed them, cutting through the rolling waves. Before two hours had passed, the surf was breaking over the jetties and another norther was full upon us. The captain of the steamer did not consider it safe to venture outside that night, and sailing was delayed until seven the next morning. All the way up the coast we had this head-wind, and despite the luxury of the steamer, those passengers who were not good sailors did not find it exactly a voyage of pleasure.

For all dangers and discomforts I found ample recompense on my arrival at Tampico. This important port lies at the mouth of the Panuco River, a magnificent waterway, in which the greatest fleet could find ample harbor room. Tampico, with a population of one hundred and sixty-three thousand, is, in fact, becoming the chief port of Mexico, even surpassing Vera Cruz; and with its safe harbor and deep water, the largest vessels can lie alongside the wharves to receive and discharge cargo, Over four hundred ocean steamers call at Tampico monthly. regular liners plying between New York, Mobile, New Orleans, Galveston, Havana and European ports, and the southern seaport cities of the Mexican Gulf coast. At a cost of over $3,000,000 a fine new custom-house has been built, and also a great wharf at which five large steamers can lie at the same time. The harbor is always full of shipping, presenting quite a lively and busy scene. The docks are situated some little distance up the river, and back of these is the city, a large part of which stands on a high bluff, rising to a height of nearly fifty feet.

While its appearance is very different from that of other Mexican cities, Tampico is an attractive-looking place. The houses usually have sloping roofs, are tinted in many colors and have wooden verandas along the fronts of each story. On the river front is a picturesque market-place, with tents and numerous white umbrellas beneath which the vendors gather; near this is the main plaza, from which tram-cars run to all parts of the city.

The rivers which join the sea at Tampico are navigable by small boats for a long distance into the interior, and pass through some fine tropical scenery. Over five thousand boats, varying in length from twenty to sixty feet, are kept on the Tameso and Panuco rivers to bring to Tampico the wild and cultivated products of the country. Almost every conceivable form of tropical plant and fruit may be found in their cargoes, as well as native-made earthenware and other manufactured articles. The Panuco River is about eighteen hundred feet wide at Tampico, and has an average breadth of eight hundred feet for several miles from its mouth. Some distance below the city are the jetties which form the harbor where the river flows into the sea; and here is La Barra, a village with a fine sandy beach on which the surf rolls invitingly. During the daytime the place is usually thronged with bathers.

Tarpon, however, was the sole object of my visit to Tampico. Many angling enthusiasts travel thither each season to fight the monstrous fish, all of whom make their headquarters at the Southern Hotel, the proprietor of which is a jovial American, Colonel Poindexter. Among the fishermen who come to Tampico are various American millionaires and many of the English and French nobility, the register of the Southern Hotel containing names that are well known in social circles the world over. Mine host, the Colonel, is himself a keen angler, and looks after his fellow-devotees of the rod and reel. For the sum of four dollars a day he provides them with all the necessary fishing-tackle, and a boat with an experienced native to row and assist in the sport.

Conducted in this way, tarpon fishing is not an expensive sport, and what is more, if the angler has ordinary good luck, he rarely leaves Tampico without landing one of these big fishes. Very different was the experience of a friend of mine, a wealthy English angler, who once spent several weeks on the gulf coast of Florida in quest of tarpon, which is popularly known there as the "silver king." He chartered two small yachts to provide quarters for himself and the members of his fishing party, while a small steam tug was also engaged for work on the fishing grounds. In addition to the crews, a staff of skilled fishermen were employed to aid in tracking the wily "silver king" to his watery lair. After cruising up and down the coast for nearly six weeks without seeing a tarpon, the chase was abandoned in disgust. This could never have happened at Tampico, in whose waters there are tarpon in plenty.

For a day after my arrival the "norther" blew on, and then the weather became fine and calm again. Under these auspicious circumstances I made a start one morning in search of tarpon, making my cruise in a boat made from the trunk of a ceiba tree. It was about twenty feet long and twenty inches wide, painted blue outside and green within, and was manned by an Indian paddler who sat in front, while

I took my seat amidships. I had a strong rod with a stout reel, while my line was braided linen, about six hundred feet long, of which four hundred and fifty feet was kept coiled inside the canoe as slack in case something took the hook, for not only tarpon but great jewfish, shark and curel (a large species of pike, weighing as much as sixty pounds) are plentiful in the river.

The tarpon has a thick, bony jaw, and when it takes the bait, the angler must give his line a strong, quick jerk, otherwise the fish is liable to get away. As soon as the bait is taken, the tarpon, rushing to the surface of the water with lightning rapidity, makes a high leap in the air. Unless the hook is driven well into the jaw, he will shake it out of his mouth, and again, if the line is held too tight, he is certain to snap it. To catch a tarpon, therefore, needs some skill as well as strength. As a well-known angling writer has very correctly said: "Tarpon fishing is the pitting of a man-sized fish against an angler whose rod and line seem utterly inadequate for the fight. It is the taking of a seven-foot giant with a slender thread, and this in a fight that may wear away an afternoon, the whole combat being accompanied by a series of thrilling leaps."

We went up the river with the tide to the south bank, and at first the fish did not bite. Along the bank I noticed extensive pastures where large herds of cattle were fattening for shipment to Cuba and Yucatan. These cattle come from the Para grass pastures of southeastern Mexico in the State of Tamaulipas (in which Tampico is situated) and the states of Vera Cruz and San Luis Potosi. Between sixty and eighty thousand head pass through Tampico every year.

Chatting with my Indian boatman, I almost forgot that I was fishing, when suddenly my float disappeared. I instantly gave a sharp jerk and threw out some slack. The next moment my line was pulled almost tight, and about a hundred feet away a large silvery fish leaped in the air. He appeared to be about seven feet long, and seemed to jump twice his length out of the water. It was a tarpon, king of game fishes. Amidst a cloud of spray up in the air he went again, his silver scales glistening with rainbow hues in the rays of the sun. Then followed a succession of leaps, none of them alike, while the head of the great fish shook angrily from side to side in his ineffectual efforts to cast out the hook. He disappeared and sulked for a time beneath the water, and then came another series of rushes and leaps, the combat taking over an hour. A half hour passed before he was tired out and I pulled him to the side of the boat for the Indian to gaff. On landing him, I found that he was only of medium size, weighing about one hundred pounds. He did not look nearly so big as when he was leaping and plunging.

Tarpon have been caught at Tampico weighing over two hundred pounds, and measuring over seven feet in length, and it has taken hours to land them. The average catches, however, range from four and a half to six and a half feet long and from seventy to one hundred and seventy pounds. One fish for a day is generally considered good sport, and has usually to be paid for by several days of tired muscles. The sport is not unattended with danger; for when a big fish has not been properly gaffed, he is sometimes stirred into fresh activity, lashing out with his tail with a force strong enough to stave in a canoe. His cutting jaws can also inflict ugly wounds. A well-known American angler, while fishing for tarpon off the Florida coast, hooked a monster weighing considerably over a hundred pounds. During the combat the great fish made a leap which landed him with a crash on the angler's back, inflicting injuries which nearly killed the unfortunate fisherman, laying him up for nearly two years. The only disappointing feature of tarpon fishing is that the dead fish is of no value whatever, the flesh being flavorless and rarely eaten. Occasionally some angling enthusiast has his big fish stuffed and mounted; the silvery scales, which measure about four inches in width, are also sometimes kept as souvenirs.

Going down to the jetties the next day, I fished with one line in the river and another in the sea, catching about twenty pounds of fish of all kinds and sizes, some of them quite gamy, especially the pargito, a fish weighing from one to five pounds, of dark color above and white below, somewhat resembling a bass and making a good fight when hooked.

The fisheries at Tampico are the finest in the Gulf of Mexico, presenting admirable opportunities for the establishment of canning factories to supply the Mexican market, which now depends on Europe and the United States. As the fish are very abundant, and the harbor improvements make the banks easy of access in all weathers, this industry could be carried on during the entire year, and at the present time almost without a competitor in Mexico.

CHAPTER XXVII

IN NORTHERN MEXICO

THAT part of Mexico which extends southward for three or four hundred miles from the border of the United States has very little resemblance to the semi-tropical regions still farther south or to the "hot lands" along the coast. It is largely a vast plateau, with great plains devoted to grazing purposes and providing pasturage for hundreds of thousands of cattle. It is in the northern states of Chihuahua, Coahuila and Durango that the greatest estates in the country are situated, one multi-millionaire in Chihuahua having a vast property of seventeen million acres. The traveller can roam for days, crossing mountains, valleys and plains without leaving this princely domain. On some of these estates there are private railways, with railway stations and numerous villages. In this region are great ranches, employing hundreds of cowboys and presenting phases of life fully as picturesque as the once famous American wild West.

As my visit to Mexico was now drawing to a close, and I had thus far confined my travels to southern Mexico, I decided to return to New York by train, and on the way through the great central plateau to stop at one or two points and see something of the country. With this object in view, I left Tampico one morning bound for San Luis Potosi, about two hundred and fifty miles distant. The branch of the Mexican Central Railway which connects the two cities is noted for its scenic attractions, the views along the way rivalling those on the Mexican Railway between Vera Cruz and the capital.

Leaving the coast and running westward, the line crosses a series of great sloping plains, extending for nearly a hundred miles, which are well adapted for grazing purposes. They are covered with a coarse, luxuriant grass known as Para, which is ever green and is a great fattener of cattle. Numerous streams are crossed, for the country is unusually well watered. Coffee, oranges, bananas, limes, ginger and other tropical fruits and plants grow luxuriantly throughout this region, and the climate is delightful.

Mounting upwards from the foot-hills, the line reaches the mountains and eventually attains an altitude of over six thousand feet; the scenery is superb, especially in the so-called Abre de Caballeros. Here the train runs along the side of a lofty mountain beneath the shadow of great cliffs which tower far above, while below is a deep, rocky cañon. From a neighboring mountain-side leaps a marvellous and beautifully colored waterfall, pouring down in one cascade after another until there are a score or more, some over a hundred feet in height and one fully three hundred feet, making together a chain of nearly a mile in length. All around are towering mountain peaks. The combined effects of water, land and sky are wonderfully grand.

Farther on from this point there are more wonderful views and magnificent distances as the line curves, turns and twists upwards among the mountains: at one point, six curves of the track are in sight, while twelve hundred feet below are the luxuriant tropical valleys, with here and there bright green fields of sugar-cane and fruits. The line winds along a shelf hewn in the side of the almost perpendicular cliffs, around curves, through a succession of tunnels, then through the wild San Ysidro Valley, the mountain-sides of which are densely wooded. It then emerges on the sloping plain of the table-land where, at an altitude of 6116 feet, is situated the city of San Luis Potosi.

Twenty years ago this old town, which was founded in 1566, was but little known to the outside world; but since the advent of the railways it has become a thriving commercial place. Situated in a fertile valley, it is surrounded by mountains rich in mineral wealth, especially silver and copper, the San Pedro mines near the city being among the most productive in Mexico. The city, in fact, derives its name from its supposed resemblance to Potosi in Peru, a famous silver-mining place. It is a bright, clean, attractive town, with handsome streets which vividly recall those of Seville, and abounds in fine old churches, rich in native decorative art. Among the public buildings are the library and museum, the mint and the state capitol, San Luis Potosi being the chief city of the State of the same name. With good hotels and theatres, public baths and lines of electric cars, the city shows every sign of progress, and has attracted a large number of foreigners who have settled there to engage in business. It is distinguished by a general appearance of neatness, which is largely due to a local law compelling the citizens to keep their dwellings in presentable condition, and prevents their becoming careless. During my stay in the city, I visited one or two of the large factories there, the machinery of which is operated by electrical power, one of these establishments, which is devoted to the manufacture of ready-made clothing, having all the latest appliances. In the workrooms the cutting, sewing, pressing and even the attaching of buttons is all done by machines driven by electrical power.

The country around San Luis Potosi is wonderfully productive, and this has done much to increase the city's prosperity. On the great haciendas throughout the State are grown a variety of crops, including wheat, barley, sugar-cane, cotton and tobacco; there are also a large number of ranches, the country being exceptionally well adapted for cattle.

From this flourishing district I made a journey of one hundred and fifty miles on the Mexican Central Railway to the picturesque old town of Aguas Calientes or Hot Springs, a popular health resort. It is a quaint, sleepy place, with a population of thirty-eight thousand, and is situated at an altitude of six thousand feet, the climate being delightful. There are several good hotels in the town, which are generally well filled, as visitors flock to the springs from all parts of Mexico. In cases of rheumatism and similar diseases the waters of Aguas Calientes are said to effect remarkable cures. At the springs the old bath-houses have been strangely named after the apostles, the figure of one of the sacred twelve being placed over each door, with figures indicating the temperature of the water within. The town is famed for its pottery, the Aguas Calientes ware; and sarapes are manufactured there in great quantities. Until recently the town was also noted for its drawn-work, which was the principal occupation of the feminine population, the finest linen being drawn in the most beautiful and complicated designs. One beautiful drawn-work costume, which was made in the town and intended for exhibition, took nine years to complete, three hundred expert needlewomen being employed on it. It is without seams, of exquisite design, and is valued at $2000. Drawn-work, however, will soon be a thing of the past in Aguas Calientes, as the women now find work in factories or other occupations which yield better wages. At the present time a great deal of imitation drawn-work is actually imported from Germany and sold to unsuspecting tourists as the work of native needlewomen. Even the gorgeous Mexican sarapes, I was told, are not all manufactured in

Aguas Calientes by patient Indian workmen, but many of them, sad to relate, are "made in Germany."

From Aguas Calientes the Mexican Central Railway runs northward through the states of Durango and Chihuahua to El Paso in Texas, a large, enterprising town which has become an important railway centre. From there California can be reached by direct train *via* New Mexico and Arizona. There are also connecting lines there which take the traveller to other parts of the United States.

Some remarkable developments are being made in this northern part of Mexico; and the rapidity with which the whole country is being transformed is only realized when one has actually been there. Lying so close to the United States, northern Mexico has naturally attracted large numbers of Americans who are settling there and engaging in mining, farming and various other branches of business. New mines are being constantly opened, factories are springing up and railways are being extended in all directions. This rush of progress has had a noticeable effect on the old cities of the north, notably Durango, Chihuahua and Zacatecas, which are being rapidly modernized. Each of these cities has from thirty to forty thousand inhabitants, and all of them are built in the same substantial manner, with large business houses and fine public buildings. Before the railways came they were sleepy, out-of-the-world places, seldom heard of; to-day, like San Luis Potosi and other towns, they have shaken off their lethargy, suddenly become busy places and are steadily increasing in size and importance.

Zacatecas is one of the most important silver-mining centres in Mexico; since the metal was first mined there, in 1546, the mines have produced an amount estimated at over $700,000,000. The present annual output is about $3,000,000.

Durango might be called the Pittsburg of Mexico, as it is the centre of an important iron industry. The smoky atmosphere and dingy back streets of Pittsburg, however, are happily non-existent, for Durango is a picturesque city, with fine, clear, mountain air. Near the city is a mountain of iron ore, averaging from seventy-five to ninety per cent of pure metal, almost solid iron! A cavalier in Cortés' time, one Señor Mercado, heard a wonderful story of a mountain of silver, and visited the present site of Durango, where it was supposed to be. To his intense disgust he found nothing but iron. His memory has been perpetuated by the name of the mountain, which is called Cerro Mercado. In the neighborhood there are a few silver mines, but iron is king. Durango, by the way, is over seven hundred miles from Mexico City, which gives some idea of the magnificent distances of Mexico.

One of the most important railway enterprises which has been carried out in northern Mexico is the building of the Kansas City, Mexican and Orient Railway, which is now approaching completion. This railway, which is the first direct line to cross the frontier between the United States and Mexico, will extend from Kansas City to the Bay of Topolobampo on the Mexican Pacific coast, a distance of 1659 miles. It runs through the states of Chihuahua and Sinaloa, opening up a magnificent country of immense area, rich in mineral and agricultural resources, and offering tempting inducements to settlers with small capital. Topolobampo is one of the most beautiful harbors in the world, having a great resemblance to the famous Bay of Rio Janeiro. The railway will connect there with steamers for the Orient, several lines having arranged to make the port a place of call; and in a few years this place, which has been named Port Stillwell, will become one of the busiest towns on the coast. Mr. Arthur E. Stillwell, who conceived the idea of this wonderful railway, has carried it out with remarkable energy, having enlisted in the enterprise a large amount of British, French and American capital.

Agriculture is making great progress in the northern states of Mexico, irrigation having been introduced very extensively, with wonderful results. To encourage this system of agriculture, the Mexican government has recently appropriated $10,000,000 to assist the owners of irrigated lands in making further improvements. The import duties on agricultural implements, cattle for breeding purposes, etc., will also be removed for a term of years for their benefit, while the export duties on the products of irrigated lands will also be taken off. Mexican lands, except those along the coast, are largely dependent upon irrigation, and by this system millions of acres of land heretofore unproductive are now producing enormous crops. Wherever irrigation is introduced, the seemingly worthless soil at once becomes wonderfully fertile.

Cotton growing is also an important industry in this part of the country, and a number of mills are in successful operation. Great quantities of wheat are grown in Chihuahua, the crop averaging about 1,500,000 bushels a year. Sheep farming is about to be undertaken in this State by an English company, which has recently purchased a tract of land fifty miles square. This is to be stocked with sheep from Australia, and by breeding and interbreeding with the best native stock, it is believed that a breed of sheep can be developed in Mexico which will equal any in the world. Several Australian sheep experts have been engaged for this great ranch. Sheep farming in Mexico has thus far been conducted in a very haphazard way, and the country has never been regarded as suitable for this industry. The work of the English company is therefore being watched with a great deal of interest.

In the extreme northwest of Mexico, beyond Durango and Chihuahua, is the rich agricultural and mining State of Sonora, which borders the Pacific Ocean. It is the second largest State in the Republic, but for some years it has continued in a condition of panic-stricken stagnation owing to the Yaqui Indians, who to the number of about five thousand have been carrying on a campaign of revenge against the whites. Mines are shut down and industries neglected, while the haciendas are fortified, and no white dare venture far from the towns or cuartels, the points where the troops are concentrated. Some idea may be formed of the interests involved in this struggle by the fact that at the banks of Guaymas and other Sonora towns there are securities representing over $50,000,000 of American capital which has been sunk in the Yaqui district of Sonora and is now, for the time at least, dead money.

There seems to be some doubt as to whether the Yaquis are the bloodthirsty savages their would-be Mexican masters like to paint them, or whether, in the language of Señor de Zayas Enriques, a well-known Mexican who has espoused their cause, they are a race of heroes. Probably the truth is somewhere between the two views. Of their bravery there can be no doubt. Wonderful stories are told of it. One Yaqui chief pursued by rurales — the Mexican country soldiers — from the vantage post of a rock, picked off his enemies one by one, till, surrounded, he had to face a mounted officer who rode at him with uplifted sabre. He parried the blow with his knife, and vaulting on the horse's back, pinioned the arms of the officer and spurred the horse to a precipice near. There the horse balked, but the Yaqui plunged his knife into its flank and the animal, with its two riders — the Yaqui crying out in triumph, the officer with terror — were hurled to death on the rocks below.

So much for their bravery. As for their savagery, it

is a fact that they have waylaid many harmless persons — Americans, for the most part — and killed them all, including women and children. There are also many cases of alleged brutality against them. Some of their own tribe, unwilling to take up arms against the Mexicans, were treated, so it is reported, in a way so horrible that the Yaquis must, if it be true, forfeit everyone's sympathy. The soles of their feet were cut off, their eyes gouged out, and they were dragged out into a waterless prairie and left to die. From such atrocities it might be supposed that the Yaquis are like the Apaches and other bloodthirsty North American redskins of former times, wearing feathers and painting their faces. The Yaquis, however, while somewhat darker, are not unlike the other Mexican Indians; they have always been an agricultural people, and to-day most of them dress in the ordinary peon costume. When left to themselves, they till their little farms and are quiet and industrious. Most of them speak Spanish as well as the Yaqui dialect.

The story of Yaqui discontent dates back to the Conquest. At that time the tribe numbered, it is related, three hundred thousand. They never submitted to Cortés, and thereafter a guerilla warfare existed in Sonora, broken by more serious uprisings, such as those in 1735 and 1825. In 1832 they successfully opposed any Mexican interference with their tribal rights, and until 1848 were left in supreme control of their lands round the Yaqui River. In that year war broke out again, lasting until 1897, when a truce was called and a treaty finally concluded. But in less than a year, owing, it is said, to the wrongful diversion of an irrigation stream by a Mexican landowner, the Yaquis flew to arms, and now hold the district by a system of terrorism. The country is covered with brush from ten to fifteen feet high, through which are trails known only to the Indians. They are all good shots, and while they never ride, can cover on foot as much as seventy-five miles a day. So keen is their system of scouting that the clumsy, ill-drilled Mexican soldiers, recruited mostly from the jails, have no chance; and in hand-to-hand fighting the government troops have so far always come off second best.

An almost incredible condition of affairs exists at the present time as the result of the Yaqui warfare. Bands of these bloodthirsty natives are constantly prowling about the country and making attacks where least expected. An instance of this occurred two or three years ago at the little town of Toledo, when the mayor gave a modest banquet, the entertainment being held on the flat roof of his house, according to the custom in that warm country. The roof, being illuminated, offered an easy mark for some Yaquis who happened to be lurking in the mountain overlooking the town. In the midst of the festivities bullets suddenly rained among the guests, killing four persons, including the mayor's wife and daughter. Several of the survivors were wounded as they hastily retreated. Similar outrages have occurred elsewhere. Even at Hermosillo, the capital of Sonora, a beautiful and progressive city, it is unsafe to venture many miles away. Not long ago, it is said, a party of Americans, while motoring near the town, were fired upon by some Yaquis concealed in the bush, and barely escaped with their lives. Hermosillo is in the centre of a rich mining region, and in the mountains near the town are a number of mines of gold, silver and copper. The soil in this part of the country is wonderfully fertile, great quantities of oranges, wheat, maize, cotton, sugar-cane and tobacco being grown. Mining and agriculture, however, have been seriously retarded by the constant dread of the Yaquis.

Short shrift is usually given to the Yaqui marauders

when caught red-handed by the Mexican soldiers. Without the semblance of a trial, a dozen or more will sometimes be stood in a line and shot down; sometimes they are hanged to trees, and their bodies left dangling by the roadside as a warning to their surviving comrades. Deportations of large numbers of inoffensive Yaquis to the swamps of Yucatan are also being carried out; and the Mexican government continues to wage a merciless war of extermination.

It was almost the end of March when I returned to San Luis Potosi to resume my journey northwards, my destination being the city of Monterey, two hundred and nine miles distant. The Mexican National Railway by which I travelled runs some comfortable trains direct to St. Louis, *via* Monterey and Laredo, the distance being about 1553 miles and the journey occupying a little over four days. The train which I took, one morning, the Mexico City-St. Louis Express, had left the capital the day before, and was composed exclusively of Pullman cars.

From the railway the country is not seen at its best, but for some miles beyond San Luis Potosi the line runs through a succession of fields and gardens planted with semitropical fruits and vegetables kept green by irrigation. In this fertile region there is a great estate through which the railway passes, and a brief view is obtained of the picturesque hacienda building of white stone, which looks like a walled fortress, surrounded with tropical gardens, bright with flowers. Near by two white church towers peep above a little village belonging to the estate, which is owned by the Frias family and is one of the finest in Mexico. Over a thousand people are employed on it. For nearly seventy miles the train ran through the great rolling plain, strewn with cactus and occasionally relieved by long stretches of cultivated land, and then reached the town of Catorce. Near the railway station at this place there is a stone monument inscribed, "Tropic of Cancer," the country south of the monument being within that zone. Passing this imaginary line brought no perceptible difference in the weather, which continued as warm as ever, with the usual amount of dust in the air. Catorce is Spanish for "fourteen," the town taking its name from a band of fourteen desperados who in ancient times had a fortress there, and levied tribute on the inhabitants of the surrounding country. From San Luis Potosi there is a gradual descent from the tableland, and at Catorce the line leaving the plains winds between the mountains, still continuing the descent.

The next important town is Saltillo, the capital of the State of Coahuila. Near it was fought the battle of Buena Vista between the Mexicans and the Americans in February, 1847, when the Mexican army was totally defeated. It is a favorite resort for well-to-do Mexicans, and during July and August life there has been described by a local American scribe as "a veritable whirl of parties, balls, concerts and burro excursions." Standing high up in the mountains at an altitude of 5249 feet, the town has one of the finest summer climates in Mexico. Saltillo is not only a health resort, but it has become an important manufacturing place, several large smelters, rubber factories and flour mills having been started there. It has some fine streets, good shops, and a magnificent club-house which contains the largest ball-room in Mexico.

From Saltillo southwards there is a succession of barren, sun-baked mountains, rocky cañons and arid valleys, dotted with cactus, but almost destitute of trees, though occasionally there is a green, irrigated patch of vegetation. It is a desolate country; for miles and miles scarcely a town or village is passed. Occasionally at small stations there are a few adobe huts where blanketed peons and some lean goats are visible, but otherwise there is little sign of life.

It is a melancholy country, and is rather depressing to the spirits. It seemed to have had an especially bad effect on two Americans who took seats near me in the smoking compartment, whither I had adjourned to try the efficacy of a good cigar in warding off the blues. They were strangers, but soon struck up an acquaintance. One of them, a dark, plump, rather Jewish-looking young man, with smoothly shaven face, had every appearance of being a "drummer." His companion was a long, lean, angular Westerner, evidently a farmer, with a scrubby gray beard which he stroked ruminatingly with one hand, while in the other he held a big, black, unlighted cigar, which he chewed vigorously from time to time.

"Well, sir," remarked the drummer, "we shall soon be seeing the last of Mexico, and getting back again into God's country. Well, I rather reckon they'll never see yours truly in Mexico again for the rest of his natural life." "You ain't done well, then," observed the Westerner. "Well?" retorted the other. "Why, I've hardly got the backbone to face my people in Chicago. I haven't even covered my expense account." "What's your line, partner?" asked the lean man, with some show of interest. "I'm travelling for a soap house," replied the drummer, with a deep groan.

The farmer gave a vindictive bite to the end of his cigar. "Well, well," he remarked, after a short silence, "I reckon we're both in the same boat, neighbor, when it comes to losing money." Here, to my horror, he actually produced a small piece of silver ore from his pocket. Surely, thought I, this cannot be another "man with a scheme." Is there no escaping them? But as I listened I heard a very different story from that which I expected. "Well, sir," continued the rural tourist, "that little chunk of metal cost me a pretty pile of money. I got it about two years ago from a fellow that came from down Guanajuato way and was a-visiting in our district. He talked me into putting up two thousand good American dollars to work a hole in the hills somewhere, that he swore was chock full of silver. We was both a-going to be millionaires in a few months. Well, I ain't never seen one cent back. Finally, I got tired o' waiting, and came down to Guanajuato to see if anything was coming out o' that hole." "What did you find in it?" asked the drummer. "Wal," dryly replied the man from the West, "I jest found that there wasn't even a hole. I've been a-trying ever since to lay my hands on that silver king; and, by gum, if I ever meet him, he won't work no more holes nor any more skin games neither." With this the two travellers relapsed into silence; both of them had painful memories of Mexico. How often during my travels had I encountered the "man with the scheme," but how little had I imagined that I should ever gaze upon one of his victims.

Later in the day, after winding for miles between the barren mountains, the train at last reached the large and important city of Monterey, situated in a beautiful valley at an altitude of fifteen hundred feet, and having a much better climate than many places farther south. Outside the station was the now familiar street-car with its two mules, still undisplaced by electrical traction, and the usual number of coches. One of the latter took me to a hotel in the middle of the town, which is nearly a mile from the railway, passing along some dusty roads lined with shed-like dwellings of tinted stucco, which give a stranger a very unfavorable first impression of the city. From this unattractive highway there was a sudden transition into the town itself, where there were good, substantial business buildings in the somewhat narrow streets, some smart shops and here and there a fine old Spanish church.

Monterey has a population of over sixty thousand, and being so close to the United States is becoming rapidly Americanized. Large numbers of Americans are living in and around the city, and a great deal of American and Canadian capital has been invested there. In strolling about the streets, I noticed signs of Americanization everywhere, the stores, for instance, having their announcements in English as well as Spanish; and at some of the street corners boys were selling a bright, well-edited American daily newspaper, the *Monterey News*. The city is the capital of the State of Nuevo Leon, and was founded in 1560. Of late years it has become an important manufacturing place; there are large iron mines not far distant, and half a dozen large smelters are in operation, where lead and silver are extracted from other ores. On the outskirts of the city are several big breweries, which manufacture the popular Monterey lager beer. As an offset to the beer, the city also does a large business in mineral water, which comes from the Topo Chico springs a few miles out; this has a great medicinal reputation and is sold all over the country.

Monterey is famous for having been the scene of an important battle in our war with Mexico in 1846, when, after a desperate, stubbornly disputed conflict lasting several days, General Taylor defeated a large force of Mexicans under General Ampudia. The old palace of the bishops of Monterey, now a picturesque ruin, standing on a hill near the town, was fortified by the Mexicans, and was the scene of fierce fighting. During the assault of the city the contest raged in the streets, the Mexican soldiers occupying the houses and shooting down the Americans from the windows and roofs.

While I was in the city, I accepted an invitation to accompany an American friend on a visit to one of the large ranches in the State of Coahuila, in which part of the country some of the largest Mexican estates are situated. Some of the ranches there have an area of two or three hundred miles and are over seventy miles wide. Much of the country is an undulating plain, with a sandy soil, covered with scrubby bushes, coarse grass and cactus.

A hot, dusty railway journey, which consumed the greater part of a day, took us to a small wayside station, where a peon awaited us with two horses. A ride of several miles brought us to the ranch. We spent the night at the ranch house, a small building of stuccoed adobe, which served as the headquarters of the manager of the estate. Early the next morning, after a good breakfast prepared by the Mexican cook, we again mounted our horses, and guided by one of the cowboys, an American, we rode about fifteen miles across the plain to a camp where a round-up was to take place.

Once a year every ranch has its round-up, when the cattle are collected and the unmarked yearlings or calves of a year old are branded, the work usually taking about a fortnight. During this interval the cowboys scour the range, gathering the bunches of cattle together and driving them towards one central point, where there is a huge stockade or corral. Towards the end of the drive there are oftentimes exciting scenes, many of the wilder animals galloping off and being brought back after a long chase. Occasionally a bull turns and charges on one of the cowboys, but although a horse is sometimes killed, the rider usually escapes. At night, too, a herd will sometimes stampede through fright and run for miles, some of the animals being killed in the mad flight.

On the way to the camp I chatted with our companion, the cowboy, a picturesque-looking fellow who wore a big straw sombrero, a blue shirt, a bright red handkerchief about his neck, while his legs were encased in skin-tight leather trousers, a protection against the thorns which abound in the low scrub. Around his waist was a well-filled cartridge belt holding a big revolver. It was a glorious morning, with a clear blue sky overhead and a mild though invigorating breeze was blowing over the great plain, which stretched for miles to a sky-line of rugged mountains.

"This is a great country," I remarked, but our cowpuncher was vigorously chewing a piece of plug tobacco and did not reply immediately. He then remarked: "Good enough for them that likes it, but I prefer God's country for mine."

"You would rather be back in Texas," I observed. "That's about it, Colonel," was the reply, "there's no fortune for a ranch hand in this part of the world." He then went on to tell me that, like many another young American, he had drifted down into Mexico in search of adventure, had got stranded, and had been obliged to take the first thing that offered in the shape of work. Cowboys on Mexican ranches, so he informed me, were supplied with a horse and saddle, paid five dollars a month and provided with food and lodging. In Texas he had earned about thirty dollars a month and his board. He was now practically a prisoner, as it was hard to save money, and Texas was a long way off. It was therefore not surprising that he sighed for God's country. Aside from his scanty wages, however, he found no fault with the work, having always done hard manual labor. I gathered from him that it was different with a good many young Americans of the better class, and quite a few young Englishmen who became stranded in Mexico and found themselves in the same position that he was in. "These tenderfeet come down here," he remarked, "expecting to find a sort of Wild West Show. Perhaps it's all very funny at first, but that soon wears off, and they find that ranching is a pretty hard life. We start work before sun-up and keep going until dark, and when a fellow has been riding miles over the range, chasing cattle all day, all he feels fit for at night is to eat his grub and turn in."

When we arrived at the camp, a large herd of cattle had just been driven into the corral by a party of cowboys or vaqueros, most of them swarthy Mexicans, with much shouting and yelling, the place being enveloped in clouds of dust. On holidays and other special occasions some of these vaqueros appear in gorgeous trappings on which all their savings are spent. Their jackets, sombreros and saddle blankets are heavily laced with gold tinsel, and they wear high boots and leather accoutrements of the finest quality. Wonderful feats of horsemanship and lassoing are exhibited by some of them.

After the cattle had been corralled, the calves or yearlings were separated from the herd and driven into a smaller enclosure, where several men were stationed with long branding-irons bearing the mark of the ranch. These were made almost red-hot in a blazing fire. One after another the yearlings were dexterously lassoed, thrown down and then held by two of the vaqueros, sometimes only after a hard struggle. The branding iron was immediately applied, burning off the hair and leaving the imprint on the skin. A peculiar clip was also given to the ear of each animal, which enables the ownership to be proved whenever they get mixed with herds belonging to another ranch. It took nearly all day to brand the yearlings in the corral; they were then turned loose with the rest of the herd, which was allowed to return to its feeding-grounds. The same process is repeated until all the cattle have been rounded up and branded.

If it were not for its monotony, there would be much worse modes of life than that on a Coahuila ranch. The country is wonderfully healthy, the climate resembling that of the southern part of the United States, but without the extremes of heat and cold which are experienced there. In the winter months the weather is quite bracing, and warm clothing is essential, especially when a "norther" swoops down through the country. I was there early in April, at which time the weather is almost perfection.

Since the great prairie lands of the United States, which once supported immense herds of cattle, have almost disappeared, the Mexican ranches have begun to attract much more attention, and a large amount of American capital is being invested in them. As feeding grounds for cattle, the Mexican ranges do not compare with the prairies, such, for instance, as formerly existed in Texas and the Indian Territory (now Oklahoma). Instead of the long, luscious prairie grass on which the American herds fattened, the Mexican cattle have to browse on coarse grass, weeds and even cactus, which they devour in spite of the prickles. In times of drought, when water and fodder are scarce, the peons sometimes gather quantities of prickly pear and partially burn off the sharp spikes, the broad, flat leaves, which are very juicy, being ravenously eaten by the cattle. Owing to the poor grazing which the Mexican ranges afford, it is estimated that about fifteen acres is required to support each animal, so that about one hundred and fifty thousand acres is needed for ten thousand head of cattle. This serves to explain the reason for the enormous extent of the great ranches.

Next to the question of food, the supply of water is of supreme importance in a country where streams are scarce and there is a long dry season. On most ranches the bulk of the water-supply is obtained from wells, the water being raised by means of windmills. It is oftentimes a long distance from the feeding grounds to the water, and in times of drought large numbers of cattle perish.

The native Mexican cattle have much the same look as the Spanish breeds, with long, wide, curving horns, but are not of much value as meat-producers. They cost about $5 each. Of foreign cattle the Swiss and Holland breeds seem to thrive best on the Mexican ranges, and these are being successfully crossed with the native stock.

On the ranch which we visited there were over a thousand head of horses, most of them small, bony, wiry animals, which hardly fetch $3 in the market. There was, however, some fine-looking stock, the result of crossing the native English and French breeds. On some of the ranches from ten to twenty thousand horses find pasturage, and for breeding purposes are divided into bunches of fifty or more, according to their color, browns, roans, grays, etc., so as to secure uniformity in the stock. After being kept together for some time, these bunches never become mixed with each other, but when roaming over the range each keeps to itself.

In addition to cattle and horses, goats are popular species of live stock on Mexican ranches, herds of five and ten thousand being quite common. Goats are very profitable, as a rule, requiring very little attention, and thriving on the poorest pasturage. Goats' flesh is much eaten by the poorer classes in Mexico, and there is always a good market for the skins.

We passed a pleasant night at the camp, where sleeping quarters were provided in two or three large tents. Out in the open, fires were kindled by the Mexican cooks, who, with the aid of sundry pans and skillets prepared a very appetizing supper for the hungry ranchmen. There was fried beef, pork and beans, freshly baked hardtack and coffee. Later in the evening, in honor of our visit, a flask of rye whiskey was produced from some place of concealment, and a homœopathic quantity subtracted by each of us.

As we sat round the fire enjoying a smoke, the scene was delightfully picturesque. Above, in the clearest of skies, was the bright moon and a blaze of stars, which lighted the great plain stretching for miles to the westward. One of a party of Mexicans who were squatting together a short distance away produced an old mandolin, and to the accompaniment of this his companions joined in singing one of those plaintive Spanish songs which seem to strangely harmonize with the life of Mexico. Stirred into activity by this burst of song, some coyotes or prairie wolves not far off set up a dismal howling, to which some of the dogs in the camp replied in wonderful imitation. In this part of the country there are not only coyotes but lynx, puma, and cinnamon bears, affording excellent sport for those who are handy with a rifle.

During the evening I entered into conversation with the ranch foreman, a very intelligent Mexican, who had been employed on one of the great ranches of northern Mexico, much larger in extent than the average American county. I had some curiosity to learn how these great estates are managed. He informed me that this particular estate was divided into farms of from one thousand to twenty-five hundred acres each, a foreman being placed in charge of each farm and managing it independently. Machinery, tools, horses, mules, wagons and money for the peons was furnished to each foreman. At certain parts of the estate there were general stores where the peons could obtain their food, clothing and other requisites on credit. Most of them remained in debt to the stores, and never saw any of the money representing their wages. In some cases an entire village would be in this condition of indebtedness. On this estate there were three thousand peons, who, with their families, made a total population of ten thousand.

Although the country seems very barren when viewed from the railway, and the ranges seem to afford very scanty subsistence for the cattle, Coahuila is nevertheless one of the richest agricultural States in Mexico. The soil in many places is wonderfully fertile, yielding large crops of wheat, cotton, sugar-cane and maize. Grapes are now being grown to some extent, and an excellent quality of wine has been produced, superior in some respects to that of California. There are also great orchards of such fruits as apples, pears and quince. As Coahuila is just below the boundary of the United States, and railway connections are steadily improving, it offers many attractions to settlers. Large numbers of Americans with capital are coming into this part of Mexico. One of the Coahuila towns, Torreon, which was until recently a small Indian village, has now a large American population and has been transformed into a thriving, busy place, with substantial buildings of brick and stone, equipped with electric light, telephones and other modern accessories.

My visit to this interesting State was a fitting close to my Mexican travels. Here, as in other parts of the Republic, I found the same development of resources in progress, the same inrush of new methods, the awakening of the people and the steady Americanization of the land. Here, too, I found that touch of the picturesque which makes Mexico, with all her faults, so fascinating to the stranger within her gates; for the deep blue, cloudless sky, the vast herds of cattle and the galloping vaqueros are things to be remembered for many a day.

The next morning I rode with my companion back to the railway, and a few hours later was again on the train returning to Monterey, with its busy streets and hum of life. Two days afterwards I boarded the St. Louis express once more and resumed my journey northwards.

It is 166 miles from Monterey to Nuevo Laredo on the Rio Grande River, which divides Mexico from the United States. The scenery for half the distance continues of the same arid description, dry valleys, with cactus and scrubby vegetation, and low, barren, sun-baked hills. Then comes a wide plain, stretching to the horizon, a desolate region, with the same scrubby bushes and dry, yellow grass. Travellers coming from the North get a very bad impression of the country in the dry season. I have heard people who have been in Texas and have gone down a few miles over the border into Mexico, denouncing the country as a perfect desert. They have simply seen a few leagues of these barren plains and sun-baked hills and call that "seeing Mexico."

At the little station of Nuevo Laredo I bade farewell, with many regrets, to old Mexico. There was a halt of a few minutes here and a cursory examination of baggage. It appeared that some serious robberies had recently occurred in the capital, and the police, thinking that the thieves might be attempting to leave the country with their plunder, had ordered a search to be made for suspicious persons and baggage at Vera Cruz and Tampico and at all railway stations along the American border. I exchanged a few words with the polite old customs officer, who, with his bronzed, bearded face and military bearing, might have stepped from a canvas by Velasquez. As I got on the train, which was already moving, he lifted his hat, and with graceful courtesy said, "Adios, señor, vaya usted con Dios."

The sun was slowly sinking over the reddish hills of Mexico as our train steamed over the long steel bridge spanning the wide, shallow Rio Grande River, to the bustling town of Laredo, Texas. Looking backwards, I could see the little station, with its group of drowsy peons loafing outside, while above it the red, white and green flag of Mexico floated idly in the evening breeze. Back there, beyond the miles of barren mountains and plains were the everlasting hills tipped with snow, overlooking many a quaint old town, with its ancient churches and its sunny plazas bright with a wealth of flowers, where a kindly though slowly progressing people were still living the life of the past. Back there, at least, the picturesque still survived; but was it to be soon obliterated by the prosaic American invasion?

As if in answer to this question, a sharp, businesslike voice greeted my ear. "All the latest books and papers—*San Antonio Express*, St. Louis and Chicago papers. Here's all of 'em." We had reached the American side of the river, and a hustling news-vendor had boarded the train with a fresh supply of literature. At the same moment another brisk voice broke in with, "Laredo; all passengers out for customs examination. Please step lively." Some local celebration happened to be in progress, and the station was decorated with masses of American flags. Just as I left the train, a brass band blared forth "Hail, Columbia," and a crowd of enthusiastic citizens rent the air with ear-piercing cheers.

Here was Laredo, the outpost of the United States, with its energy, its push, and its inspiring patriotism; and there, across that wide, shallow river was Mexico, the old, the romantic, the picturesque, slowly but surely awakening into new life through the oncoming host of American invaders.

INDEX

Adobe houses, 40.
Advertisements, Mexico City, 64.
Agriculture, on haciendas in Cuautla, 322–326, 329–330; in the hot lands, 385–386; in northern Mexico, 410, 425.
Aguadores, 34, 99.
Aguas Calientes, 407.
Ajusco, Mount, 221.
Alameda, the, Mexico City, 48–49.
Alban, Monte, ruins on, 300–302.
Alvarado, Pedro, peon millionaire, 365–366.
Ambassadors, Hall of, National Palace, 90.
Amecameca, town of, 328, 330–331; sacred mountain and Passion Play at, 335–336.
Americanization of Mexico, 176.
American quarter, Mexico City, 171, 182.
Americans, in Mexico City, 59–60; invasion of Mexico by tourists, and their characteristics, 170–173; good feeling between English residents and, 173; promoters of "schemes," 173–174; Mexican feeling against, 174–175; called "gringos," 175; capital invested by, 175, 297; at Cuernavaca, 227; at Puebla, 244; at Oaxaca, 265–266, 298; at Cuautla, 318; at Guadalajara, 343; in northern Mexico, 408, 425.
Amusements, public, Mexico City, 130–131.
Animals, blessing of the, 155–156.
Annexation, possibility of, 176.
Apam, plains of, 40, 44.
Aqueduct, remains of, Mexico City, 99.

Arcade Hotel, Puebla, 238.
Archæological researches, 301, 308.
Armor, exhibit of, Mexico City, 91.
Arms of Mexico, 210.
Army, system of education in, 149; training of officers, statistics concerning, etc., 217–218.
Art, specimens of, National Museum, Mexico City, 93; in church buildings, 114; works of, in churches, 246–247; Murillo's "Assumption," Guadalajara, 342; Titian's "Entombment of Christ," 372–375.
Artists, prominent, 128.
Art students, public assistance of, 128.
Atequiza, village of, 349.
Atlacomulco, hacienda of, 225.
Australian sheep in Chihuahua, 410.
Automobile roads, 129, 220–221.
Automobiles, Mexico City, 103, 105, 129.
Aztecs, history of tribe of, 71–77; descendants of the, 184–185; remains of, about Cuernavaca, 230–231.

Baird, W. H., 272–278.
Ball-playing, Mexican, 291, 292.
Banana raising, 383, 385, 405.
Baronial estates, 322–325, 350, 404, 414.
Barranca, the, at Cuernavaca, 228; at Guadalajara, 347.
Bathing, compulsory, 137.
Beans, as staple food, 32.
"Bear, playing the," 161–165, 327; Young America's views on, 363.
Beggars, 15–16, 40, 109, 227; in Mexico City, 66; check placed on, under Diaz régime, 213.

INDEX

Blake, W. W., researches of, 92.
Blessing of the animals, custom of, 155–156.
Borda, Jose de la, 225–226.
Borda Garden and mansion, 225–227.
Bosque, park in Mexico City, 102.
Boulevard, Mexico City, 99–100.
Breweries, 129, 418.
Brigandage, extinction of, 203–204.
British in Mexico, 177–178, 276–277. *See* English.
British Club, Mexico City, 183.
Buena Vista, battle of, 415.
Bull-fights, Mexico City, 105–106.
Burden-bearers, Mexican, 4–5, 45.
Burial customs, 154, 360–361.

Cabs (*coches*), 20, 45–46.
Cacahuamilpa, caves of, 231–233.
Cacti, Mexican, 256–257; fibre-producing qualities of, 330.
Cafés, Vera Cruz, 6; Mexico City, 139.
Calendar Stone, Aztec, 92.
Calle Cinco de Mayo, Mexico City, 60.
Calle San Francisco, Mexico City, 62.
Campeche, State of, 383.
Canada, large interests of, in Mexico, 178.
Cañons. *See* Barranca.
Capital, foreign, in Mexico, 175, 206–207; opportunity for men with small, 180–181.
Cargadores, 4–5, 45.
Carriages, Mexico City, 103.
Casino Español, Mexico City, 183.
Catacomb, at Guanajuato, 360–362.
Cathedral, Vera Cruz, 2, 6; Orizaba, 25; Mexico City, 87; of San Francisco, at Cuernavaca, 224; Puebla, 240–241; Oaxaca, 264, 270; Guadalajara, 342.
Catholicism, tenacity of, 151–152.
Catorce, town of, 414–415.
Cattle, native and foreign, 423.
Caves of Cacahuamilpa, 231–233.
Ceremonial, tendency to, 132.
Chapala, town of, 350–352.
Chapala, Lake, 350, 351–354.

Chapalteco Indians, 354.
Chapultepec, military college at, 217.
Chapultepec, Castle of, Mexico City, 101.
Chapultepec Café, 103.
Charcoal, use of, Mexico City, 59.
Charles IV, statue of, Mexico City, 100.
Charnay, French archæologist, 109–110.
Cherubusco, Country Club at, 183.
Chihuahua, State of, 404, 409, 410.
Children, education and training of, 126.
Chimneys, absence of, Mexico City, 58, 59.
Chinese, resemblance of Mexican Indians to, 185–186.
Chinese club, Mexico City, 183.
Cholula, town of, 244–247.
Christian Science in Mexico, 153.
Christmas festivities, 242–244; at Los Reyes, 290–294.
Church, governmental interference with the, 151.
Church, the oldest, in America, 248.
Church of —
 Jesus Maria, Mexico City, 113.
 Jesus Nazareno, Mexico City, 111.
 La Compania, Puebla, 241.
 La Piedad, Mexico City, 116.
 Nuestra Señora de los Angeles, Mexico City, 112.
 Nuestra Señora de los Remedios, Cholula, 246–247.
 Our Lady of Guadalupe, Guadalupe Hidalgo, 117–122.
 Our Lady of Succor, Los Remedios, 116.
 San Cristobal, Puebla, 241.
 San Diego, Mexico City, 49.
 San Francisco, Jalapa, 397.
 San Francisco, Puebla, 241.
 San Francisco, Tlaxcala, 248.
 San Francisco, Vera Cruz, 6.
 San Hipólito, Mexico City, 113.
 Santa Cruz, Queretaro, 375.
 Santa Domingo, Oaxaca, 270.
 Santa Rosa, Queretaro, 375.
 Santa Teresa, Orizaba, 25.

INDEX   431

Churches, at Orizaba, 25; Mexico City, 111–115; Cuautla, 319; Queretaro, 375.
Church-bell nuisance, 24, 152, 241.
Church pictures, 246–247, 342, 372.
Church property, state appropriation of, 151, 319.
Cinematograph shows, 130, 241.
City of Churches, 236.
City of temples, a, 245.
Climate, 17–18, 53; in Mexico City, 50; of Guadalajara, 341–342.
Clothes, 20–22, 27–28; of priests, 25, 151; cost of peons', 33; expense of, 65; ladies', 168.
Clubs, foreign residents', 183.
Coahuila, State of, 404, 415 ff., 425; a ranch in, 418–425.
Coal, small quantity of, produced, 369.
Cock-fighting, 191–192.
Coffee, Mexican, 142.
Coffee raising, 383, 405.
Colima, State of, 348.
Colima volcano, 348.
Columbus statue, Mexico City, 100.
Congress, the Federal, 210.
Contras, Jose Peon y, poet, 128.
Convent of San Francisco, at Tzintzuntzan, 372.
Convolvulus, 223.
Copper mines, 369.
Cordier, Columbus statue by, 100.
Cordoba, town of, 14–16.
Corn, production of, 237; in hot lands, 385.
Corral, Vice-President, 208.
Cortés, 3, 19, 54, 87; conquest of Mexico by, 74–79; absence of monuments to, 100; death and burial-place of, 111–112; traces of, at Cuernavaca, 224–225; title of Marquis of the Valley of Oaxaca, 271.
Cosio, General, 208.
Cost of living, Mexico City, 136.
Cotton growing, northern Mexico, 410.
Country Club, Mexico City, 183.
Courtship, method of, 161.

Courts of law, 211 ff.
Creel, Ambassador, 180, 208.
Creelman, James, quoted, 202, 208–209.
Criadors, 263.
Cuauhnahuac, 221.
Cuauhtemoc, Aztec prince, statue of, 100.
Cuautla, mineral springs and haciendas at, 314–327.
Cuernavaca, 219–230.
Curanderas, wise women, 311.
Currency, Mexican, 7.
Customs officials, Mexican and American, 426, 427.

Dances, peons', at Christmas festivities, 293; of Zapotec Indians, 312–313.
Death-rate, Mexico City, 55.
Degollado theatre, Guadalajara, 343–344.
Dentists, American, in Mexico, 23.
Devil Dance of Zapotec Indians, 312–313.
Diaz, Porfirio, defeats forces of Maximilian, 84; becomes President of Mexico (1876), 85; receptions held by, 90; residence of, 91; disapproval of bull-fighting by, 106; the President and his wife as social leaders, 126; at the Circo Teatro, 131; weekly baths enforced by, 137; treatment of newspaper editors, 143–144; educational system inaugurated by, 148–150; keenness on religious toleration, 153; affection of natives for, 198; sketch of career of, 199–202; personal appearance of, 202; habits, 202–203; family, 203; progress of country under, 203–207; question of successor to, 207–208; danger from prolonged rule of, 208; views on education, 209; reception given to Mystic Shriners by, 337; and the Western widows, 338.
"Dick, the Chinaman," 260.

Diplomatic corps, Mexico City, 127.
Divorces, absence of, 158.
Drainage system, Mexico City, 54.
Drawnwork of Aguas Calientes, 407.
Dress, change in women's, to French styles, 168. *See* Clothes.
Drinking, by Indians, 40–43, 193–195.
Drinking-places, 6–7, 28.
Drinks in restaurants, 141.
Duck-shooting, Chapala, 353.
Duels, 164.
Durango, State and city of, 404, 408–409.

Eating-places, Mexico City, 63, 138–143.
Education, progress in, 148–150; lack of, in women, 167; of Indians, 192; President Diaz on, 209.
Educational institutions, Mexico City, 149.
Enchiladas, 140.
English customs, Mexico City, 125.
English in Mexico, 173; called "Americans," 176; loss of first place in trade in Mexico by, 177–178; as mining men, 276–277.
"Entombment of Christ," Titian's, 372–375.
Escandon, Señor Landa y, 126–127, 208.
Escandon mansion, Mexico City, 61.
Esperanza, town of, 38.
Estates, baronial (haciendas), 322–325.
Executions, method pursued in, 216–217.
Exports of Mexico, 179.

Fair God legend, 69, 93.
Family life, 158.
Farming estates, 322–326, 350, 404, 414.
Farming in the hot lands, 382 ff.
Federal District, Mexico City, government of, 96–97.
Felipe, patron saint of Mexico City, 98–99.

Fernandez, Señor, 208.
Festival of Our Lady of Guadalupe, 117, 120.
Festivals, Christmas, 243–244.
Fibre plants, cultivation of, 326, 329–330.
Fiestas, 189.
Fifth of May Street, Mexico City, 60.
Fishing, in Lake Chapala, 353; at Tampico, 399–403.
Flirtations, 161–162.
Flores, Manuel, poet, 128.
Flower Market, Mexico City, 95.
Food, cost of, 136; in restaurants, Mexico City, 138–141.
Foreigners in Mexico, 170 ff.; capital invested by, 175; Americans, Spanish, French, Germans, English, and Canadians, 177–178; influence exercised by children of, 179–180; colonies and clubs of, Mexico City, 182–183; mining properties of, 272.
Foreign quarters, Mexico City, 181–182.
Fortune-telling, 229.
French, occupation of Mexico by, 83–84; clubs of, Mexico City, 183.
French business men in Mexico, 177.
Frias family, 414.
Frijoles, 140.
Fruits, 141, 267, 383, 385, 405, 425.
Funeral customs, 154.
Funerals, street-cars used for, 97–98; prevalence of Catholic rites in, 154.
Fuster, Alberto, artist, 128.

Gambling, 61, 65–66, 297–298; by Indians, 191–192.
Game, land of the big, 381–382.
Games, Christmas, 242–244, 292–293; gambling, 297–298 (*see* Gambling).
Germans in Mexico, 177; affiliation of, with Mexicans, 180; club and club building of, Mexico City, 183.
Gillow, Archbishop, 270.

INDEX 433

Goat raising, 423.
Gold, undiscovered mines of, 368; annual output of, 369.
Gold mining, 272-282; in State of Jalisco, 348-349.
Government, autocracy of, 205-206; machinery of, 210 ff.
Government Palace, Cuernavaca, 224.
Granadita, the, 32.
Graphite from Mexico, 369.
Grazing land, American vs. Mexican, 422.
"Greasers," 174.
"Gringos," 175.
Grocery stores, Spanish ownership of, 298-299.
Guadalajara, 339-349.
Guadalajara ware, 346-347.
Guadalupe, festival of Our Lady of, 117, 120.
Guanajuato, the "silver city," 355-367.
Guernsey, Frederick, 145.
Guerrero, President, 187.
Guerrero, ruins in, 233.

Haciendas, 322-326; near Guadalajara, 350; in San Luis Potosi, 406-407.
Hacienda system, an obstacle to progress, 325.
Hall of Monoliths, Mitla, 306-310.
Health resorts, 249-257, 314-322, 407, 415.
Hearse-cars, 97-98, 154.
Heating of houses, 182.
Hemp trade, 329-330.
Henequen, growth of, 329-330.
Hermosillo, capital of Sonora, 413.
Hidalgo, Miguel, insurrection of, 79-80, 90, 359.
Highwaymen, treatment of, 216-217.
Hill of the Frogs, Guanajuato called, 357.
Horse races, Mexico City, 130.
Horse raising, 423.
Hospicio, Guadalajara, 345-346.
Hotel de France, 23.
Hotel Diligencia, Vera Cruz, 395.

Hotel Morelos, Cuautla, 317-318.
Hotels, Mexican, 23-24, 46-48; at Orizaba, 23; at Cuernavaca, 223; at Puebla, 238; at Tehuacan, 251-253; at Oaxaca, 262-263; at Cuautla, 317-318; at Chapala, 351; at Vera Cruz, 395; at Tampico, 400.
Hot lands, 233, 259-260, 380, 382-393; products and great future of, 383.
Hot springs, 407.
Housekeeping, absence of good, 166.
House of Tiles, Mexico City, 61.
Houses, Mexico City, 124; rental of, 136; heating of, 183; at Puebla, 239.
Huitzilopochtli, Aztec War-god, 87, 91.
Hunting grounds, 381-382.

Idols, Aztec, 92-93.
Indian corn, 237; growth of, in hot lands, 385.
India rubber, extraction of and prospects for, 384-385.
India rubber plantations, 382, 384.
Indians, Mexican, 20-21, 22, 184-186; politeness of, 133-134; Yaqui, 185; resemblance of, to Chinese and Japanese, 185-186; Mayan, 186; numbers of, 187; women of, 192-193; drink the curse of, 193-195; bathing and non-bathing habits of, 195; stories of stupidity of, 195-197; in the army, 218; as pottery-makers, 228-229; of San Antone, 229; Yaqui, 411-414. *See* Mayans, Yaquis, Zapotecs, *etc.*
Infant mortality, 193.
Influenza in Mexico, 314.
Inquisition, victims of the, 49.
Investment, field for, in Mexico, 179.
Investments, opportunity for small, 180-181; grand total of foreign, 206-207.
Iripuato, town of, 355.
Iron deposits, 369.
Irrigation of land, 410.

2 F

Isthmus of Tehuantepec, 378-393.
Iturbide, Augustin, career of, 80-81; burial-place, 88.
Ixtaccihuatl, Mount, 102, 224; shortening of name, by Americans, 177; legend of, 332.
Ixtle, fibre-producing qualities of, 330.
Ixtlilxochitli, Indian poet, 127.
Izaguirre, Leandro, artist, 128.

Jaguar, country of the, 381-382.
Jalapa, city of, 395-397.
Jalisco, State of, 348.
Jalisco Times, the, 343.
Japanese, resemblance of Mexican Indians to, 185-186.
Jiminez, Francisco, statue by, 100.
Jockey Club, Mexico City, 61.
Juarez, Benito, 82-85, 94, 187.

Kansas City, Mexican and Orient Railway, 409.

La Cima, 220.
Lakes, about Mexico City, 53; Chapala and Patzcuaro, 350, 351-354, 370-371.
Language, the Spanish, as spoken in Mexico, 128-129.
La Trinidad mine, 367.
Law courts, 211 ff.
Lead deposits, 369.
Legends of miracles, 115-119.
Lerma River, 352.
Letter-writers, public, 34.
Libel laws, 144.
Liberty Bell of Mexico, 90.
Libraries, public, 6, 149.
Limantour, J. Y., 127, 208.
Literature, leaders in, 127-128.
Lopez, Gregorio, 88.
Los Reyes, gold-mine at, 287, 294; Christmas celebration at, 290-294.
Lotteries, 65.
Love-making, method of, 161-165.
Luna Park, Mexico City, 102.
Lunchrooms, railway, 38, 260, 315-317.

Maguey plant, the, 40-41; other uses for, than drink, 330.
Maguey plantations, 329.
Mahogany, 383.
Maltrata, village of, 37.
Mango, the Mexican, 32.
Mantilla, the, 89.
Manzanillo, railway to, 348.
Mariscal, Señor, statesman and writer, 128.
Market, at Oaxaca, 267-270.
Markets, public, 31.
Mark Twain, quotation from, 230.
Marriage, charges by priests, 152; ideas about, 161; Indians' disregard of, 193.
Martinez, Ramos, artist, 128.
"Mashers," Mexico City, 104, 160; and the Western widows, 338.
Maximilian, Archduke, Emperor of Mexico, 83-84; relics of, in National Museum, 93; municipal improvements in Mexico City under, 100-101; surrender and execution of, at Queretaro, 376-377.
Mayan Indians, 186, 391.
Meat, Mexican, 33.
Merida, city of, 389.
Mexican Central Railway, scenic attractions of, 219-220; between Mexico City and Guadalajara, 340; from Guadalajara westward to Manzanillo, 347-348.
Mexican Herald, the, 145.
Mexican Railway, 13-14.
Mexican Southern Railway, 261-262.
Mexican War, the, 81.
Mexico, past history of, 67 ff.; derivation of the name, 72.
Mexico, Valley of, 220.
Mexico City, 44-66, 86 ff.; government of, 96-97; consideration of the name, 177; visit of Shriners to, 336-337.
Meztizos, 187.
Military college, Mexico City, 102.
Militia, national, 217-218.
Mineral productions, 179.

Mineral springs, 249-257, 320-322. See Health resorts.
Mines, inaccessibility of, 272.
Mining, in Guerrero, 233-234; around Oaxaca, 272-282, 296-297; in Jalisco, 348-349.
Mining expert, a so-called, 263.
Mining laws, 280-281.
Mining possibilities, 369.
Miracles, 115-119.
Mitla, ruins of, 302-310.
Model city, near Cuernavaca, 222.
Money, Mexican, 7.
Monterey, city of, 417-418; battle of, 418.
Monterey News, the, 418.
Montezuma I, King, 72.
Moon Pyramid, 107-108.
Morals, laxity in, 161.
Morelos, Jose Maria, insurrection of, 80, 319.
Morelos, Hotel, 317.
Morelos, State of, 224.
Motoring, interest in, 129. See Automobiles.
Motor roads, 129, 220-221.
Mummies, in catacomb at Guanajuato, 361-362.
Murillo, the "Assumption" by, 342.
Music, Mexican fondness for and indulgence in, 131-132.

National Library, Mexico City, 149.
National Museum, Mexico City, 91.
National Palace, Mexico City, 89-91.
National Pawn-shop, 94.
Natividad mine, 272.
Negroes in Mexico, 9.
Newspaper readers, public, 28-29.
Newspapers, 143-146.
New Year's at Oaxaca, 299.
Nicknames by Americans, 177.
Nitzahualcoyotl, Indian poet, 127.
Niven, William, archæologist, 233.
Novelists, 128.
Nueva Laredo, station of, 426.

Oaxaca, President Diaz' birth and early years at, 198-199, 271; prison in, 217; pronunciation and location, 250; railway to, 261-262; visit at, 262-271; mining about, 272-282, 296-297; prehistoric remains about, 300-310.
Oaxaca, State of, 283-284.
Oil, production of, 369; for fuel on railways, 379.
Onyx quarries, Puebla, 240.
Opera-house, Mexico City, 57.
Organs in churches, 115.
Orizaba, Mount, 2, 26, 37, 38.
Orizaba, town of, 12, 19-35.
Our Lady of the Angels, church and shrine of, Mexico City, 112-113.
Oxen, teams of, 267.

Pachuca, silver mining at, 367.
Paganism, survivals of, 150.
Palacio, Vincent Riva, novelist, 128.
Palenque, ruins at, 390.
Pan-American Railway, 389-390.
Pankhurst, Señor, 180.
Paper pulp from cacti, 330.
Para grass, 405.
Parks, 49.
Paseo de la Reforma, Mexico City, 99-100.
Passion Play at Amecameca, 335-336.
Patio process of silver extraction, 366.
Patzcuaro, Lake, 350, 370-371.
Patzcuaro, town of, 370-371.
Pawn-shop, National, 94.
Paz, Irenio, novelist, 128.
Pearson and Sons, works of, at Rincon Antonio, 386.
Pears' Soap anecdote, 196-197.
Peons, 184, 350; dress of, 20-21, 33; wretched living conditions of, Mexico City, 136-137; good qualities and faults, 187-188; on large haciendas, 324-326, 424. See Indians.
Periodicals, 145.
Pesa, Juan de Dios, poet, 128.
Petroleum, supply of, 369.
Physicians, American, in Mexico, 23.
Picture-cards, game of, 297-298.
Pictures in churches, 246-247, 342, 372.

Picture-writings, 70.
Pilgrimages, remarks on, 236.
Piñates, 242-243.
"Playing the bear," 161-165, 327, 363.
Plazas in cities, 25-26.
Pneumonia, in Mexico City, 55.
Poets and poetry, 127-128.
Poindexter, Colonel, 400.
Police, in Vera Cruz, 10; at Orizaba, 34; Mexico City, 50-52; Republican Guard, Mexico City, 100-101; enforced baths by, 137; work of, under Diaz régime, 213-214; abuses by, 214-216.
Politeness, Spanish style of, in Mexico City, 132; of Indians, 133-134, 192.
Polygamy, 193.
Popocatepetl, Mount, 102, 220, 224; shortening of name, by Americans, 177; ascent and description of, 328, 331-335; legend of, 332; sulphur mining on, 334.
Popo Park, 331.
Posadas, 243-244.
Post-office, Mexico City, 57.
Pottery, 33-34; from Guadalajara, 346-347; Aguas Calientes ware, 407.
Pottery industry, San Antone, 228-229.
Prehistoric relics, 390.
Prescott, W. H., quoted, 245, 308.
Press, Mexican, 143-146.
Priests, Mexican, 25; influence of, 150-151.
Prisons, compulsory education in, 149; conditions in, 217.
Procrastination, prevailing habit of, 132-133.
Products of Mexico, 179.
Protestantism, slight hold of, 153.
Puebla, city of, 235-247.
Puebla, State of, 239.
Puerto Mexico, port of, 379, 388.
Pullman cars, 13.
Pulque, national drink, 40-43, 141; consumption of, by Indians, 193-195.

Pulquerias, 194.
Pyramid at Cholula, 245-246.
Pyramids of the Sun and Moon, 107-108.

Queretaro, surrender and execution of Emperor Maximilian at, 84-85, 376-377; visit to, 375-377.
Quero, Don Felix, 304.
Queroga, Bishop, 373.
Quetzalcoatl, legend of, 69; idol called, 93; emblem of, 231; temple of, Cholula, 245-246.

Railway, Mexican, 13-14; Mexican Central, 219-220, 340, 347-348; Tehuantepec National, 378 ff., 388-389; a Pan-American, 389-390; Kansas City, Mexican and Orient, 409.
Railway possibilities, 389.
Railway restaurants, 38, 260, 315-317.
Railways, government policy concerning, 146-147, 204; changes effected by, 148.
Railway stations, 45, 147.
Railway trains, 12-13, 35.
Railway travel, cost of, 35.
Ranches, in State of Coahuila, 418-425. See Haciendas.
Ranch life, 418-425.
Real estate investments, 182.
Rebeccas, Indian, 274.
Refresco, Mexican drink, 6.
Religion, state of, 151-154; of the peons, 189-190.
Religious practices, 150, 155-156.
Religious toleration, 152-153.
Rent, cost of, Mexico City, 136.
Republican Guard, Mexico City, 100-101.
Restaurants, railway, 38, 260, 315-317; in Mexico City, 63, 138-143.
Reyes, General, 208.
Rincon Antonio, railway shops at, 386.
Rubber. See India rubber.
Rurales, mounted police, 213.

INDEX

Salina Cruz, port of, 379, 387-388.
Saltillo, town of, 415.
Salvation Army, barred from Mexico, 153.
San Antone, 228-229.
San Francisco Street, Mexico City, 62.
San Juan Teotihuacan, town of, 107-108.
San Juan de Ulloa, island of, 3.
San Luis Potosi, city of, 406.
San Miguel Peras, village of, 287, 289-290.
San Pedro, village of, 346.
Santa Ana, General, 81.
Santa Lucrezia, village of, 383.
Sapodilla, the, 32.
Sarape, the, 21; an Indian word, 129; "made in Germany," 407-408.
"Schemes," men with, 173-174, 263, 264, 295, 363; a victim of, 416-417.
Sculptors at San Pedro, 346-347.
Sculpture, Mexico City, 100.
Seasons, dry and rainy, 53.
Servants, 48; force of custom among, 134; wages of, 166; numbers of household, and customs, 166-167.
Sheep farming in Chihuahua, 410.
Shooting, at Chapala, 353; jaguar, puma, tapir, deer, etc., 382.
Shops, at Orizaba, 22-23; at Mexico City, 62.
Shriners in Mexico, 336-337; at Guadalajara, 344-345.
Sierra, Justo, poet, 128.
Signs, American, in Mexico City, 59.
Silver, the mining of, 364-367, 408; processes of extraction of, 366; annual output of, 369.
Silver king, tarpon called, 400.
Silver kings, 225-226, 364-366.
Slavery, 184-185, 188-191, 424.
Slum districts, Mexico City, 136-137.
Smith, F. Hopkinson, quoted, 190, 373-375.
Smoking by women, 165.
Soap-manufacture, 239.

Social leaders, Mexico City, 126-127.
Social life, Mexico City, 124.
Soldiers, Mexico City, 57; on guard at National Palace, 90; compulsory education for, 149; training of, statistics of army, uniform, etc., 217-218.
Sombrero, Danza de, 293.
Sombreros, 21.
Sonora, Yaqui Indian war in, 411-414.
Sorrowful Night, the, 107, 113.
Southern Hotel, Tampico, 400.
Spaniards in Mexico, 177; clubs of, Mexico City, 183.
Stage-coaches, 350-351, 370.
Statues, Mexico City, 100.
Steamship lines, 395.
Stephens, J. L., cited, 390.
Stillwell, Arthur E., 409-410.
Stone of Sacrifice, 87, 91.
Storekeeping methods, 298-299.
Strawberries at Iripuato, 355.
Street-car fares, 97.
Street-cars, Vera Cruz, 6; Orizaba, 27; Mexico City, 46, 57, 97; Cuernavaca, 222; Puebla, 238; Guadalajara, 344, 346; Guanajuato, 356.
Street of the Dead, Teotihuacan, 110.
Streets, Mexico City, 58; names of, 64.
Suburban life, growth of, 107.
Suffrage, severely limited, 210.
Sugar-cane regions, 322-326, 385.
Sulphur mining on Mt. Popocatepetl, 334.
Sun Pyramid, 107-108.
Sun-worship, 72.
Swamps of hot lands, 383.

Tabasco, State of, 383.
Tacubaya, town of, 107.
Tamales, 139.
Tampico, 3, 394, 398-403.
Tarpon fishing, 394, 399-403.
Teatro Juarez, el, 358.
Tehuacan, Mexican Carlsbad, 249-257.

Tehuantepec, Isthmus of, 378–393; city of, 390–393.
Tehuantepec National Railway, 378 ff., 388–389.
Telsa, Manuel, statue by, 100.
Temples, at Cholula, 245.
Tezozomoc, Indian poet, 127.
Theatre, at Guanajuato, 358.
Theatres, Mexico City, 50, 131; Guadalajara, 343–344.
Thieves' Market, 95.
Thompson, David E., American ambassador, 127.
Titian, painting by, at Tzintzuntzan, 372–375.
Tlacolula, town of, 303–304.
Tlapanecos, gold in land of, 368.
Tlaxcala, town and State of, 247–248.
Tobacco raising, 382.
Toledo, Juan Telles, portrait painter, 128.
Toltecs, race of, 68–69; mementos of the, 107–109.
Toluca, town of, 129.
Topobolampo, harbor of, 409.
Topo Chico springs, 418.
Toro, station of, 220.
Torreon, town of, 425.
Tortilla, native bread, 32.
Tourists, 171–173; at Cuernavaca, 227–228; visit of the Mystic Shriners, 336–337, 344–345; visit of Western widows, 337–338.
Tower, Reginald T., British representative, 127.
Tree of "la Noche Triste," 107; big tree of Tula, 303.
Tres Marias, station of, 220, 221.
Tropical Mexico, 378–393. *See* Hot lands.
Tropic of Cancer, 415.
Tula, village of, 302–303.
Tumbago, 61; in cathedral, Mexico City, 88.
Turkey vendors, 345.
Typhoid, prevalence of, at Mexico City, 55.
Tzintzuntzan, village of, 371–372; the Titian at, 372–375.

Uniforms, military, 90, 218.
United States. *See* Americans.

Valencia, Martin de, 335.
Valenciana, Conde de, silver king, 365.
Vera Cruz, harbor of, 2; importance commercially, 3; early history of, 3–4; description of, 5–12, 394–395.
Vera Cruz, State of, 383.
Volcano, Colima, 348.

Wages, of servants, 166; of peons, 188; of native miners, 369; of cowboys, 420.
Warner, Charles Dudley, quoted, 375–376.
Water-carriers, 34, 99.
Watering-places, 249–257, 314–322, 407, 415.
Water supply, Mexico City, 99.
Wheat, raising of, 237; in Chihuahua, 410.
Wines, absence of native, 141.
Witchcraft, belief in, 311.
Witches, Indian, 229.
Women, in business, 56, 167–168; jealous protection of, 123, 157–159; lack of housekeeping knowledge, 125, 166; concern of, in church matters, 151, 165; appearance of, 159, courtship of, 161–162; smoking by, 165–166; lack of education in, 167; dress of, 168–169; Indian, 192–193; the Zapotec, at Tehuantepec, 391–393.
Women's rights, tabooed, 159.
Woods, valuable, 383.

Xochicalco, ruins of, 231.

Yaqui Indians, 185; warfare conducted by, in Sonora, 411–414.
Yellow fever, extinction of, 11, 388.
Y.M.C.A. in Mexico, 153.
Young men, lack of responsibility of, 178–179.
Young Mexican party, 205.

INDEX

Yucatan, Mayan Indians in, 186, 391; cultivation of henequen in, 329; railway possibilities in, 389.

Zacatecas, silver mining at, 408.
Zambrano, silver king, 364–365.
Zapote, the, 32.
Zapotec Indians, 271, 309, 311–313, 391–393.
Zaragoza, General, 83, 239.
Zavaleta, scenic and climatic attractions of, 284–285.
Zavaleta gold mine, 272–282.
Zayas Enriques, Señor de, champion of Yaquis, 411.
Zocalo, park in Mexico City, 97.
Zopilotes, in Vera Cruz, 11.
Zyaboa, Mitla called, 309.

By Dr. WILFRED T. GRENFELL and Others

Labrador

Illustrated, cloth, 8vo, $2.25 net

In this volume Dr. Grenfell supplies a need that has long been felt for a volume containing a full and adequate account of Labrador — the country, its natural resources, the climatic conditions, and its people. In addition to the main body of the book with its chapters on Physiography, the People of the Coast, the Missions, the Dogs, the various Fisheries, there are short chapters on the Flora, the Fauna, the Geology, etc., each by a scientific author of standing. The volume, profusely illustrated from photographs in the author's own collection, reveals an unknown land to the vast majority of readers. Few of us hitherto have been aware of what this peninsula has to offer to the world, either in material resources or beauty of scenery. All of this, and more, Dr. Grenfell makes clear and interesting.

By ELLA HIGGINSON

Alaska : The Great Country

Illustrated, cloth, 12mo, $2.25 net

"No other book gives so clear an impression of the beauty and grandeur and vastness of our northernmost territory, nor so inspires one to explore its vastnesses. She has mingled enough of history and statistics to make it authoritative, and has embellished the tale with stories and anecdotes to prevent its being dull and has succeeded in writing what might well be called a great book on a great subject." — *The Boston Evening Transcript.*

"Mrs. Higginson has put the very soul of picturesque Alaska into her pages and done it with a degree of truth, sympathy, and enthusiasm that will make her volume a classic in its domain. The volume is well illustrated." — *Chicago Record-Herald.*

PUBLISHED BY

THE MACMILLAN COMPANY

64-66 Fifth Avenue, New York

By E. V. LUCAS

A Wanderer in Holland
Illustrated, cloth, 8vo, $2.00 net

"Mr. Lucas assures us that Holland is one of the most delightful countries to move about in, everything that happens in it being of interest. He fully proves his statement, and we close his book with the conviction that we shall never find there a more agreeable guide than he. For he is a man of taste and culture, who has apparently preserved all the zest of youth for things beautiful, touching, quaint, or humorous — especially humorous — and his own unaffected enjoyment gives to his pages a most endearing freshness and sparkle. . . . In short, the book is a charming one." — *New York Tribune.*

A Wanderer in London
Illustrated, cloth, 8vo, $1.75 net

"We have met with few books of the sort so readable throughout. It is a book that may be opened at any place and read with pleasure by readers who have seen London; and those who have not, will want to see it after reading the book of one who knows it so well." — *New York Evening Sun.*

A Wanderer in Paris
Illustrated, cloth, 8vo, $1.75 net

Mr. Lucas in his wanderings in many lands plays the part of an intellectual lecturer absorbing the atmosphere of the country and the soul of its people rather than that of a hustling reporter content with diagrammatic descriptions. He is as much at home in Paris as he is in his native London, and he enters into the life of the Parisians with the same intimacy and the same charm that have characterized all his previous works. The volume is profusely illustrated.

PUBLISHED BY

THE MACMILLAN COMPANY
64-66 Fifth Avenue, New York

ILLUSTRATED DESCRIPTIONS OF AMERICAN PLACES AND PEOPLE

BY M. A. DeWOLFE HOWE

Boston : The Place and the People

With over one hundred illustrations, including many from pen drawings executed especially for this volume by L. A. HOLMAN.

Decorated cloth, boxed, $2.00 net; by mail, $2.20

BY MRS. ST. JULIEN RAVENEL

Charleston : The Place and the People

Illustrated from photographs and drawings by VERNON H. BAILEY.

Decorated cloth, boxed, $2.00 net; by mail, $2.20

BY GRACE KING

New Orleans : The Place and the People

With eighty-three illustrations from drawings by FRANCES JONES.

Decorated cloth, boxed, $2.00 net; by mail, $2.20

BY AGNES REPPLIER

Philadelphia : The Place and the People

With eighty-two illustrations from drawings by ERNEST C. PEIXOTTO.

Decorated cloth, boxed, $2.00 net; by mail, $2.20

BY JOHN C. VAN DYKE

The New New York : The Place and the People

With one hundred and twenty-six illustrations, including twenty-four in color, by JOSEPH PENNELL.

Decorated cloth, $4.00 net; by mail, $4.22

Welcome books, either for the traveller's use during his visit, or as a pleasant reminder of bygone days, or to bring the different districts vividly before the minds of intending travellers, or before those who are unable to leave home.

PUBLISHED BY

THE MACMILLAN COMPANY

64-66 Fifth Avenue, New York

By CECIL HEADLAM

Venetia and Northern Italy
Old World Travel Series *Illustrated, cloth, 8vo, $2.50 net*

"Cecil Headlam has a happy art of making books about places, in which he mingles history and art with scenery and personal impressions. . . . The impression he makes is that of an intelligent and sympathetic companion, who never discourses long enough on any subject to weary his hearers. . . . There are twenty-five full-page illustrations in color by Gordon Home." — *The New York Post.*

By GORDON HOME

Along the Rivieras of France and Italy
Old World Travel Series *Illustrated, cloth, 8vo, $2.50 net*

"It has always been Mr. Home's pleasant habit to illustrate his books of travel with his own pictures, and its pursuance in 'Along the Rivieras of France and Italy' has produced a volume in which the brilliant descriptions of the text are rivalled by twenty-five colored plates, many of them extraordinarily happy in their reproduction, and about twenty drawings in black and white. . . . A better guide for comfortable library or study travel could not be devised." — *The Boston Transcript.*

Color Books

A series of over one hundred and fifty elegantly bound and decorated books of travel and description, each volume distinguished for its exquisite illustrations in color and the interest of its information. Among the new additions to the series are: Essex, described by A. R. H. Moncrieff, painted by Burleigh Bruhl; Hampshire, described by Rev. Telford Varley, painted by Wilifred Ball; Hungary, described by Adrian Stokes, painted by Mr. and Mrs. Adrian Stokes; Kashmir, described by Sir Francis Younghusband, painted by Major E. Molyneaux; The Lake of Geneva, described by Francis Gribble, painted by J. H. and M. H. Lewis; and The Rivers and Streams of England, described by A. G. Bradley, painted by Sutton Palmer.

A full descriptive list of this series, with prices, will be gladly sent on request to any address.

PUBLISHED BY

THE MACMILLAN COMPANY
64-66 Fifth Avenue, New York

www.ingramcontent.com/pod-product-compliance
Lightning Source LLC
Chambersburg PA
CBHW070945160426
43193CB00012B/1804